Exploring Bentley STAAD.Pro V8i

SELECTseries 6

(2nd Revised and Updated Edition)

Sham Tickoo
Professor
Purdue University Northwest
Hammond, Indiana, USA

Contributing Authors
Tickoo Institute of Emerging Technologies (TIET)
Gurgaon, India

CADCIM Technologies
Indiana, USA

REPRINT 2023

ISBN: 978-93-86551-10-8
2nd Revised and Updated Edition
(For Distribution in SAARC countries only)

Limits of Liability and Disclaimer of Warranty

Distributors

COMPUTER BOOK CENTRE
12, Shrungar Shopping Centre
M.G. Road
BENGALURU–560001
Ph: 25587923/25584641

DECCAN AGENCIES
4-3-329, Bank Street
HYDERABAD-500195
Ph: 24756967/24756400

MICRO MEDIA
Shop No. 5, Mahendra Chambers
150 DN Rd. Next to Capital Cinema
V.T (C.S.T.) Station
MUMBAI-400001

BPB BOOK CENTRE
376 Old Lajpat Rai Market
DELHI-110006
Ph: 23861747

INFOTECH
G-2, Sidhartha Building, 96 Nehru Place
NEW DELHI-110019
Ph: 26438245

BPB PUBLICATIONS
20, Ansari Road, Darya Ganj
New Delhi-110002
Ph: 23254990/23254991

Published by Manish Jain for BPB Publications, 20 Ansari Road, Darya Ganj
New Delhi-110002 and Printed at Manipal Technologies Limited, Manipal

DEDICATION

*To teachers, who make it possible to disseminate knowledge
to enlighten the young and curious minds
of our future generations*

*To students, who are dedicated to learning new technologies
and making the world a better place to live in*

THANKS

*To employees of CADCIM Technologies and
Tickoo Institute of Emerging Technologies (TIET)
for their valuable help*

Note

If you are a faculty member, you can register by clicking on the following link to access the teaching resources: ***http://www.cadcim.com/Registration.aspx****. The student resources are available at* ***http://www.cadcim.com****.*

Table of Contents

Chapter 3: Structural Modeling Using Tools

Chapter 4: Defining Material Constants and Section Properties

Chapter 5: Specifications and Supports

Chapter 6: Loads

Chapter 7: Performing Analysis, Viewing Results, and Preparing Report

Chapter 8: Structural Modeling Using Building Planner

Conversion Table

Conversion Table-Metric/Imperial			
	Unit	**Multiply By (Factor)**	**To Obtain**
Length	Inch	2.54	Centimeter
	Centimeter	0.393	Inch
	Feet	0.301	Meter
	Meter	3.281	Feet
	Kilometer	0.54	Nautical Mile
	Nautical Mile	1.852	Kilometer
	Feet	0.000304	Kilometer
Weight and Mass	Ounce	28.35	Gram
	Gram	0.0353	Ounce
	Pound	0.453	Kilogram
	Kilogram	2.205	Pounds
	Metric Ton	1.102	Ton
Liquid Measures	Fluid Ounce	0.0296	Liter
	Gallon	3.785	Liter
	Liter	0.264	Gallon
Thrust / Pressure	Pounds Force	4.448	Newton
	Newton	0.225	Pound
	Pound per square inch (psi)	6.895	KiloPascal
Temperature	Kelvin	1	Degree Celsius-273.15
	Degree Celsius	1.8	Degree Fahrenheit +32

Preface

STAAD.Pro V8i (SELECTseries 6)

STAAD.Pro V8i (SELECTseries 6), developed by Bentley Systems, is a powerful software used for structural analysis and design. It has various tools that help in modeling 2D and 3D models. These tools analyze and virtually design any type of structure. This enables the users to automate their tasks, and remove the tedious long procedures involved in the manual methods. STAAD.Pro is an effective tool for structural engineers and construction professionals.

STAAD.Pro has an extremely flexible modeling environment that helps in creating accurate models quickly and accurately. It supports broad ranges of Steel, Concrete, Aluminium, and Timber design codes. It is capable of analyzing any structure for static loads, dynamic response, soil-structure interaction, wind, earthquake, and moving loads. STAAD.Pro supports Bentley Rebar, AutoPipe, RAM Connection, STAAD.Foundation, and other software.

Exploring Bentley STAAD.Pro V8i (SELECTseries 6) is a comprehensive textbook that has been written to cater to the needs of the students and professionals. The chapters in this textbook are structured in a pedagogical sequence, which makes the learning process very simple and effective for both the novice as well as the advanced users of STAAD.Pro. In this textbook, the author explains in detail the procedure of creating 2D and 3D models, assigning material constants, assigning cross-section properties, assigning supports, defining different loads, performing analysis, viewing results, and preparing report. The chapters in the book are punctuated with tips and notes, wherever necessary, to make the concepts clear, thereby enabling the user to create his own innovative projects.

The highlight of this textbook is that each concept introduced in it is explained with the help of suitable examples to facilitate better understanding. The simple and lucid language used in this textbook makes it a ready reference for both the beginners and the intermediate users.

- **Concepts explained with Examples**
  The author has explained the concepts in detail with examples for better comprehension of the processes involved.

- **Tips and Notes**
  The additional information related to topics is provided to the users in the form of tips and notes.

- **Learning Objectives**
  The first page of every chapter summarizes the topics that are covered in that chapter.

- **Self-Evaluation Test and Review Questions**
  Every chapter ends with Self-Evaluation Test so that the users can assess their knowledge of the chapter. The answers to Self-Evaluation Test are given at the end of the chapter. Also, the Review Questions are given at the end of chapters and they can be used by Instructors as test questions.

- **Heavily Illustrated Text**
  The text in this book is heavily illustrated with screen capture images.

Symbols Used in the Textbook

Note

The author has provided additional information related to various topics in the form of notes.

Tip

The author has provided a lot of information to the users about the topic being discussed in the form of tips.

New

This symbol indicates that the command or tool being discussed is new in this release.

Enhanced

This symbol indicates that the command or tool being discussed has been enhanced in this release.

Unit System Followed in the Textbook

In this book, the Metric system has been used as the default unit system.

Formatting Conventions Used in the Textbook

Please refer to the following list for the formatting conventions used in this textbook.

- Names of tools, buttons, options, menu, command, pages, and tabs are written in boldface. Example: The **Add Beams** tool, the **OK** button, the **File** menu, the **Modeling** tab, the **General** page, and so on.
- Names of dialog boxes, menus, windows, edit boxes, check boxes, and radio buttons are written in boldface. Example: The **Property** dialog box, the **Density** edit box of the **Property** dialog box, and so on.
- Values entered in edit boxes are written in boldface. Example: Enter **Buildings** in the **Name** edit box.
- Names of the files are italicized. Example: *c03_staad_v8i_ex1*

Naming Conventions Used in the Textbook

Tool

If you click on an item in a toolbar and a command is invoked to create/edit an object or perform some action, then that item is termed as tool. For example: **Insert Node** tool and **Translational Repeat** tool, refer to Figure 1.

Figure 1 *The tools available in a toolbar*

Button

The item in a dialog box that has a 3d shape is termed as Button. For example, **OK** button, **Cancel** button, **Apply** button, and so on.

Dialog Box

In this textbook, different terms are used to indicate various components of a dialog box, refer to Figure 2.

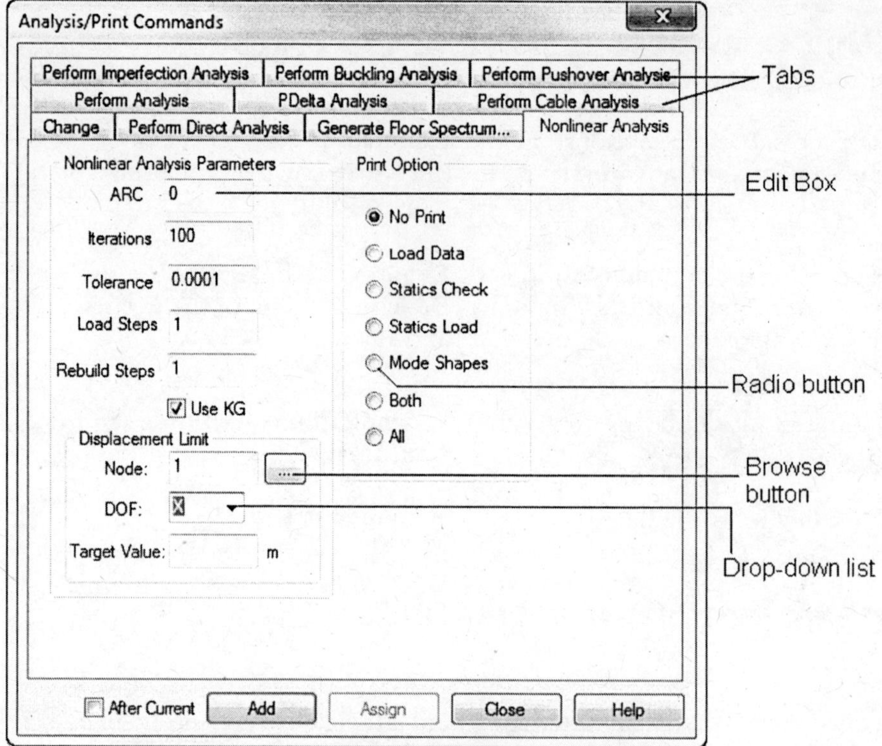

***Figure 2** Different components of a dialog box*

Menu

A menu is the one in which a set of common tools and options are grouped together. These menus are given a name based on the tools grouped in them. For example, **Mode** menu, **Geometry** menu, and so on, refer to Figure 3.

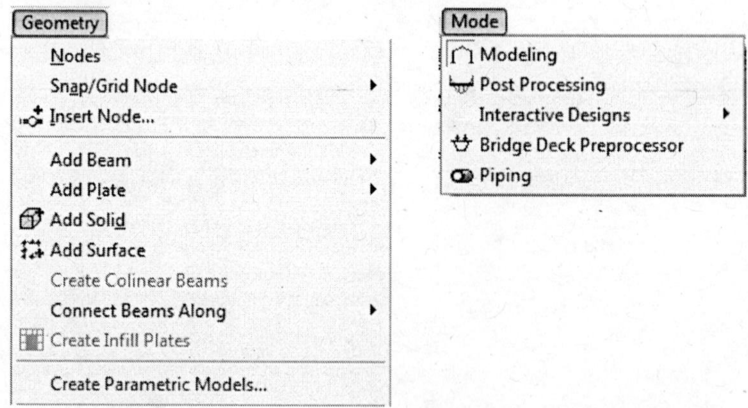

***Figure 3** The partial view of **Geometry** and **Mode** menus*

Options

Options are the items that are available in shortcut menus, dialog boxes, drop-down lists, and so on. For example, choose the **Orientation** option from the shortcut menu displayed on right-clicking in the Main Window, refer to Figure 4.

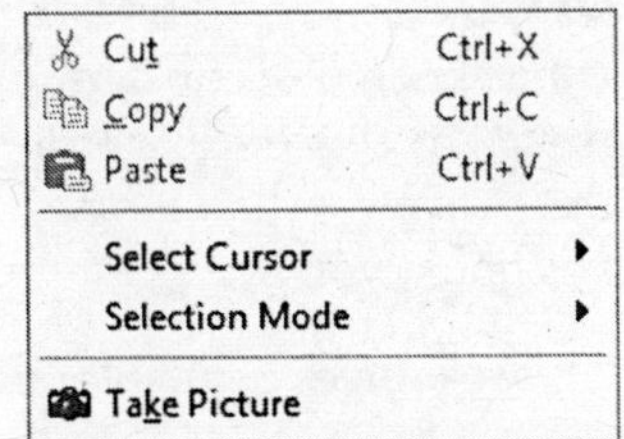

***Figure 4** The shortcut menu displayed in the main window*

Free Companion Website

It has been our constant endeavor to provide you the best textbooks and services at affordable price. In this endeavor, we have come out with a Free Companion website that will facilitate the process of teaching and learning of STAAD.Pro V8i (SELECTseries 6). If you purchase this textbook, you will get access to the files on the Companion website.

The resources available for the faculty and students in this website are as follows:

Faculty Resources

- **Technical Support**
  You can get online technical support by contacting ***info@tiet.in***.

- **Instructor Guide**
  Solutions to all review questions and exercises in the textbook are provided in the instructor guide to help the faculty members test the skills of the students.

- **PowerPoint Presentations**
  The contents of the book are arranged in PowerPoint slides that can be used by the faculty for their lectures.

- **Example Files**
  The example files used are available for free download.

Student Resources

- **Technical Support**
  You can get online technical support by contacting ***info@tiet.in***.

- **Example Files**
  The example files used are available for free download.

If you face any problem in accessing these files, please contact the publisher at ***info@tiet.in*** or the author at ***stickoo@purduecal.edu*** or ***tickoo525@gmail.com***.

Stay Connected

You can now stay connected with us through Facebook and Twitter to get the latest information about our textbooks, videos, and teaching/learning resources. To stay informed of such updates, follow us on Facebook (***www.facebook.com/cadcim***) and Twitter (@cadcimtech). You can also subscribe to our YouTube channel (***www.youtube.com/cadcimtech***) to get the information about our latest video tutorials.

Chapter 1

Introduction to STAAD.Pro V8i

Learning Objectives

After completing this chapter, you will be able to:

- *Understand the basic features of STAAD.Pro V8i*
- *Start STAAD.Pro V8i software*
- *Use different components of the user interface of STAAD.Pro V8i*
- *Start a new project in STAAD.Pro V8i*
- *Import different files to STAAD.Pro V8i*

INTRODUCTION TO STAAD.PRO V8i

STAAD.Pro V8i is used to create, analyze, and design any type of virtual structure through its flexible modeling environment. The three basic activities which are to be carried out to achieve this goal are: model generation, calculations to obtain the analytical results, and result verification. All these activities are discussed individually in different chapters. STAAD.Pro is designed for engineers who understand the process of modeling, analyzing, and designing a structure.

BASIC FEATURES OF STAAD.PRO V8i

The basic features of STAAD.Pro V8i are listed below:

1) State-of-the art 2D/3D graphical environment.

2) Ability to perform structural analysis and design such as static, P-delta, pushover, response spectrum, time history, cable (linear and non-linear), buckling, and steel, concrete and timber design.

3) Ability to generate 2D/3D CAD models.

4) Modeling of truss and beam members, plates, solids, linear and non-linear cables, and curvilinear beams.

5) Advanced automatic load generation facilities for wind, area, floor, and moving loads.

6) Customizable structural templates for creating a model.

7) Toggle display of loads, supports, properties, and structural elements.

8) User-controlled numbering scheme for structural elements.

STARTING BENTLEY STAAD.PRO V8i

You can start STAAD.Pro V8i by double-clicking on the STAAD.Pro V8i icon available on the desktop. Alternatively, choose **Start > All Programs > STAAD.Pro v8i > STAAD.Pro** from the task bar (for Windows 7), refer to Figure 1-1; the interface will be displayed.

USER INTERFACE

The user interface of STAAD.Pro is divided into five areas: **Project Tasks**, **Recent Files**, **Help Topics**, **License Configuration**, and **STAAD News**, refer to Figure 1-2. These areas are discussed next.

Project Tasks

The **Project Tasks** area contains several options which are used for creating a new project, opening an existing project, opening a STAAD model from a project wise repository, configuring settings, and so on.

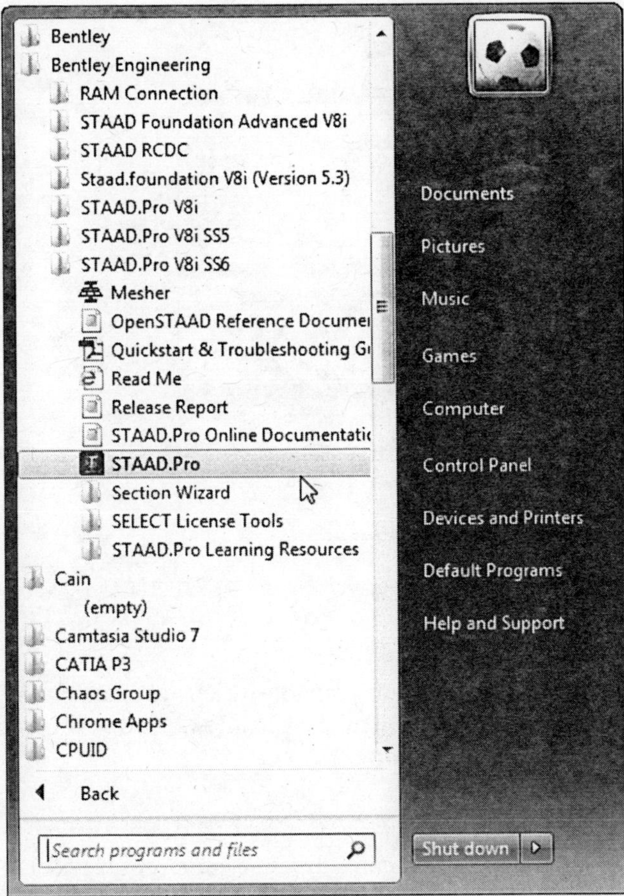

Figure 1-1 *Starting* ***STAAD.Pro*** *from the task bar*

The **New Project** option is used to create a new project. The process of creating a new project is discussed in detail later in this chapter. The **Open Project** option is used to open an existing project in STAAD.Pro. The **Open From ProjectWise** option is used to open a model from a project wise repository. The **Configuration** option is used to configure the program settings such as units, color, input/output file formats, default design codes, and so on. The **Backup Manager** option is used to view and edit the backup options such as the settings for backups and auto save.

Recent Files

In the **Recent Files** area, six recently used files will be displayed. You can open any of these files by clicking on the required file. When you place cursor on any of the recently used files, its preview and location will be displayed on the right side of the area.

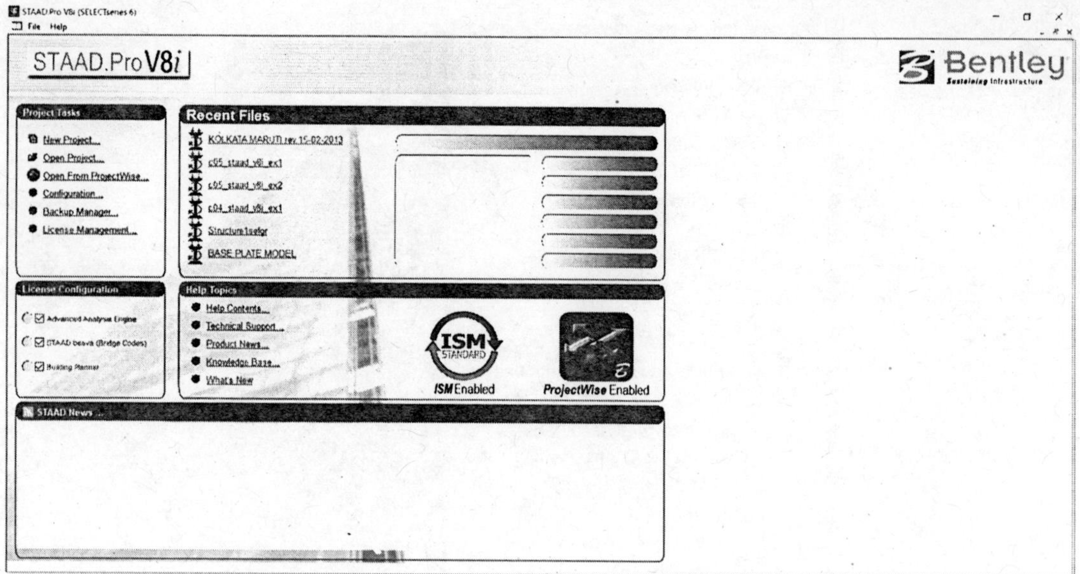

Figure 1-2 The user interface of STAAD.Pro V8i

Help Topics

In the **Help Topics** area, several options are available which are used for accessing help documents online and offline, technical support services, product news, and so on. You can access the offline help by clicking on the **Help Contents** option.

License Configuration

In the **License Configuration** area, you can select the code required for the project by selecting the check box beside the code. If the license is available, the circle beside the check box will be green otherwise it will be red.

STARTING A NEW PROJECT

In STAAD.Pro, you can start a new project. To do so, choose the **New Project** option from the **Project Tasks** area; the **New Model** dialog box will be displayed, as shown in Figure 1-3. In this dialog box, you need to provide some essential data which is necessary for creating the model such as the structure type to be created. Select the **Space**, **Plane**, **Floor**, or **Truss** check box to specify the structure type. For example, for space structure type, select the **Space** check box and then specify the name of the file in the **File Name** text box. Next, specify the location where the file will be saved. To do so, choose the Browse button available next to the **Location** edit box; the **Browse For Folder** dialog box will be displayed. In this dialog box, select the folder in which you want to save the file and then choose the **OK** button; the path of the location will be displayed in the **Location** edit box. In the **Length Units** area, specify the length unit by selecting the corresponding radio buttons. Similarly, specify the force unit by selecting the corresponding radio button in the **Force Units** area.

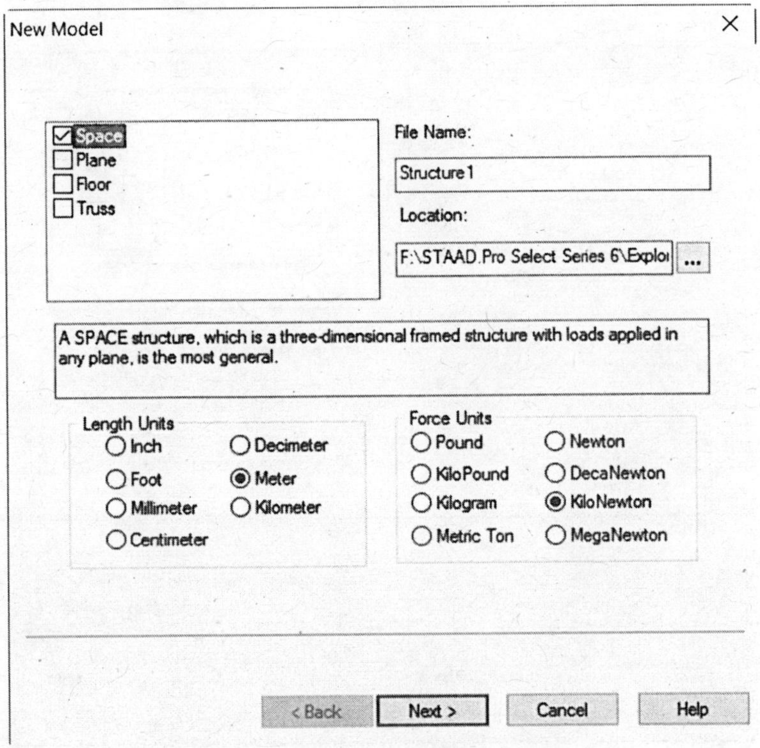

Figure 1-3 The ***New Model*** *dialog box*

After specifying all the data, choose the **Next** button; the **Where do you want to go?** dialog box will be displayed, as shown in Figure 1-4. In this dialog box, you will specify the method to be used for creating the model. These methods are discussed next.

You can select the **Add Beam** check box to create the model by creating nodes and members using the construction grid. Select the **Add Plate** check box to create the model by creating new joints, 3-noded and 4-noded plate elements using the construction grid. Select the **Add Solid** check box to create the model by creating new joints and 8-noded solid/brick elements using the construction grid. Select the **Open Structure Wizard** check box to create model by using standard, parametric structural templates for trusses, surfaces, bay frames, and so on. Select the **Open STAAD Editor** check box to create model using STAAD syntax commands through the **STAAD Editor** window. Select the **Edit Job Information** check box to provide information about the client's name, job title, engineer involved, and so on before creating the model. All these methods are discussed in detail in further chapters. You can choose the **< Back** button to go back to the previous page and make any changes in the unit and other settings in the **New** dialog box. After specifying all the options, choose the **Finish** button; the STAAD.Pro user interface will be displayed, as shown in Figure 1-5.

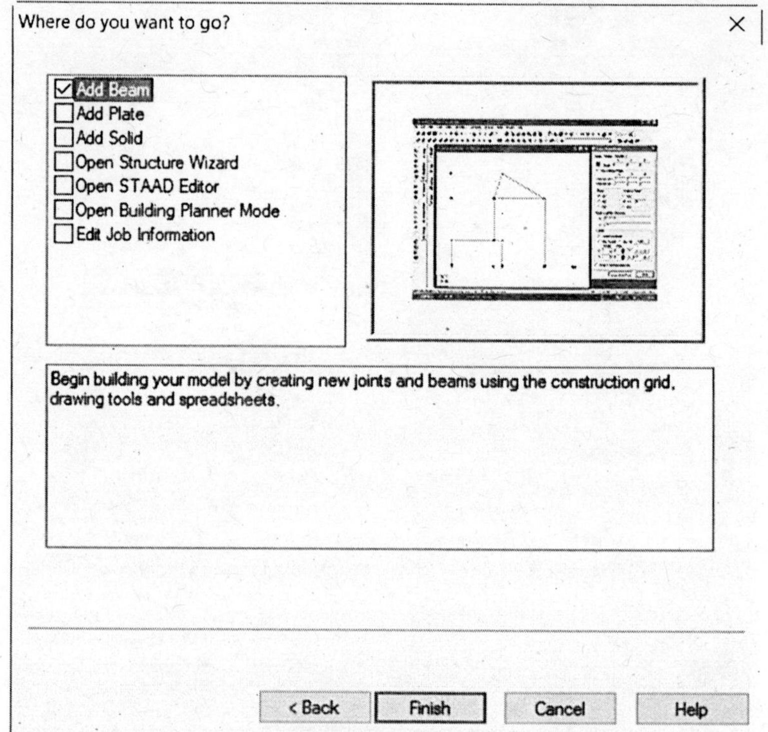

*Figure 1-4 The **Where do you want to go?** dialog box*

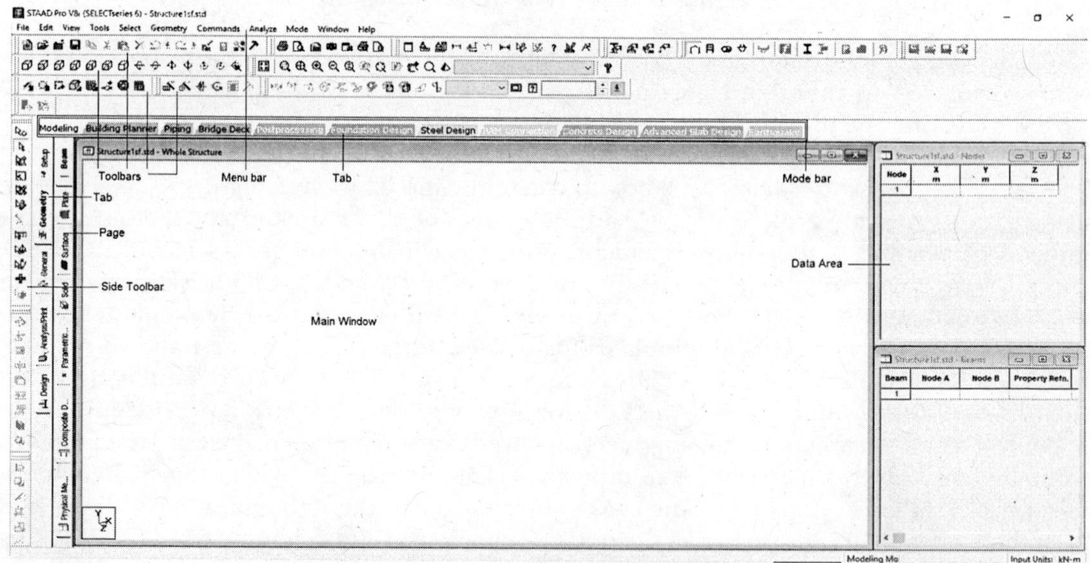

Figure 1-5 The user interface of STAAD.Pro V8i

WORKING IN USER INTERFACE

The user interface of STAAD.Pro V8i comprises of several elements such as the **Menu bar**, **Toolbar**, **Side Toolbar**, **Tabs**, **Pages**, **Snap Node/Beam Window**, **Data Area**, and **Main Window**, refer to Figure 1-5. The interface elements are exclusively designed to provide an easy access to the tools and windows. These elements are discussed next.

Menu Bar

The menu bar is located at the top of the interface. It comprises of different menus: **File**, **Edit**, **View**, **Tools**, **Select**, **Geometry**, **Command**, **Analyze**, **Mode**, **Window**, and **Help**. These menus will be available in the **Modeling** mode. When you switch to different mode, such as **Postprocessing**, different menus will appear in the Menu Bar. These modes are discussed in later chapters. The different menus in the menu bar are discussed next.

File

The **File** menu contains the options which are used for performing different file operations such as creating new structure, opening an existing model, saving files, printing files, and so on. Figure 1-6 shows different options in the **File** menu.

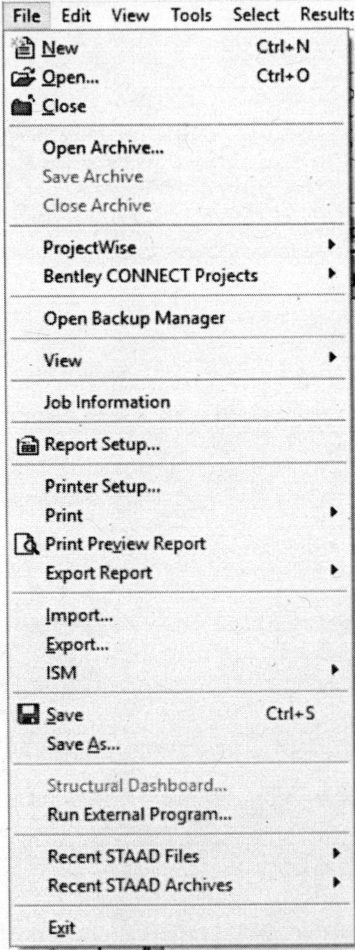

*Figure 1-6 Different options in the **File** menu*

The **New** option in the menu is used for creating a new structure. On choosing this option, the **New** dialog box will be displayed. The options in this dialog box have already been discussed. The **Open** option is used for opening an existing file. The **Report Setup** option is used to create a customized output report. The **Print** option is used to print different files. The **Export Report** option is used to export the output file in Word or Text file. The **Import** option is used to import data from other formats, such as DXF. The **Save** option is used to save the input data. The **Recent STAAD Files** option shows a list of the most recently used or created STAAD input files. The **Exit** option is used to exit STAAD graphical environment.

Edit

The **Edit** menu contains the options that are used to perform editing operations such as copy, paste, undo, redo, editing input command file, and so on. Figure 1-7 shows the different options in the **Edit** menu. You can use the **Undo** and **Redo** options to undo/redo an operation. The **Cut** option is used to cut the selected object and then paste that object at the desired place by pressing CTRL+V from the keyboard or by using the **Paste** option. The **Copy** option is used to copy the selected object to clipboard. The **Paste** option is used to paste an object from the clipboard into the STAAD. The **Delete** option is used to delete the selected object. The **Take Picture** option is used to take a snapshot of the current view. The **Edit Input Command File** option is used to edit the input command file.

View

The **View** menu contains the options used to perform various view-related tasks such as zooming, panning, setting colors, fonts, and so on. Figure 1-8 shows different options in the **View** menu. The **Zoom** option is used to magnify or reduce the size of the structure in the main window.

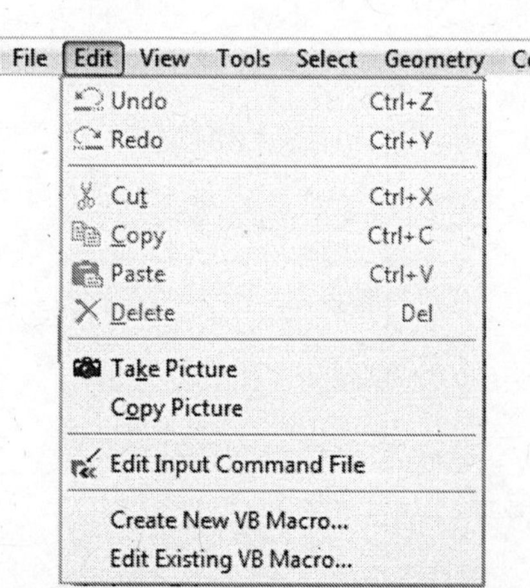

***Figure 1-7** Different options in the **Edit** menu*

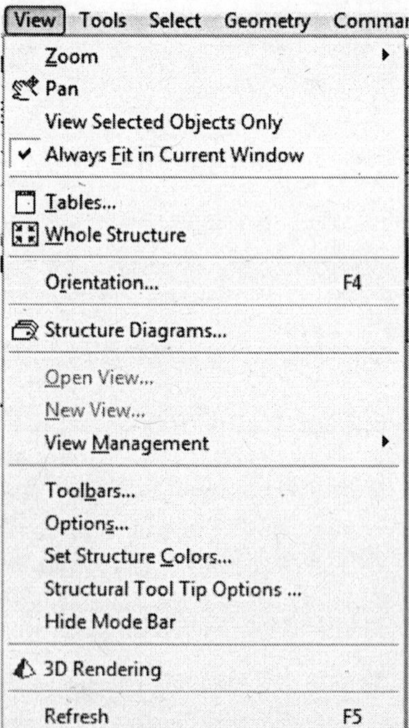

***Figure 1-8** Different options in the **View** menu*

The **Pan** option is used to move the structure in the current view window in any direction. The **View Selected Objects Only** option is used to view the selected objects only. The **Orientation** option is used to modify the settings for various view orientations of the structure, such as plan view, elevation view, and perspective view. The **Set Structure Colors** option is used to specify colors for different items such as structure color and analysis results. The **3D Rendering** option is used to view the rendered view of the structure.

Tools

The **Tools** menu contains the miscellaneous tools and options which are used for performing different tasks such as checking orphan nodes, checking overlapping members, performing simple calculations, inserting text, changing units, and so on. Figure 1-9 shows different options in the **Tools** menu.

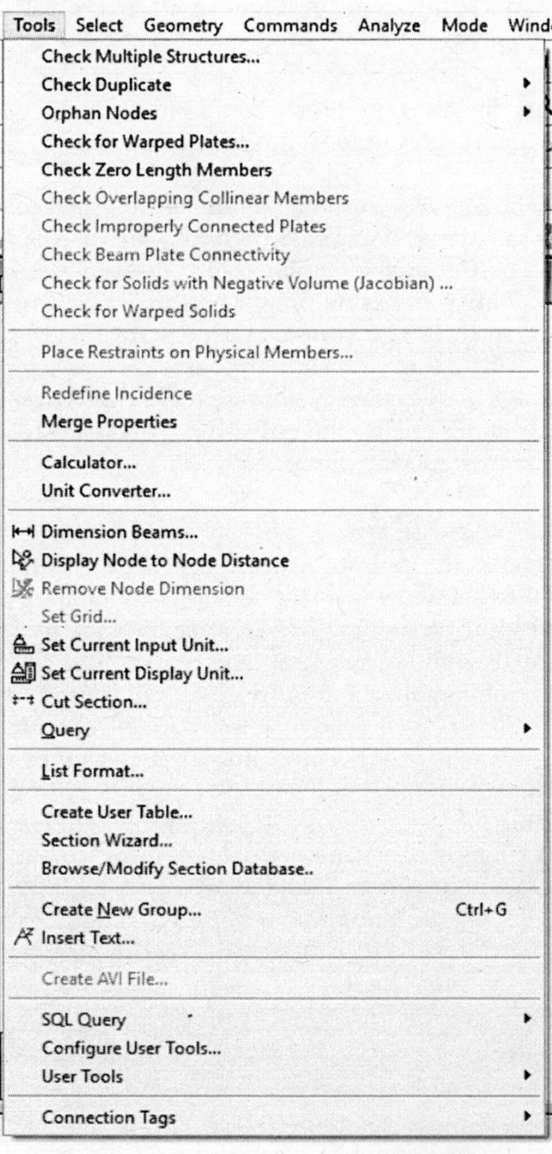

*Figure 1-9 Different options in the **Tools** menu*

The **Check Multiple Structures** option is used to check for more than one unconnected structure in a model. The **Check Duplicate** option is used to check for duplicate entities such as two nodes having same coordinates. The **Orphan Nodes** option is used to check for the unconnected nodes in a structure. The **Unit Converter** option is used to convert data from one unit system into another. The **Calculator** option is used to display **STAAD.Pro Calculator** which can be used for performing calculations. The **Dimension Beams** option is used to display the dimension of beams in a view. The **Set Current Input Unit** option is used to set the unit while creating structure, assigning properties, and so on. The **Section Wizard** option is used to display the **Section Wizard** window. In this window, you can calculate section property values such as area, moment of inertia, and so on for cross sections. These cross sections can be assembled from pre-existing standard shapes, user-created shapes, and parametric shapes. The **Insert Text** option is used to add comments and titles to pictures and result diagrams.

Select

The **Select** menu contains the tools used for selecting nodes, members, plate/elements, solids, and so on. Figure 1-10 shows different tools in the **Select** menu.

The **Nodes Cursor** tool is used for selecting nodes in a structure. The **Beams Cursor** tool is used for selecting beams in a structure. The **Plates Cursor** tool is used for selecting plate element in a structure. The **Geometry Cursor** tool is used for selecting the nodes, members and elements of the structure at the same time. The **Load Edit Cursor** tool is used to change any load applied on the structure. The **Support Edit Cursor** tool is used to modify any support applied on the structure. The **Beams Parallel To** tool is used to select the members parallel to any of the specified global axis. The **Entity at node** tool is used to select beam, plates, or solid attached to any particular node. The **By Specification** tool is used to select nodes and members based on the specifications assigned to them.

Geometry

The **Geometry** menu contains the tools used for creating and modifying a structure. Figure 1-11 shows different tools in the **Geometry** menu. The **Nodes** tool is used to display the **Nodes** table in which you can add and edit the nodes. The **Snap/Grid Node** tool is used to specify the grid and snap settings for creating nodes, beams, plates, and solids. The **Insert Node** tool is used to insert node on an existing member. The **Add Plate** tool is used to add plates by connecting nodes. The **Create Infill Plates** tool is used to automatically generate the floor slab by selecting some or all beams in a structure. The **Translational Repeat** tool is used to copy the entire structure linearly. The **Circular Repeat** tool is used to copy the entire structure in circularly. The **Generate Surface Meshing** tool is used to create a finite element mesh. The **Rotate** tool is used to rotate the selected portions of the structure or the entire structure about the specified axis through a specified distance. The **Merge Selected Members** tool is used to merge two members and replace them with one. The **Renumber** tool is used to renumber nodes, members, or plates starting with a specified number. The **Run Structure Wizard** tool is used to display the **StWizard** window which is discussed in later chapter.

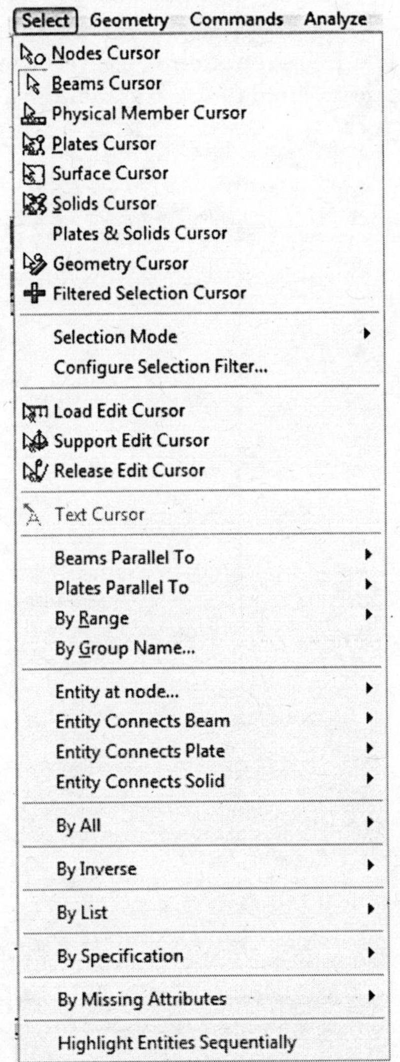

*Figure 1-10 Different tools in the **Select** menu*

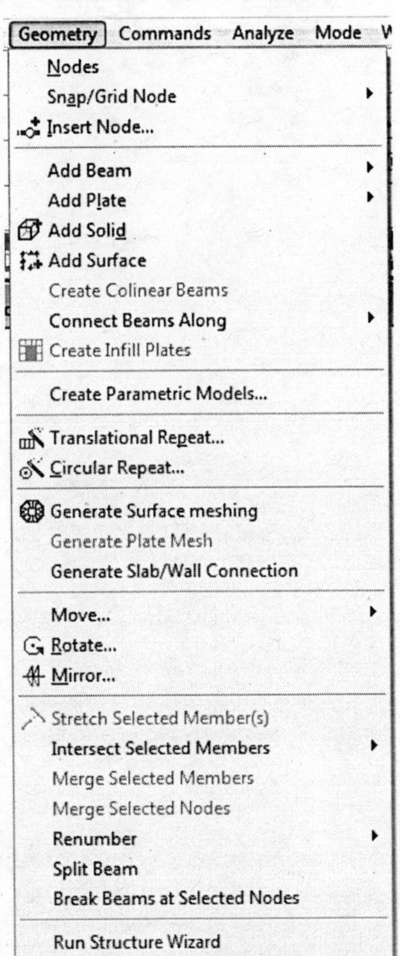

*Figure 1-11 Different tools in the **Geometry** menu*

Command

The **Command** menu contains different options that allow you to define supports, loads, specifications, and so on. Figure 1-12 shows different options in the **Command** menu. The **Plate Thickness** option is used to specify the plate thickness. The **Member Property** option is used to define the cross-sectional properties of the members such as prismatic sections, steel sections, aluminium sections, and so on. The **Material Constants** option is used to define and assign material constants such as Density, Elasticity, Poisson's Ratio, Coefficient of Thermal Expansion, and so on. The **Geometric Constants** option is used to define and assign geometric constants such as Beta Angle, Reference Point, and so on. The **Pre Analysis Print** option is used to define the commands for printing input data information in the STAAD Output file.

The **Loading** option is used to define and apply loads on a structure. The **Analysis** option is used to define the type of analysis to be performed. The **Post-Analysis Print** option is used to print analysis results in the STAAD Output file. The **Design** option is used to specify design parameters and commands. The **Miscellaneous** option is used to add commands such as **Input Width, Output Width, Set Z Up**, and so on.

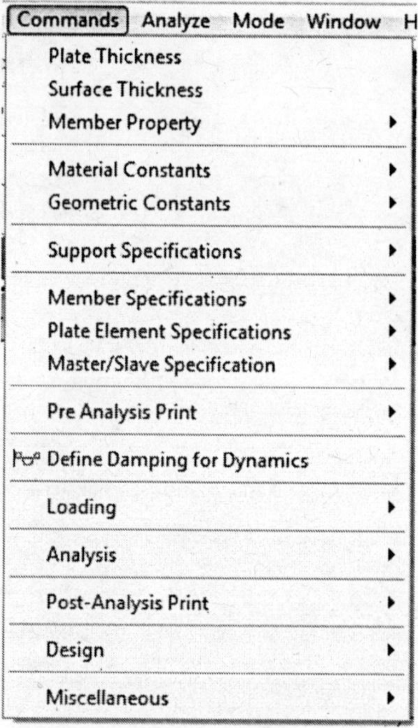

*Figure 1-12 Options in the **Command** menu*

Analyze

The **Analyze** menu contains the **Run Analysis** command that is used to perform the analysis. This analysis is carried out to calculate support reactions, member forces, joint displacements, and so on. All these are discussed in detail in later chapters. Figure 1-13 shows the **Run Analysis** option in the **Analyze** menu.

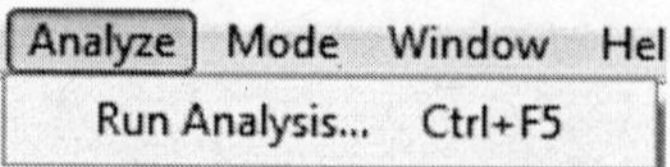

*Figure 1-13 The **Run Analysis** option in the **Analyze** menu*

Mode

The **Mode** menu contains the options that allow you to switch among the **Modeling**, **Post Processing**, **Interactive Designs**, **Bridge Deck Preprocessor**, and **Piping** modes. In this menu, the **Post Processing** option will be enabled only after the analysis has been performed. Figure 1-14 shows different options in the **Mode** menu.

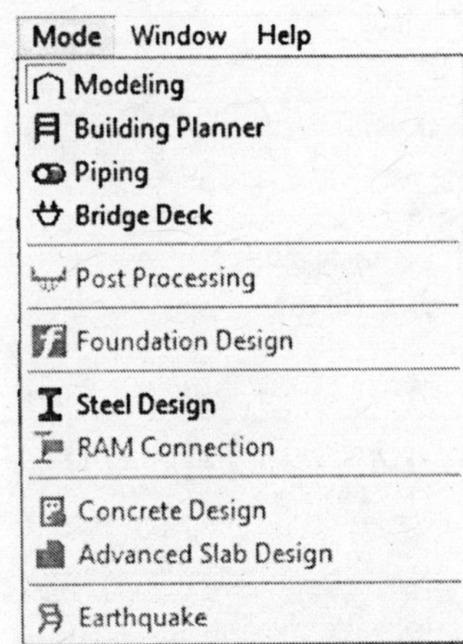

*Figure 1-14 Options in the **Mode** menu*

Window

The options in the **Window** menu allow you to position the Main Window and Data Area window. The **Tile Horizontal** option is used to place the windows horizontally. The **Tile Vertical** option is used to place the windows vertically. The **Structure Only** option is used to view the Main Window only. Figure 1-15 shows various options in the **Window** menu.

Window Help
Cascade Shift+F5
Tile Horizontal Shift+F4
Tile Vertical Ctrl+Shift+F4
Structure Only
✔ 1 Structure2.std - Whole Structure
2 Structure2.std - Job Info

*Figure 1-15 Options in the **Window** menu*

Help

The **Help** menu contains different options which are used to access offline help document, technical support services, and so on. The **Contents** option is used to access the help document. The **Technical Support** option is used to access the information about the technical support. When you choose the **About STAAD.Pro** option, the **STAAD.Pro for Windows** dialog box is displayed. This dialog box contains information about the STAAD.Pro version being used such as product name, release number and build number. Figure 1-16 shows various options in the **Help** menu.

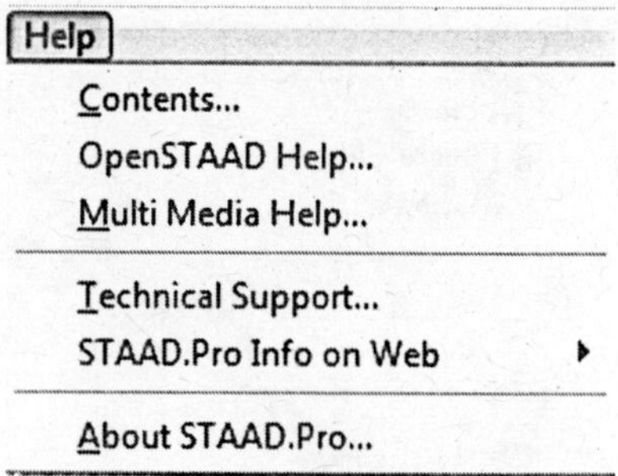

Figure 1-16 Options in the **Help** menu

Toolbars

STAAD.Pro comprises of various toolbars available at the top of the interface. These toolbars are dockable and can be placed anywhere in the interface. These toolbars contain various tools which are used for creating new structure, opening an existing structure, changing views, printing, rotating tools, viewing results, and so on. Figure 1-17 shows various tools in the toolbar.

Figure 1-17 Various tools in the toolbar

Side Toolbar

The Side Toolbar is located on the left side of the interface. It contains different tools which are used for selecting structural entities such as editing loads, supports, member specifications, toggling node labels, beam labels, solid labels, and plate labels. Figure 1-18 shows different tools in the Side Toolbar.

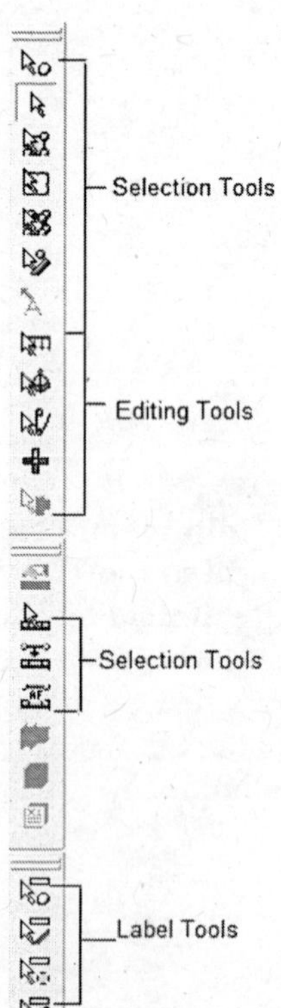

Figure 1-18 Various tools in the Side Toolbar

Mode bar

The STAAD.Pro user interface comprises of various tabs such as **Modeling**, **Postprocessing**, **Steel Design**, **Concrete Design**, **RAM Connection**, **Bridge Deck**, **Advanced Slab Design**, and **Piping**. The options in these tabs are used for creating structure, assigning properties, assigning supports, defining loads, viewing results, steel design, concrete design, and so on. Some of these tabs are discussed next. Figure 1-19 shows different tabs.

Modeling

The **Modeling** tab is located at the top of the Main Window, refer to Figure 1-19. This tab contains different tabs which are used for creating structure, assigning properties, assigning supports, defining loads, and so on. This tab is chosen by default and it displays five different tabs: **Setup**, **Geometry**, **General**, **Analysis/Print**, and **Design**. These tabs are located at the left side of the Main Window and are discussed next.

Setup

In the **Setup** tab, the **Job** page will be displayed, refer to Figure 1-19. In the **Job** page, you can specify general information about the job such as job description, job number, persons responsible for creation, checking, and approving the job. The information is entered in the **Job Info** dialog box which will be available at the right side of the interface, refer to Figure 1-20.

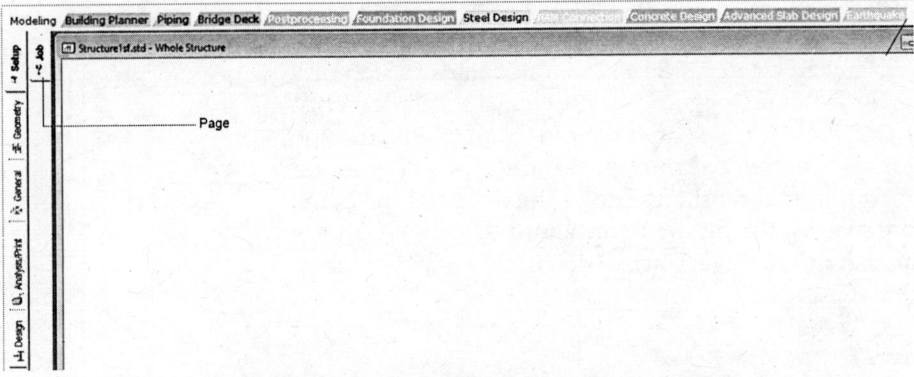

Figure 1-19 Tabs in STAAD.Pro user interface

Structure1sf.std - Job Info
Job
Client
Job No.
Rev.
Part
Ref
File
Filename : Structure1sf.std
Directory : F:\STAAD.Pro Select Series
Date / Time : 19-Oct-2016 05:12 PM
File size : 106 More...
Engineer Checker Approved
Name
Date 19-Oct-16
Comment
Help

*Figure 1-20 The **Job Info** dialog box*

Geometry

Using the options in the **Geometry** tab, you can create nodes, members, plates, surface, solid models, parametric models, and composite deck. This tab comprises of five pages: **Beam**, **Plate**, **Surface**, **Solid**, **Parametric Models**, and **Composite Deck**, refer to Figure 1-21. These pages are discussed next.

In the **Beam** page, you can create frame members such as beams, columns, and truss members. In the **Plate** page, you can create 3 or 4 noded plate elements. In the **Surface** page, you can create surface elements such as a slab or a wall. In the **Solid** page, you can create solid elements. Solid elements are 4 or 8 noded isoparametric type elements. In the **Parametric Models** page, you can preview the final meshed state of the wall, slab or panel before placing the meshed entity into the model. In the **Composite Deck** page, you can define the composite floor deck system.

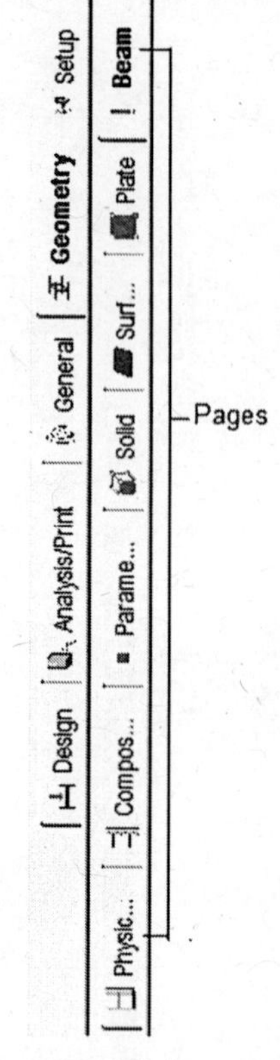

Figure 1-21 Various pages in the Geometry tab

General

In the **General** tab, you can define and edit the material and cross-section properties for a structure, provide structural conditions of a joint, member, or plate, define and assign supports, and define and apply loads. This tab comprises of five pages: **Property**, **Spec**, **Support**, **Load & Definition**, and **Material**. These pages are discussed in detail in later chapters.

Analysis/Print

The **Analysis/Print** tab is used to define pre-print, analysis, and post-analysis print commands. This tab comprises of 3 pages: **Pre-Print**, **Analysis**, and **Post-Analysis**.

In the **Pre-Print** page, you will define the input data information to be printed in the output file. In the **Analysis** page, you will define the type of analysis to be performed. In the **Post Analysis** page, you will define the analysis results to be printed in the output file.

Design

In the **Design** tab, you will define the concrete, steel, aluminium, timber, footing, and shear wall design parameters and commands on the basis of their codes. This tab comprises of six pages: **Steel**, **Concrete**, **Timber**, **Aluminium**, and **Shearwall**.

Post Processing

In the **Post Processing** tab, you can verify the analysis results graphically and numerically. It comprises of four tabs: **Node**, **Beam**, **Animation**, and **Reports**. These tabs allows you to view displacements, reactions, stresses, and so on. These tabs are discussed next.

Node
The **Node** tab allows you to view the displacements at nodes and support reactions. This tab comprises of two pages: **Displacement** and **Reactions**, refer to Figure 1-22.

Beam
The **Beam** tab allows you to view the member end forces and member stresses both graphically and in tabular form. It also allows you to view the bending moment diagram and shear force diagram of individual members at a time. This tab comprises of three pages: **Forces**, **Stresses**, and **Graphs**. These pages are discussed in detail in later chapters.

Animation
The **Animation** tab allows you to graphically view deflections, section displacements, mode shapes and stresses in an animated mode. It contains only the **Animate** page which is discussed in detail in later chapters.

Reports
The **Reports** tab allows you to create customized report. This report will include structural elements, properties, load cases, mode shapes, numerical and graphical results, and so on.

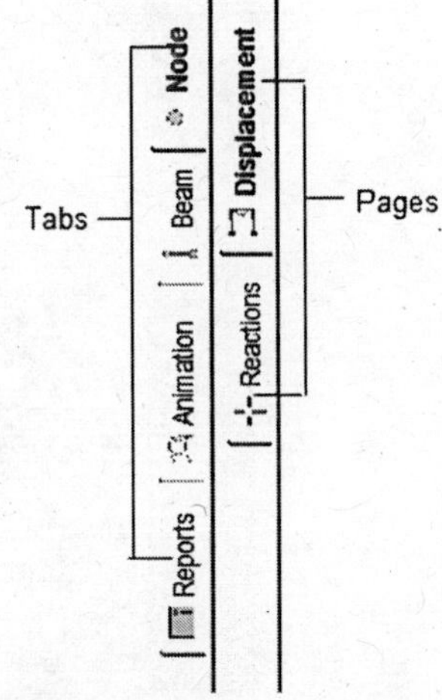

***Figure 1-22** Tabs and pages in the **Post Processing** tab*

Snap Node/Beam Window
The **Snap Node/Beam** window allows you to define snap and grid settings which will be used to create nodes and members simultaneously. Using the options in this tab, you can create linear and circular structures. Figure 1-23 shows the **Snap Node/Beam** window. This window is discussed in detail in later chapters.

Data Area
In STAAD.Pro, the Data Area is located at the right side of the interface. This area contains different windows and tables. In this area, you can provide the coordinates for creating nodes and members, define member properties, define supports, define loads, and so on. This area will be displayed after closing the **Snap Node/Beam** window. Figure 1-24 shows the Data Area which contains the **Nodes** and **Beams** tables.

Main Window
The Main Window covers the largest area in the interface. In the Main Window, the created structure along with the assigned properties, loads, supports, and specifications will be displayed. The analysis results and diagrams will also be displayed in this area. In this window, the global coordinate system axes will be displayed at the left corner. Figure 1-25 shows the structure along with loads and supports in the Main Window.

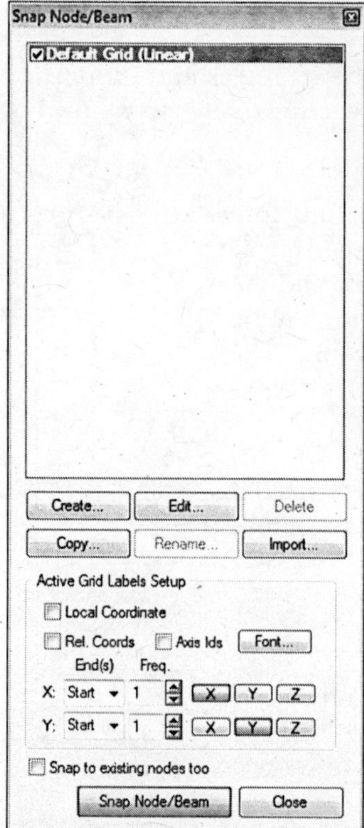

Figure 1-23 The ***Snap Node/Beam*** window

Structure2.std - Nodes

Node	X m	Y m	Z m
1			

Nodes Table

Structure2.std - Beams

Beam	Node A	Node B	Property Refn.
1			

Beams Table

Figure 1-24 The ***Nodes*** and ***Beams*** table in the Data Area

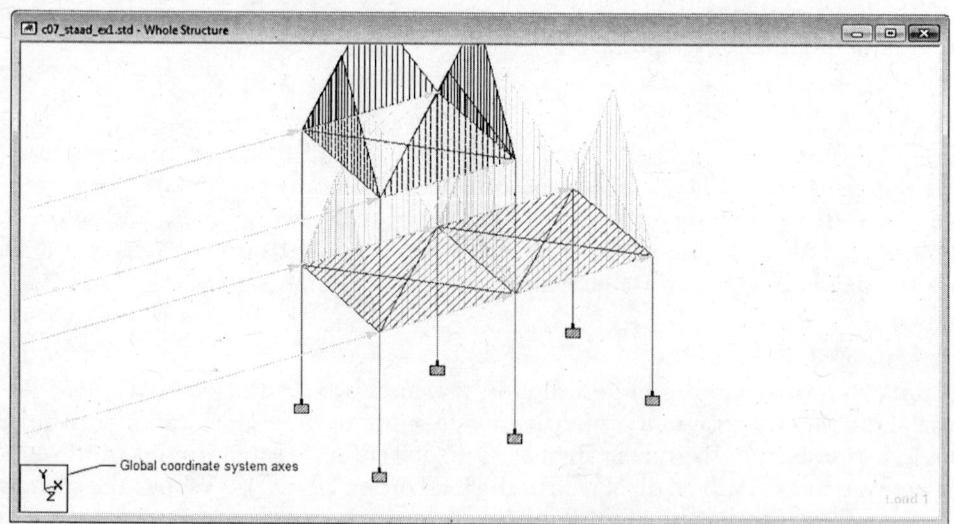

Figure 1-25 Structure displayed in the ***Whole Structure*** window

OPENING AN EXISTING PROJECT

In STAAD.Pro, you can open an existing project by clicking on the **Open Project** option available in the **Project Tasks** area, refer to Figure 1-2. Alternatively, choose the **Open** option from the **File** menu. On doing so, the **Open** dialog box will be displayed, as shown in Figure 1-26. In this dialog box, first browse to the required location and then select the required file from the available list of files. Next, choose the **Open** button; the project will be loaded and structure will be displayed in the **Whole Structure** Window.

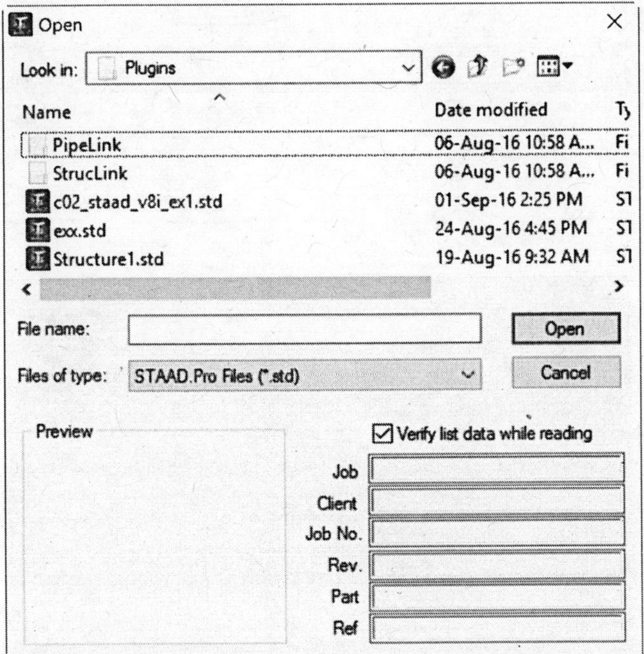

*Figure 1-26 The **Open** dialog box*

SAVING A PROJECT

In STAAD.Pro, you can save a file by choosing the **Save As** option from the **File** menu. On doing so, the **Save As** dialog box will be displayed, as shown in Figure 1-27. Now, browse to the location where the file will be saved. Next, specify the file name in the **File name** text box and then choose the **Save** button; the file will be saved at the specified location.

CONFIGURING UNITS

In STAAD.Pro, there are two base unit systems: english (imperial) and metric. The default unit system will be the one which you have selected while installing the program. You can also change the base units in the program. To do so, click on the **Configuration** option available in the **Project Tasks** area, refer to Figure 1-2. On doing so, the **Configure Program** dialog box will be displayed, as shown in Figure 1-28. In this dialog box, the **Base Unit** tab will be chosen by default. In this tab, the current base unit will be displayed at the top, refer to Figure 1-28. You change the unit by selecting the **English** or **Metric** option from the **Select Base Unit** drop-down list.

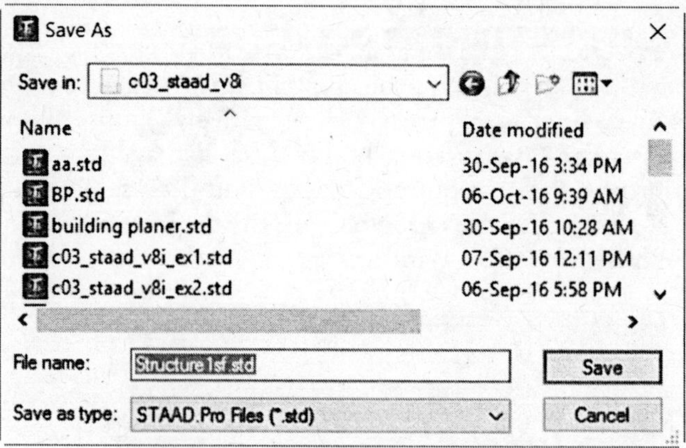

***Figure 1-27** The **Save As** dialog box*

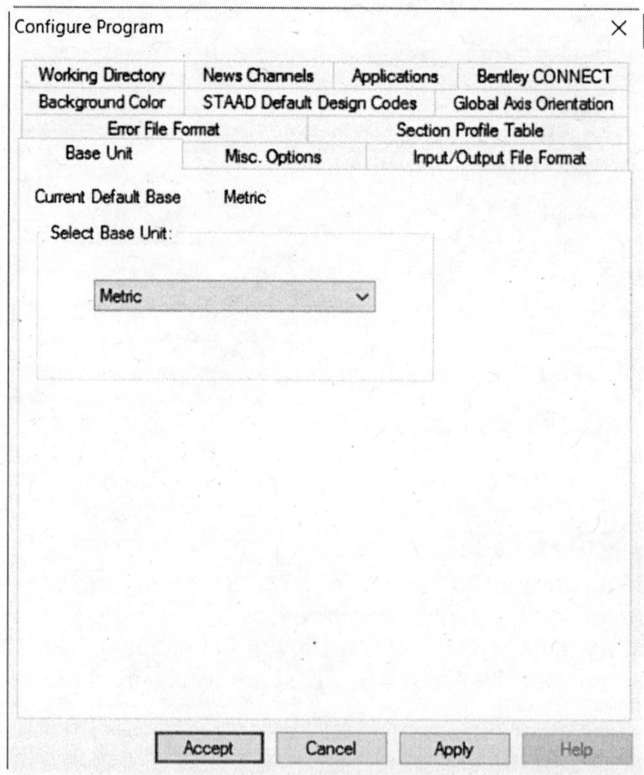

***Figure 1-28** The **Base Unit** tab chosen in the **Configure Program** dialog box*

KEYBOARD SHORTCUTS

In STAAD.Pro, keyboard shortcuts have been assigned to some of the frequently used commands. These shortcuts can be typed using the keyboard to invoke the corresponding command. These shortcut keys are also available in the **Labels** tab of the **Diagrams** dialog box, as shown in Figure 1-29. To invoke the **Diagrams** dialog box, right-click in the main window; a shortcut menu will be displayed. Choose the **Labels** option from the menu to display the **Diagram** dialog box. Table 1-1 shows some of the frequently used shortcut keys in STAAD.Pro.

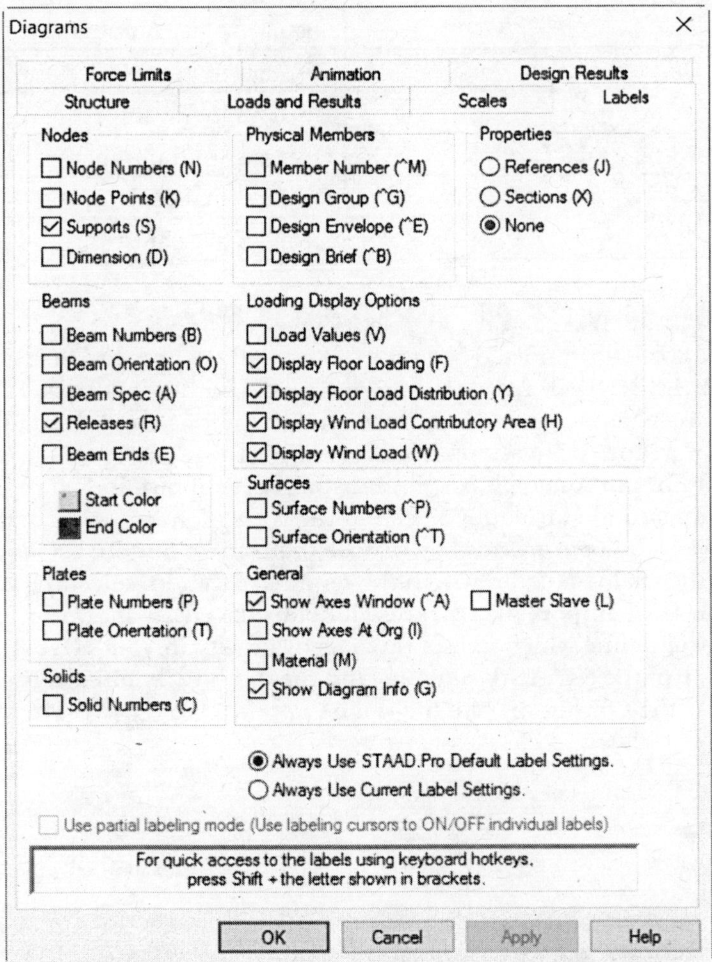

Figure 1-29 *Various shortcut keys displayed in the* ***Labels*** *tab of the* ***Diagrams*** *dialog box*

Table 1-1 Various shortcut keys used in STAAD.Pro

Keyboard Shortcut	Description
SHIFT+N	Displays node numbers
SHIFT+B	Displays beam numbers
SHIFT+S	Displays support icons
SHIFT+E	Displays member ends
SHIFT+O	Displays beam orientation
SHIFT+P	Displays plate numbers
SHIFT+L	Displays master slave node
SHIFT+V	Displays load values
SHIFT+C	Displays solid numbers
SHIFT+M	Displays material
SHIFT+I	Displays axes at origin

IMPORTING A MODEL IN STAAD.Pro

In STAAD.Pro, data can be imported from the following file types: 3D DXF, QSE ASA, Stardyne, and CIS/2. From the 3D DXF file only line diagrams can be imported. From the CIS/2 file, member properties, material constants, member end conditions, support conditions, and loading information can be imported. To import data from any of the files, choose the **Import** option from the **File** menu; the **Import** dialog box will be displayed, as shown in Figure 1-30. In this dialog box, select the required file format by selecting the corresponding radio button. For example, select the **3D DXF** radio button and then choose the **Import** button; the **Open** dialog box will be displayed. In this dialog box, browse to the required location, select the file, and choose the **Open** button; the **DXF Import** dialog box will be displayed, as shown in Figure 1-31. In this dialog box, you will define which axis is the axis of gravity in your STAAD.Pro model. If the axis system is same in the STAAD.Pro model and the dxf file, then select the **No Change** radio button and choose the **OK** button; the file will be imported to STAAD.Pro.

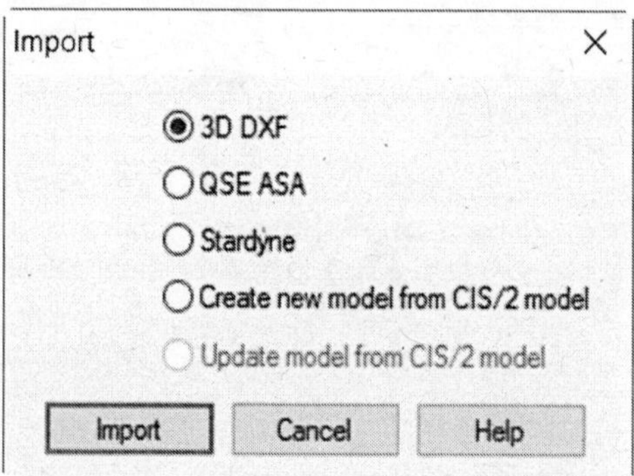

***Figure 1-30** The **Import** dialog box*

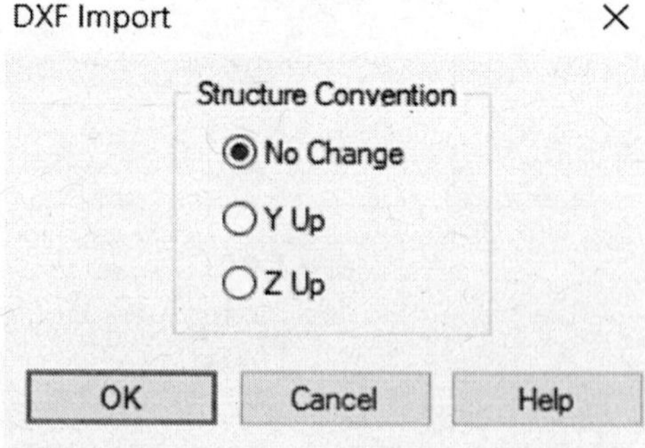

***Figure 1-31** The **DXF Import** dialog box*

Self-Evaluation Test

Answer the following questions and compare them to those given at the end of this chapter:

1. In which of the following menus, does the cursor appear?

   (a) **Tools** (b) **Geometry**
   (c) **Select** (d) None of these

2. Which of the following options is located in the **Tools** menu?

   (a) **Rotate** (b) **Cut Section**
   (c) **Mirror** (d) All of these

3. The _________ shortcut key is used to display the load values.

4. The _________ shortcut key is used to display the member ends.

5. STAAD files are saved in the _________ format.

6. Job information is provided in the **Job Info** dialog box. (T/F)

7. In the **Postprocessing** mode, you can verify the analysis results graphically and numerically. (T/F)

Answers to Self-Evaluation Test

1. c, **2.** b, **3.** SHIFT+V, **4.** SHIFT+E, **5.** .std, **6.** T, **7.** T

Chapter 2

Structural Modeling in STAAD.Pro

Learning Objectives

After completing this chapter, you will be able to:
- *Create structures using STAAD Editor*
- *Create structures using STAAD GUI*
- *Create structures using the Structure Wizard*

INTRODUCTION

Before erecting a structure, you need to run a stability check for the structure. To check the structural stability, you need to model the structure virtually. The virtual structural models comprise of various components such as beams, columns, walls, slabs, and so on. In STAAD.Pro, you can model a structure and then check its structural stability. A structural model in STAAD.Pro is represented as a line structure which consists of nodes and members. Before modeling a structure, you need to determine the nodes and the connection between them.

In STAAD.Pro, nodes are the joints which are capable of resisting forces and moments. Nodes are located at the end of beams, columns, or plates. A node is always represented by a node number. To create nodes, you need to determine its coordinates in the XYZ space. After creating nodes, you can form members or plate elements by connecting the nodes. A member may be a column, beam, or truss, which is generated by connecting two nodes and is represented by a member number. Figure 2-1 shows the nodes and members in a portal frame structure.

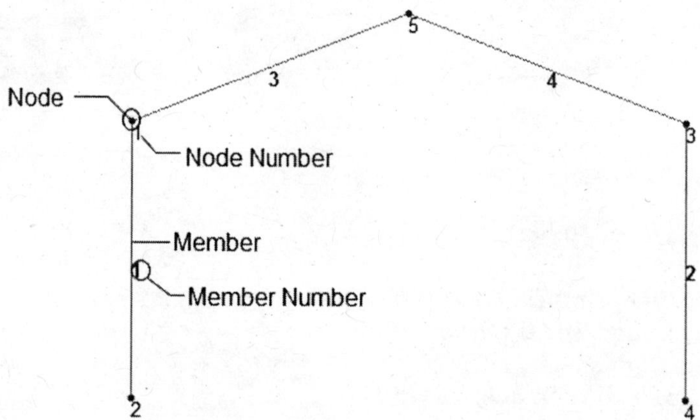

Figure 2-1 *Nodes and members in a portal frame structure*

A plate element is formed by connecting three or four nodes and is represented by a plate number. A plate element can be triangular or quadrilateral. These members and plate elements are represented by member number and element number.

In STAAD.Pro, you can create a structural model by using any of the following methods:

1) Using STAAD Editor
2) Using STAAD GUI
3) Using Structure Wizard
4) Building planner

These methods are discussed next.

STRUCTURAL MODELING USING STAAD EDITOR

In STAAD.Pro, the **STAAD Editor** window contains a list of commands required to model, analyze, and design a structure. These commands are the instructions related to the analysis and design of a structure and are executed consecutively. The **STAAD Editor** window can be invoked by choosing the **STAAD Editor** button from the toolbar. Figure 2-2 shows the default commands in the **STAAD.Pro Editor** window.

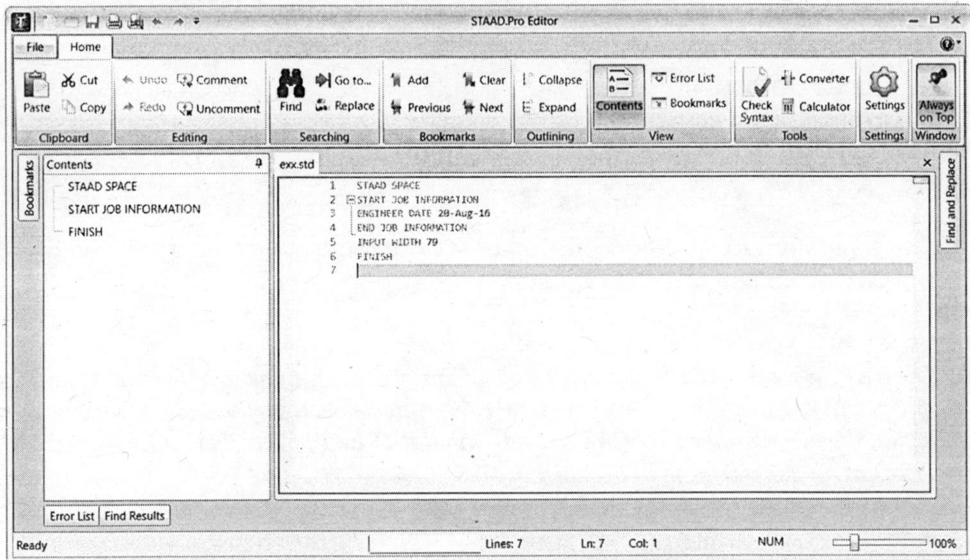

Figure 2-2 The ***STAAD Editor*** *window*

To start the structure geometry, the nodes must be created first and then other elements can be created like beams, plates, surfaces, and solids. The command for creating the nodes is discussed next.

Creating Nodes

Nodes are created by specifying the X, Y, and Z coordinates of the joints in a structure. The command used for specifying the coordinates is **JOINT COORDINATES**. This command will be specified after specifying the unit command. The general format for specifying the coordinates is given below:

```
JOINT COORDINATES
n x y z
```

In the above command, **n** represents the node number and **x**, **y**, and **z** represent the coordinates of the nodes in a structure. To create nodes, first you need to specify the command **JOINT COORDINATES** in the **STAAD Editor** window. Next, you will specify the node number and coordinates for the first node. After specifying the first node, you need to put a semi-colon and then specify the node number and coordinates of the second node, and so on. After specifying the command, choose the **Save** button from the toolbar in the **STAAD Editor** window and then close the window. You can view the node numbers of the created nodes by pressing SHIFT+N.

Note

*The **JOINT COORDINATE** command is not case sensitive. You can also write the initial three letters for the command. For example, enter **JOI COO** for this command. In case you forget to choose the **Save** button before closing the window, then the **Save** dialog box will be displayed. You can save the changes by choosing the **Yes** button.*

You can also generate multiple nodes at a time by using the REPEAT and REPEAT ALL commands. These commands generate the nodes in a repetitive pattern. The general format for specifying the REPEAT and REPEAT ALL commands is given below:

```
JOINT COORDINATES
n x y z
REPEAT n xi yi zi
REPEAT ALL n xi yi zi
```

In the above command, **n** represents the number of times the nodes will be repeated and $\mathbf{x_i}$, $\mathbf{y_i}$, and $\mathbf{z_i}$ represent increments in the **x**, **y**, and **z** coordinates.

Note

*The **REPEAT** command repeats the previous line of input n number of times with the increments specified in x, y, and z directions. The **REPEAT ALL** command repeats all the previously specified inputs. When you use the **REPEAT** command after **REPEAT** or **REPEAT ALL**, then the **REPEAT** command is will create the last created node.*

Note

1. In this chapter, you need to download the c02_staad_v8i.zip file from http://www.cadcim.com for working on the examples. The path of the file is as follows: Textbook > Civil/GIS > STAAD. Pro > Exploring Bentley STAAD.Pro V8i.

2. Before starting the examples, you need to create a folder with the name STAAD Examples in C: drive and then extract the downloaded zip folder to this folder.

Example 1

In this example, you will create nodes for a portal frame structure. This structure will be created as a plane frame structure.

Steps required to complete this example are given below:

Step 1: Start STAAD.Pro and choose the **New Project** option from the **Project Tasks** area in the STAAD.Pro interface; the **New Model** dialog box is displayed. In this dialog box, select the **Plane** check box and specify the name *c02_staad_v8i_ex1* in the **File Name** edit box and browse to the location *C:\ STAAD Examples\c02_staad_v8i* in the **Location** area.

Step 2: Select the **Meter** and **KiloNewton** radio buttons from the **Length Units** and **Force Units** area, respectively and choose the **Next** button; the **Where do you want to go?** window is displayed. In this window, select the **Open STAAD Editor** check box and choose the **Finish** button; the **STAAD.Pro Editor** window is displayed.

Tip

*You can also invoke the **STAAD Editor** window by choosing the **STAAD Editor** button from the toolbar.*

Step 3: In this window, specify the commands, refer to in Figure 2-3.

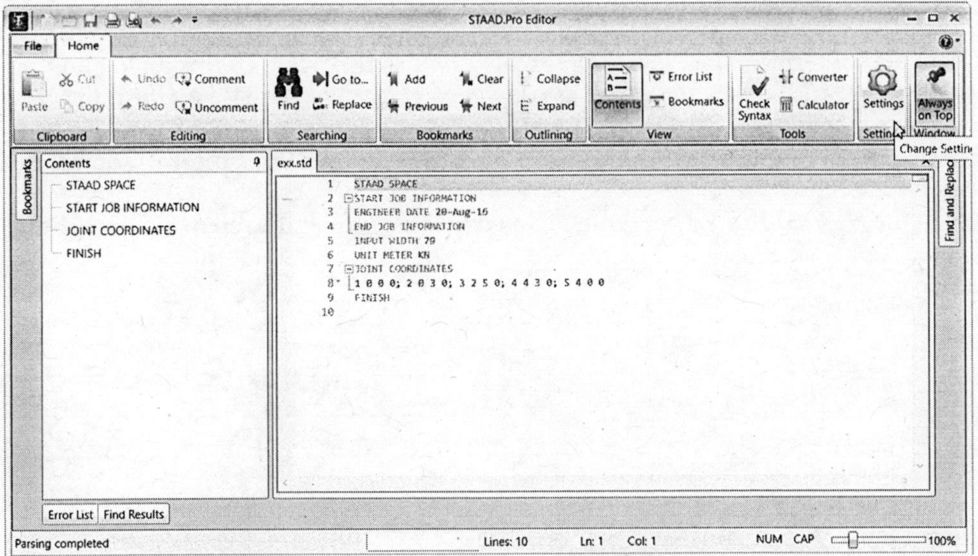

Figure 2-3 *Commands specified in the **STAAD Editor** window*

Step 4: Choose the **Save** button from the toolbar in the **STAAD Editor** window and then close it; the nodes are generated. Press SHIFT+N to view the node numbers, refer to Figure 2-4.

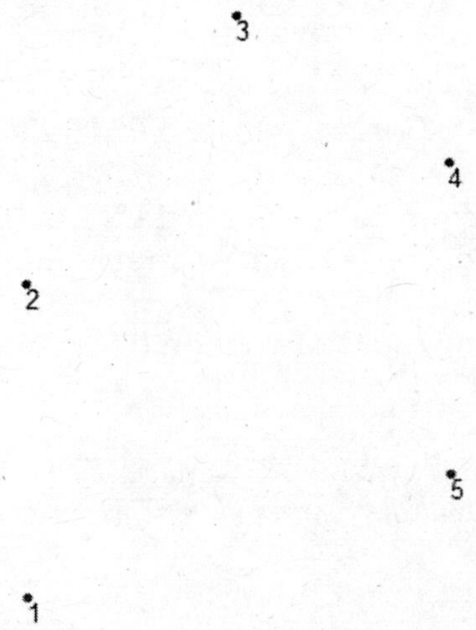

Figure 2-4 *Nodes created using commands*

Example 2

In this example, you will create the nodes for a structure using the **REPEAT** and **REPEAT ALL** commands. The structure will be created as a space frame structure.

Steps required to complete this example are given below:

Step 1: Start STAAD.Pro and then choose the **New Project** option from the **Project Tasks** area in the STAAD.Pro interface; the **New Model** dialog box is displayed. In this dialog box, select the **Space** check box and specify the name as *c02_staad_v8i_ex2* in the **File Name** edit box. Choose the **Next** button and select the **Open STAAD Editor** check box from the **Where do you want to go?** dialog box and then choose the **Finish** button; the **STAAD.Pro Editor** window is displayed.

Step 2: In the **STAAD.Pro Editor** window, specify the commands, refer to Figure 2-5.

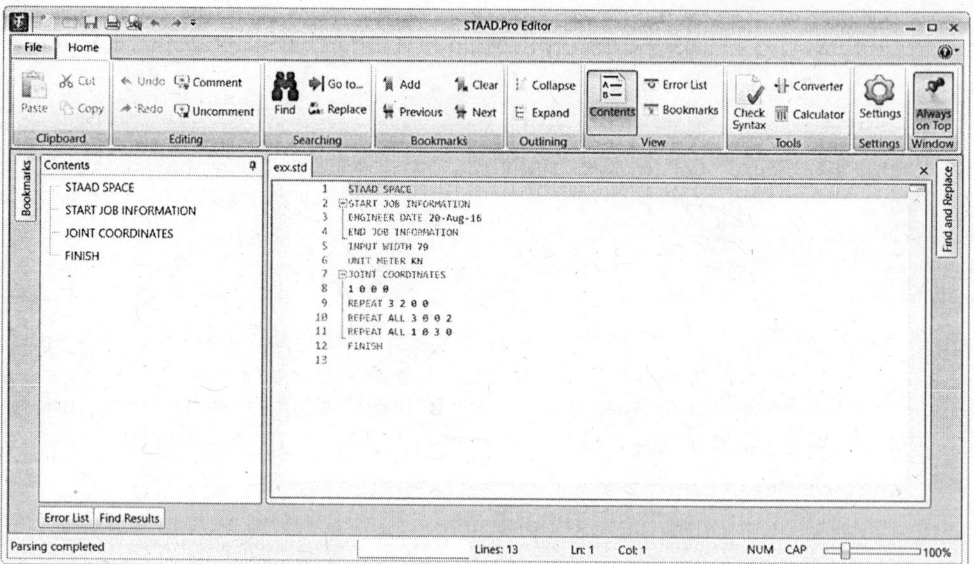

*Figure 2-5 Commands in the **STAAD Editor** window*

Step 3: Choose the **Save** button from the toolbar in the **STAAD Editor** window and then close the window; the nodes are generated. Press SHIFT+N to view the node numbers, refer to Figure 2-6.

Step 4: Close the file by choosing the **Close** option from the **File** menu.

Note

*Whenever you save a project in STAAD.Pro, the **REPEAT** and **REPEAT ALL** commands are converted into comments and the coordinates of each node are generated in the **STAAD Editor** window.*

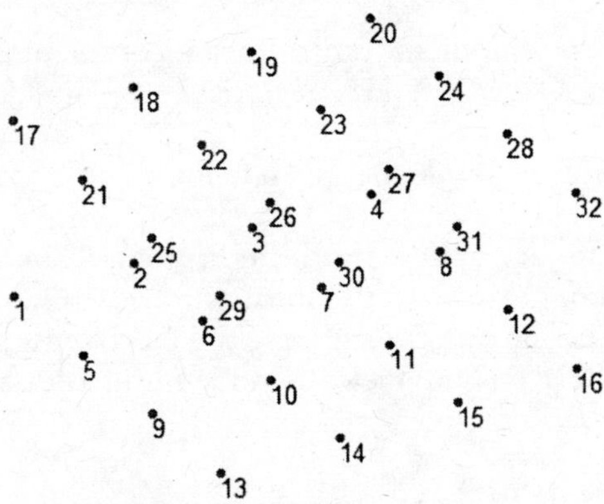

Figure 2-6 Nodes of the space frame structure

Creating Members

You can create members by specifying their start and end nodes. The command for creating a member is **MEMBER INCIDENCES**. The general format for creating members is given below:

```
MEMBER INCIDENCES
m i j
```

Here, **m** represents the member number and **i, j** represents the start and end nodes, respectively. After creating nodes, you need to create members by specifying the connectivity between nodes. The **REPEAT** and **REPEAT ALL** commands can also be used for easy generation of the members. The general format to use the **REPEAT** and **REPEAT ALL** commands for creating members is given below:

```
MEMBER INCIDENCES
m i j
REPEAT   n i_i j_i
REPEAT ALL   n i_i j_i
```

In the above command, **n** represents the number of times the previously created member will be repeated, $\mathbf{i_i}$ represents the member number increment, and $\mathbf{j_i}$ represents the node number increment.

In this case, the **REPEAT** command will create the previously created member for specified number of times with specified increment in node numbers and member numbers. The **REPEAT ALL** command will create all the previously created members for specified number of times with specified increment in node numbers and member numbers.

Note

*To use the **REPEAT** and **REPEAT ALL** commands for creating members, you need to number the members in consecutive order.*

Example 3

In this example, you will create the members to form a complete portal frame structure. The file used in this example is *c02_staad_v8i_ex1.std*.

Steps required to complete this example are given below:

Step 1: Choose the **Open Project** option from the **Project Tasks** area; the **Open** dialog box is displayed. In this dialog box, browse to the location: *C:\ STAAD Examples\c02_staad_v8i* and select the *c02_staad_v8i_ex1.std* file and then choose the **Open** button; the *c02_Staad_v8i_ex1.std* window is displayed. Press SHIFT+N to view the node numbers, refer to Figure 2-7.

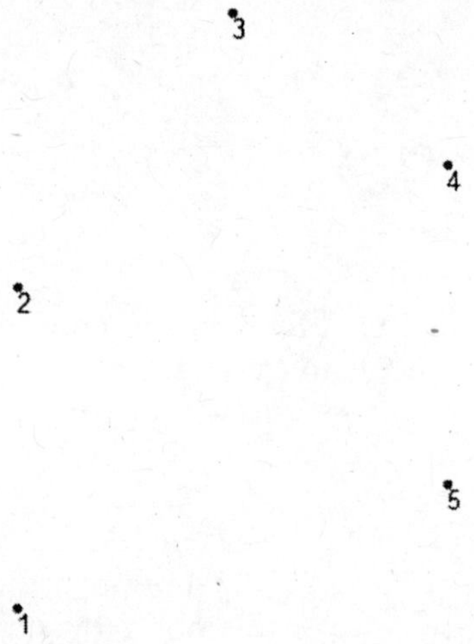

3

4

2

5

1

Figure 2-7 *Node numbers for the nodes*

Step 2: Invoke the **STAAD Editor** window and specify the commands for creating the members, refer to Figure 2-8.

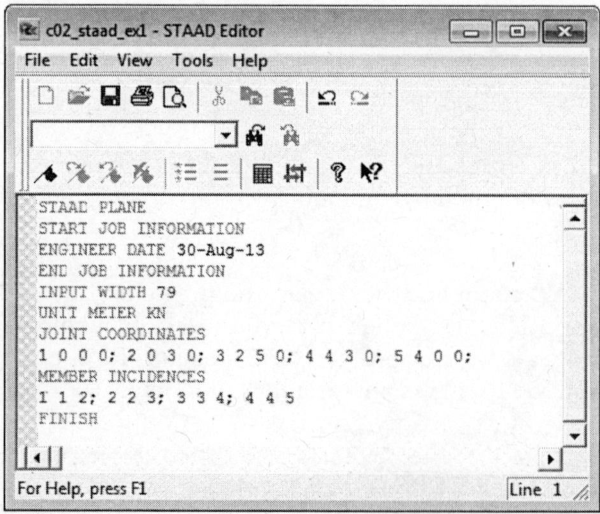

Figure 2-8 *Commands for creating the members in the* ***STAAD Editor*** *window*

Step 3: Choose the **Save** button from the toolbar in the **STAAD Editor** window and then close it; the members are generated. Press SHIFT+B to view the member numbers, refer to Figure 2-9.

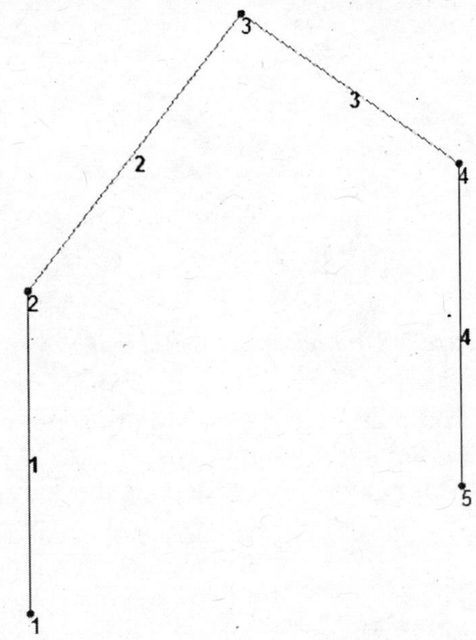

Figure 2-9 *Members created to complete the structure*

Step 4: Choose the **Save As** option from the **File** menu; the **Save As** dialog box is displayed. In this dialog box, specify the name *c02_staad_v8i_ex3* in the **File name** edit box and save it at an appropriate location.

Example 4

In this example, you will create members using the **REPEAT** and **REPEAT ALL** commands and form a complete space frame structure. The file used in this example is *c02_staad_v8i_ex2.std*.

Steps required to complete this example are given below:

Step 1: Open the *c02_staad_v8i_ex2.std* file, as discussed in Example 3. Choose the **Geometry** tab and press SHIFT+N to view the node numbers.

Step 2: Invoke the **STAAD Editor** window and specify the commands given below after the **Joint Coordinates** command:

```
MEMBER INCIDENCES
1 1 17
```

Step 3: After specifying the above command, choose the **Save** button and close the **STAAD Editor** window; the member 1 will be created, as shown in Figure 2-10. Click on working area and then Press SHIFT+B to view the member number.

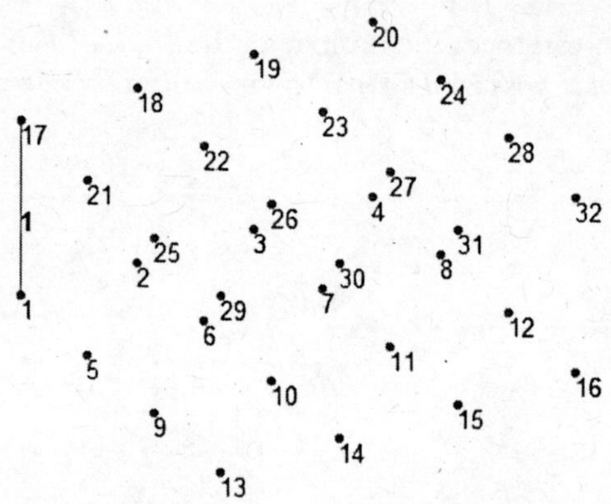

Figure 2-10 Member 1 created using commands

Step 4: Specify the **REPEAT** command after specifying the command in step 2 in the **STAAD Editor** window, as given below. After specifying the command, choose the **Save** button and close the **STAAD Editor** window; the members are created, as shown in Figure 2-11.

```
REPEAT 3 1 1
```

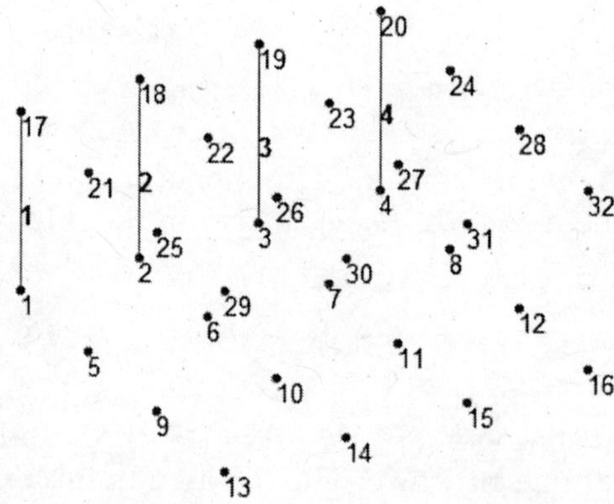

*Figure 2-11 Members created using the **REPEAT** command*

Step 5: Specify the next command given below in the **STAAD Editor** window. Next, choose the **Save** button and close the **STAAD Editor** window; the members are created, as shown in Figure 2-12.

```
REPEAT ALL 3 4 4
```

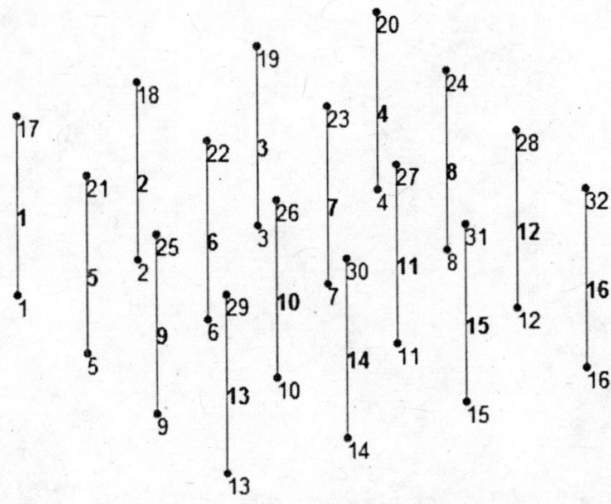

*Figure 2-12 Members created using the **REPEAT ALL** command*

Step 6: Next, create the horizontal members by specifying the command given next.

```
17 17 18
REPEAT 2 1 1
REPEAT ALL 3 3 4
```

Step 7: Choose the **Save** button and close the **STAAD Editor** window; the members are created, as shown in Figure 2-13.

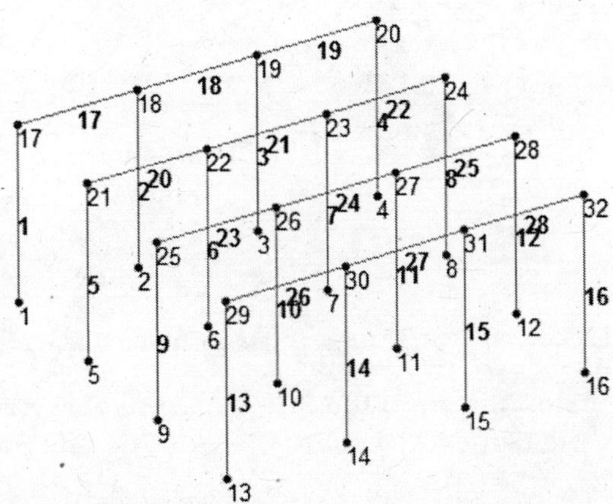

Figure 2-13 Horizontal members created

Step 8: Next, specify the command to create the remaining members as given below and the structure is completed, as shown in Figure 2-14. Figure 2-15 shows the **STAAD Editor** window with all the commands.

```
29 17 21
REPEAT 3 1 1
REPEAT ALL 2 4 4
```

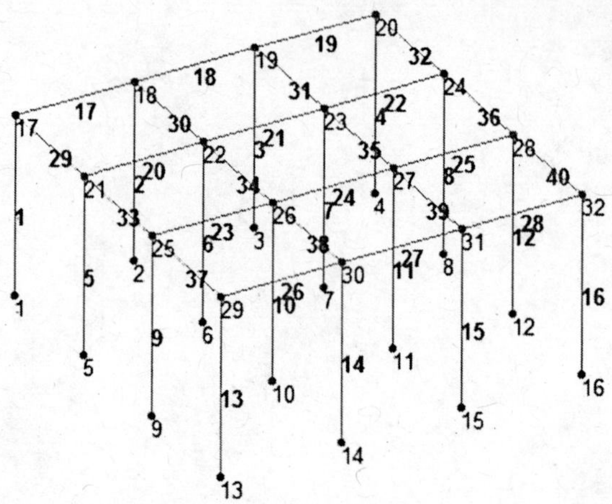

***Figure 2-14** The complete structure after creating members*

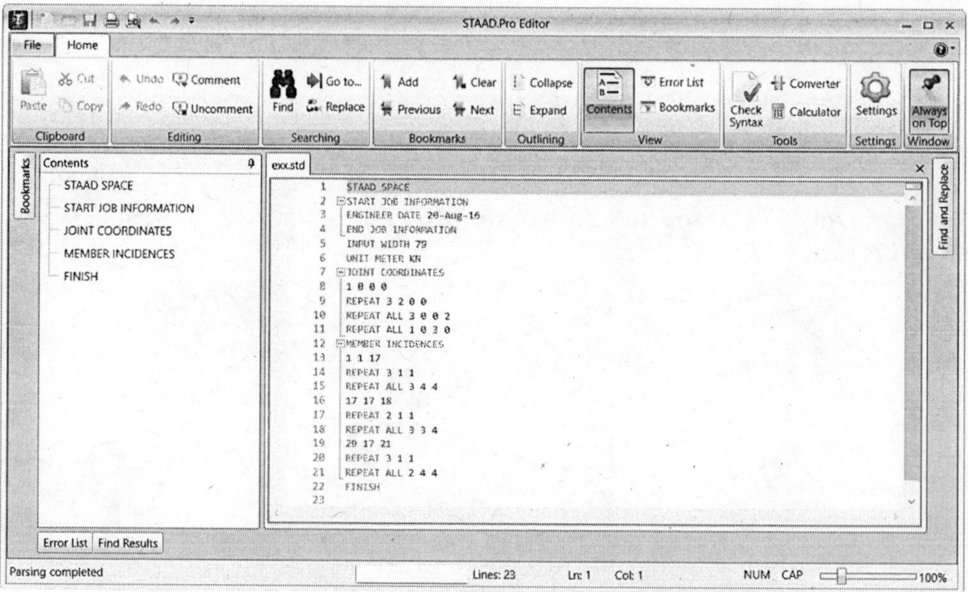

***Figure 2-15** Commands for creating members in the **STAAD Editor** window*

Step 9: Choose the **Save As** option from the **File** menu; the **Save As** dialog box is displayed. In this dialog box, specify the name *c02_staad_v8i_ex4* in the **File name** edit box and save it at an appropriate location.

The commands for creating members can also be written as given below:

```
MEMBER INCIDENCES
1 1 17 4
REPEAT ALL 3 4 4
17 17 18 19
REPEAT ALL 3 3 4
29 17 21 32
REPEAT ALL 2 4 4
```

In the first line of the above command, the span of the member 1 is from node 1 to node 17 and the new members will be generated with the member number increment and the node number increment as 1. Thus, the spans of the members numbered as 2, 3, and 4 are from nodes 2 to 18, 3 to 19, and 4 to 20, respectively.

Similarly, in the third and fourth line of the command, the members 17 to 19 and 29 to 32 will be formed.

Creating Plate Elements

In STAAD.Pro, a plate is a thin shell with multi-noded shape. It can have three or four nodes. A plate is used to model a floor slab, roof, or wall that does not need to be designed as a shear wall. For modeling a shear wall, you need to use the **Add Surface** tool. This tool will be discussed later in this chapter. But, to model a slab, roof, or wall, you need to create several plates which can be done by meshing. The process of meshing will be discussed later in this chapter.

To create a plate, first you need to create nodes. Next, identify connectivity between the nodes and create the plates. The command for creating a plate is given next.

ELEMENT INCIDENCES

p i_1 i_2 i_3 i_4

In the above command, **p** represents plate number, $\mathbf{i_1}$, $\mathbf{i_2}$, $\mathbf{i_3}$, and $\mathbf{i_4}$ represent node numbers. The order of these node numbers can be clockwise or anti-clockwise

If the plate is 3-noded, then i_4 node is not needed. Note that, if you have created members in the project then the member numbers and element numbers must be distinct. You can also create plate elements by using the **REPEAT** and **REPEAT ALL** commands. The general format for using these commands is given below:

ELEMENT INCIDENCES

p i_1 i_2 i_3 i_4

REPEAT n e_i j_i

REPEAT ALL n e_i j_i

In the above command, **n** represents number. of times the plate will be repeated, $\mathbf{e_i}$ represents the element number increment, and $\mathbf{j_i}$ represents the node number increment.

In this case, the **REPEAT** and **REPEAT ALL** commands will generate the previously created plate n number of times, with the specified plate and node number increment.

Example 5

In this example, you will create plate elements for the plane structure using the **REPEAT** and **REPEAT ALL** commands.

Steps required to complete this example are given below:

Step 1: Create a new file in STAAD.Pro with the name *c02_staad_v8i_ex5* and invoke the **STAAD Editor** window, as discussed earlier. Specify the commands to create nodes and members, as shown in Figure 2-16.

Step 2: Choose the **Save** button and close the **STAAD Editor** window; the nodes and members are created, as shown in Figure 2-17. Press Shift+N and Shift+B to view the number of nodes and beams respectively.

Step 3: Next, invoke the **STAAD Editor** window and specify the command for creating plates, as given below:

```
ELEMENT INCIDENCES
18 1 2 6 5
```

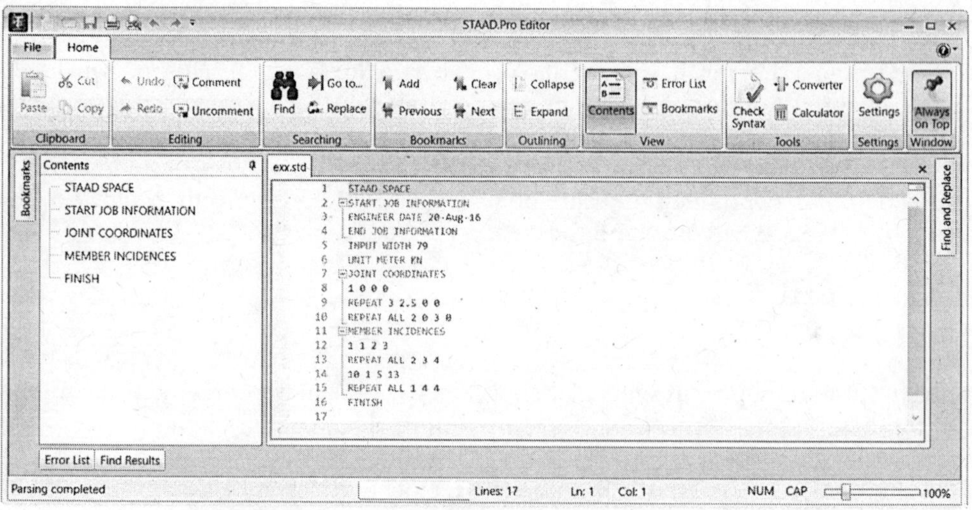

Figure 2-16 Commands for creating nodes and members

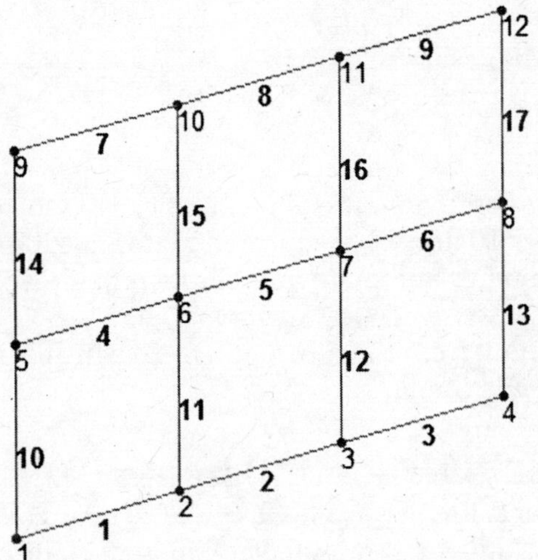

Figure 2-17 Nodes and members created

Note

*You can view the created plate elements in the **Rendered View** window. This window can be invoked by choosing the **3D Rendered View** button from the toolbar.*

Step 4: Specify the commands in the **STAAD.Pro Editor** window as given below to create the remaining plates, as shown in Figure 2-18. Press SHIFT + P to view the plate numbers.

```
REPEAT 2 1 1
REPEAT ALL 1 3 4
```

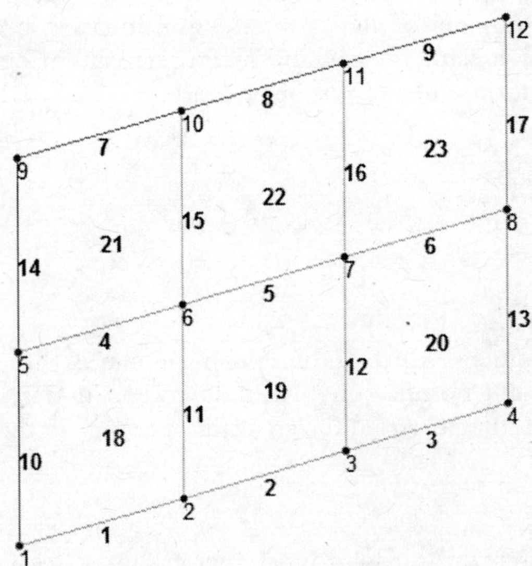

Figure 2-18 Plates created using commands

The commands used for creating plates can also be written as given below:

```
ELEMENT INCIDENCES
18 1 2 6 5 TO 20
REPEAT ALL 1 3 4
```

In the first line of the above command, the plate number 18 is formed by connecting the nodes 1, 2, 6, and 5. Plate number 19 and 20 are formed by connecting the node numbers 2, 3, 7, 6 and 3, 4, 8, 7. The node number and plate number increment is 1.

Step 5: Choose the **Save** option from the **File** menu to save the file and then close it by choosing the **Close** option from the **File** menu.

Creating Solid and Surface Elements

In STAAD.Pro, solid elements are used to analyze the structures which include 3 dimensional stresses such as concrete gravity dams. A solid element is an eight-noded element and has three translational degrees of freedom per node. To create solid elements, first you need to create the nodes. The command for creating the solid elements is given below:

```
ELEMENT INCIDENCES SOLID
c i1 i2 i3 i4 i5 i6 i7 i8
REPEAT ni ei ji
REPEAT ALL ni ei ji
```

Here, **c** is the element number or solid number. $\mathbf{i_1}$ to $\mathbf{i_8}$ represent the node numbers, and **n**, $\mathbf{e_i}$, $\mathbf{j_i}$ are same as for plate elements discussed earlier.

In STAAD.Pro, a surface is used to model slab, shear walls, bridge deck, and so on. A surface element is a collection of number of plates which makes it easier for the users to apply a single element to the entire wall or slab. You can also insert rectangular openings to the surface. The command for creating a surface element is given below:

```
SET DIVISION m
SURFACE INCIDENCE
n1,....., ni SURFACE s DIV sd1,.....,sdj
RECOPENING x1 y2 z3 x2 y2 z2 x3 y3 z3 x4 y4 z4
```

Here, **m** represents number of divisions to be generated between each pair of adjacent nodes, $\mathbf{n_1}$,....,$\mathbf{n_j}$ represent node numbers which defines the perimeter of the surface, **s** represents surface number, $\mathbf{sd_1}$,....,$\mathbf{sd_j}$ represent number of divisions between nodes, and $\mathbf{x_1}$ $\mathbf{y_2}$ $\mathbf{z_3}$.... represents coordinates of the corners that are used for creating openings in the surface.

Example 6

In this example, you will create the solid block element in space frame by using the **STAAD Editor** commands.

Steps required to complete this example are given below:

Step 1: Create a new STAAD file with the name *c02_staad_v8i_ex6.std* and invoke the **STAAD. Pro Editor** window. Specify the commands for creating nodes as given below:

```
UNIT METER KN
JOINT COORDINATES
1 0 0 0 3 3 0 0
4 0 0 2 6 3 0 2
REPEAT ALL 1 0 2 0
```

Step 2: Next, specify the commands for creating solid elements as given below:

```
ELEMENT INCIDENCES SOLID
1 4 5 11 10 1 2 8 7 TO 2
```

In the above command, 1 represents the solid number which will be created by connecting the eight nodes in a sequence and TO represents the solid number 2 which will be created automatically by connecting its corresponding nodes in the same manner.

Step 3: Choose the **Save** button and close the **STAAD.Pro Editor** window; the solid elements are created, press SHIFT+C to view the solid element numbers. As shown in Figure 2-19.

Note

*You can view the element in the **Rendered View** window. The **Rendered View** window can be invoked by choosing the **3D Rendered View** button from the toolbar.*

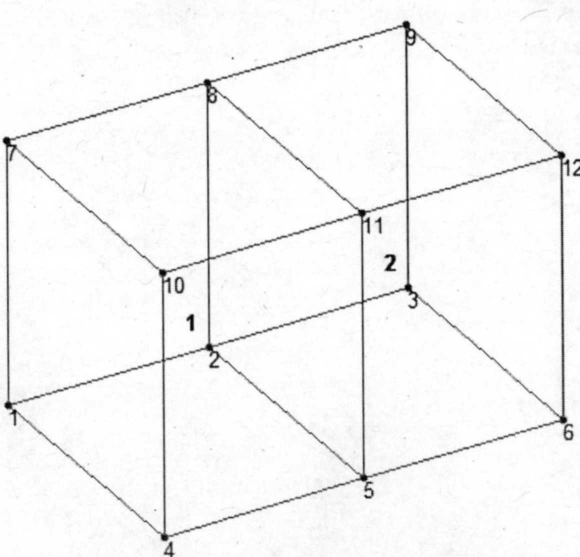

Figure 2-19 Solid elements created using commands

Step 4: Choose the **Save** option from the **File** menu to save the file and then close it by choosing the **Close** option from the **File** menu.

STRUCTURAL MODELING USING STAAD GUI

You can model the structural geometry using the STAAD Graphical User Interface (GUI). The STAAD GUI comprises of various graphical tools that are used to generate the structure. Whenever you model the structure using the graphical tools, the **STAAD Editor** window will be automatically updated with the associated commands. Thus, the graphical model generation and the command file methods are interrelated to each other. The changes made in the former will be reflected in the latter and vice-versa. It is essential for the users to learn both the methods so that they can easily make any change and update it in the model. There are various tools and methods available for modeling a structure. Some important methods are discussed next.

Creating Nodes and Members Using Snap Node/Beam Method

In the Snap Node/Beam method, the nodes and members are generated simultaneously. In this method, to create nodes and members, first you need to specify the grid and snap settings. The options related to the grid and snap settings will be available in the **Snap Node/Beam** window. This window will be displayed in the **Beam** page of the **Geometry** tab. When you open a new file in STAAD.Pro, ensure that the **Add Beam** check box is selected in the **Where do you want to go?** window. On doing so, the **Snap Node/Beam** window will be displayed, as shown in Figure 2-20. You can also invoke the **Snap Node/Beam** window by choosing the **Snap Node/Beam** button from the toolbar.

In this window, the **Create** button is used to create new grids. The **Edit** button is used to configure the settings of an existing grid. The **Delete** button is used to remove an existing grid from the window. The **Copy** button is used to create a copy of an existing grid. You can change the name of the grid by using the **Rename** button. You can import a grid setting created in AutoCAD by using the **Import** button.

In the **Snap Node/Beam** window, you need to specify the settings of construction lines for creating nodes and members. In STAAD.Pro, there are three grid systems which can be used for specifying the settings of the construction lines. By default, the linear grid system is defined in the window, refer to Figure 2-20. In this window, the active grid system will be selected and highlighted. The three different grid systems available in STAAD.Pro are discussed next.

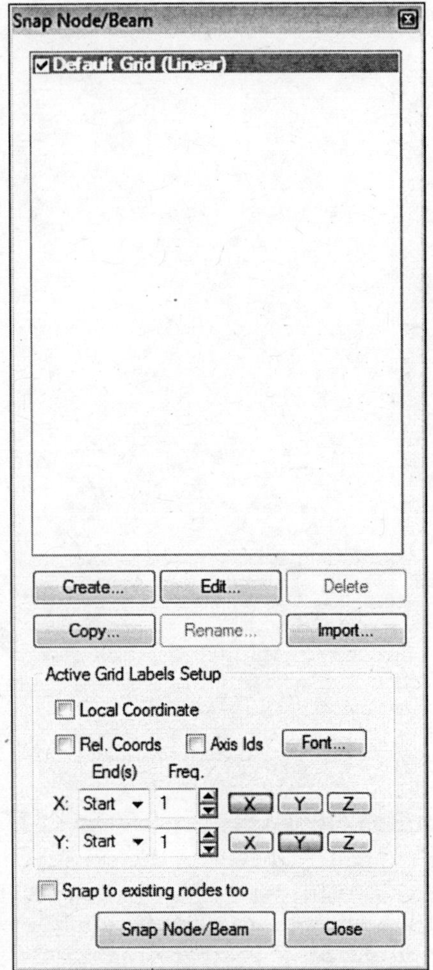

***Figure 2-20** The **Snap Node/Beam** window*

Linear Grid

In the linear grid system, the construction lines are perpendicular to each other. You can also create a new linear, radial, and irregular grid system. To create a linear grid system, choose the **Create** button in the **Snap/Node Beam** window; the **Linear** dialog box will be displayed, as shown in Figure 2-21.

In the **Linear** dialog box, the **Linear** option will be selected by default in the drop-down list available at the top of the dialog box. You can specify the name of the grid system in the **Name** edit box. Specify the required plane for the grid lines in which the structure will be drawn from the **Plane** area. For example, if a structure is to be drawn in the XY plane, select the **X-Y** radio button. Specify the angle of rotation of a plane about an axis in the corresponding edit box in the **Angle of Plane** area. Next, specify the coordinates of the origin of the grid in the **X**, **Y**, and **Z** edit boxes in the **Grid Origin** area. In the **Construction Lines** area, you can adjust the settings of the construction lines. To display the coordinates on the negative direction of X and Y axes, specify the required values in the **Left** column of the **X** and **Y** edit boxes by using the spinner. Specify the spacing between the grids in the **Spacing** edit box. To place the axes at an angle, specify the required value in the edit boxes corresponding to **Skew**. Figure 2-22 shows a linear grid system.

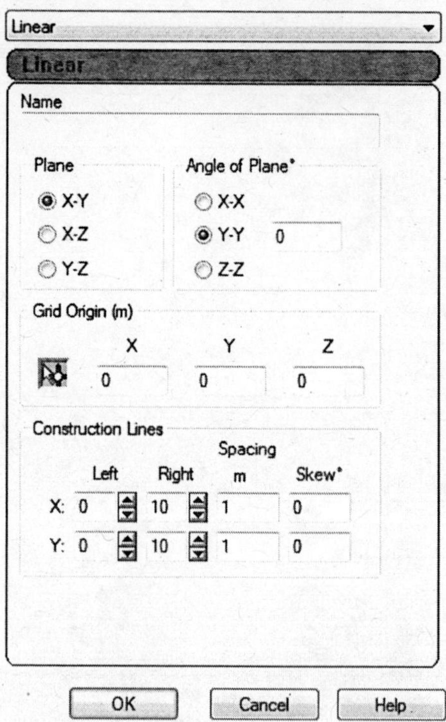

Figure 2-21 *The* ***Linear*** *dialog box*

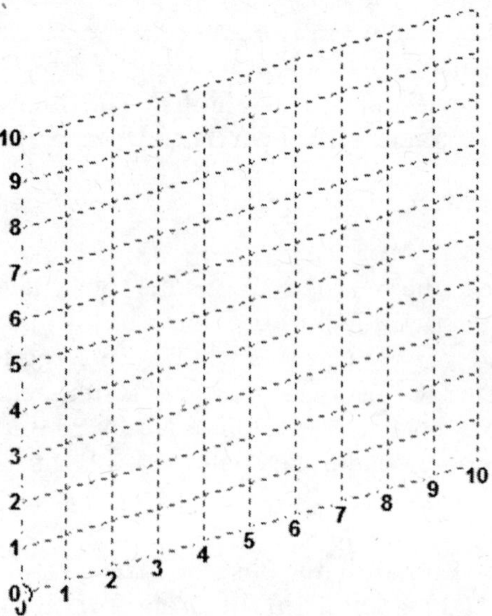

Figure 2-22 *The linear grid*

Radial Grid

In a radial grid system, the construction lines will appear in a spider-web style. In this grid style, you can create circular structures by creating small linear members. To create a radial grid system, choose the **Create** button from the **Snap/Node Beam** window; the **Linear** dialog box will be displayed, refer to Figure 2-21. Select the **Radial** option from the drop-down list available at the top; the **Radial** dialog box will be displayed and the options related to the radial grid system will be displayed, as shown in Figure 2-23.

In the **Radial** dialog box, you can specify the plane, angle of plane, and grid origin for the radial grid system in the same way as discussed for the linear grid system. In the **Construction Lines** area, specify the start angle of the grid in the **Start Angle** edit box. Specify the total angle of sweep in the **Sweep** edit box. Specify the inner and outer radius in the **Radius 1** and **Radius 2** edit boxes, respectively. Specify the number of bays in the **Bays** edit box. Figure 2-24 shows the radial grid system.

Note

Increasing the number of bays in the first ***Bays*** *edit box produces a better circular structure.*

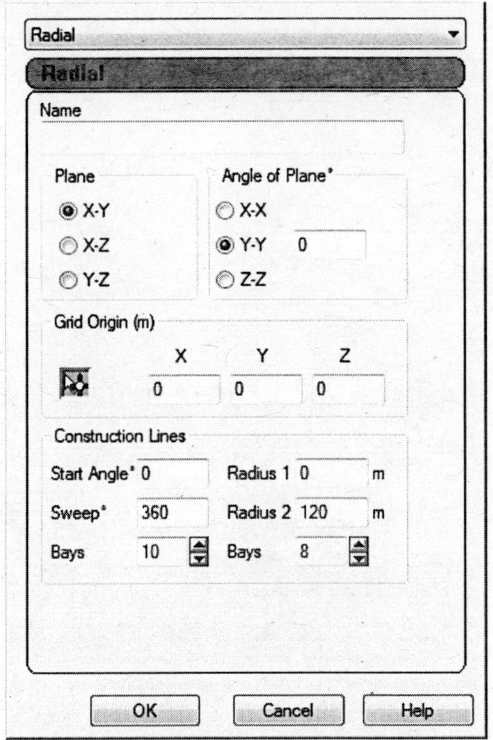

*Figure 2-23 The **Radial** dialog box*

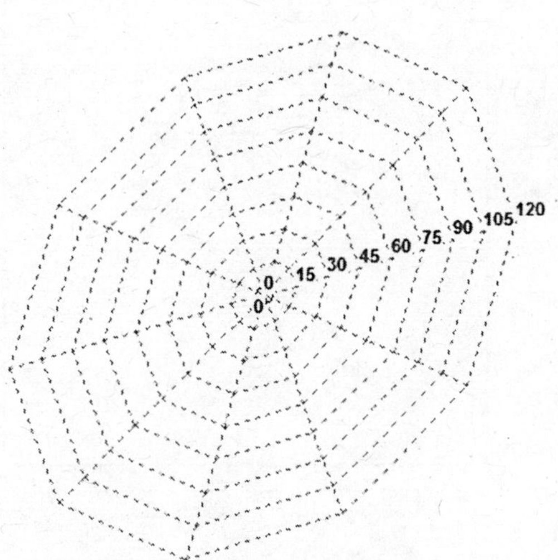

Figure 2-24 The radial grid system

Irregular Grid

In the irregular grid system, you can create the grid lines with unequal spacing. The process of creating an irregular grid is the same as discussed above for the linear and radial grid system. In this case, you can specify the relative grid distance in the X and Y edit boxes of the **Relative gridline distances** area in the **Irregular** dialog box, refer to Figure 2-25.

After creating the required grid system, choose the **OK** button; the **Snap Node/Beam** window will be displayed. Using this window, you can choose the desired grid system. For example, to create a linear structure, select the check box corresponding to the linear grid system. Next, choose the **Snap Node/Beam** button, if not chosen by default; a plus cursor will appear on the grids displayed in the main window area. Next, to create the nodes, click on the intersection point of the grids; the members will also be created along with the nodes. Figure 2-26 shows an irregular grid system.

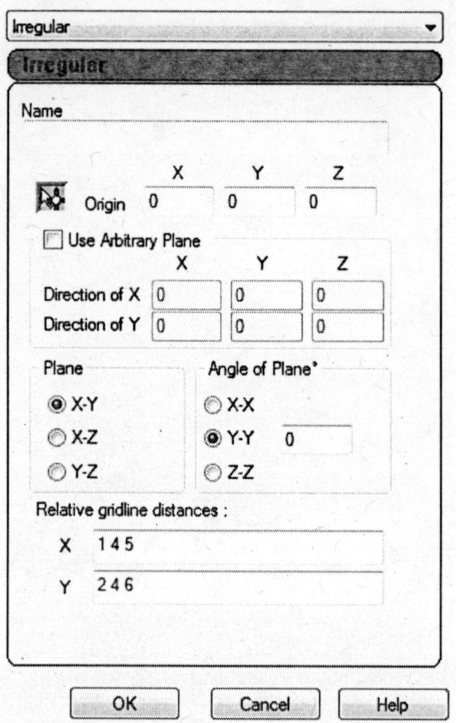

Figure 2-25 *The* ***Irregular*** *dialog box*

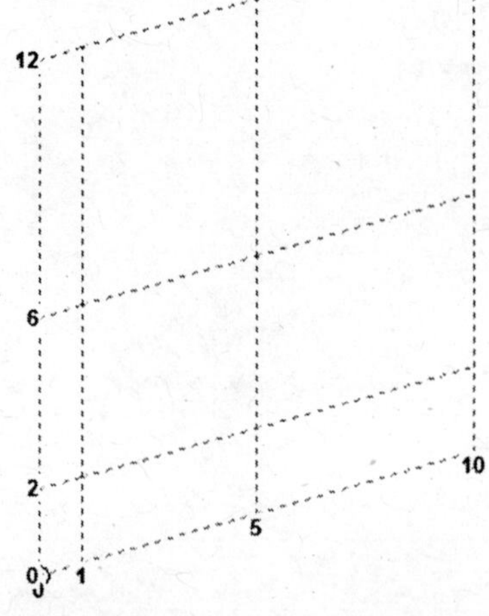

Figure 2-26 *The irregular grid system*

Example 7

In this example, you will create a structure, as shown in Figure 2-27 using the **Snap Node/Beam** method.

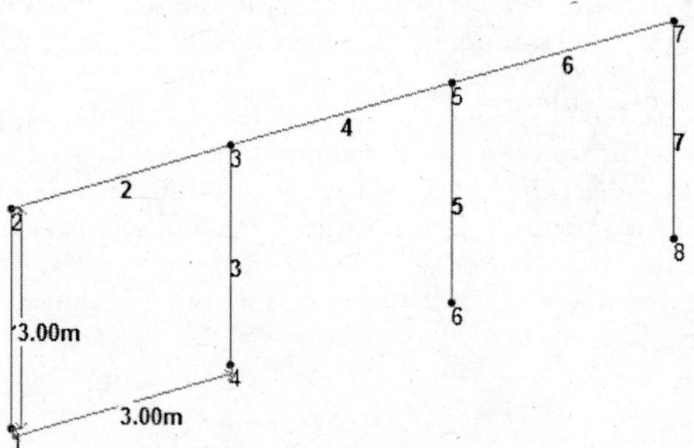

Figure 2-27 *Portal frame structure*

Steps required to complete this example are given next:

Step 1: Choose the **New Project** option from the **Project Tasks** area in the STAAD.Pro interface; the **New Model** dialog box is displayed. In this dialog box, select the **Plane** check box and specify the name *c02_staad_v8i_ex7* in the **File Name** edit box and choose the **Next** button; the **Where do you want to go**? window is displayed.

Step 2: Ensure that the **Add Beam** check box is selected in the **Where do you want to go?** window. Next choose the **Finish** button; the **Snap Node/Beam** window is displayed. In this window, choose the **Edit** button; the **Linear** dialog box is displayed.

Step 3: In this dialog box, ensure that the spacing between grids is **1** and other default settings are retained. Choose the **OK** button to close the dialog box.

Step 4: Place the cursor at the origin and click; node1 is created and a member is attached to the cursor, refer to Figure 2-28.

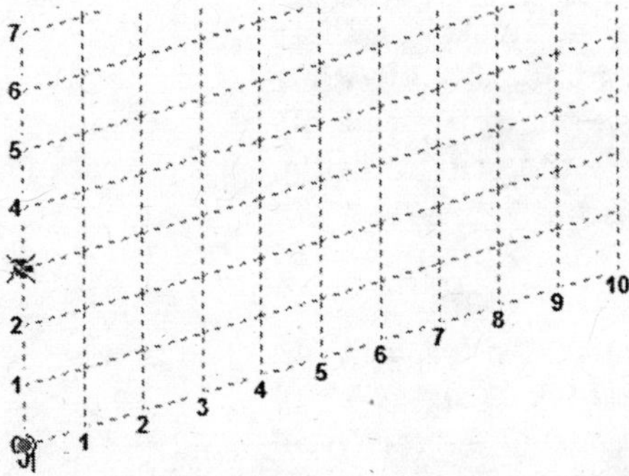

Figure 2-28 *Node 1 created at the origin*

Step 5: Next, move the cursor in the Y direction and click at (0,3) coordinates; the node 2 is created along with the member 1, refer to Figure 2-29.

Step 6: Now, move the cursor in the X direction and click at the coordinates (3,3); the node 3 is created along with the member 2, refer to Figure 2-29.

Step 7: Move the cursor in the negative Y direction and create node 4 at coordinates (3,0), along with member 3. Press **SHIFT+B**, refer to Figure 2-29.

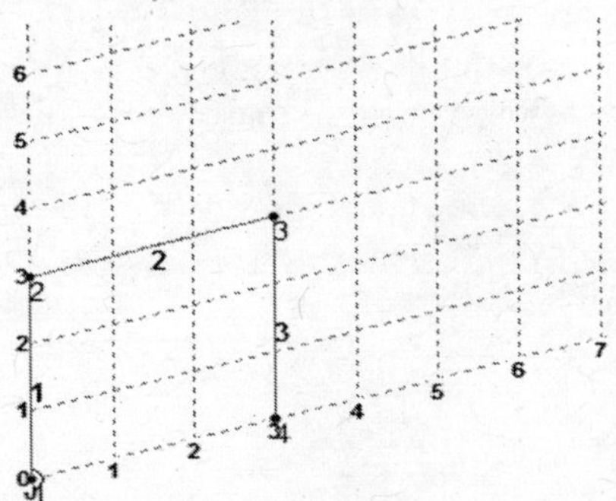

Figure 2-29 *Nodes 2, 3, and 4 created alongwith the members*

Step 8: Now, press the ESC key to deactivate the **Snap Node/Beam** mode.

Step 9: Again, choose the **Snap Node/Beam** button from the **Snap Node/Beam** window; the **Snap Node/Beam** mode will be activated. Repeat the previous steps to create nodes 5, 6, 7, and 8 with members 4, 5, 6, and 7.

Step 10: Next, close the **Snap Node/Beam** window; the structure is created, refer to Figure 2-27.

Step 11: Choose the **Save** option from the **File** menu to save the file and then close it by choosing the **Close** option from the **File** menu.

Creating Plate Elements Using the Snap Node/Plate Method

In the Snap Node/Plate method, you can create nodes and plates simultaneously. Before creating the nodes and the plates, first you need to specify the grid and snap settings. To do so, invoke the **Plate** page in the **Geometry** tab; the **Snap Node/Plate** window will be displayed, as shown in Figure 2-30. In this window, you can specify the grid and snap settings, which are same as discussed above.

Note

*While working in an existing drawing, the **Snap Node/Plate** window will not be displayed. In that case, in the menu bar, choose the **Quad** option from **Geometry > Snap Grid/Node > Plate**.*

Now, choose the **Snap Node/Plate** button to create the plates. To specify the coordinates for the nodes, click at the appropriate places in the clockwise or anti-clockwise direction in the grid.

Note that the displayed **Snap Node/Plate** window can be used for the quadrilateral plates. To create triangular (3 noded) plates, choose **Geometry > Snap Grid/Node > Plate > Triangle**; the **Snap Node/Plate** window for triangular plates is displayed. Now, using this window, you can create triangular (3 noded) plates.

*Figure 2-30 The **Snap Node/Plate** window*

Creating Solid Elements Using the Snap Node/Solid Method

You can create the solid elements by using the Snap Node/Solid method. To do so, invoke the **Solid** page in the **Geometry** tab; the **Snap Node/Solid** window is displayed. You can also display this window by selecting the **Add Solid** check box while opening a new project in STAAD.Pro. In this window, specify the required settings for the grid system and choose the **Snap Node/ Solid** button; the plus cursor appears in the Main Window. Next, click at the appropriate places in the grid to create solid elements. Note that, if you will click at the random places then the created solid element will be irregular in shape. So, you need to specify the nodes in a proper order. Figure 2-31 shows an irregular solid element which has been created by specifying the nodes randomly.

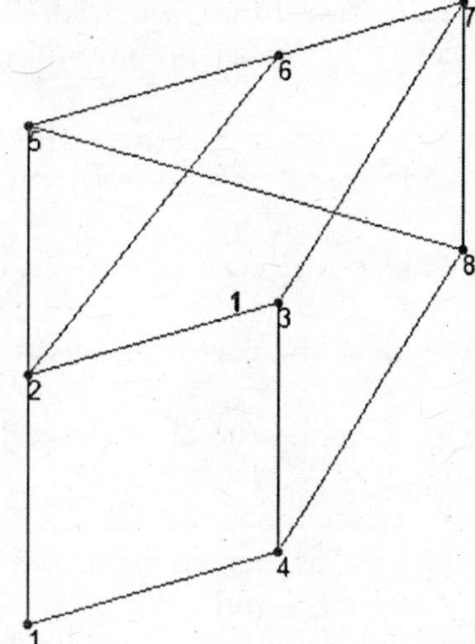

Figure 2-31 *An irregular solid element*

Note

*In case, the **Snap Node/Solid** window is not displayed, choose the **Solid** option from the **Geometry > Snap Grid/Node** to display the window.*

Example 8

In this example, you will create the plate elements using the Snap Node/Plate method. Figure 2-32 shows the structure to be created in this example.

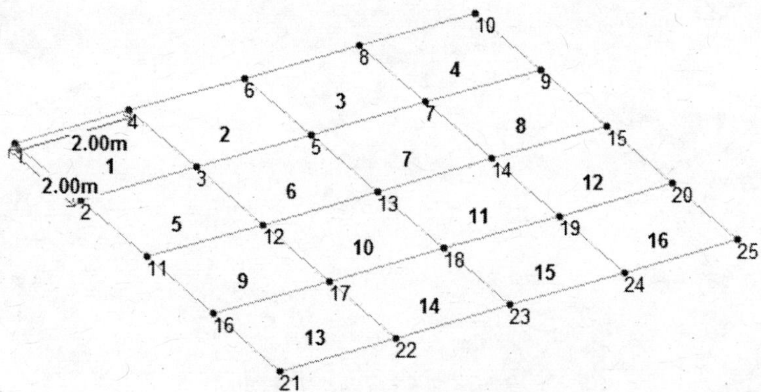

Figure 2-32 *The roof slab*

Steps required to complete this example are given below:

Step 1: Create a new file in STAAD.Pro with the name *c02_staad_v8i_ex8.std* and choose the **Next** button; the **Where do you want to go?** window is displayed. Ensure that the **Add Plate** check box is selected in the **Where do you want to go**? window. Next, choose the **Finish** button; the **Snap Node/Plate** window is displayed in data area.

Step 2: In this window, choose the **Edit** button; the **Linear** dialog box is displayed. In this dialog box, select the **X-Z** radio button in the **Plane** area to activate the XZ plane.

Step 3: Next, enter **8** in the **X** and **Z** edit boxes in the **Right** spinner of the **Construction Lines** area and choose the **OK** button to apply the changes.

Step 4: Place the cursor at the origin and click; the first node is created.

Step 5: Move the cursor in the Z direction and click at the point (0,0,2); the node 2 is created.

Step 6: Move the cursor in the X direction and click at the point (2,0,2); the node 3 is created.

Step 7: Again, move the cursor in the negative Z direction and click at the point (2,0,0); node 4 and plate 1 is created, as shown in Figure 2-33. Press the ESC key to exit the tool selection. Press SHIFT+N and SHIFT+P to view the nodes and plates, respectively. Choose **Snap Node/ Plate** button from the **Snap Node/Plate** dialog box.

Step 8: Place the cursor at (4,0,2) and click; node 5 is created.

Step 9: Move the cursor in negative Z direction and click at the coordinate (4,0,0); node 6 is created.

Step 10: Click on node 2 and then on node 3; plate 2 is created.

Step 11: Repeat the previous steps and create plates 2 to 16, refer to Figure 2-32.

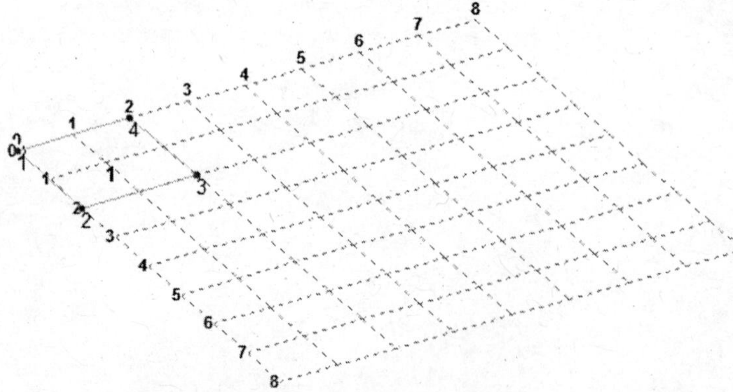

Figure 2-33 *Plate 1 created*

Step 12: Choose the **Save** option from the **File** menu to save the file and then close it by choosing the **Close** option from the **File** menu.

Example 9

In this example, you will create the solid block element using the Snap Node/Solid method. Figure 2-34 shows the concrete block to be created.

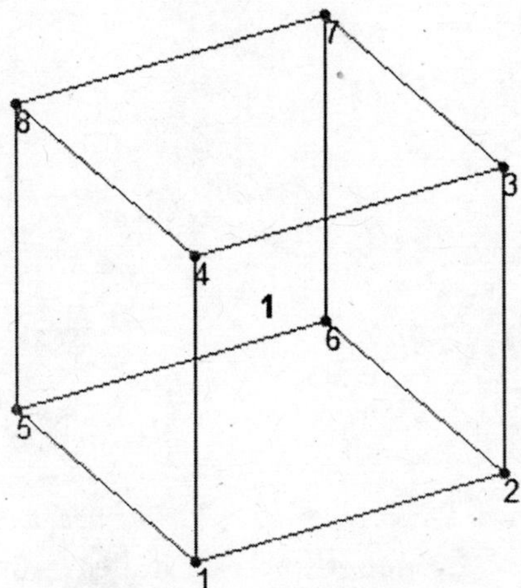

***Figure 2-34** The concrete block*

Steps required to complete this example are given below:

Step 1: Create a new file in STAAD.Pro with the name *c02_staad_v8i_ex9.std* and choose the **Next** button; the **Where do you want to go**? window is displayed. Ensure that the **Add Solid** check box is selected in this window.

Step 2: Choose the **Finish** button; the **Snap Node/Solid** window is displayed.

Step 3: Move the cursor to the point (0, 0) and click to create node 1.

Step 4: Move the cursor in the X direction and click at the point (4, 0) to create node 2.

Step 5: Similarly, click at the point (4, 4) and (0, 4) to create nodes 3 and 4, respectively.

Step 6: Next, choose the **Edit** button from the **Snap Node/Solid** window; the **Linear** dialog box is displayed.

Step 7: In this dialog box, specify **-4** in the **Z** edit box under the **Grid Origin(m)** area and then choose the **OK** button; the grid is moved to a new location, as shown in Figure 2-35.

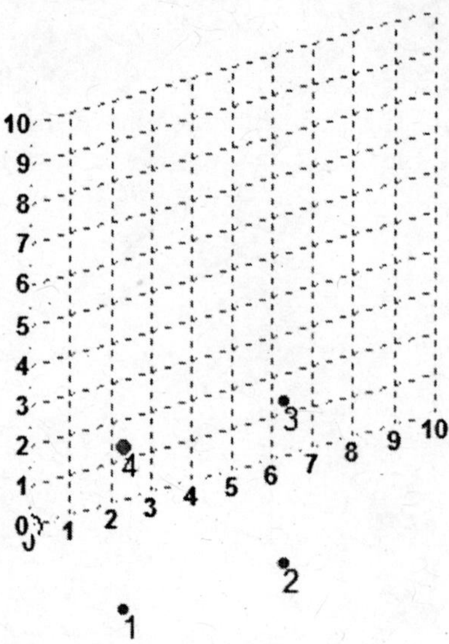

Figure 2-35 *Grids moved to the new location*

Step 8: Now, repeat the steps 2 through 4 to create nodes 5, 6, 7, and 8; the solid element is created, refer to Figure 2-34. Press the ESC button to exit the command. Press SHIFT+N and then SHIFT+C to view the node and the solid number, respectively.

Step 9: Choose the **Save** option from the **File** menu to save the file and then close it by choosing the **Close** option from the **File** menu.

STRUCTURAL MODELING USING THE STRUCTURE WIZARD

Structure wizard contains pre-defined prototype models and templates such as truss models, frame models, surface models, solid models, and so on. Using these templates and prototype models, you can create a structure model by specifying the parameters such as length, width, height, radius, and so on. After creating the model in Structure wizard, you can transfer or import it into STAAD.Pro to start a project. To access the Structure Wizard, choose the **Run Structure Wizard** option from the **Geometry** menu; the **default.stp - StWizard** window will be displayed, as shown in Figure 2-36.

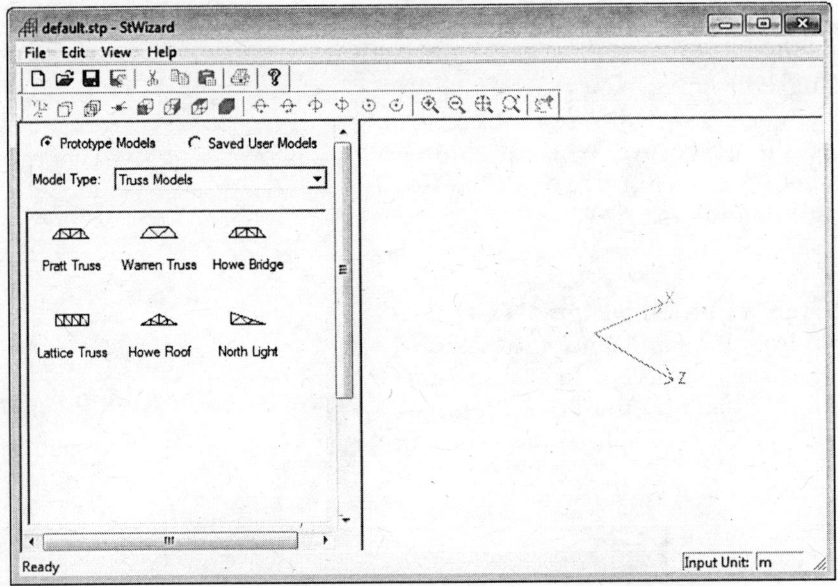

Figure 2-36 The ***default.stp - StWizard*** *window*

In this window, you can access both type of models, the prototype models and the models saved by the user. To access the prototype models, select the **Prototype Models** radio button. A list of different prototype models will be displayed in the **Model Type** drop-down list such as trusses, plates, solids, surfaces, and so on. To access the saved user models, select the **Saved User Models** radio button. Before generating a structure, you need to specify the units. To do so, choose the **Select Units** option from the **File** menu; the **Select Units** dialog box will be displayed. In this dialog box, select the appropriate unit and choose the **OK** button. The process of generating various types of structures is discussed next.

Truss Models

In the **Structure Wizard** window, you can create truss models. To do so, select the **Truss Models** option from the **Model Type** drop-down list of the **default.stp - StWizard** window; various prototype truss models will be displayed in the left pane of the window. In this pane, select an appropriate truss template. For example, select the **Howe Bridge** truss template and double-click on it; the **Select Parameters** dialog box will be displayed, as shown in Figure 2-37.

Select Parameters

Model Name: Howe Bridge

Length: 50 m No. of bays along length: 6

Height: 10 m

Width: 10 m No. of bays along width: 1

Apply Cancel

Figure 2-37 *The* ***Select Parameters*** *dialog box for* ***Howe Bridge***

In this dialog box, specify the name for the truss model in the **Model Name** edit box. Next, specify the length, width, height, and no. of bays in their corresponding edit boxes. Choose the **Apply** button; the structure will be generated and displayed in the **Structure Wizard** window. Figure 2-38 shows the howe bridge model created with the default values.

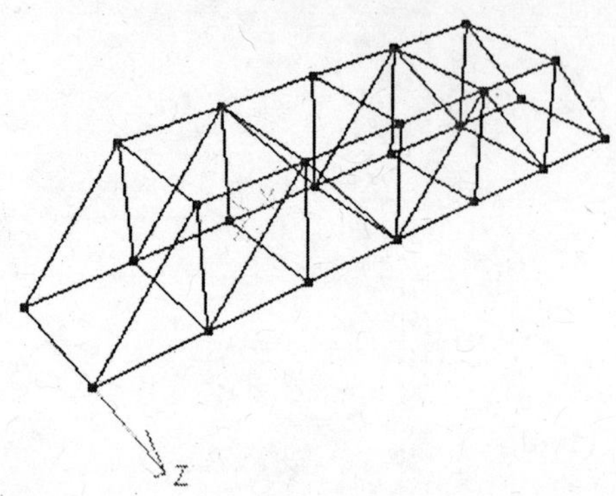

Figure 2-38 *The Howe Bridge model created*

Next, choose the **Merge Model with STAAD.Pro Model** option from the **File** menu; the **StWizard** message box will be displayed. In this message box, choose the **Yes** button; the **Paste Prototype Model** dialog box will be displayed, as shown in Figure 2-39.

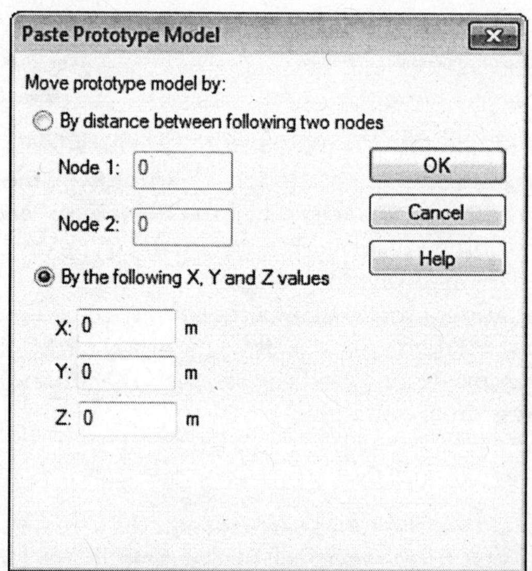

Figure 2-39 *The* ***Paste Prototype Model*** *dialog box for a new model*

Note

The ***Paste Prototype Model*** *dialog box will be displayed only when there is no existing structure in STAAD.Pro. If there is already a structure in STAAD.Pro, then the* ***Paste Prototype Model*** *dialog box will be displayed with the* ***Reference Pt*** *button added, as shown in Figure 2-40.*

In this dialog box, you can specify the coordinate values to move the prototype model. To move the model by a specified distance, select the **By distance between following two nodes** radio button; the **Node1** and **Node2** edit boxes will be enabled. Specify the desired values and choose the **OK** button to merge the model. To move the model to a specified coordinate, select the **By the following X, Y, and Z values** radio button; the **X**, **Y**, and **Z** edit boxes will be enabled. Specify the required values and choose the **OK** button to apply the changes. If you will merge a new model with an existing one then the **STAAD.Pro V8i (SELECTseries 6)** message box will be displayed, as shown in Figure 2-41.

Paste Prototype Model
Move prototype model by:
By distance between following two nodes
Node 1: 0
Node 2: 0
By the following X, Y and Z values
X: 0 m
Y: 0 m
Z: 0 m
OK
Cancel
Help
Reference Pt

***Figure 2-40** The **Paste Prototype Model** dialog box for an existing model*

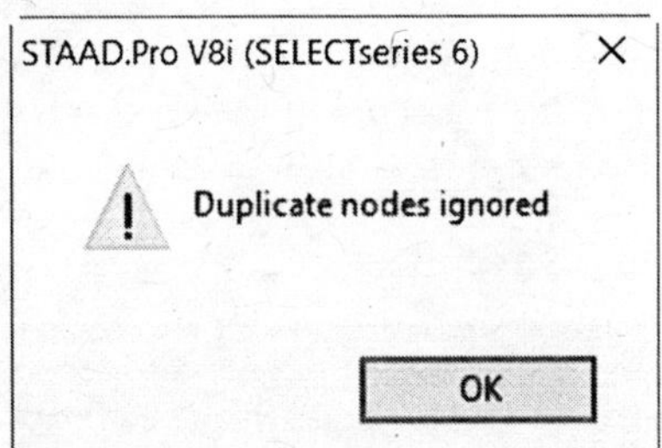

***Figure 2-41** The **STAAD.Pro V8i (SELECTseries)** message box*

Choose the **OK** button to close the message box. You can choose the **Reference Pt** button in case of merging one model with other. In that case, you need to specify the node which will act as the reference point. Choose the **OK** button to close the dialog box. On doing so, all the members and nodes will be generated automatically.

Frame Models

You can create the frame models by selecting the **Frame Models** option from the **Model Type** drop-down list in the **Structure Wizard** window. On selecting this option, various prototype frame models will be displayed in the left pane of the window. Using these models, you can create different structures such as continuous beam, bay frame, cylindrical structure, circular beam, floor grid, and so on. In the left pane, double-click on the required prototype model; the **Select Parameters** dialog box for the selected model will be displayed, refer to Figure 2-42. In this dialog box, specify the desired values and choose the **Apply** button; the dialog box closes and the structure is created. Figure 2-43 shows a bay frame structure created with default values.

Select Parameters
Model Name: Bay Frame
Length: 12 m No. of bays along length: 4
Height: 15 m No. of bays along height: 5
Width: 12 m No. of bays along width: 4
Apply Cancel

***Figure 2-42** The **Select Parameters** dialog box for the bay frame structure*

Next, you can transfer the model in STAAD.Pro by following the same method as discussed for the truss model.

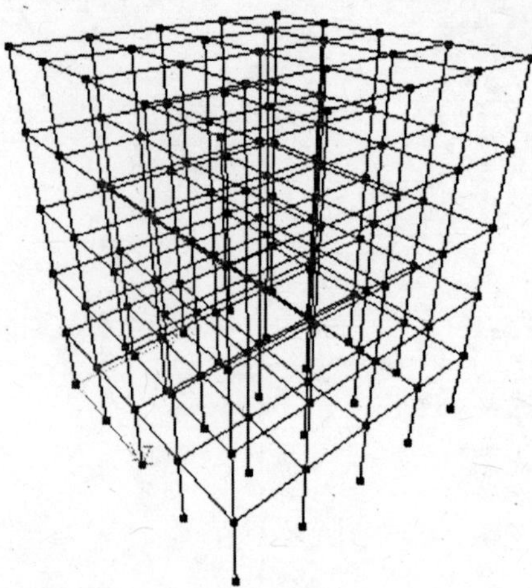

Figure 2-43 The bay frame structure

Surface/Plate Models

Using the **Structure Wizard** window, you can create surface/plates models like quadrilateral plates, cylindrical surfaces, polygonal plates with holes, spherical surface, cooling tower, and so on. To do so, select the **Surface/Plate Models** option from the **Model Type** drop-down list in the **Structure Wizard** window; various prototype models will be displayed in the left pane of the window. In the left pane, double-click on the required model; the dialog box related to the selected model will be displayed. Note that the dialog box displayed for each prototype model will be different. Figure 2-44 shows the dialog box for the Polygonal Plate With Holes model.

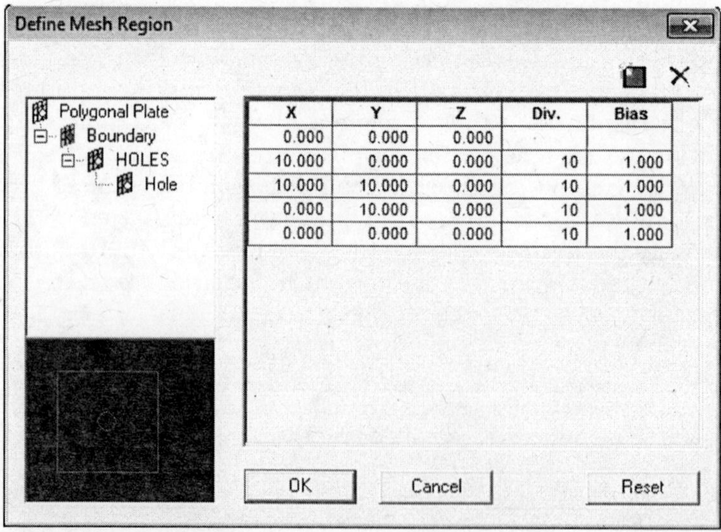

Figure 2-44 The ***Define Mesh Region*** *dialog box for the Polygonal Plate With Holes model*

In this dialog box, the parameters for the boundary will be displayed by default. You can consider the default values or can change them as per your requirement. Specify the locations for corners of the boundary, number of divisions for each side, and bias for each side division in their respective cells. You can also add a new row in the right pane by choosing the **Add New**

Row button available at the top right in the dialog box. To delete a row, first select it and then choose the **Delete Row** button.

Next, click on the **Hole** sub node under the **HOLES** node in the left pane; the corresponding parameters will be displayed in the right pane. Using the options in this pane, you can create circular, polygonal, and elliptical holes. To do so, select the desired option from the **Region Type** drop-down list in the right pane of the dialog box; various parameters will be displayed in the left pane of the dialog box. The options displayed in the dialog box depend upon the options selected from the **Region Type** drop-down list. Specify the values as required and choose the **OK** button; the structure will be created and displayed in the right pane of the window. Figure 2-45 shows the polygonal plate with hole created using the default values. Now, merge the model in STAAD.Pro as discussed before.

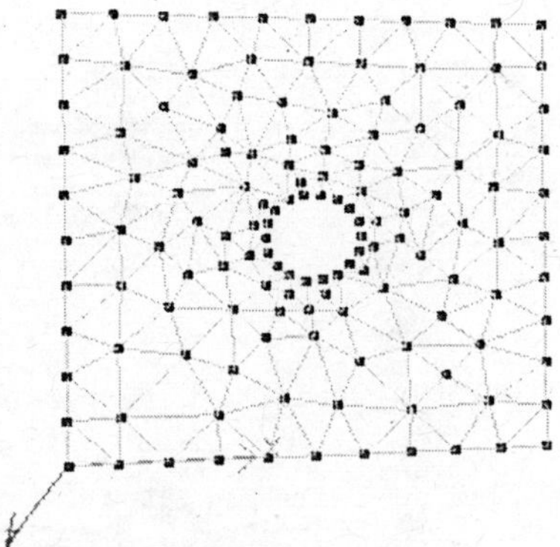

Figure 2-45 *Polygonal plate with hole*

Solid Models

You can also generate solid block models using the Structure Wizard. To do so, select the **Solid Models** option from the **Model Type** drop-down list; the **Solid Block** prototype model will be displayed in the left pane. Double-click on the **Solid Block** option; the **Select Meshing Parameters** dialog box will be displayed, as shown in Figure 2-46.

In this dialog box, specify the length and division along the axes in their corresponding edit boxes. Then, choose the **Apply** button; the solid block is created. Next, transfer it to STAAD.Pro by following the same procedure as discussed before. Figure 2-47 shows the solid block created using the default values.

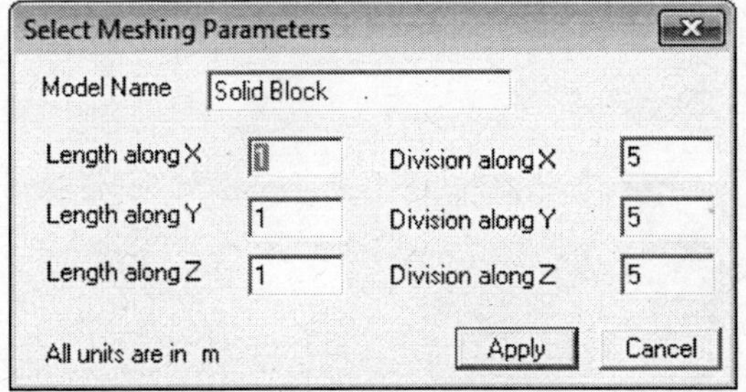

Figure 2-46 *The* ***Select Meshing Parameters*** *dialog box*

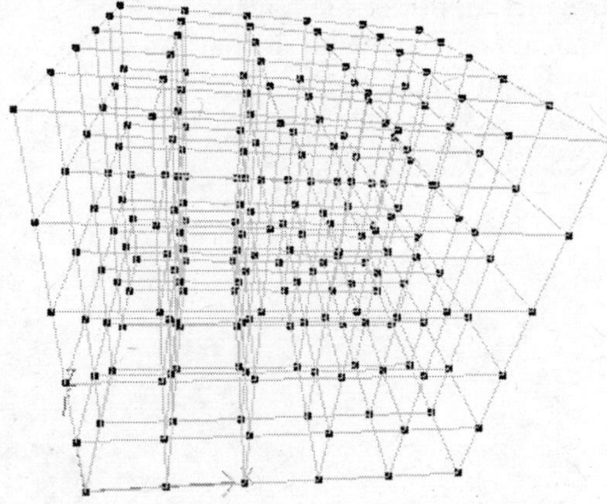

Figure 2-47 *The solid block created*

Composite Models

You can also generate composite models such as bunker or silo using Structure Wizard. To do so, select the **Composite Models** option from the **Model Type** drop-down list; the **Bunker or Silo** prototype model will be displayed in the left pane of the window. Double-click on the **Bunker or Silo** option; the **Select Meshing Parameters** dialog box will be displayed, as shown in Figure 2-48.

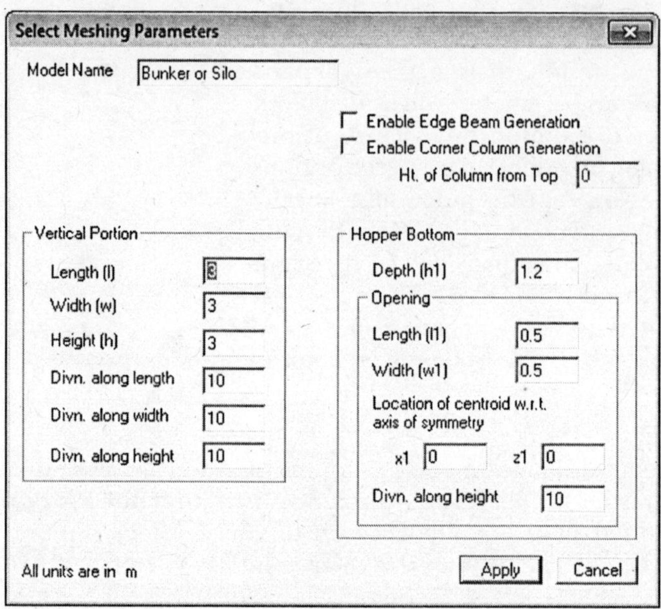

Figure 2-48 *The* ***Select Meshing Parameters*** *dialog box*

In this dialog box, you can define the geometry of the vertical portion. To do so, specify the required values in the corresponding edit boxes in the **Vertical Portion** area. Similarly, you can specify the depth of the hopper bottom in the corresponding edit boxes in the **Hopper Bottom** area. After specifying all the parameters, choose the **Apply** button; the structure will be created, as shown in Figure 2-49.

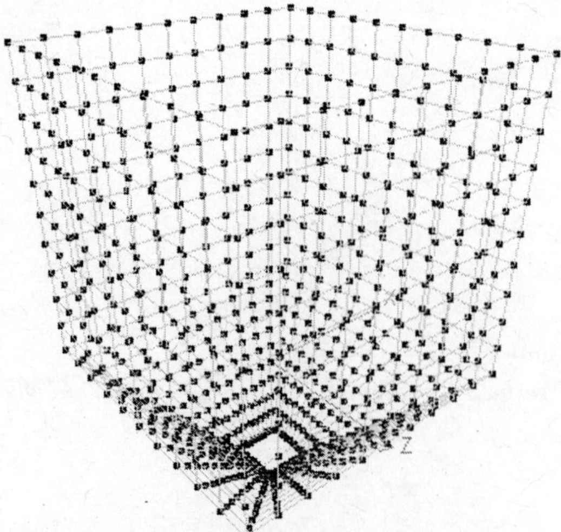

Figure 2-49 *The Bunker or Silo model*

Import CAD Models

Using the **Import CAD Models** option, you can import the AutoCAD models, which are saved in DXF format. To do so, select the **Import CAD Models** option from the **Model Type** drop-down list; the **Scan DXF** and **STAAD Model** options will be displayed in the left pane of the window. To import the AutoCAD models, double-click on the **Scan DXF** option in the right pane; the **Open** dialog box will be displayed. In this dialog box, browse to the required location, select the .dxf file, and then choose the **OK** button; the model will be displayed in the right pane. Using this option, you can import line, 3D-Polyline, and 3D-Face.

To import STAAD models, double-click on the **STAAD Model** option in the right pane; the **Open** dialog box will be displayed. In this dialog box, browse to the required location, select the file, and then choose the **OK** button; the file will be displayed in the window.

VBA Macro Models

Using the **VBA Macro Models** option, you can create models such as stadium roof. To do so, select the **VBA-Macro Models** option from the **Model Type** drop-down list; the **Stadium Roof** and **A Simple Tower** options will be displayed in the left pane of the window. Using these two options, you will be able to model a stadium roof and tower. The procedures to create a stadium roof and a tower are discussed next.

To create a stadium roof, select the **Stadium Roof** option from the left pane of the **default.stp - StWizard** window and drag it to the right pane; the **Stadium Roof** dialog box will be displayed, as shown in Figure 2-50. In this dialog box, you can specify the length, width, depth, number of panels along length, and number of panels along width in their corresponding edit boxes. Next, choose the **OK** button; the stadium roof is created and displayed in the window. Figure 2-51 shows the stadium roof model created using default values.

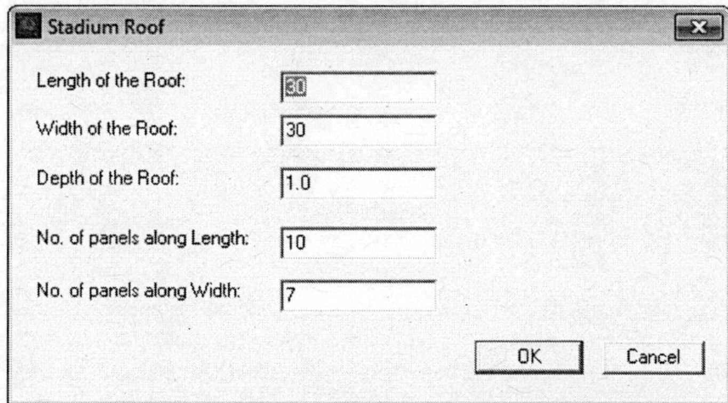

Figure 2-50 *The* ***Stadium Roof*** *dialog box*

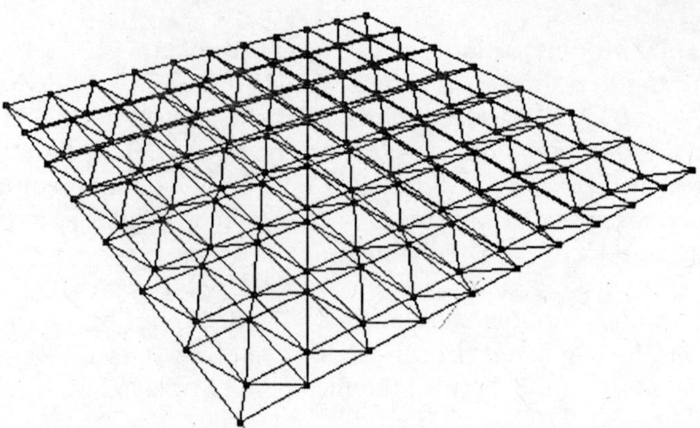

Figure 2-51 *Stadium roof created with default values*

To create a tower, select the **A Simple Tower** option from the left pane of the **default.stp - StWizard** window and drag it to the right pane; the **Tower Parameters** dialog box will be displayed, as shown in Figure 2-52. In this dialog box, you can specify the base dimension, top dimension, height, and number of bays along height in their corresponding edit boxes. Next, choose the **OK** button; the dialog box is closed and the tower will be created. Figure 2-53 shows a simple tower modeled using default values.

Tower Parameters

Base Dimension: 8

Top Dimension: 4

Height: 50

No. of Bays Along Height: 6

Cancel OK

Figure 2-52 *The* ***Tower Parameters*** *dialog box*

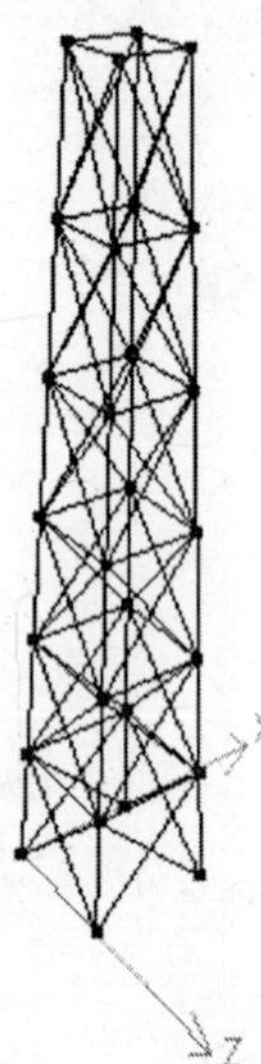

Figure 2-53 *A simple tower created using default values*

Example 10

In this example, you will create Howe Bridge in Structure Wizard and transfer it to STAAD.Pro. Figure 2-54 shows the structure of Howe Bridge to be created in this example.

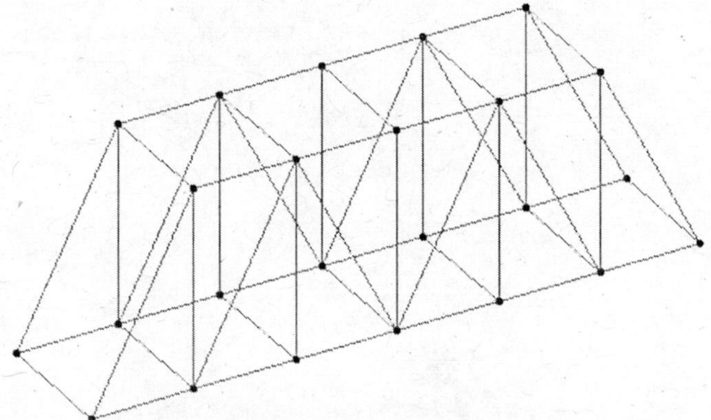

***Figure 2-54** The Howe Bridge model*

Steps required to complete this example are given below:

Step 1: Create a new file in STAAD.Pro with the name *c02_staad_v8i_ex10.std* and choose the **Next** button; the **Where do you want to go?** window is displayed. Ensure that the **Open Structure Wizard** check box is selected in this window.

Step 2: Choose the **Finish** button; the **default.stp - StWizard** window is displayed.

Step 3: In this window, ensure that the **Truss Models** option is selected in the **Model Type** drop-down list.

Step 4: Double-click on the **Howe Bridge** option in the left pane; the **Select Parameters** dialog box is displayed.

Step 5: In this dialog box, specify the length, height, width, and number of bays parameters, as shown in Figure 2-55.

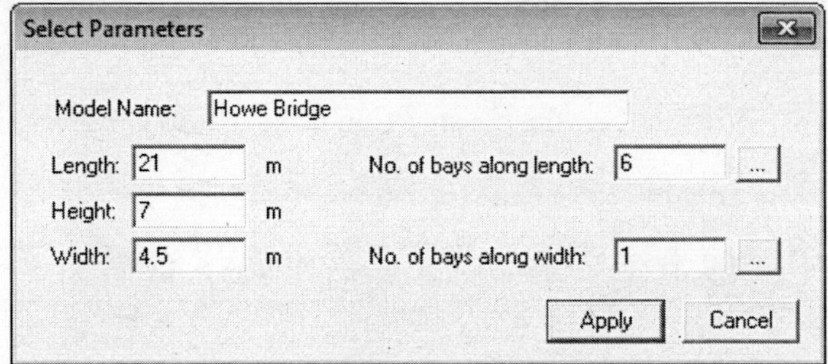

***Figure 2-55** The **Select Parameters** dialog box*

Step 6: Choose the **Apply** button; the model is created and displayed in the window, as shown in Figure 2-56.

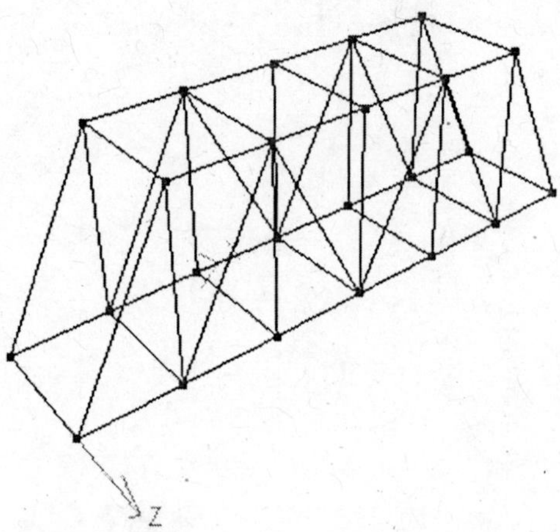

Figure 2-56 *The howe bridge model*

Step 7: Choose the **Add/Paste Model in STAAD.Pro** option from the **Edit** menu in the **StWizard** window; the **StWizard** message box appears.

Step 8: Choose the **Yes** button; the **Paste Prototype Model** dialog box is displayed. Choose the **OK** button; the model is displayed in the main area of the STAAD.Pro window, refer to Figure 2-54.

Step 9: Choose the **Save** option from the **File** menu to save the file and then close it by choosing the **Close** option from the **File** menu.

Self-Evaluation Test

Answer the following questions and then compare them to those given at the end of this chapter:

1. The command used for creating nodes is __________.

2. The __________ command repeats the previous line of input specified in the **STAAD Editor** window.

3. In the __________ grid system, the construction lines are perpendicular to each other.

4. The command for creating solid elements is __________.

5. In STAAD.Pro, plates are used to model slabs and shear walls. (T/F)

6. You can create nodes and members simultaneously using the Snap/Node Beam method. (T/F)

7. In STAAD.Pro, the Structure Wizard contains the prototype models. (T/F)

Review Questions

Answer the following questions:

1. Which of the following commands is used to create members?

   (a) **Joint Coordinates** (b) **Element Incidences**
   (c) **Member Incidences** (d) None of these

2. Which of the following commands repeats all the previously defined inputs?

   (a) **Finish** (b) **Repeat**
   (c) **Repeat All** (d) All of the above

3. Which of the following methods is used to create the nodes and members simultaneously?

   (a) Snap/Node Plate (b) Snap/Node Beam
   (c) Snap/Node Solid (d) None of these

4. Which of the following grid style can be used to create circular structures?

   (a) **Radial** (b) **Linear**
   (c) **Irregular** (d) All of these

5. In STAAD.Pro, you can create members before creating the nodes. (T/F)

6. Solid elements are the eight-noded elements. (T/F)

7. The Truss Model template contains various prototype truss models. (T/F)

Answers to Self-Evaluation Test

1. Joint Coordinates, 2. Repeat, 3. Linear, 4. Element Incidences Solid, 5. T, 6. T, 7. T

Chapter 3

Structural Modeling Using Tools

Learning Objectives

After completing this chapter, you will be able to:

- *Create additional structural elements*
- *Edit the structural elements*

INTRODUCTION

In STAAD.Pro, there are tools which make the modeling process easier and faster. Using these tools, you can add additional nodes, members, plates, and so on. You can also modify an existing structure by using these tools or by modifying the commands. In this chapter, these tools are categorized into two topics which are listed below:

1) Essential tools for structural modeling
2) Other miscellaneous tools

Before using these tools, you need to create nodes and members which has been discussed in the second chapter.

ESSENTIAL TOOLS FOR STRUCTURAL MODELING

STAAD.Pro has some essential tools to create the model geometry. These tools can also be used to modify an existing structure. Using these tools, you can add additional beams, plates, solids, and other structural elements. The procedure for adding beams is discussed next.

Adding Beams Using Tools

In STAAD.Pro, you can add beams to an existing structure using various tools. A beam can also be added to a structure if there are no existing nodes or between the mid-points of the existing members. The process of adding beams and corresponding tools are discussed next.

Add Beam from Point to Point

You can add a beam between two existing nodes in a structure by using the **Add Beams** tool.To do so, invoke the **Add Beams** tool from the toolbar; the **Add Beams** cursor will be displayed in the window. Alternatively, choose **Add Beam > Add Beam from Point to Point** tool from the **Geometry** menu; the cursor will be displayed in the Main Window. Click on the start node; the beam will be attached to the cursor. Next, click on the end node; the beam will be added.

You can also create a beam when you have an existing member in the drawing but do not have the start and end node for the new beam to be created. To create beams with the help of existing members, choose the **Add Beams** tool from the toolbar and then click at any point on the member where the start node of the beam will lie; the **STAAD.Pro V8i (SELECTseries 6)** message box will be displayed prompting you to add a new node. Choose the **Yes** button; the **Insert Nodes into Beam** dialog box will be displayed, as shown in Figure 3-1. In this dialog box, the beam length will be displayed at the top. In the **New Insertion Point** area, specify the distance of the node to be created from the start node in the **Distance** edit box. As you specify the required value in the **Distance** edit box, the proportion of the specified distance with respect to the length of the member will automatically be modified in the **Proportion** edit box. Next, choose the **Add New Point** button; the node location will be added to the **Insertion Points** area.

You can also divide a member into two equal parts by creating a mid-point node. To do so, choose the **Add Beams** tool from the toolbar and select the beam; the **STAAD.Pro V8i (SELECT series 6)** message box will be displayed. Choose the **Yes** button from this message box; the **Insert Nodes into Beam** dialog box will be displayed. Choose the **Add Mid Point** button; the mid-point node location will be added to the **Insertion Points** area. Choose the **OK** button; the node will be created.

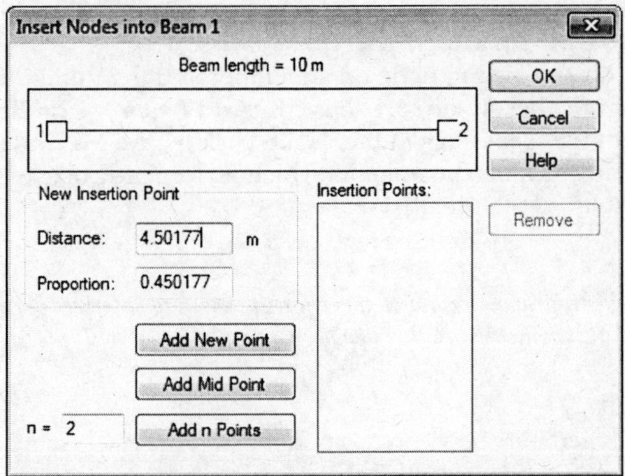

Figure 3-1 *The* ***Insert Nodes into Beam*** *dialog box*

To create a member at the mid point of existing members, choose the **Add Beams** tool from the toolbar and select the mid point of the beam; the **STAAD.Pro V8i (SELECT series 6)** message box will be displayed. Choose the **Yes** button from this message box; the **Insert Nodes into Beam** dialog box will be displayed. Choose the **Add Mid Point** button; the mid-point node location will be added to the **Insertion Points** area. Choose the **OK** button; the node will be created with an attached beam. Next, click at the mid point of the other member where the end node of the beam will lie. Again the **STAAD.Pro V8i (SELECTseries 6)** message box will be displayed prompting you to create a new node. Choose the **Yes** button; the **Insert Nodes into Beam** dialog box will be displayed. Choose the **Add Mid Point** button; the mid-point node location will be added to the **Insertion Points** area. Choose the **OK** button; a node will be created and the member will be attached at the mid point of another member.

You can also divide beams into any number of equal parts by specifying the required value in the **n** edit box. Next, choose the **Add n Points** button; the location of n number of nodes will be specified in the **Insertion Points** area. To remove a node from the **Insertion Points** area, select the required insertion point and choose the **Remove** button. After specifying the required values, choose the **OK** button; members will be created depending upon the number of nodes inserted.

Note

*You can also insert nodes in an existing member by using the **Add Beams** and **Insert Node** tools. The **Insert Node** tool is available in the toolbar.*

Add Beam between Mid-Points

Using the **Add Beams between Mid-Points** tool, you can add a beam between the mid-points of two existing members. To do so, choose **Add Beam > Add Beam between Mid-Points** tool from the **Geometry** menu. Click on the first member where start node of the beam will lie; the start node of the beam will be created at the mid-point of the member and beam will be attached along with the cursor. Next, click on the member where end node of the beam will lie; the beam will be created between the mid-points of the two existing members.

Add Beam by Perpendicular Intersection

To add a beam between an existing node on a member and the node which is perpendicularly intersecting the other member. To do so, choose the **Add Beam > Add Beam by Perpendicular Intersection** tool from the **Geometry** menu. Next, click on the existing node which will be the start node of the beam. Click on the member which is perpendicular to the beam; a beam will be created perpendicular to the members.

Note

If there is no existing node on the member for the beam to intersect perpendicularly, then a node will be created automatically on the member where the beam will intersect.

Add Curved Beam

You can create curved members between two nodes using the **Add Curved Beam** tool. To do so, choose the **Add Beam > Add Curved Beam** tool from the **Geometry** menu; the tool cursor will be displayed in the Main Window. Next, click on the two nodes; the **Curved Beam Properties** dialog box will be displayed, as shown in Figure 3-2. In this dialog box, specify the radius of curvature and gamma angle in the corresponding edit boxes and choose the **OK** button; the beam will be created according to the specified values.

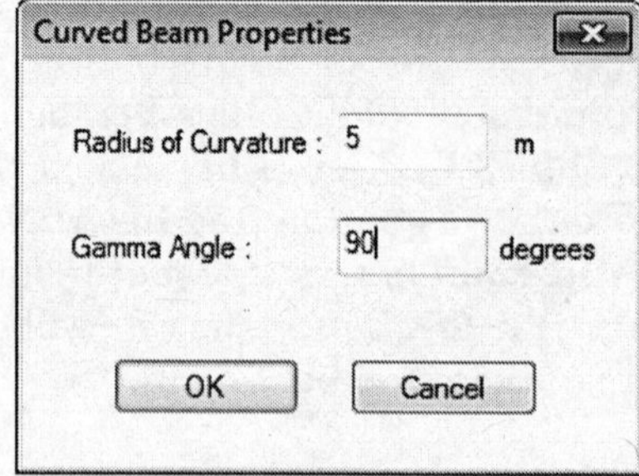

Figure 3-2 The ***Curved Beam Properties*** *dialog box*

Note

In this chapter, you need to download the c03_Staad_v8i_ex.zip file for the examples from http://www.cadcim.com. The path of the file is as follows: Textbook > Civil/GIS > STAAD.Pro > Exploring Bentley STAAD.Pro V8i.

Example 1

In this example, you will create the portal plane frame structure shown in Figure 3-3 using the **Add Beams** tool.

Steps required to complete this example are given next.

Step 1: Create a new file in STAAD.Pro with the name *c03_staad_v8i_ex1* and create a portal frame structure of **9m*9m** using the **Snap Node/Beam** tool, as shown in Figure 3-4.

Step 2: Invoke the **Add Beams** tool and move the cursor in the Main Window area; the Add Beams cursor is displayed.

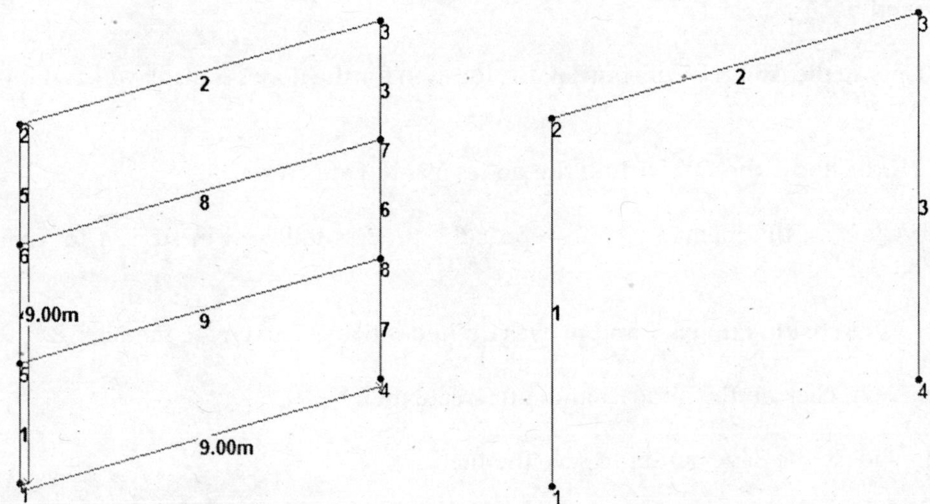

Figure 3-3 *The portal frame structure*

Figure 3-4 *Portal frame structure*

Step 3: Next, place the cursor on the member 1 and click; the **STAAD.Pro V8i (SELECTseries 6)** message box is displayed.

Step 4: Choose the **Yes** button; the **Insert Nodes into Beam 1** dialog box is displayed. In this dialog box, specify the values shown in Figure 3-5.

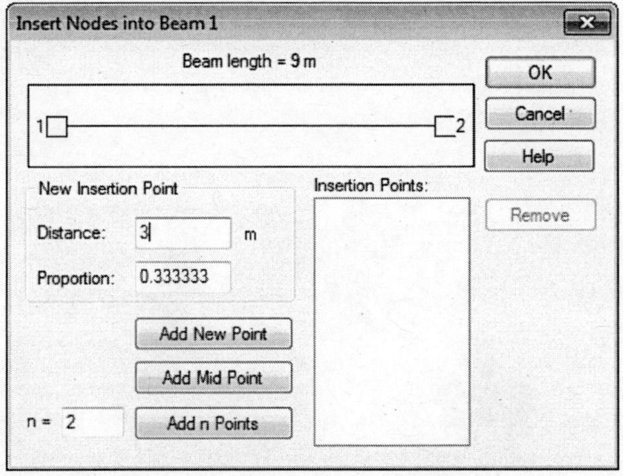

Figure 3-5 *The* ***Insert Nodes into Beam 1*** *dialog box*

Step 5: Choose the **Add n Points** button; the location for the nodes is displayed in the **Insertion Points** area.

Step 6: Next, choose the **OK** button; the nodes 5 and 6 are created.

Step 7: Click on the member 3 and repeat the process followed in steps 4 and 5 and create nodes 7 and 8.

Step 8: Choose the **Add n Points** button; the location for the nodes is displayed in the **Insertion Points** area.

Step 9: Next, choose the **OK** button; the nodes 5 and 6 are created.

Step 10: Click on the member 3 and repeat the process followed in steps 4 to 6 and create nodes 7 and 8.

Step 11: After creating nodes 7 and 8, click on nodes 6 and 7 to create member 8.

Step 12: Next, click on the nodes 5 and 8 to create member 9.

Step 13: Choose the **Save** button to save the file.

Example 2

In this example, you will create a curved beam using the **Add Curved Beam** tool.

Steps required to complete this example are given below:

Step 1: Create a new file in STAAD.Pro with the name *c03_staad_v8i_ex2* and create a portal frame structure of dimension **6m*6m** using the **Snap Node/Beam** tool, refer to Figure 3-6.

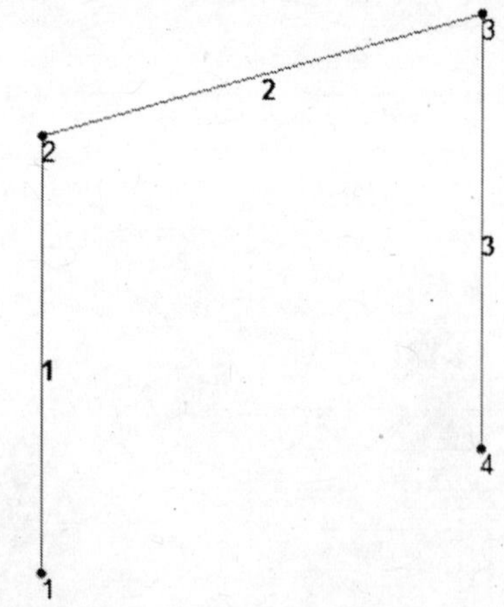

Figure 3-6 *The portal frame structure*

Step 2: Delete the member 2 and choose the **Add Beam > Add Curved Beam** tool from the **Geometry** menu. Move the cursor in the Main Window area; the **Add Curved Beam** tool cursor is displayed.

Step 3: Place cursor on node 2 and click; the member is attached with the cursor. Next, click on the node 3; the **Curved Beam Properties** dialog box is displayed.

Step 4: In this dialog box, specify the values, as shown in Figure 3-7 and choose the **OK** button; the curved beam is created, as shown in Figure 3-8.

Step 5: Choose the **Save** button to save the file.

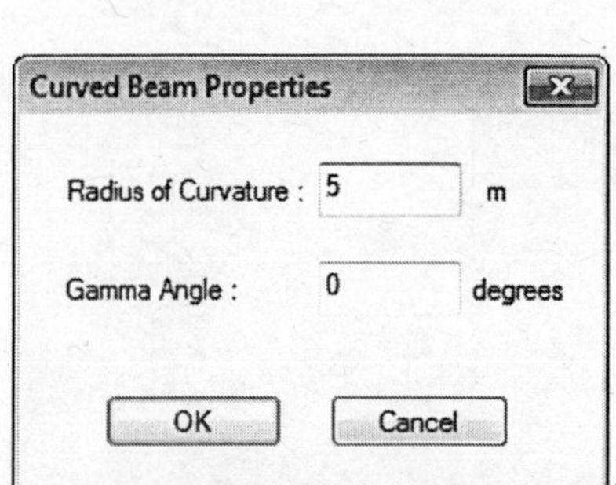

*Figure 3-7 The **Curved Beam Properties** dialog box*

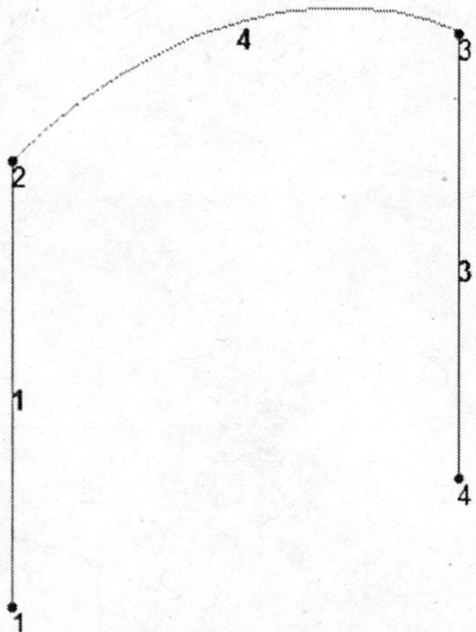

Figure 3-8 Curved beam created

Creating Colinear Beams

You can create colinear beams (members) along three or more nodes by connecting them along a straight line. To do so, first select the colinear nodes along which members will be created. Next, select the **Create Colinear Beams** option from the **Geometry** menu; the members will be created. Note that if you select more than two nodes then the **STAAD.Pro V8i (SELECTseries 6)** window will be displayed prompting you about the created members. Choose the **OK** button; the members will be created along the colinear nodes. If there are no colinear nodes then the **STAAD.Pro V8i (SELECTseries 6)** window will display a message prompting you that no three colinear nodes were found to create new beams.

Creating Beams Along Axes

Members can also be created by connecting colinear points along a selected global axis. To do so, first select the required nodes along which the members will be created. Next, choose the required global axis along which the members will be created from the flyout displayed when you select **Geometry > Connect Beams Along** option; the **STAAD.Pro V8i (SELECTseries 6)** window will be displayed. Choose the **OK** button; the members will be created along the selected axis. If there are no colinear points along the selected global axis then the **STAAD.Pro V8i (SELECTseries 6)** window will display a message prompting you that no members is created.

Example 3

In this example, you will create the structure shown in Figure 3-9 using the tools explained above. Steps required to complete this example are as follows:

Step 1: Open the *c03_staad_v8i_ex1.std* file in STAAD.Pro; the model is displayed in the main window, as shown in Figure 3-9.

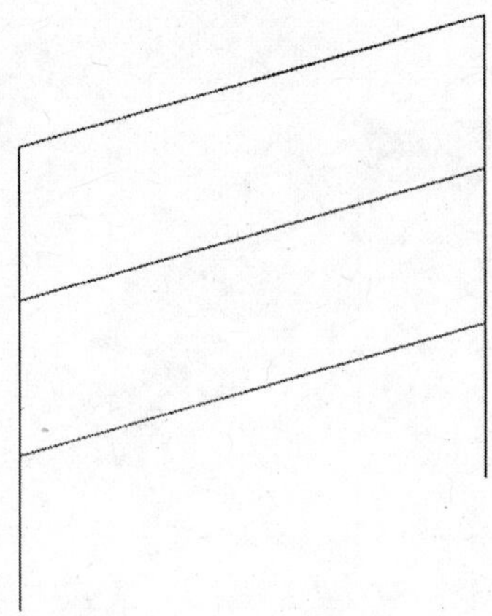

Figure 3-9 *The portal frame structure*

Step 2: Select member 2 and right-click; a shortcut menu is displayed. Choose the **Insert Node**; the **Insert Nodes Into Beam 2** dialog box is displayed. Choose the **Add Mid Point** button; the location for the node is displayed in the **Insertion** area. Next, choose the **OK** button; the node 9 is created.

Step 3: Select all the beams in the structure and press **Delete**; a **STAAD.Pro V8i (SELECTseries 6)** message box is displayed, as shown in Figure 3-10. Choose the **OK** button; the **STAAD.Pro V8i (SELECTseries 6)** message box is displayed, as shown in Figure 3-11. Choose the **No** button; all beams are deleted, as shown in Figure 3-12. Ensure that the **Geometry** tab is selected.

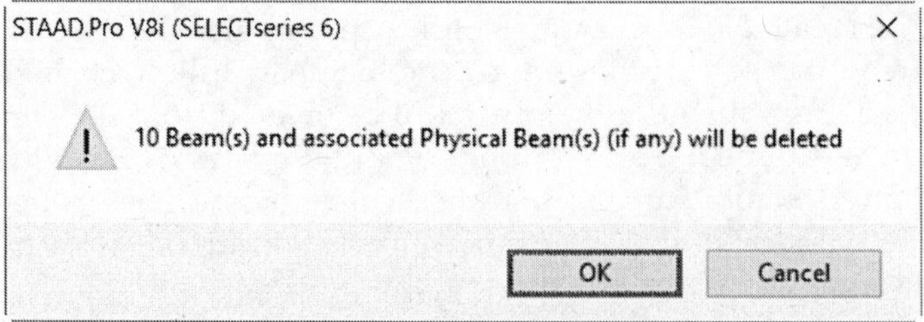

Figure 3-10 *The **STAAD.Pro V8i (SELECTseries 6)** message box*

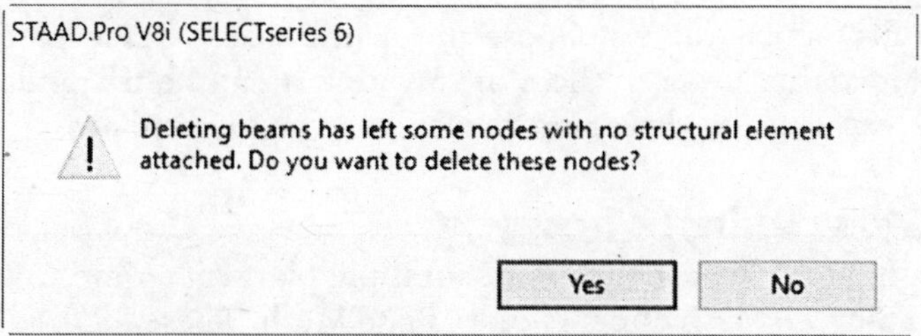

Figure 3-11 STAAD.Pro V8i (SELECTseries 6) message box

Step 4: Invoke the **Nodes Cursor** from the side toolbar and select all the nodes; the selected nodes get highlighted.

Step 5: Next, choose the **Create Colinear Beams** option from the **Geometry** menu; the **STAAD. Pro V8i (SELECTseries 6)** window is displayed. Choose the **OK** button; eight members are created along the collinear points, refer to Figure 3-13.

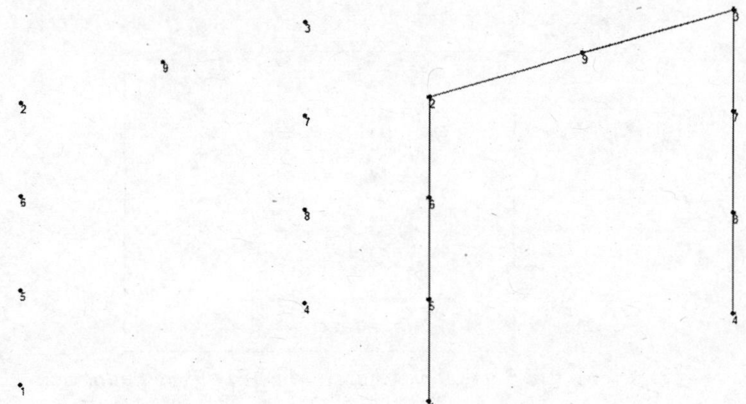

Figure 3-12 *Nodes displayed in the main window after deleting beams*

Figure 3-13 *Created members*

Step 6: Next, using the CTRL key, select the nodes numbered 5, 6, 7, and 8 and choose the **X Axis** option from **Geometry > Connect Beams Along**; the **STAAD.Pro V8i (SELECTseries 6)** window is displayed. Choose the **OK** button; two members are created along the x axis and the structure gets completed, refer to Figure 3-9. Choose the **Save** button to save the file.

Creating Plates Using Tools

You can add quadrilateral or triangular plates by connecting the existing nodes using certain tools. These tools are discussed next.

To add quadrilateral plates, choose the **Add Plate > Quad** tool from the **Geometry** menu. Move the cursor in the Main Window area; the tool cursor will be displayed. Next, click on the four nodes in a proper sequence; the plate will be created.

Similarly, to create triangular plates, choose the **Add Plate > Triangle** tool from the **Geometry** menu. Move the cursor in the Main Window area; the triangular tool cursor will be displayed. Next, click on three nodes to create triangular plates.

Creating Plates Using Meshing

In STAAD.Pro, meshing can be used to create multiple plates at a time. You can create mesh in two ways: Generate Surface Mesh and Generate Plate Mesh. These methods are discussed next.

Generate Surface Mesh

The Generate Surface Meshing method is used to generate finite element mesh. In this case, you need to define the outer boundary of the mesh to be generated by connecting the existing nodes. To create surface meshing, choose the **Generate Surface Meshing** tool from the toolbar and move the cursor in the Main Window area; the tool cursor will be displayed. Next, click on the nodes either in the clockwise or anti-clockwise direction; a line will be formed while clicking, which indicates the boundary of the mesh. To close the boundary, click on the first node again. If the boundary is formed by connecting four nodes, then the **Choose Meshing Type** dialog box will be displayed, as shown in Figure 3-14.

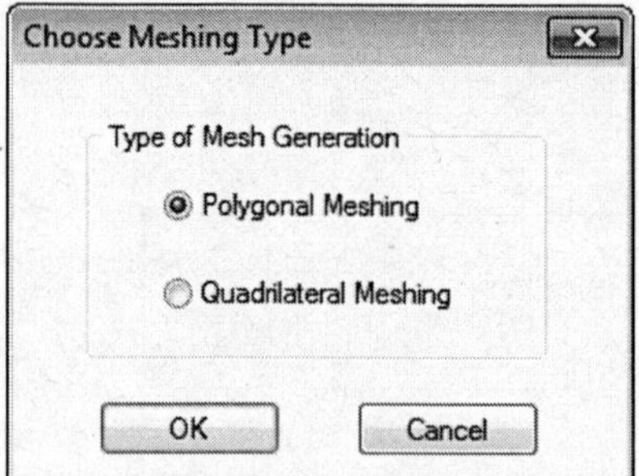

Figure 3-14 *The **Choose Meshing Type** dialog box*

In this dialog box, select the **Polygonal Meshing** radio button to create only triangular elements. Next, choose the **OK** button; the **Define Mesh Region** dialog box will be displayed, as shown in Figure 3-15. Various options in this dialog box are discussed next.

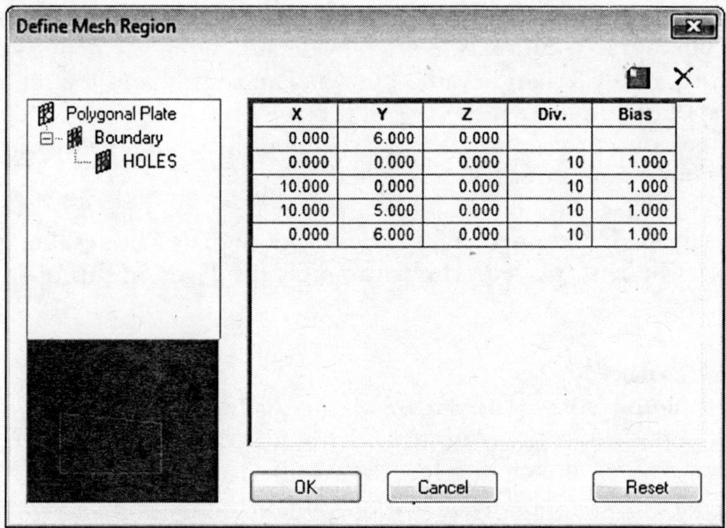

Figure 3-15 *The* ***Define Mesh Region*** *dialog box*

In this dialog box, the coordinates of the selected nodes will be displayed in the **X**, **Y**, and **Z** columns in the right pane. In the **Div.** column, you can specify the number of plates to be created along the sides. By default, the value in the **Div.** column is **10**. In the **Bias** column, you can specify a value for the increase or decrease in the size of element along a certain edge. To create a hole in the mesh, click on the **HOLES** node in the left pane in the dialog box and then right-click on it; a shortcut menu is displayed. To create a new hole, choose the **Create New Hole** option; the **Hole 1** will be added under the **HOLES** node and parameters to create a hole will be displayed in the right pane. In this pane, you can define the type of hole to be created by selecting the required option from the **Region Type** drop-down list; the parameters for the hole will be displayed in the right pane. Specify the required values for the option selected and choose the **OK** button; a mesh will be generated.

To create quadrilateral and triangular plates, select the **Quadrilateral Meshing** radio button, refer to Figure 3-14. Next, choose the **OK** button; the **Select Meshing Parameters** dialog box will be displayed, as shown in Figure 3-16.

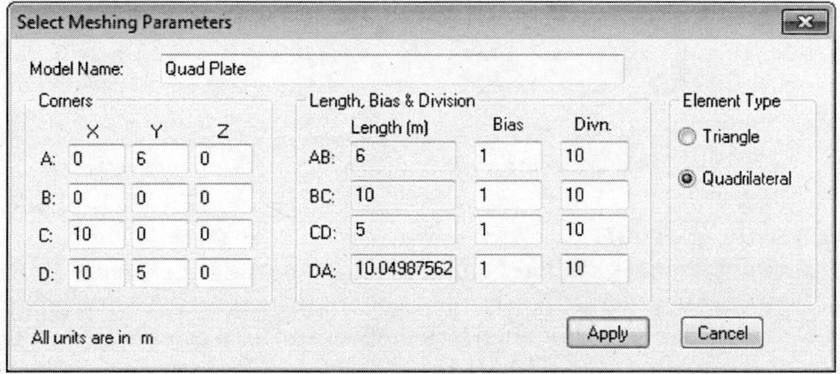

Figure 3-16 *The* ***Select Meshing Parameters*** *dialog box*

In this dialog box, you can specify the name of the model, if required, in the **Model Name** text box. The **Quadrilateral** radio button is selected by default in the **Element Type** area. To create triangular plates, select the **Triangle** radio button. The coordinates for the four corners and side lengths are specified in their respective edit boxes. You can specify the required division value in the **Divn** column corresponding to the required sides. After specifying the parameters, choose the **Apply** button; meshing will be created.

If the boundary is formed by connecting 3 nodes or more than 4 nodes then the **Define Mesh Region** dialog box will be displayed. The parameters displayed in this dialog box have been discussed earlier.

Generate Plate Mesh

The generate plate mesh method is used to divide an existing plate into multiple plate elements. To create a plate mesh, invoke the plates cursor from the side toolbar. Then, move the cursor in the Main Window area and select the required plate. Next, right-click in the Main Window; a shortcut menu will be displayed. Choose the **Generate Plate Mesh** option from the menu; the **Choose Meshing Type** dialog box will be displayed along with the **Generating Mesh** dialog box, as shown in Figure 3-17. Select the required radio button from the **Choose Meshing Type** dialog box and choose the **OK** button. The process of creating mesh has been discussed earlier.

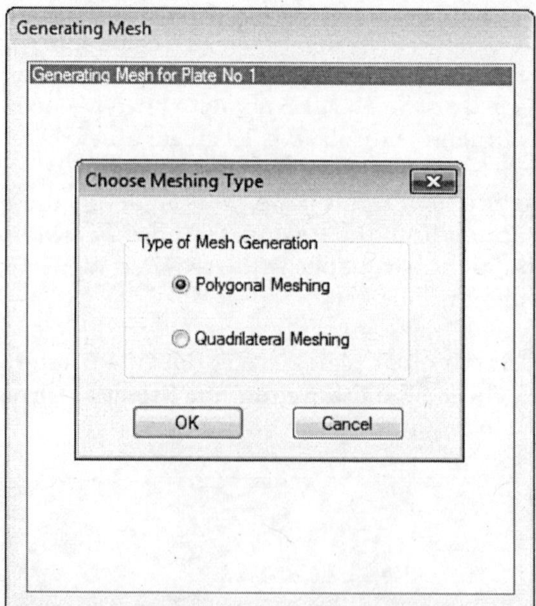

*Figure 3-17 The **Choose Meshing Type** and **Generating Mesh** dialog boxes*

Creating Infill Plates

In STAAD.Pro, multiple plates can be created at a time by using the **Create Infill Plates** tool. In this case, the plates are generated in a closed boundary surrounded by members. To use this tool, first select the panel which is bounded by members and then choose the **Create Infill Plates** tool from the toolbar; the **STAAD.Pro V8i (SELECTseries 6)** window will be displayed prompting you to create plates. Choose the **OK** button; the plates will be generated. You can view the plates in 3D view.

Example 4

In this example, you will generate finite element mesh to create a roof slab. Figure 3-18 shows the portal frame structure to be created.

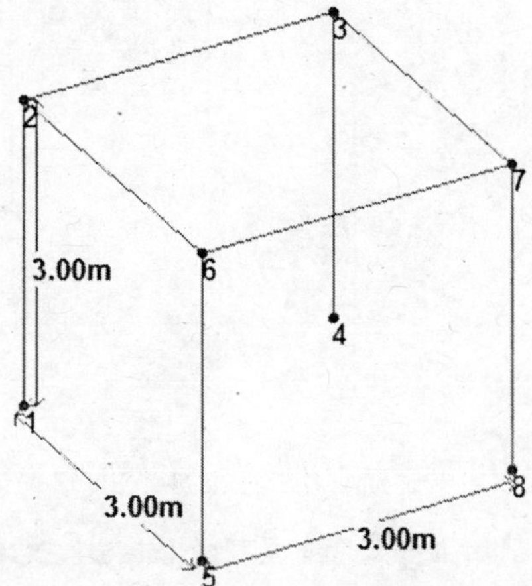

Figure 3-18 *The portal frame structure*

Steps required to complete this example are given below:

Step 1: Create a new file in STAAD.Pro with the name *c03_staad_v8i_ex4* and create the structure shown in Figure 3-18 using any of the model generation methods discussed in Chapter 2.

Step 2: After creating the structure, choose the **Generate Surface Meshing** tool in the toolbar and move the cursor in the Main Window area; the surface meshing cursor appears.

Step 3: Click on the node 2; a line is attached with the cursor. Next, click on node 6, 7, and 3. Click on the node 2 again to close the boundary; the **Choose Meshing Type** dialog box is displayed.

Step 4: Select the **Quadrilateral Meshing** radio button in the dialog box and choose the **OK** button; the **Select Meshing Parameters** dialog box is displayed.

Step 5: In this dialog box, specify **6** as the value in the **Divn** column of each side.

Step 6: Next, choose the **Apply** button; the mesh is created. Figure 3-19 shows the created slab. You can also view the generated plates in the rendered view. Press SHIFT+P to view the plate numbers and save the file by choosing the **Save** button.

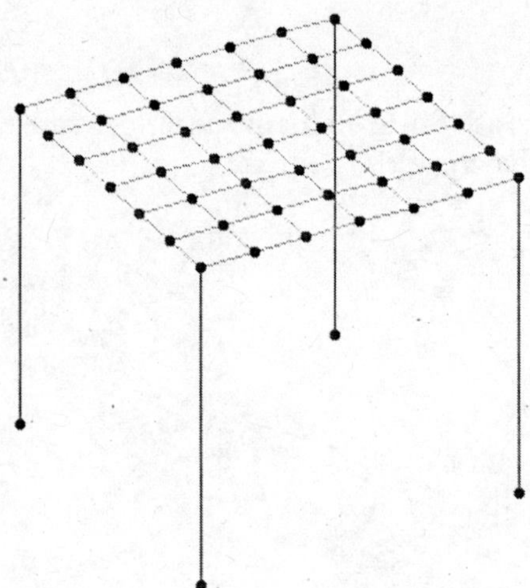

Figure 3-19 *The roof slab created*

Creating a Surface Using the Add Sueface Tool

You can create a surface by connecting existing nodes. To create a surface, choose the **Add Surface** tool from the toolbar and move the cursor in the Main Window; the surface cursor will be displayed. Next, click on the existing nodes in the clockwise or counter clockwise direction and to complete the surface, click on the first node again; the surface will be created.

After creating the surface, you can insert an opening in it. For example, you can create an opening for windows, lifts, and so on. To add an opening in a surface, first select the surface by choosing the surface cursor from the side toolbar. Next, choose the **Insert Openings in the Surface** tool from the toolbar; the **Snap Node/Opening** window will be displayed. Next, create openings by clicking at appropriate points in the surface.

Example 5

In this example, you will model a shear wall with door openings. The model used in this example has been saved in Example 4 of Chapter 2. Figure 3-20 shows the final model after creating surfaces.

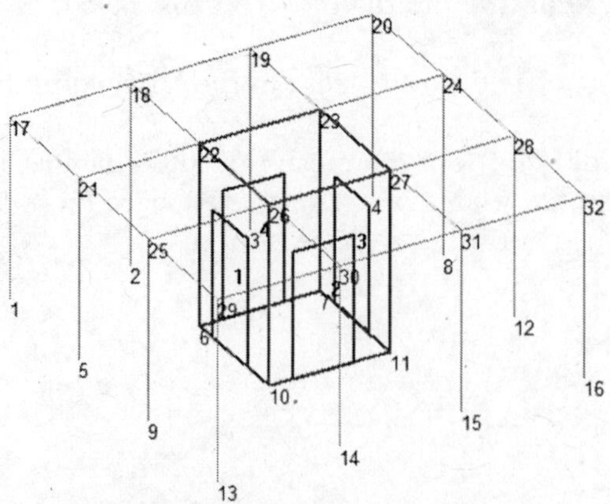

Figure 3-20 *Model to be created*

Steps required to complete this example are given below:

Step 1: Open the *c02_staad_v8i_ex4.std* file in STAAD.Pro; the model is displayed in the Main Window.

Step 2: Select the beams 6, 10, 7, and 11 using the CTRL key and then choose the **View Selected Objects Only** option from the **View** menu; only the selected beams will be displayed in the Main Window, refer to Figure 3-21.

Step 3: Choose the **Add Surface** tool from the toolbar and move the cursor in the main window; the surface cursor appears.

Step 4: Click on the nodes 22, 6, 10, 26, and 22 to create surface 1. Press CTRL+SHIFT+P to view the surface numbers. Similarly, create surface 2, 3, and 4 by connecting the respective nodes, as given in Table 3-1. Figure 3-22 shows the created surface.

Table 3-1 *Various nodes required to create surface*

Surface	Nodes
2	26, 10, 11, 27, and 26
3	23, 7, 11, 27, and 23
4	22, 6, 7, 23, and 22

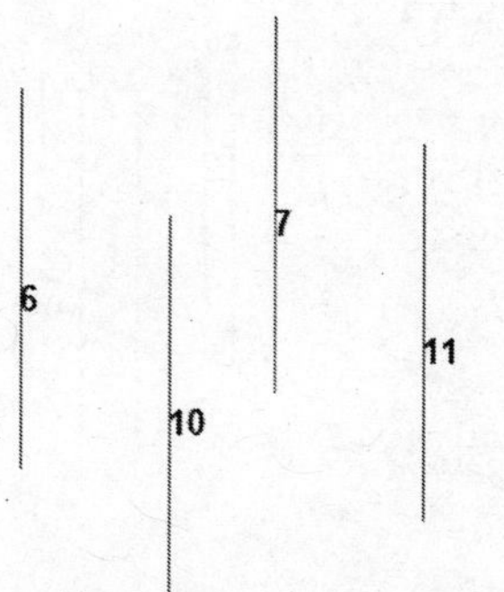

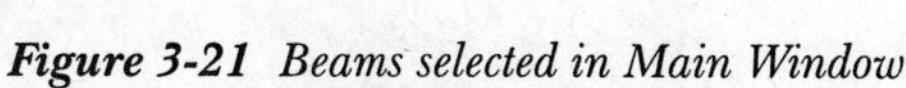

Figure 3-21 *Beams selected in Main Window*

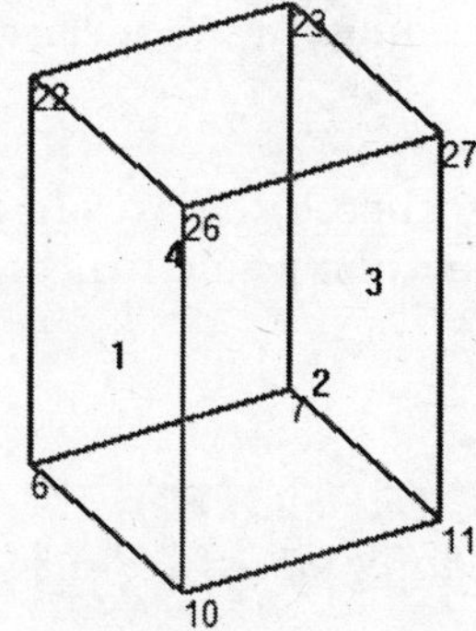

Figure 3-22 *The created surfaces*

Step 5: Invoke the surface cursor from the side toolbar and select surface 1. Choose the **Insert Openings in the Surface** tool from the toolbar; the **Snap Node/Opening** window and the grid is displayed, refer to Figure 3-23.

Step 6: Click at the appropriate places in the grid to create an opening, as shown in Figure 3-24.

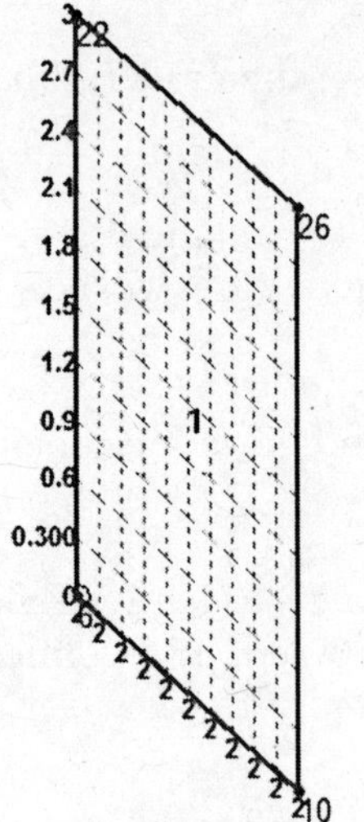

Figure 3-23 *Grid displayed*

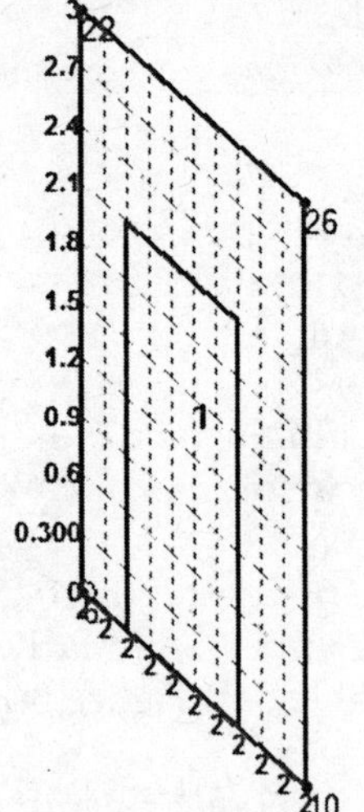

Figure 3-24 *Opening created*

Step 7: Close the **Snap Node/Opening** window and select the surface 2.

Step 8: Repeat the procedure followed in steps 5 and 6 and create openings in the surfaces 2, 3, and 4, as shown in Figure 3-25.

Step 9: Now, choose the **Whole Structure** option from the **View** menu; the whole structure is displayed, refer to Figure 3-20.

Note

To select the third and fourth surfaces, you can rotate the model using the left and right arrow keys.

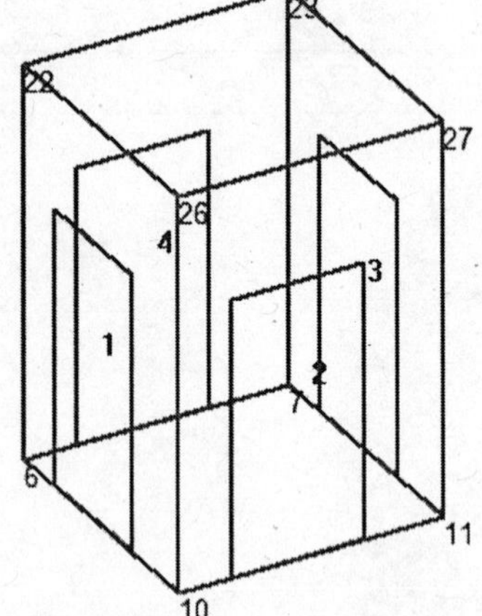

Figure 3-25 *Openings created*

Step 10: Choose the **Save As** option from the **File** menu; the **Save As** dialog box is displayed. In this dialog box, specify the name *c03_staad_v8i_ex5* in the **File name** edit box and save it at an appropriate location.

Creating Solid Elements Using the Add Solid Tool

The solid elements can be created by connecting the existing nodes in a proper sequence. Solid elements are minimum four to eight noded so you first need to create the nodes. Next, invoke the **Add Solid** tool from the toolbar. Alternatively, choose the **8 Noded Brick**, **7 Noded Degenerated Brick**, **6 Noded Wedge**, **5 Noded Pyramid**, **4 Noded Tetrahedra** tool from the **Geometry** menu as per your requirement. Now, move the cursor in the Main Window; the solid cursor will be displayed. Click on the nodes in a proper sequence to connect them; the solid element will be created.

Creating a Structure Using the Translational Repeat Tool

In STAAD.Pro, modeling a tall structure or any complex model is a tedious task. But it can be made simpler by using the **Translational Repeat** tool. Using this tool, you can duplicate and repeat the entire structure or the required portion of the structure n number of times in a linear direction by specifying certain parameters, which are discussed next.

To create a copy or multiple copies of an existing structure, first select the structure and then choose the **Translational Repeat** tool from the toolbar; the **Translation Repeat** dialog box will be displayed, as shown in Figure 3-26.

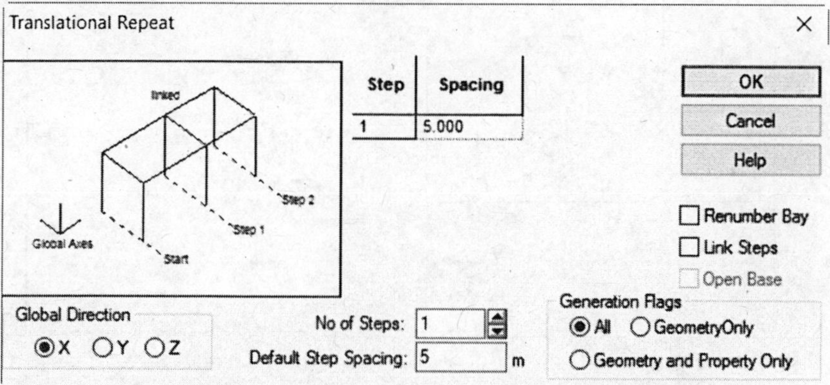

***Figure 3-26** The **Translation Repeat** dialog box*

In this dialog box, to specify the direction in which the structure will be duplicated, select the **X**, **Y**, or **Z** radio button in the **Global Direction** area. Next, specify the number of times the structure will be copied in the **No. of Steps** edit box. As you define the number of steps, the specified number of steps will be added as rows in the **Step Spacing** table. Specify the spacing value between the structure and its copy in the **Default Step Spacing** edit box. You can change the spacing of any step by specifying a value in the **Spacing** column of the **Step Spacing** table. Select the **Renumber Bay** check box to specify the starting number of the members created in each step. On selecting the **Renumber Bay** check box, the **Number From** column will be added to the **Step Spacing** table in which you can specify the desired number. Select the **Link Steps** check box to connect the copied structures by creating members between each copied structure. On selecting the **Link Steps** check box, the **Open Base** check box will be enabled. Select the **Open Base** check box to keep the base of the copied structures open. While generating copies of a structure, either you can duplicate the structure with all its properties and loads acting on it or you can create the copy of the structure only. To duplicate the structure with all its properties and loads, select the **All** radio button in the **Generation Flags** area. To repeat the structure geometry only and not its other properties, select the **GeometryOnly** radio button. To duplicate the structure geometry along with the properties, select the **Geometry and Property Only** radio button. After specifying all the parameters, choose the **OK** button to close the dialog box. All changes will be applied.

Creating a Structure Using the Circular Repeat Tool

Using the **Circular Repeat** tool, you can repeat the entire structure or a small portion of it in a circular direction. To do so, first select the required structure and then choose the **Circular Repeat** tool from the toolbar; the **3D Circular** dialog box will be displayed, as shown in Figure 3-27. Various parameters displayed in this dialog box are discussed next.

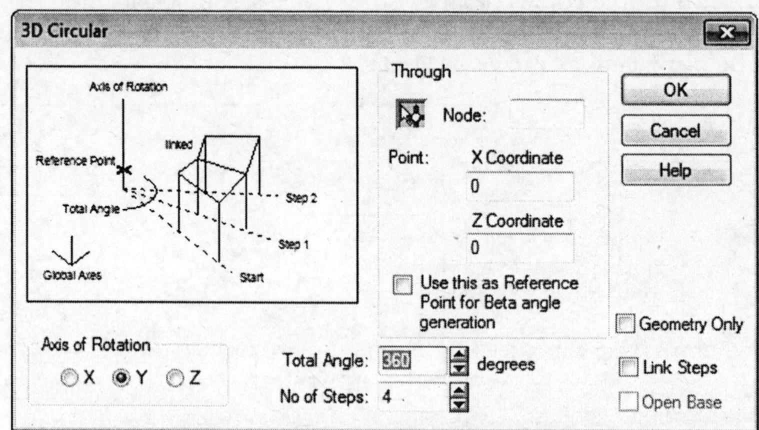

Figure 3-27 The ***3D Circular*** *dialog box*

To specify the axis of rotation for repeating the structure, select the **X**, **Y**, or **Z** radio button in the **Axis of Rotation** area. In the **Through** area, you can specify the coordinates for the axis of rotation. To do so, choose the node button; the node cursor will be displayed in the Main Window. Next, select the required node in the Main Window area; the coordinates of the selected node will be filled automatically in the **X Coordinate** and **Z Coordinate** edit boxes. Next, select the **Use this as Reference Point for Beta angle generation** check box to consider the member orientation. Specify the total angle of rotation of the copied structure and original structure in the **Total Angle** edit box. The other parameters in this dialog box are same as for the **Translational Repeat** tool. After specifying all the parameters, choose the **OK** button; the dialog box will be closed and changes will be applied.

Example 6

In this example, you will create a multi-storeyed building using the **Translational Repeat** and **Circular Repeat** tools. Figure 3-28 shows the circular structure to be created in this example.

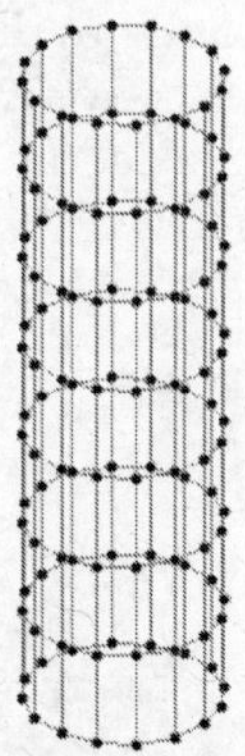

Figure 3-28 The circular structure

Steps required to complete this example are given next.

Step 1: Create a new file in STAAD.Pro with the name *c03_staad_v8i_ex6* and create a member using the **Snap Node/Beam** method, refer to Figure 3-29.

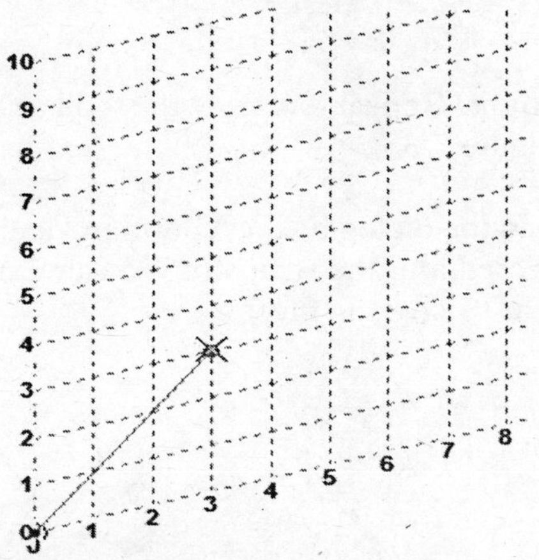

Figure 3-29 *Member created using the Snap Node/Beam method*

Step 2: Next, close the **Snap Node/Beam** window and select the created member.

Step 3: Choose the **Circular Repeat** tool from the toolbar; the **3D Circular** dialog box is displayed.

Step 4: In this dialog box, specify the values, as shown in Figure 3-30.

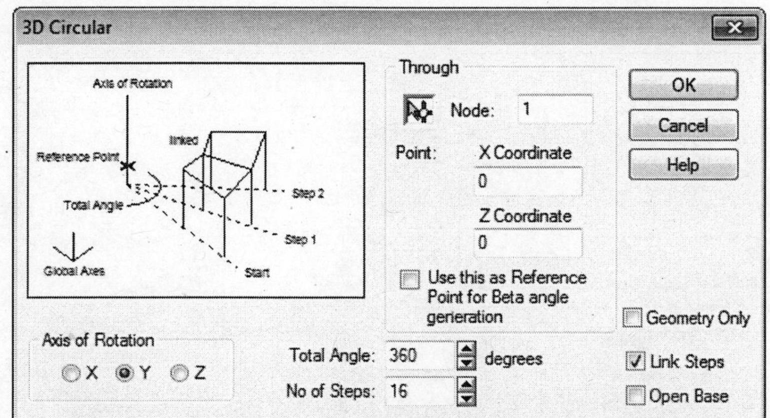

Figure 3-30 *Values speicifed in the **3D Circular** dialog box*

Step 5: Next, choose the **OK** button; the dialog box is closed and the member is repeated in the circular direction, refer to Figure 3-31.

Step 6: Select the members 1, 3, 5, 7, 9, 11, 13, 15, 17, 19, 21, 23, 25, 27, 29, and 31, refer to Figure 3-32 and delete them.

Step 7: On deleting all beams, a message box is displayed. Choose the **OK** button; another message box is displayed. Choose the **Yes** button.

Step 8: Invoke the **Beams Cursor** from the side toolbar and select all the members in the Main Window area.

Step 9: Invoke the **Translational Repeat** tool from the toolbar; the **Translational Repeat** dialog box is displayed, refer to Figure 3-33.

Step 10: Specify the values in the dialog box, as shown in Figure 3-33, and then choose the **OK** button; the dialog box is closed and the structure is created, refer to Figure 3-28. Choose the **Save** button from the toolbar to save the file.

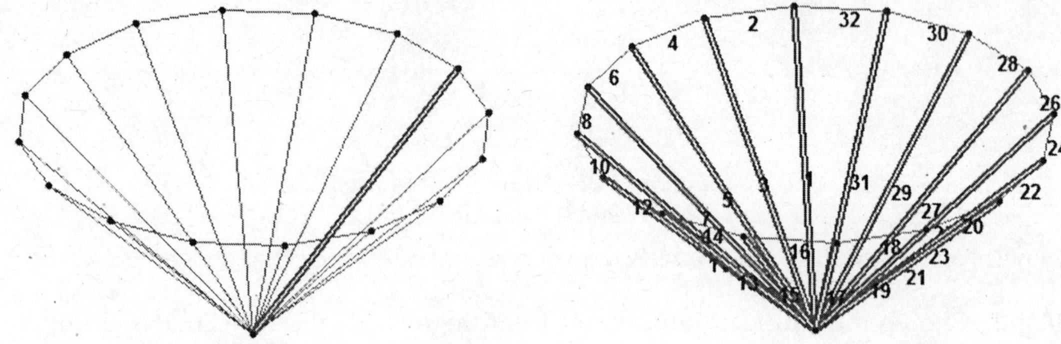

Figure 3-31 Member repeated in circular direction

Figure 3-32 Selected members

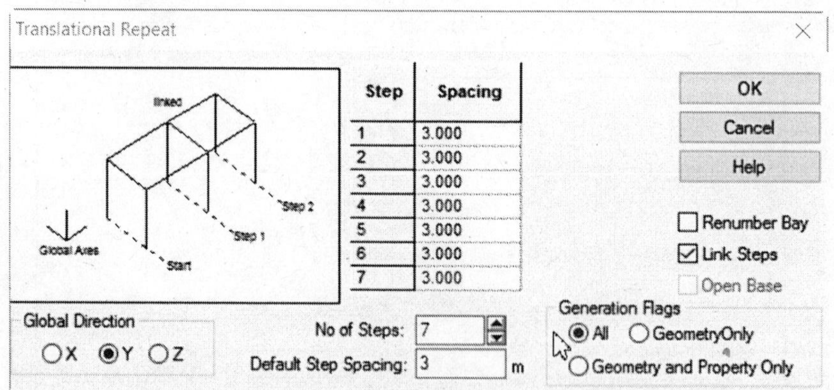

*Figure 3-33 Values specified in the **3D Repeat** dialog box*

Shifting Structure Using Move Tool

In STAAD.Pro, you can shift the entire structure to a new location by specifying the coordinates of that location. Similarly, the location of beams, nodes, and plates can also be changed. This can be achieved by specifying the coordinates in the data area and you can also use the **Move** tool to move the structure which is discussed next.

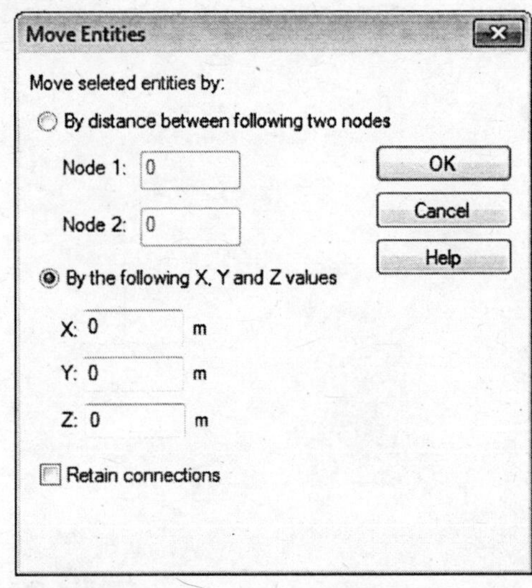

Figure 3-34 The ***Move Entities*** *dialog box*

First select the required nodes, members, plates, or the entire structure. Next, choose **Geometry > Move** from the menu bar; a cascading menu will be displayed. In this cascading menu, you can choose the required option. For example, choose the **Joint** option from the cascading menu; the **Move Entities** dialog box will be displayed, as shown in Figure 3-34. You can move the selected entities by specifying the distance between two nodes.

To do so, select the **By distance between following two nodes** radio button in the **Move selected entities by** area; the **Node 1** and **Node 2** edit boxes will be enabled. Next, specify the desired node numbers in the **Node 1** and **Node 2** edit boxes. You can also move the selected entities by specifying the required coordinates. To do so, select the **By the following X, Y, and Z values** radio button and specify the desired values in the **X**, **Y**, and **Z** edit boxes. After specifying the values, choose the **OK** button; the dialog box will be closed and the selected entities will move to a new position.

Rotating Structure Using the Rotate Tool

You can rotate an entire structure or a small portion of a structure using the **Rotate** tool. To rotate a structure, first select the required structure and choose the **Rotate** tool from the **Geometry** menu; the **Rotate** dialog box will be displayed, as shown in Figure 3-34. Various parameters displayed in this dialog box are discussed next.

In this dialog box, specify the angle of rotation in the **Angle** edit box. To define the axis of rotation, choose the node button from the **Axis Passes Through** area; the select node cursor will be displayed. Select the required nodes from the Main Window area; the node numbers will be filled automatically in the **Node 1** and **Node 2** edit boxes in the **Axis Passes Through** area. The coordinates of the selected nodes will also be filled in the $\mathbf{X_1}$, $\mathbf{Y_1}$, $\mathbf{Z_1}$, $\mathbf{X_2}$, $\mathbf{Y_2}$, and $\mathbf{Z_2}$ edit boxes in the **Points** area. Select the **Copy** radio button if you want to create a copy of the selected structure. Select the **Move** radio button to save the rotated structure and delete the original one. To connect the original and the copied structures, select the **Link Bays** check box. After specifying all the parameters, choose the **OK** button; the dialog box will be closed and all the changes will be applied to the structure.

Example 7

In this example, you will create a structure using the **Rotate** tool. Figure 3-35 shows the structure to be created in this example.

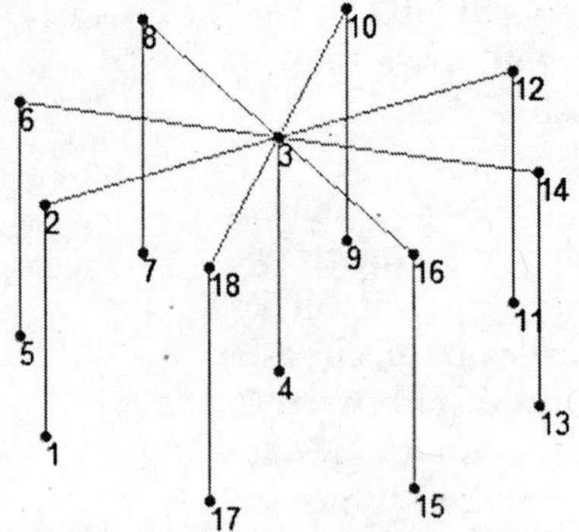

Figure 3-35 Structure to be created

Steps required to complete this example are given below:

Step 1: Create a new file in STAAD.Pro with the name *c03_staad_v8i_ex7* and create a portal plane frame structure of 3m height and 3m width using the **Snap Node/Beam** tool, refer to Figure 3-36. Close the **Snap Node/Beam** window.

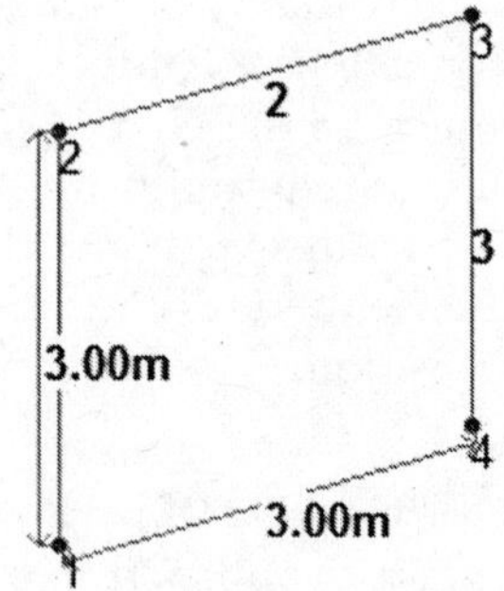

Figure 3-36 The portal frame structure

Step 2: Select the entire structure and choose the **Rotate** tool from the **Geometry** menu; the **Rotate** dialog box is displayed.

Step 3: Specify the parameters in the dialog box, as shown in Figure 3-37.

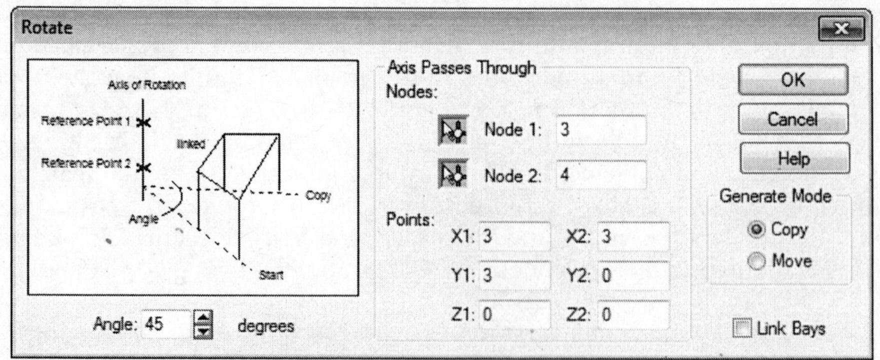

*Figure 3-37 The **Rotate** dialog box*

Step 4: Next, choose the **OK** button; the **STAAD.Pro V8i (SELECTseries)** message box is displayed. Choose the **OK** button from the message box; the structure is rotated and copied, as shown in Figure 3-38.

Step 5: Again, select the entire structure and invoke the **Rotate** dialog box. Next, specify the values as per your need, refer to Figure 3-38. Choose the **OK** button; the **STAAD.Pro V8i (SELECTseries 6)** message box is displayed. Choose the **OK** button from the message box; the structure is rotated and copied, as shown in Figure 3-39.

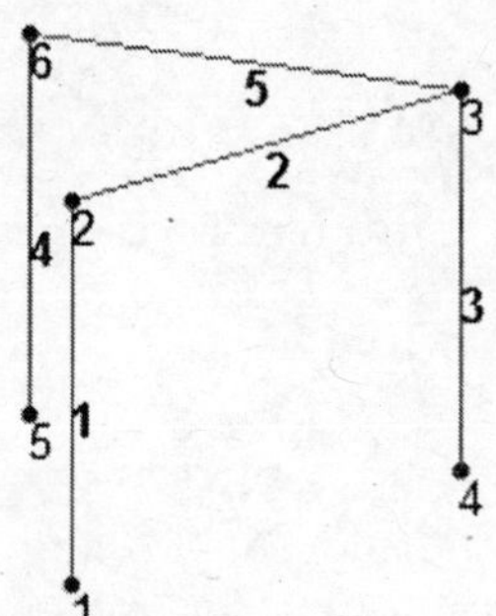

Figure 3-38 *Structure after using the* ***Rotate*** *tool*

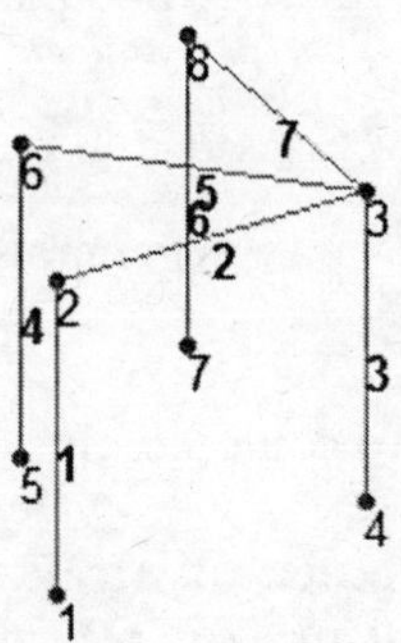

Figure 3-39 *Structure after using the* ***Rotate*** *tool*

Step 6: Repeat the procedure followed in steps 5 and create the structure, refer to Figure 3-35. Choose the **Save** button to save the file.

Mirroring a Structure

You can generate a mirror image of the entire structure or a small portion of the structure by using the **Mirror** tool. To do so, first select the required structure and then choose the **Mirror** tool from the **Geometry** menu; the **Mirror** dialog box will be displayed, as shown in Figure 3-40. Various parameters of this dialog box are discussed next.

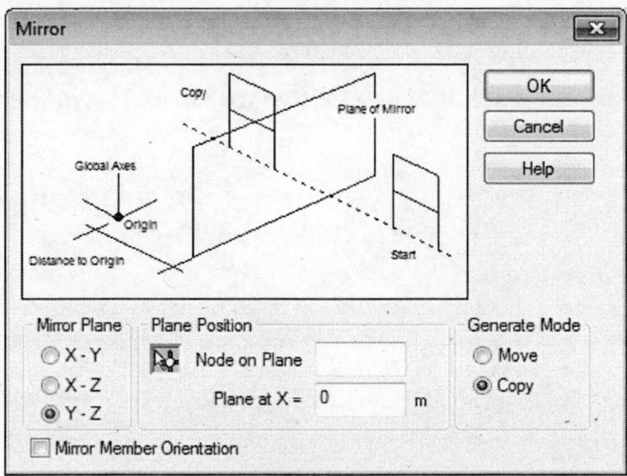

Figure 3-40 *The* ***Mirror*** *dialog box*

To define the plane about which the selected geometry will be mirrored, select the radio button corresponding to the required plane from the **Mirror Plane** area. To define the position of the plane, choose the node button and then select the node. Alternatively, specify the node number in the **Node on Plane** edit box. If you want to generate the mirror image of the original structure and do not want the original one, select the **Move** radio button in the **Generate Mode** area. If you want to keep the original structure with the newly created one, then select the **Copy** radio button. To mirror the member orientation, select the **Mirror Member Orientation** check box. After specifying all the parameters, choose the **OK** button; the selected geometry will be mirrored about the specified plane.

Example 8

In this example, you will generate the mirror image of a portal frame structure using the **Mirror** tool.

Steps required to complete this example are given below:

Step 1: Create a new file in STAAD.Pro with the name *c03_staad_v8i_ex8* and create a portal plane frame structure of **3m*3m** using the **Snap Node/Beam** tool, refer to Figure 3-41.

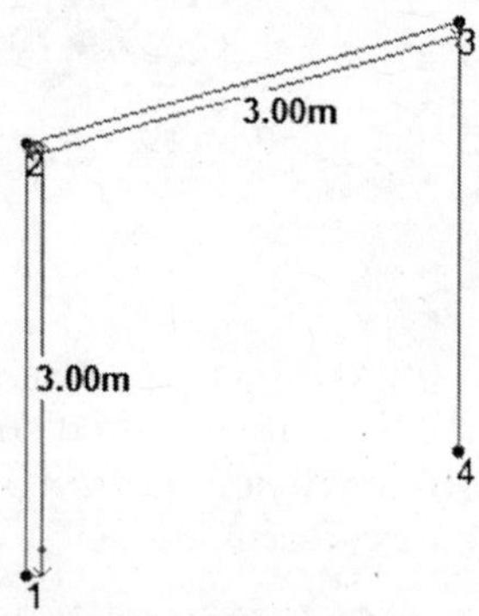

***Figure 3-41** The portal frame structure*

Step 2: Select the entire structure and choose the **Mirror** tool from the **Geometry** menu; the **Mirror** dialog box is displayed.

Step 3: In this dialog box, specify the parameters, as shown in Figure 3-42. Choose the **OK** button; the mirror image is generated, as shown in Figure 3-43.

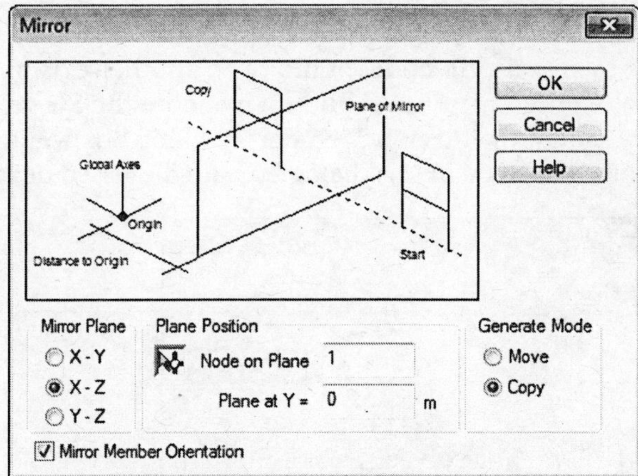

***Figure 3-42** The **Mirror** dialog box*

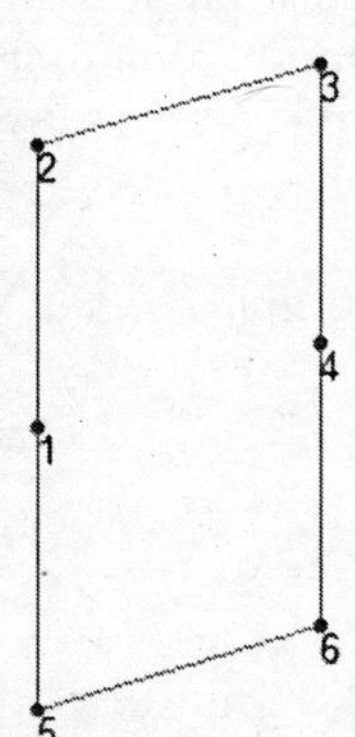

***Figure 3-43** Mirror image of the structure*

Step 4: Again, select the entire structure and invoke the **Mirror** tool; the **Mirror** dialog box is displayed.

Step 5: In this dialog box, select the **Y - Z** radio button in the **Mirror Plane** area. Specify **3** in the **Node on Plane** edit box in the **Plane Position** area and then select the **Copy** radio button. Next, choose the **OK** button; the mirror image is generated, as shown in Figure 3-44. Choose the **Save** button to save the file.

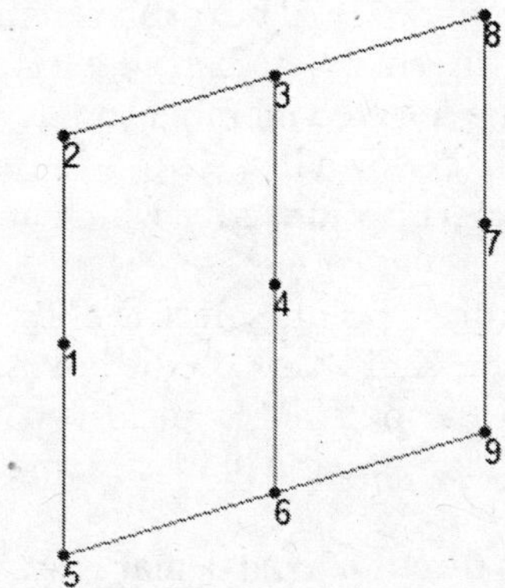

***Figure 3-44** Mirror image of the structure*

OTHER MISCELLANEOUS TOOLS

Earlier in this chapter, you have learned some of the essential tools used for structural modeling. You can also use some of the miscellaneous tools to reduce time and effort while modeling. These tools are discussed next.

Stretching Members Using Stretch Tool

In STAAD.Pro, you can stretch the length of the members in various ways. For example, a member can be stretched through a distance to an existing node, point, or to another existing member. To stretch a member, first select the required member(s) and then choose the **Stretch Selected Member(s)** tool from the **Geometry** menu; the **Stretch Member(s)** dialog box will be displayed, as shown in Figure 3-45. The options displayed in this dialog box are discussed next.

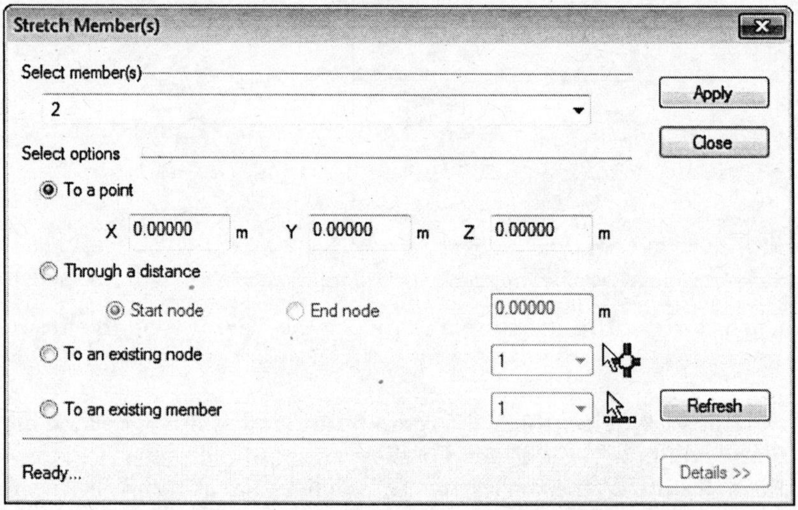

***Figure 3-45** The **Stretch Member(s)** dialog box*

In this dialog box, the selected member(s) will be displayed in the **Select member(s)** drop-down list. If you have selected more than one member, then all selected members will be displayed in the drop-down list. You can deselect the selected members by clearing the check box corresponding to the members displayed in the drop-down list. Next, to stretch the selected members, you can use the options available in the **Select options** area which are discussed next.

To stretch the selected members to a point, select the **To a point** radio button and specify the coordinates of the point in the **X**, **Y**, and **Z** edit boxes. Next, choose the **Apply** button; the member(s) will be stretched to a specified point. In that case, STAAD.Pro will determine automatically that which end of the member will be stretched.

To stretch the selected member(s) through a particular distance, select the **Through a distance** radio button. Next, specify the start or end node along which the member will be stretched by selecting the **Start node** or **End node** radio button, respectively. Then, specify the distance through which the member will be stretched in the edit box adjacent to the **End node** radio button. Next, choose the **Apply** button; the selected member(s) will be stretched through the specified distance.

To stretch the selected member(s) to an existing node, select the **To an existing node** radio button. Next, select the required node from the drop-down list available next to the radio button. You can also select the node directly from the Main Window. To do so, choose the **Pick node** button and then move the cursor in the Main Window; the nodes cursor will be displayed. Now, select the node from the Main Window and then choose the **Apply** button; the selected member(s) will be stretched to the selected node.

To stretch the selected member(s) to an existing member, select the **To an existing member** radio button and then select the required member from the drop-down list available next to the radio button. In that case, you can also specify the member by choosing the **Pick member** button.

Note

To stretch a member, there must be an intersection point, on the axis of the existing member to be stretched.

Intersecting Members Using the Intersect Tool

Sometimes during the modeling of a structure, the members intersect each other without creating a connection point at the intersection. As a result, there is no transfer of forces between the intersecting members. To avoid this, you can physically connect the intersecting members by creating a common connecting node. To do so, first select the required intersecting members from the Main Window. Next, choose **Intersect Selected Member(s) > Intersect** from the **Geometry** menu; the **Intersect Members** dialog box will be displayed. In this dialog box, you can specify the tolerance value to find the intersecting members. Next, choose the **OK** button; the **STAAD.Pro V8i (SELECTseries 6)** message box will be displayed containing information about the newly created members. Choose the **OK** button; new members will be created by splitting the intersecting members at the intersection point.

Merging Members and Nodes

You can merge the collinear members. To merge the members, first select the required members. Next, choose the **Merge Selected Members** option from the **Geometry** menu; the **Merge Selected Beams** dialog box will be displayed, as shown in Figure 3-46.

In this dialog box, the selected members will be displayed and highlighted in blue, refer to Figure 3-46. You can specify the name to be assigned for the new member by selecting a member number from the **Beam No. to Keep** drop-down list. Similarly, you can specify the required sectional property, elasticity, poisson, and density by selecting the required values from the respective drop-down lists. After specifying all properties, choose the **Merge** button; the **STAAD.Pro V8i (SELECTseries 6)** message box will be displayed prompting you to merge the members. Choose the **Yes** button from the message box and then the **Close** button from the **Merge Selected Beams** dialog box; the dialog box will be closed the two members will be merged into one.

Similarly, you can merge the selected nodes. To do so, select the required nodes and choose the **Merge Selected Nodes** option from the **Geometry** menu; the **Select Node** dialog box will be displayed, as shown in Figure 3-47. In this dialog box, select the node to be assigned from the **Node To Keep** drop-down list. Next, choose the **OK** button; the selected nodes will be merged into one.

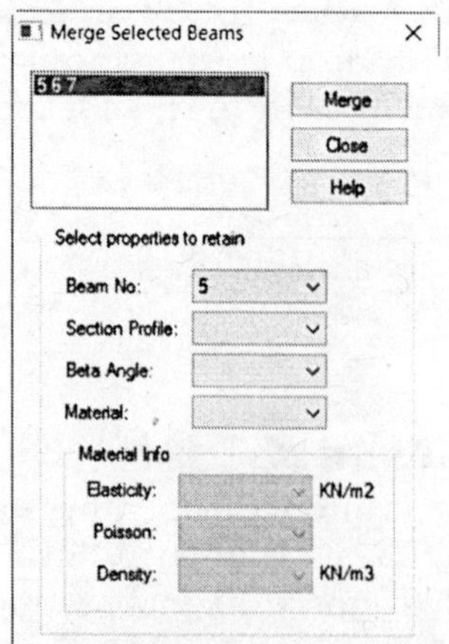

*Figure 3-46 The **Merge Selected Beams** dialog box*

*Figure 3-47 The **Select Node** dialog box*

Renumbering Nodes, Members, and Elements

STAAD.Pro allows you to renumber the nodes, members, plate elements, and solids. To renumber the existing nodes, first select the required nodes from the Main Window. Next, choose **Renumber > Nodes** from the **Geometry** menu; the **STAAD.Pro V8i (SELECTseries 6)** warning message will be displayed prompting you to renumber the nodes. Choose the **Yes** button; the **Renumber** dialog box will be displayed, as shown in Figure 3-48.

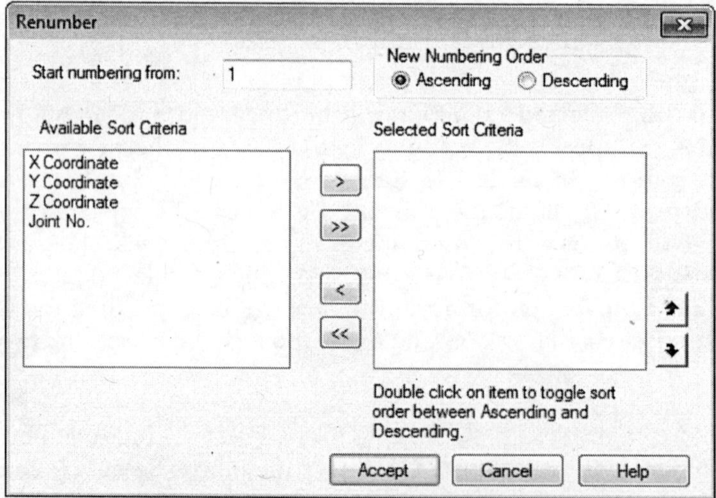

*Figure 3-48 The **Renumber** dialog box*

In this dialog box, you can specify the starting number of the node in the **Start numbering from** edit box. Next, specify the numbering order (ascending or descending) by selecting the **Ascending** or **Descending** radio button in the **New Numbering Order** area. You can also specify the sequence of numbering by selecting the required criteria available in the **Available Sort Criteria** area. For renumbering nodes, select the **Joint No.** option and then choose the forward button to shift the selected option in the **Selected Sort Criteria** area. Next, choose the **Accept** button; the nodes will be renumbered. Similarly, you can renumber the members, plates, and solids.

Splitting and Breaking Beams at Selected Nodes

There are some tools available in STAAD.Pro which allow you to split a single member into two parts, and also allow you to break a beam at selected nodes.

While splitting a beam, you need to select the member first. Next, choose the **Split Beam** option from the **Geometry** menu; the **Insert Nodes** dialog box will be displayed. Using the options in the dialog box, you can create a node on the member which will split it at that particular node.

Note

While splitting a member, the member properties and loads will be automatically generated.

If some nodes are created on the line of a member, then you can break the member at those nodes which creates smaller members connecting all the nodes. To break a beam at selected nodes, first select the required node(s) and then choose the **Break Beams at Selected Nodes** option from the **Geometry** menu; the **STAAD.Pro V8i (SELECTseries 6)** message box will be displayed informing about the created beams. Choose the **OK** button; the selected beam will be broken at the specified nodes.

CUTTING SECTIONS

Assigning properties and loads to complex structures becomes a tedious task. In that case, you can slice off the structure along the global XY, YZ, and XZ planes to create its sectional view. To create a sectional view, choose the **Cut Section** tool from the toolbar; the **Section** dialog box will be displayed, as shown in Figure 3-49. This dialog box comprises of three tabs: **Range By Joint**, **Range By Min/Max**, and **Select to View**. These tabs are discussed next.

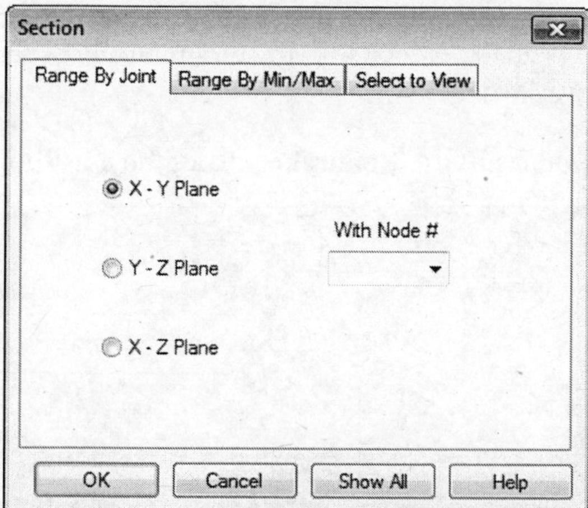

*Figure 3-49 The **Section** dialog box*

The **Range By Joint** tab is chosen by default. In this tab, you can specify the section plane by selecting the **X - Y Plane**, **Y - Z Plane**, or **X - Z Plane** radio button. Next, select the node which lie on the section plane from the **With Node #** drop-down list.

In the **Range By Min/Max** tab, you can define a range along the axis perpendicular to the section plane. Thus the portion of structure lying in this range will be displayed in the Main

Window. You can specify a plane by selecting the corresponding radio button. Next, specify the minimum and maximum range for the section in the **Minimum** and **Maximum** edit boxes.

In the **Select to View** tab, you can specify the portion of the structure to be displayed in the Main Window. Select the **Window / Rubber Bound** radio button to select the portion of structure to be displayed by drawing a selection window. To display only the selected objects, select the **View Highlighted Only** radio button. To view only the beams, plates, solids, and nodes, select the **Select to View** radio button. Next, select the corresponding check boxes to display the required object.

Choose the **OK** button from the **Section** dialog box; the required section will be displayed.

After creating the sectional views, you can view the whole structure by choosing the **Whole Structure** option from the **View** menu; the entire structure will be displayed in the Main Window.

Example 9

In this example you will renumber the nodes and members of a structure. The model used in this example is in the file *c02_staad_v8i_ex4.std.*

Steps required to complete this example are given below:

Step 1: Open the *c02_staad_v8i_ex4.std* file in STAAD.Pro and press SHIFT+N to view the node numbers.

Step 2: Invoke the **Nodes Cursor** from the side toolbar and select all the nodes. Choose **Renumber > Nodes** from the **Geometry** menu; the **STAAD.Pro V8i (SELECTseries 6)** message box is displayed prompting you to proceed with the renumbering process. Choose the **Yes** button; the **Renumber** dialog box is displayed.

Step 3: Next, specify the values in the **Renumber** dialog box, as shown in Figure 3-50.

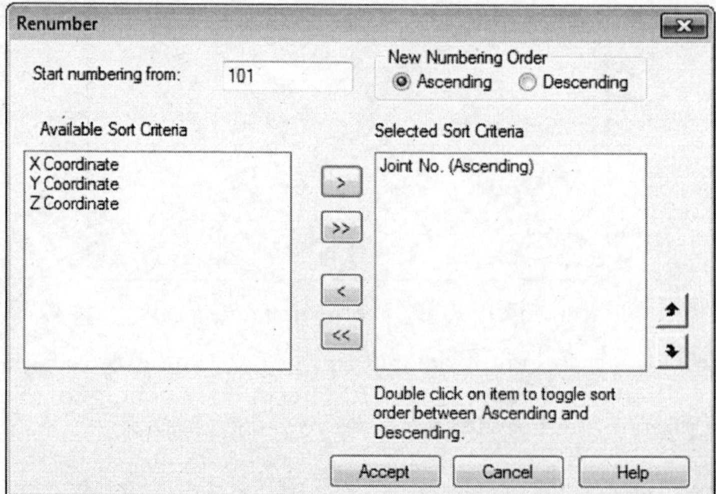

***Figure 3-50** Values specified in the **Renumber** dialog box*

Step 4: Choose the **Accept** button; the **STAAD.Pro V8i (SELECTseries 6)** message box is displayed. Choose the **OK** button; the selected nodes are renumbered.

Step 5: Press SHIFT+N to hide the node numbers and press SHIFT+B to view the member numbers.

Step 6: Choose **Beams Parallel To > X** from the **Select** menu; members parallel to **X** axis are selected and highlighted in red in the Main Window.

Step 7: Next, choose **Renumber > Members** from the **Geometry** menu; the **STAAD.Pro V8i (SELECTseries 6)** message box is displayed. Choose the **Yes** button; the **Renumber** dialog box is displayed.

Step 8: Specify the values in the dialog box, as shown in Figure 3-51.

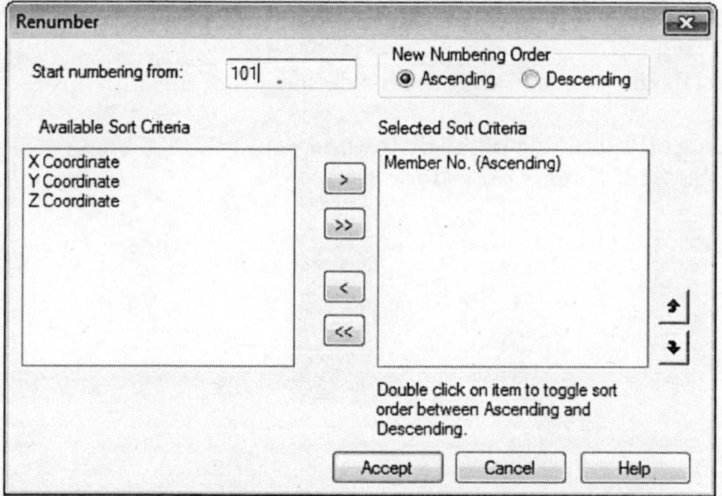

Figure 3-51 *Values specified in the* ***Renumber*** *dialog box*

Step 9: Choose the **Accept** button; the **STAAD.Pro V8i (SELECTseries 6)** message box is displayed prompting you about the renumbered members. Choose the **OK** button; the members are renumbered.

Step 10: Choose **Beams Parallel To > Y** from the **Select** menu; members parallel to Y axis are selected and highlighted in red in the Main Window.

Step 11: Repeat the procedure followed in steps 7 through 9 and renumber the members. In this case, enter 301 in the **Start numbering from** edit box in the **Renumber** dialog box.

Step 12: Choose **Beams Parallel To > Z** from the **Select** menu; members parallel to Z axis are selected and highlighted in red in the Main Window.

Step 13: Repeat the procedure followed in steps 7 through 9 and renumber the members. In this case, specify **401** in the **Start numbering from** edit box of the **Renumber** dialog box.

Step 14: Choose the **Save As** option from the **File** menu; the **Save As** dialog box is displayed. In this dialog box, specify the name *c03_staad_v8i_ex9* in the **File name** edit box and save it at an appropriate location.

Example 10

In this example, you will cut the structure along some of the global planes to view the sections. The model used in this example is in the file *c02_staad_v8i_ex4.std*.

Steps required to complete this example are given below:

Step 1: Open the file *c02_staad_v8i_ex4.std* in STAAD.Pro and press SHIFT+N to view the node numbers.

Step 2: Invoke the **Cut Section** tool from the toolbar; the **Section** dialog box is displayed.

Now, you will specify the values to view the inside section of the structure.

Step 3: In the **Range By Joint** tab of the dialog box, select the **Y-Z Plane** radio button and node number **2** from the **With Node#** drop-down list.

Step 4: Next, choose the **OK** button; the dialog box closes and the section is displayed, as shown in Figure 3-52.

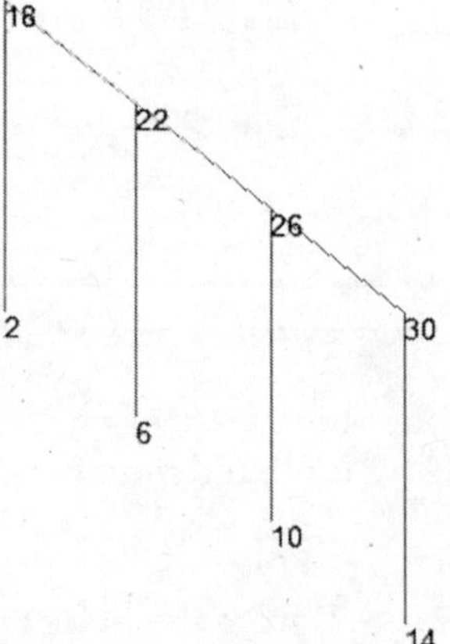

Figure 3-52 *Section after cutting*

Step 5: Now, select the **Whole Structure** option from the **View** menu bar; the whole structure is displayed.

Step 6: Repeat the previous steps to cut off the section along the other global planes.

Self-Evaluation Test

Answer the following questions and compare them to those given at the end of this chapter:

1. The __________ tool is used to add beam between two nodes.

2. The __________ tool is used to add curved beams between two nodes.

3. The __________ tool is used to create surface meshing.

4. The collinear members can be created by using the **Create Colinear Beams** option. (T/F)

5. In STAAD.Pro, only quadrilateral plates can be created. (T/F)

6. In STAAD.Pro, you cannot divide a single plate into multiple plates. (T/F)

7. The **Translational Repeat** tool is used to repeat the structural elements in a circular direction. (T/F)

Review Questions

Answer the following questions:

1. Which of the following tools is used to repeat the structure n number of times in a linear direction?

   (a) **Rotate** (b) **Circular Repeat**
   (c) **Translational Repeat** (d) **Copy**

2. Which of the following tools is used to connect the intersecting members?

   (a) **Mirror** (b) **Rotate**
   (c) **Intersect** (d) None of these

3. Which of the following tools is used to split a member into two parts?

   (a) **Insert Node** (b) **Split Beam**
   (c) **Move** (d) **Add Beam**

4. In STAAD.Pro, only nodes can be renumbered. (T/F)

5. Using the **Move** tool, you can shift the structure to a new position. (T/F)

6. Openings can be inserted only in surfaces. (T/F)

7. You can create multiple plates at a time by using the **Create Infill Plates** tool. (T/F)

Answers to Self-Evaluation Test

1. Add Beam from Point to Point, **2**. Add Curved Beam, **3**. Generate Surface Meshing, **4**. T, **5**. F, **6**. F, **7**. F

Chapter 4

Defining Material Constants and Section Properties

Learning Objectives

After completing this chapter, you will be able to:

- *Define material constants and cross-section properties*
- *Define and assign section properties*

INTRODUCTION

After modeling a structure, you need to define its material constants and cross-section properties. In STAAD.Pro, there are two types of materials: Isotropic and Orthotropic 2D. The Isotropic materials have same values of a property in all directions whereas in Orthotropic 2D materials, properties vary in primary direction.

It helps to keep the bending and shear stresses within the allowable limits. The process of defining and assigning constants and cross-section properties is discussed next.

MATERIAL CONSTANTS

The material constants include elastic constants such as Poisson's ratio, Young's modulus, and Shear modulus as well as density, thermal coefficient, and critical damping ratio. You can define the material constants in the **Material** page of the **General** tab. In this page, the **Material - - Whole Structure** window will be displayed in the Data Area, as shown in Figure 4-1.

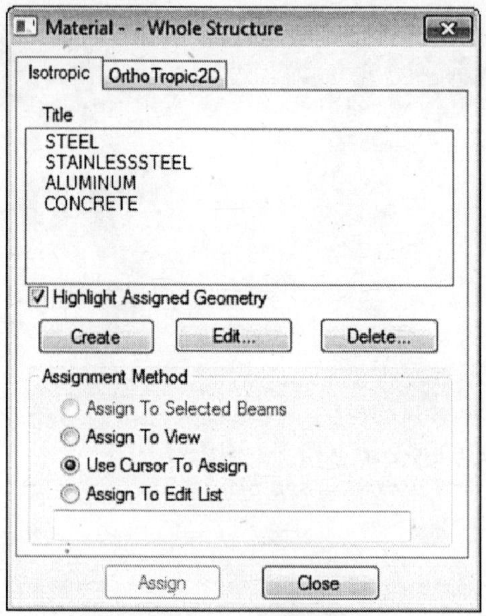

Figure 4-1 *The* ***Material - - Whole Structure*** *window*

In this window, the **Isotropic** tab is chosen by default. In this tab, four pre-defined materials are displayed. To view the values of different properties of a material, double-click on the corresponding material. For example, if you double-click on **CONCRETE**, the **Isotropic Material** dialog box will be displayed, as shown in Figure 4-2. In this dialog box, the name of the material is displayed in the **Title** edit box of the **Identification** area. The material properties and its values are displayed in the **Material Properties** area. You cannot edit the values displayed in this dialog box except the values of compressive strength.

You can use the options displayed in the **Isotropic** tab of the **Material - - Whole Structure** window to create new materials, edit existing materials, change the values of material properties, and to assign the material properties to the structure. This is discussed next.

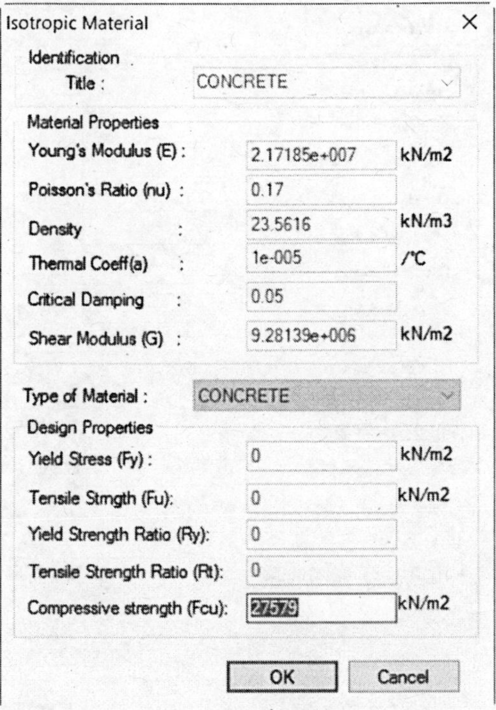

*Figure 4-2 The **Isotropic Material** dialog box*

Creating New Materials

You can create a new material and define its properties. To do so, choose the **Create** button in the **Material - - Whole Structure** window; the **Isotropic Material** dialog box will be displayed, as shown in Figure 4-3. In this dialog box, you can specify a name for the material in the **Title** edit box. In the **Material Properties** area, specify values of the properties in their respective edit boxes. Next, choose the **OK** button; the **Isotropic Material** dialog box will be closed and the name of the newly created material will be displayed in the **Title** area of the **Material - - Whole Structure** window. You can also create a material tag from the available pre-defined materials. To do so, click on the down-arrow in the **Title** edit box of the **Isotropic Material** dialog box; a list of material names will be displayed. Select the required material from the displayed list; the values of the properties of the selected material will be automatically filled in the edit boxes corresponding to them in the **Material Properties** area, refer to Figure 4-3. Note that these values will not be in the editable mode. To change the values of the properties of existing material, specify a new name in the **Title** edit box; the material properties will be enabled for editing. Now, you can enter the desired property values in the edit boxes and close the dialog box by choosing the **OK** button.

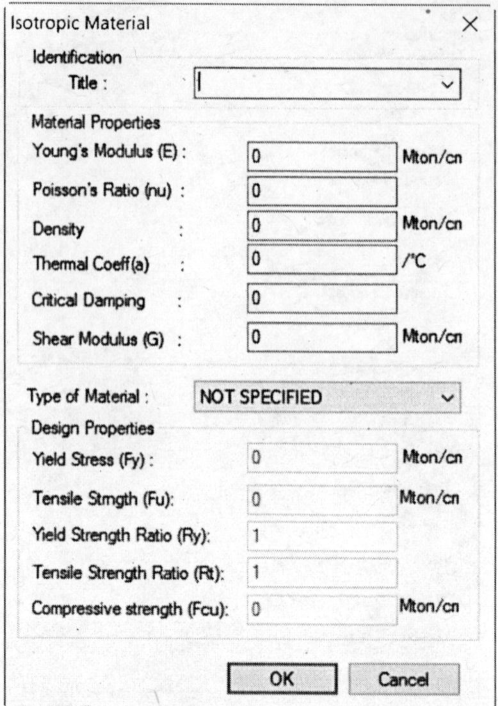

*Figure 4-3 The **Isotropic Material** dialog box*

Editing Material Properties

You can edit the newly created material properties. To do so, first select the material from the **Title** area and then choose the **Edit** button in the **Material - - Whole Structure** window; the **Isotropic Material** dialog box will be displayed. In this dialog box, specify the property values as required and choose the **OK** button to apply the changes. You can use the **Delete** button to delete any material from the materials available in the **Title** area.

Assigning Materials to the Structure

You can assign the required material to the structure. To do so, you can use any of the radio buttons available in the **Assignment Method** area of the **Material - - Whole Structure** window. These radio buttons are discussed next.

Assign To Selected Beams

This radio button is used to assign the desired material to the members selected in the structure. For assigning material to the structural members, you first need to select the required material from the **Title** area. Next, select the structural members or elements from the main window. The **Assign To Selected Beams** radio button is selected by default in the **Assignment Method** area. Now, choose the **Assign** button; the **STAAD.Pro V8i (SELECTseries 6)** message box will be displayed. Choose the **Yes** button; the **STAAD.Pro V8i (SELECTseries 6)** message box will close and the material will be assigned to the selected structural members.

Assign To View

This radio button is used to assign a material to an entire structure. For assigning material to the whole structure, first select the desired material and then select the **Assign To View** radio button. Now, choose the **Assign** button; the **STAAD.Pro V8i (SELECTseries 6)** message box will be displayed. Choose the **Yes** button; the **STAAD.Pro V8i (SELECTseries 6)** message box will close and the material will be assigned to the entire structure.

Use Cursor To Assign

This radio button is used to assign material to a structural element by using the cursor. For assigning material to a structural element one by one, first select the material and then select the **Use Cursor To Assign** radio button. Next, choose the **Assign** button; the **Assigning** label will appear on it. Now, click on the structural elements to which you want to assign the material. Choose the **Assigning** button to terminate the assigning process.

Assign To Edit List

This radio button is used to assign material by specifying a list of members to which material will be assigned. For assigning material to the structural members, first select the material and then select the **Assign To Edit List** radio button; the edit box below the radio button will be enabled. In this edit box, specify the member numbers and then choose the **Assign** button; the material will be assigned to the specified members.

After assigning material constants, you can view the commands for the defined material constants. To do so, choose the **STAAD Editor** button from the toolbar; the **Warning** message box will be displayed. In this message box, choose the **Save** button; the **STAAD Editor** window will be displayed. The commands for the material constant will be displayed below the **Member Incidences** command. For example, if you have assigned concrete material to the structure then the command for the concrete material will be as follows:

```
DEFINE MATERIAL START
ISOTROPIC CONCRETE
E 2.17185e+007
POISSON 0.17
DENSITY 23.5616
ALPHA 1e-005
DAMP 0.05
END DEFINE MATERIAL
CONSTANTS
MATERIAL CONCRETE ALL
```

Defining OrthoTropic Material

You can define the material property of the Orthotropic 2D materials as well. To do so, choose the **OrthoTropic 2D** tab in the **Material -- Whole Structure** window. In this tab, choose the **Create** button; the **2-D OrthoTropic Material Property** dialog box will be displayed, as shown in Figure 4-4. In this dialog box, specify the name of the material in the **Title** edit box. Specify the values for **Young's Modulus** and **Thermal Coefficient** in local x and y directions in the **Property in Element X direction** and **Property in Element Y direction** areas. Specify the values for **Density, Critical Damping** and **Poisson's Ratio** in their corresponding edit boxes in the **General** area. You can specify the values for shear modulii in the **Gxy, Gyz** and **Gzx** edit boxes from the **Shear Modulii** area. After specifying the values, choose the **Add** button to add material properties to the **Material - - Whole Structure** window.

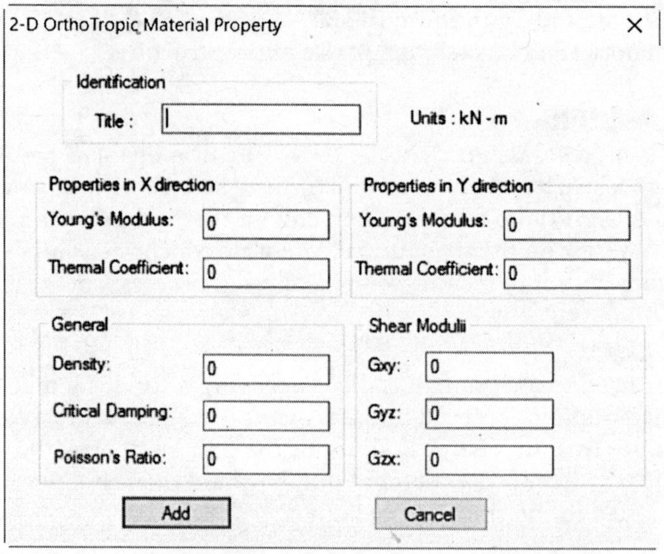

***Figure 4-4** The **2D OrthoTropic Material Property** dialog box*

Note

For doing the examples of this chapter, you need to download the c04_Staad_v8i.zip file from http://www.cadcim.com. The path of the file is as follows: Textbook > Civil/GIS > STAAD.Pro > Exploring Bentley STAAD.Pro V8i.

Example 1

In this example, you will open the file *c02_staad_v8i_ex4* file. Next, you will create a material and assign it to a structure.

The steps required to complete this example are given below:

Step 1: Start STAAD.Pro and open the file *c02_staad_v8i_ex4*; the model is displayed in the main window, refer to Figure 4-5.

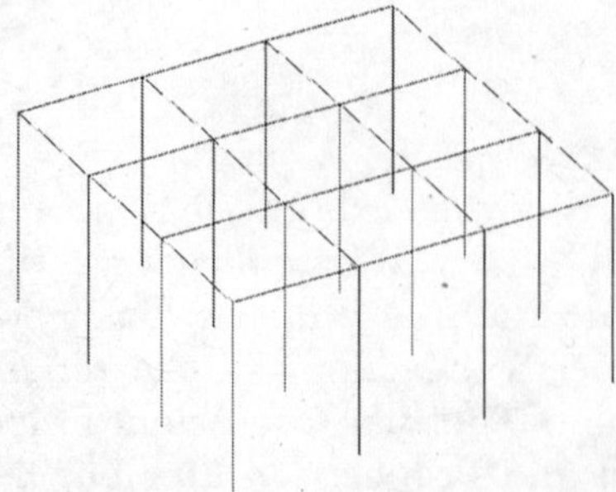

***Figure 4-5** Model displayed in the Main Window*

Step 2: Select all members and choose the **Translational Repeat** tool from the tool bar; the **Translational Repeat** dialog box is displayed. Specify the values in this dialog box, as shown in Figure 4-6. Next Choose the **OK** button; the members are repeated, as shown in Figure 4-7.

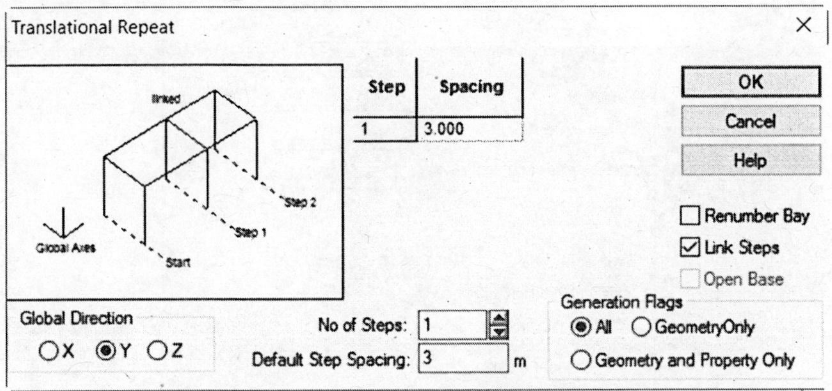

Figure 4-6 The **Translation Repeat** dialog box

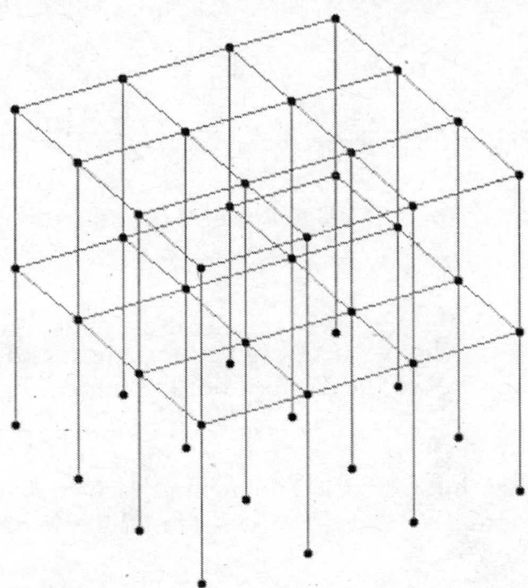

Figure 4-7 Model displayed in the Main Window

Step 3: Choose the **General** tab from the main window and then open the **Material** page from it; the **Material - - Whole Structure** window is displayed.

Step 4: In this window, choose the **Create** button; the **Isotropic Material** dialog box is displayed.

Step 5: In this dialog box, select the **CONCRETE** option from the **Title** drop-down list in the **Identification** area.

Step 6: Now specify a new name **CONC** in the **Title** edit box and specify the values for the properties, as shown in Figure 4-8.

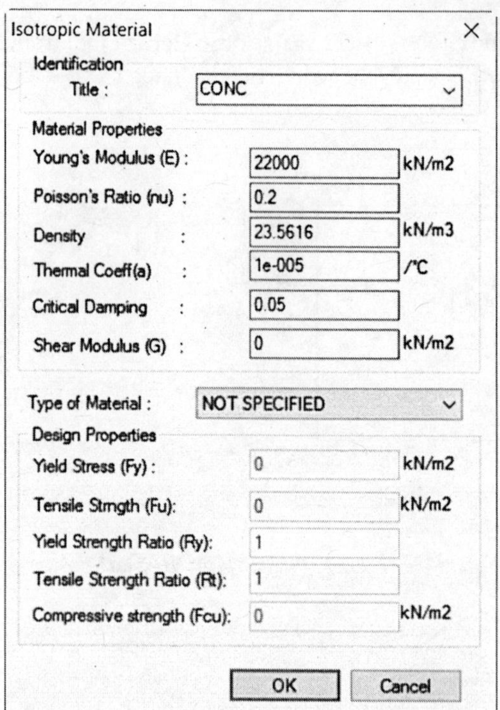

*Figure 4-8 The **Isotropic Material** dialog box*

Step 7: Choose the **OK** button; the **CONC** material is created and displayed in the **Title** area of the **Isotropic** tab.

Step 8: Select the **CONC** material and then select the **Assign To View** radio button in the **Assignment Method** area. Next, choose the **Assign** button; the **STAAD.Pro V8i (SELECTseries 6)** message box is displayed. Choose the **Yes** button; the material gets assigned to the entire structure.

Step 9: Choose the **Save As** option from the **File** menu; the **Save As** dialog box is displayed. In this dialog box, specify the name *c04_staad_v8i_ex1.std* in the **File name** edit box and save it at an appropriate location.

SECTION PROPERTIES

After assigning the materials to the structure, you need to define the section properties for the structure and then assign those properties to the structure. In STAAD.Pro, you can define the section properties for prismatic sections, steel sections, tapered sections, steel joist, and joist girders from the available database in the software. This is discussed next.

Prismatic Section

You can define the prismatic section properties in the **Property** page of the **General** tab. In this page the **Properties - Whole Structure** window will be displayed in the Data Area, refer to Figure 4-9. In this window, the **Section** tab is chosen by default. In this tab, choose the **Define** button; the **Property** dialog box is displayed with the **Circle** page selected by default, refer to Figure 4-10. For the circular section, specify the diameter in the **YD** edit box. You can define the rectangular section as well. To do so, choose the **Rectangle** option in the left pane of the dialog box; the **Rectangle** page will be displayed. In this page, specify the length and width of the rectangle in the **YD** and **ZD** edit boxes, respectively.

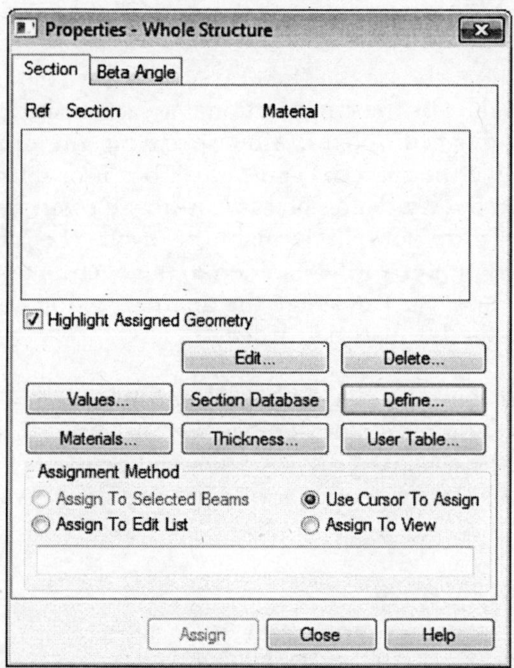

Figure 4-9 *The* ***Properties - Whole Structure*** *window*

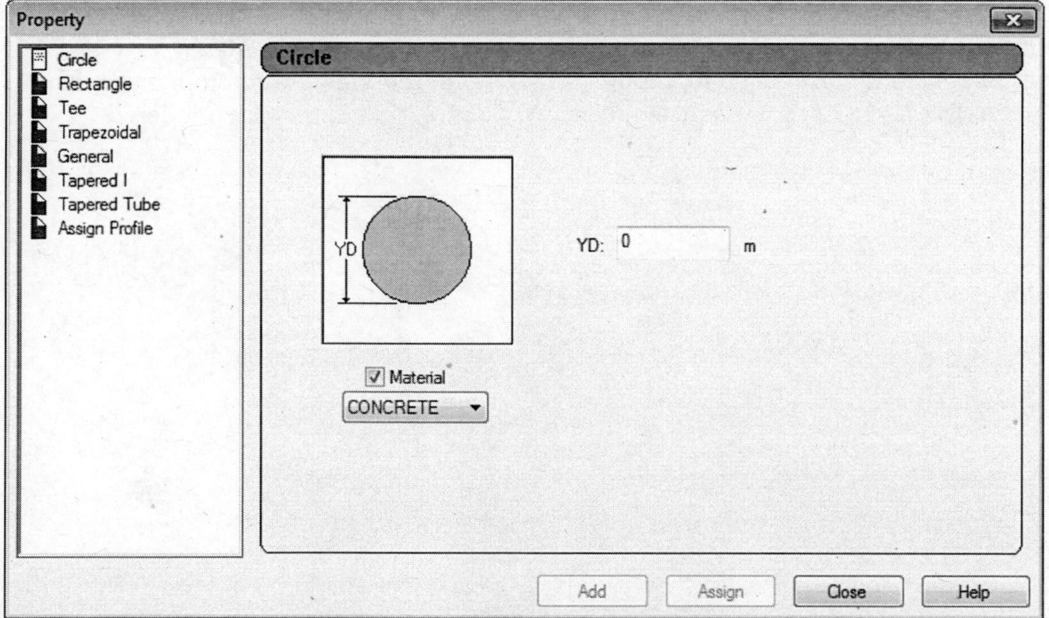

Figure 4-10 *The* ***Property*** *dialog box*

To define the Tee section, choose the **Tee** option; the **Tee** page will be displayed. Next, specify the dimension of the web and flange in the **YD**, **ZD**, **YB**, and **ZB** edit boxes.

To define the trapezoidal section, choose the **Trapezoidal** option; the **Trapezoidal** page will be displayed. Next, specify values in the **YD**, **ZD**, and **ZB** edit boxes to define the geometry of trapezoid.

To define an arbitrary section, choose the **General** option; the **General** page will be displayed. In this page, specify the value for the cross-sectional area, the shear area, and the moment of inertia in their corresponding edit boxes. After specifying the dimensions for the required section, you need to include the material constants. To do so, select the **Material** check box in the right pane of the **Property** dialog box if it is not selected by default. Then, select the required material from the drop-down list available below the check box. Next, choose the **Add** button; the defined section property will be added to the **Section** tab with the tag number and the property description. Now, you can assign the defined section to the structure by using any of the four assignment methods discussed earlier.

You can also view the commands for the section properties assigned to the structure. To do so, choose the **STAAD Editor** button from the toolbar; the **Warning** message box will be displayed. Choose the **Save** button; the **STAAD Editor** window will be displayed with all the commands. The commands for creating the prismatic rectangular section is given next.

```
MEMBER PROPERTY
1 TO 7 PRIS YD 0.25 ZD 0.35
```

Note

The commands for the section properties will be displayed after the ***Material Constants*** *command in the* ***STAAD Editor*** *window.*

After assigning cross-sections to the structure, you can view the rendered view in the **Rendered View** window. To do so, choose the **3D Rendered View** button from the toolbar; the **Rendered View** window will be displayed. Figure 4-11 shows the rendered view of the structure.

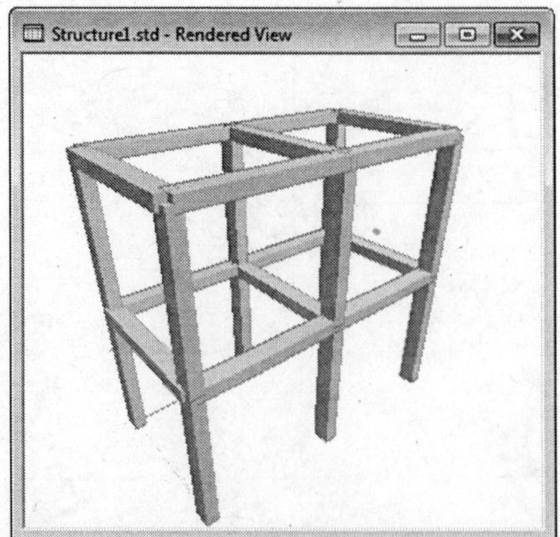

Figure 4-11 *Rendered view of the structure*

Example 2

In this example, you will open the *c04_staad_v8i_ex1.std* file in STAAD.Pro. Next, you will define a prismatic section and then assign it to the structure.

Steps required to complete this example are given below:

Step 1: Start STAAD.Pro and open the file *c04_staad_v8i_ex1.std*; the model is displayed in the main window.

Step 2: Choose the **General** tab from the main window; the **Property** page and the **Property - Whole Structure** window are displayed in the Data Area.

Step 3: In the **Properties - Whole Structure** window, choose the **Define** button; the **Property** dialog box is displayed.

Step 4: In this dialog box, choose the **Rectangle** option from the left pane; the **Rectangle** page is displayed. In this page, specify the values **0.250** and **0.350** in the **YD** and **ZD** edit boxes, respectively. Next, select the material **CONC** from the **Material** drop-down list.

Step 5: Choose the **Add** button to add the rectangular section and close the dialog box. Next, select the added section from the **Section** tab of the **Properties - Whole Structure** window.

Step 6: Select the **Assign To View** radio button from the **Assignment Method** area and then choose the **Assign** button; the **STAAD.Pro V8i (SELECTseries 6)** message box is displayed. Choose the **Yes** button; the section is assigned to the entire structure.

Step 7: Right-click in the main window and choose the **Structure Diagrams** option from the shortcut menu; the **Diagrams** dialog box is displayed.

Step 8: In this dialog box, select the **Full Sections** radio button from the **3D Sections** area and choose **Apply** and then the **OK** button to close the dialog box. Figure 4-12 shows the rendered view of the structure.

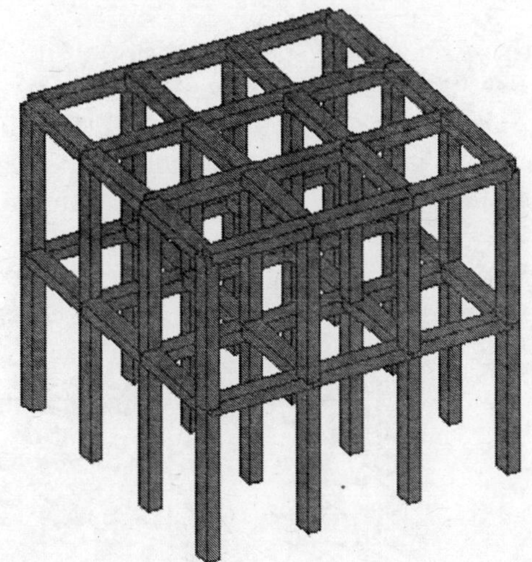

***Figure 4-12** The rendered view of the structure*

Step 9: Choose the **Save As** option from the **File** menu; the **Save As** dialog box is displayed. In this dialog box, specify the name *c04_staad_v8i_ex2.std* in the **File name** edit box and save it at an appropriate location.

Tapered Sections

You can define the tapered I and tube section properties and assign them to a structure. The tapered I section has varying depth along the length of the member. To define the tapered I section, choose the **Define** button from the **Properties - Whole Structure** window and invoke the **Property** dialog box. In this dialog box, choose the **Tapered I** option; the **Tapered I** page will be displayed, as shown in Figure 4-13.

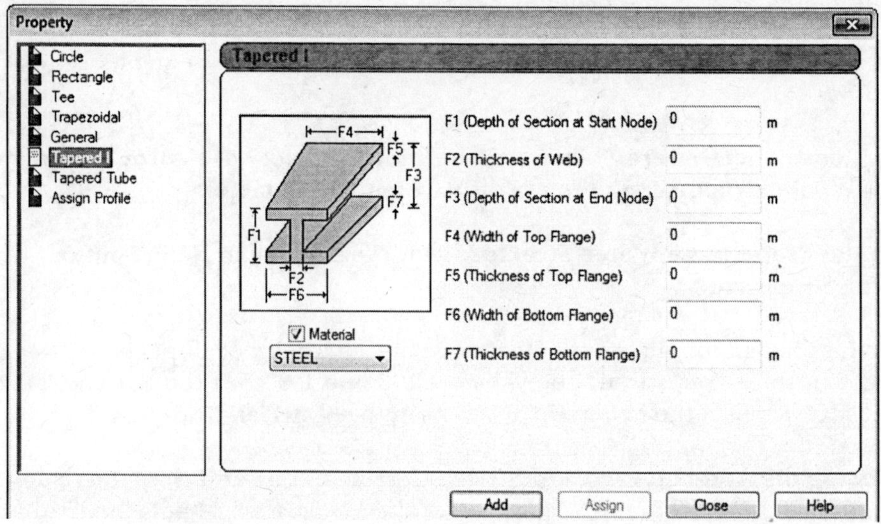

*Figure 4-13 The **Tapered I** page in the **Property** dialog box*

In this page, specify the dimension of the web and flange in the **F1 (Depth of Section at Start Node, F2 (Thickness of Web), F3 (Depth of Section at End Node), F4 (Width of Top Flange), F5 (Thickness of Top Flange), F6 (Width of Bottom Flange)**, and **F7 (Thickness of Bottom Flange)** edit boxes. You can include the material constant by selecting the **Material** check box. Next, choose the **Add** button to add the material and then assign it to the structure.

Similarly, to add the tapered tube section properties, choose the **Tapered Tube** option from the left pane of the dialog box; the **Tapered Tube** page will be displayed, as shown in Figure 4-14.

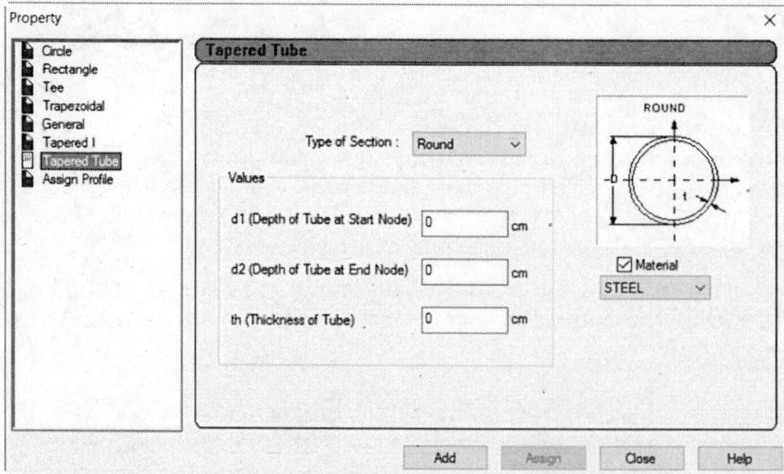

*Figure 4-14 The **Tapered Tube** page in the **Property** dialog box*

In this page, select the type of tube from the **Type of Section** drop-down list. Next, specify the depth of the tube at the start and end nodes in the **d1** and **d2** edit boxes, respectively. Specify the thickness of tube in the **th** edit box. Now, choose the **Add** button to add the structure to the **Section** tab and then close the dialog box by choosing the **Close** button. After adding the section, you can assign it to the structure.

To assign a profile to the structure, select **Assign Profile** from the left pane of the **Property** dialog box; the **Assign Profile** page will be displayed, as shown in Figure 4-15. You can asign the desired profile by selecting the radio button corresponding to that option from the **Select Profile Specification** area and then choosing the **Add** button. On doing so, the selected profile will be added to the **Properties - Whole Structure** window in the **Section** tab. Once a section is added, it can be assigned to the structure.

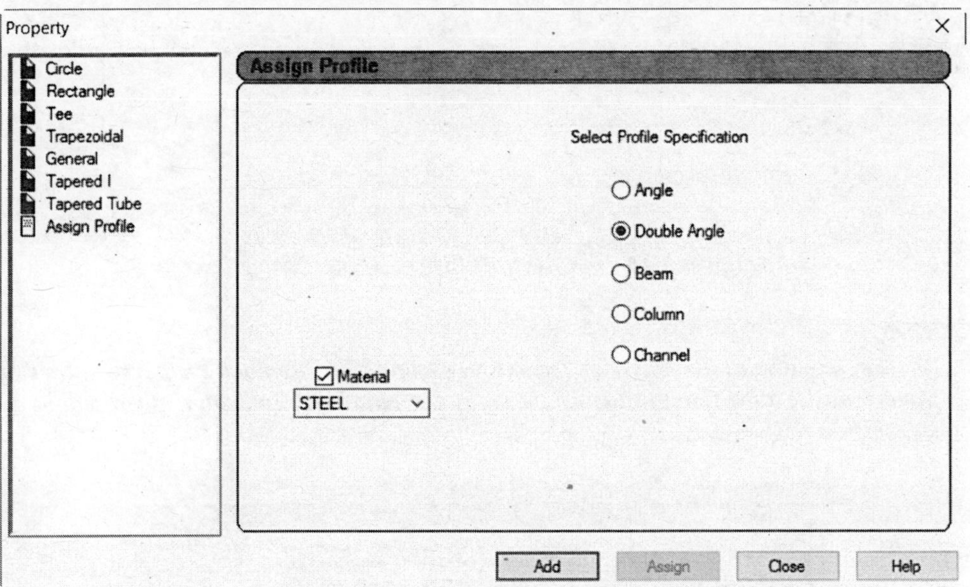

*Figure 4-15 The **Assign Profile** page in the **Property** dialog box*

Steel Sections

STAAD.Pro has in-built steel tables which are used in different countries. It contains thousands of steel sections. To access the steel library, choose the **Section Database** button from the **Properties - Whole Structure** window; the **Section Profile Tables** dialog box will be displayed with the **Steel** tab chosen by default, as shown in Figure 4-16. This dialog box comprises of four tabs: **Steel**, **Coldformed Steel**, **Timber**, and **Aluminum**. In the left pane of the **Steel** tab, you can view various sections of different shapes. These sections are grouped into different folders according to their country name. For example, in **American** folder, you can view the American sections. By default, **W Shape** is selected in the left pane and the **W Shape** page is displayed in the right pane of the **Steel** tab. In this page, you can select the required beam from the **Select Beam** list box. You can also specify additional specifications such as Single section, Tee section, Composite section, Top & Bottom Cover plate, and so on in the **Type Specification** area. To include the material constants, select the **Material** check box if it is not selected by default. Next, choose the **Add** button to add the material in the **Material -- Whole Structure** window. Now, you can assign the added material to the structure.

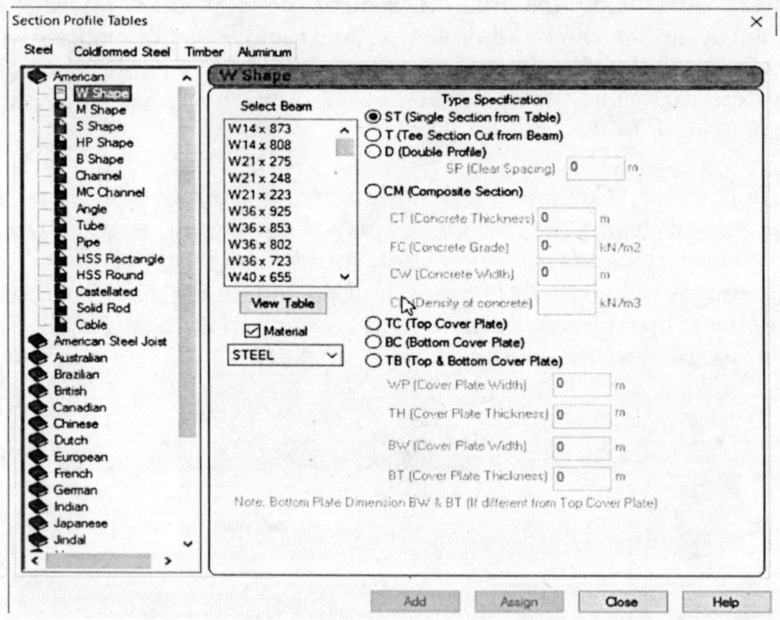

***Figure 4-16** The **Section Profile Tables** dialog box*

Note

*You can also display the American sections by choosing the **Member Property > Steel Table > American** from the **Commands** menu; the **American Steel Table** dialog box will be displayed, as shown in Figure 4-17.*

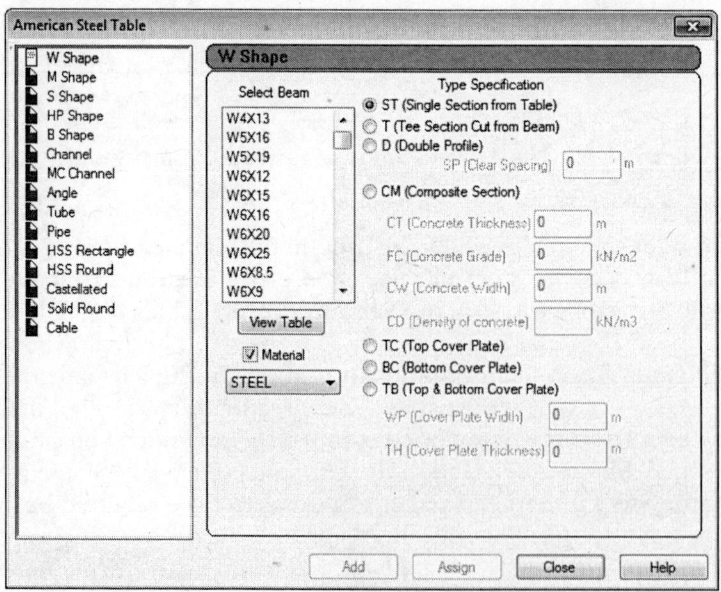

***Figure 4-17** The **American Steel Table** dialog box*

To add the cold formed steel sections to the structure, choose the **Coldformed Steel** tab. In this tab, expand the **American Cold Formed** folder in the left pane if it is not selected by default and select the required shape. Next, select the required section from the right pane of the dialog box. In this pane, specify the type of specification and then choose the **Add** button to add the specification to the **Material - - Whole Structure** window. Next, close the dialog box by choosing the **Close** button. Assign the added section to the structure.

After assigning the section to the structure, you can view the associated commands. To do so, choose the **STAAD Editor** button from the toolbar; the **Warning** message box will be displayed. Next, choose the **Save** button; the **STAAD Editor** window will be displayed. In this window, the command for the assigned steel section is given below the material constants command. The command for the assigned steel section is given next.

```
MEMBER PROPERTY AMERICAN
MEMBER-LIST TABLE ST {CROSS-SECTION TYPE}
```

In the above command, the first line will initiate the command. The Member-List command represents the list of members to which the steel section has been assigned. The Table ST command represents the command for the steel table, and the command in brackets represents the cross section to be assigned.

After assigning the steel section, you can view the rendered view in the **Rendered View** window. Figure 4-18 shows the **Rendered View** window with the rendered view of a structure on which the steel section has been applied. You can also view the rendered view of the structure in the main window. To do so, right-click in the main window; a shortcut menu will be displayed. From this menu, choose the **Structure Diagrams** option; the **Diagrams** dialog box will be displayed. In this dialog box, the **Structure** tab is chosen by default. In this tab, select the **Full Sections** radio button in the **3D Sections** area and choose the **Apply** and then the **OK** button; the dialog box will be closed and the rendered view of the structure will be displayed, refer to Figure 4-19.

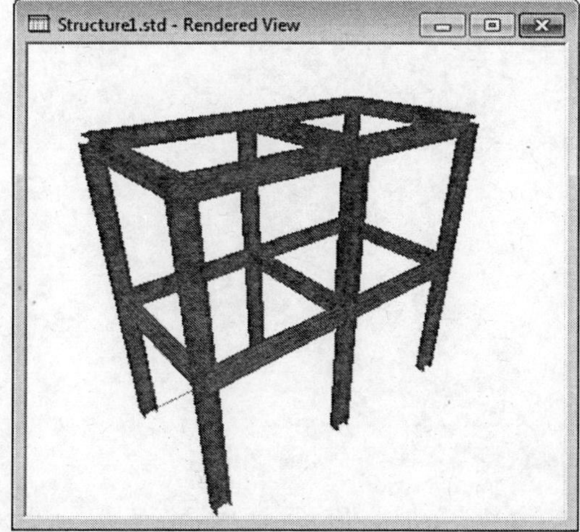

Figure 4-18 *Rendered view of the structure in the* ***Rendered View*** *window*

Figure 4-19 *Rendered view of a structure in the Whole Structure Window*

Steel Joist and Joist Girders

Similar to sections, you can also assign the steel joist and joist girder sections to a structure. These sections are available in the **Section Profile Tables** dialog box. Expand the **American Steel Joist** node in the left pane of the dialog box; the **K Series** page will be displayed in the right pane. In this page, you can select the required profile from the **Select Profile** list box. After specifying all necessary options, choose the **Add** button to add the section to the **Properties - Whole Structure** window and then close the **Section Profile Tables** dialog box. Now, you can assign the added section to the structure.

You can also find the suitable joist by specifying the values for **Span of Joist**, **Depth of Joist**, **Total Load** and **Live Load** in their corresponding edit boxes in the **Find suitable joist section** area. After specifying the values, choose the **Find Section** button; the appropriate profile will be selected and highlighted in the **Select Profile** list box. Next, choose the **Add** button to add the section and then assign it to the structure.

Plate/Surface Thickness

In STAAD.Pro, you need to specify the thickness for plates and surface elements. To do so, choose the **Thickness** button in the **Properties - Whole Structure** window; the **Plate Element/Surface Property** dialog box will be displayed. In this dialog box, the **Plate Element Thickness** option will be selected in the left pane with the **Plate Element Thickness** page is displayed by default in the right pane, refer to Figure 4-20. In the **Plate Element Thickness** page, you can specify the thickness at each node in the **Node 1**, **Node 2**, **Node 3**, and **Node 4** edit boxes, respectively. For the plates of uniform thickness, specify the value in the **Node 1** edit box and the values in the other edit boxes will be filled automatically. Select the **Material** check box to include the material constants and then select the required material from the drop-down list available below it. Next, choose the **Add** button to add the plate thickness in the **Section** tab. Close the dialog box and then assign thickness to the plates.

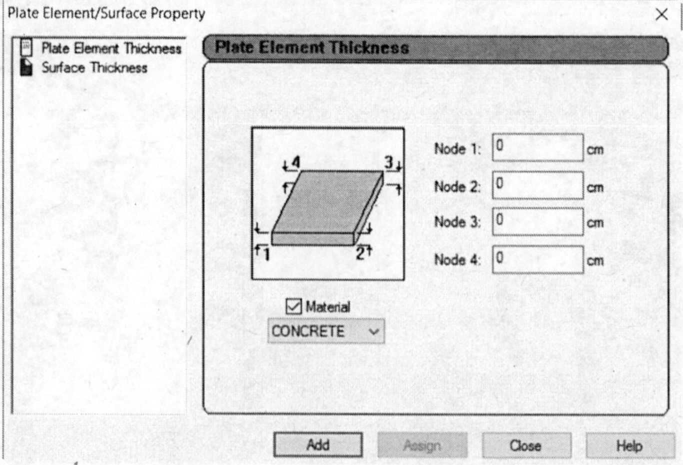

***Figure 4-20** The **Plate Element Thickness** page in the **Plate Element/Surface Property** dialog box*

Similarly, you can add and assign thickness to the surface. To do so, select the **Surface Thickness** option from the left pane of the **Plate Element/Surface Property** dialog box; the **Surface Thickness** page is displayed. In this page, specify the thickness value in the **Node 1** edit box. In the **Properties - Whole Structure** window, you can choose the **Materials** button to view the values of material constants. On choosing this button, the **Materials** window will be displayed. In this window, the material constants and their properties are listed in a table. Similarly, you can view the section property information by choosing the **Values** button. On doing so, the **Section Properties** table will be displayed. In this table, the added section properties are categorized into tabs. Using the **User Table** button, you can access the user defined sections if they have been defined by the user. If there are no user defined sections, then on choosing this button, the **STAAD.Pro V8i (SELECTseries 6)** message box will be displayed prompting you to create a section. If you want to create a user defined section, choose the **Yes** button, otherwise choose the **No** button. A cross-section can be removed from the **Section** tab, by choosing the **Delete** button. On doing so, the cross-section will be removed from the structure as well. To modify the cross-section properties, choose the **Edit** button.

In the **Beta Angle** tab, you can change the orientation of a member. To do so, choose the **Beta Angle** tab and then choose the **Create Beta Angle** button; the **Beta Angle** dialog box will be displayed, as shown in Figure 4-21. In this dialog box, select the **Angle in Degrees** radio button to specify the angle in degrees. Next, specify the angle in the edit box displayed next to the radio button. Next, choose the **OK** button; the beta angle will be added to the **Beta Angle** tab. Now, select the added angle and then assign it to the required structure by using any of the assignment methods. You can view the oriented members in the rendered view.

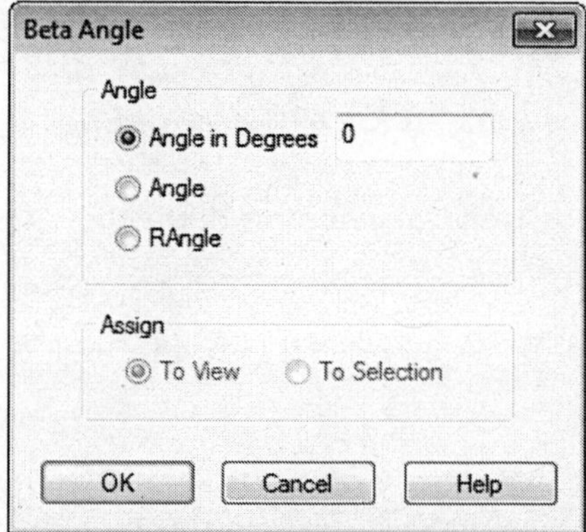

*Figure 4-21 The **Beta Angle** dialog box*

Example 3

In this example, you will add and assign steel sections to the structure. After assigning the steel sections, you will orient the member.

Steps to complete this example are given below:

Step 1: Create a new file *c04_staad_v8i_ex3* and create a portal frame structure of 5*5m using the **Snap Node/Beam** tool, refer to Figure 4-22.

Step 2: Choose the **General** tab from the main window; the **Property** tab and the **Properties - Whole Structure** window is displayed.

Step 3: Choose the **Section Database** button from the **Properties - Whole Structure** window; the **Section Profile Tables** dialog box is displayed.

Step 4: In this dialog box, ensure that the **W Shape** option is selected under the **American** head in the left pane of the dialog box. Select the **W10X26** option from the **Select Beam** area. Ensure that the **Material** check box is selected and the **STEEL** option is selected in the drop-down list below this check box. Next, choose the **Add** button.

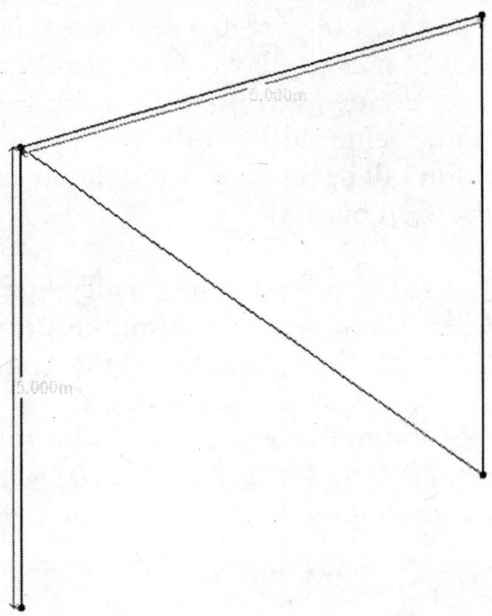

Figure 4-22 *The portal frame structure*

Step 5: Select the **Angle** option from the left pane of the dialog box; the **Angle** page is displayed in the right pane of the dialog box.

Step 6: Select the **L40406** option from the **Select Angle** area. Next, choose the **Add** button and close the dialog box.

Step 7: In the **Section** tab of the **Properties - Whole Structure** window, select the **W10X26** option and from the **Select** menu. Next, choose the **Beams Parallel To > X** option; beams parallel to x axis get selected.

Step 8: Choose **Select > Beams Parallel To > Y** option from the menu bar; all the members parallel to x and y axes get selected.

Step 9: Ensure that the **Assign To Selected Beams** radio button is selected in the **Assignment Method** area of the **Properties - Whole Structure** window. Choose the **Assign** button; the **STAAD.Pro V8i (SELECTseries 6)** message box is displayed. Choose the **Yes** button; the selected section is assigned to the selected members.

Step 10: Select the **L40406** option and choose **By Missing Attributes > Missing Property** option from the **Select** menu; beam is selected.

Step 11: Choose the **Assign** button; the **STAAD.Pro V8i (SELECTseries 6)** message box is displayed. Choose the **Yes** button; the selected section gets assigned. Choose the **3D Rendered View** button from the toolbar; the rendered view of the structure is displayed.

Step 12: Choose the **Beta Angle** tab from the **Properties - Whole Structure** window and then choose the **Create Beta Angle** button; the **Beta Angle** dialog box is displayed.

Step 13: Specify **90** in the edit box next to the **Angle in Degrees** radio button and choose the **OK** button.

Step 14: Select the members parallel to x axis and assign **Beta 90** to the selected member using the Assign To Selected Beams method discussed in the previous steps. Figures 4-23 and 4-24 show the structure members before and after orientation.

Step 15: Choose the **Save** button to save the file.

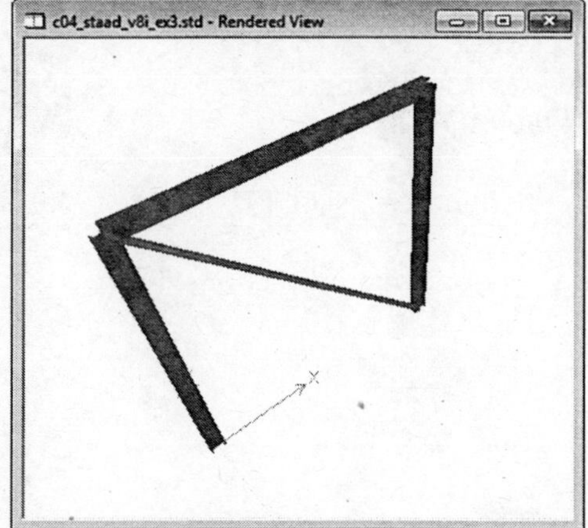

***Figure 4-23** Structure before orientation*

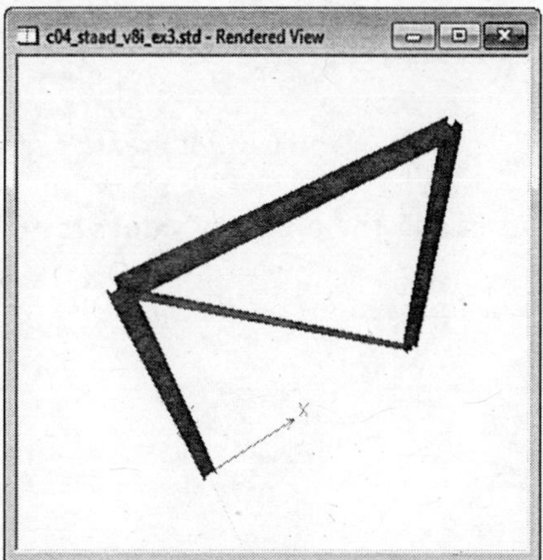

***Figure 4-24** Structure after orientation*

Self-Evaluation Test

Answer the following questions and then compare them to those given at the end of this chapter:

1. The __________ tool is used to assign material to the selected members.

2. The prismatic sections are defined in the __________ dialog box.

3. In the __________ page, you can define the section properties.

4. You cannot define the tapered sections in STAAD.Pro. (T/F)

5. In STAAD.Pro, you need to specify thickness for the plates. (T/F)

6. In STAAD.Pro, you cannot change the orientation of a member. (T/F)

Review Questions

Answer the following questions:

1. Which of the following buttons is used to invoke the **Section Profile Tables** dialog box?

   (a) **Define** (b) **Section Database**
   (c) **Edit** (d) **Delete**

2. Which of the following buttons is used to invoke the **Property** dialog box?

   (a) **Value** (b) **Define**
   (c) **Materials** (d) None of these

3. In STAAD.Pro, you cannot create user-defined tables. (T/F)

4. You can edit the property values for the pre-defined materials. (T/F)

5. In isotropic materials, the material properties vary in primary directions. (T/F)

Answers to Self-Evaluation Test

1. Assign To Selected Members, **2.** Property, **3.** Property, **4.** F, **5.** T, **6.** F

Chapter 5

Specifications and Supports

Learning Objectives

After completing this chapter, you will be able to:

- *Use different specifications for nodes, members, and plates*
- *Use different types of supports*

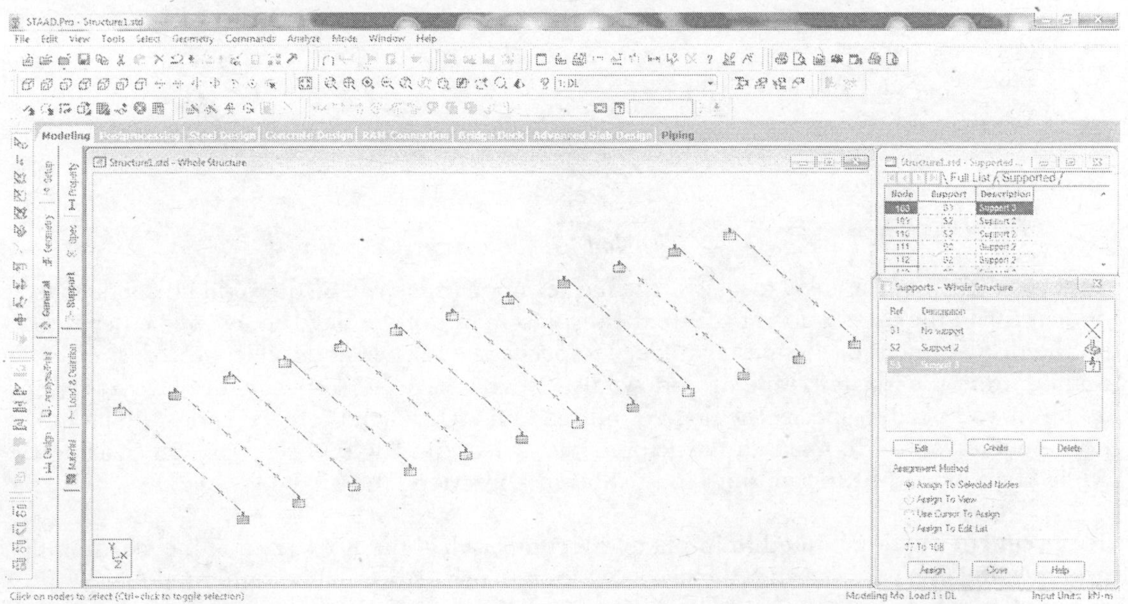

INTRODUCTION

In this chapter, you will learn about various structural conditions and methods of creating and assigning supports to a structure.

In a structural model, you can define the structural conditions of a node, member, and plates. These conditions include specifications such as master/slave nodes, plane stress, fire proofing, member offsets, and so on. In this chapter, these specifications have been categorized under the joint, member, and plate categories. These specifications are discussed next.

NODE SPECIFICATION

In STAAD.Pro, you can assign Master/Slave specification to nodes in a structure. These nodes will act as rigid links in the structure. These structures can be called as rigid diaphragm structures. A rigid diaphragm transfers lateral load to frames or shear walls. A lateral load can be wind load, earthquake load, hydrostatic pressure, and so on. You can define a rigid diaphragm by specifying the rigid links in the structure. In STAAD.Pro, these rigid links are represented as master nodes. To specify a rigid link, choose the **General** tab and then select the **Spec** page from the STAAD.Pro interface; the **Specifications - Whole Structure** window will be displayed in the Data Area. In this window, choose the **Node** button; the **Node Specification** dialog box will be displayed, as shown in Figure 5-1.

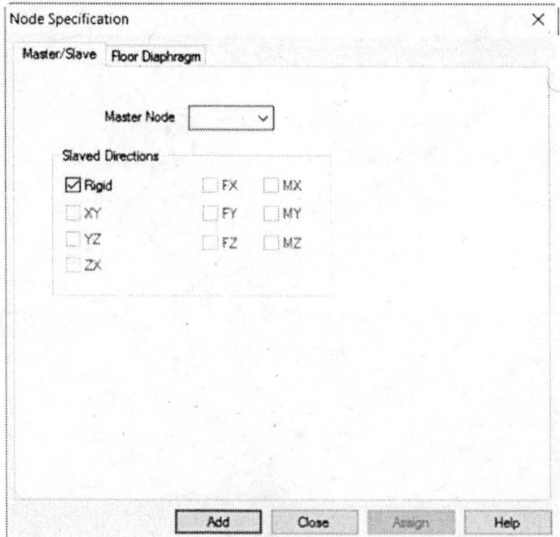

***Figure 5-1** The **Node Specification** dialog box*

In this dialog box, you need to specify the master node which will be the rigid link. The master node is called the master node because the displacements of the slave nodes will be dependent on the displacement of the master node. To specify the master node, select the desired node number from the **Master Node** drop-down list. Next, you need to specify the slave directions. To do so, you need to specify the degrees of freedom with which the slave nodes will be linked to the master node. To make the structure rigid, select the **Rigid** check box. On clearing the **Rigid** check box, the other options in the **Slaved Direction** area will be enabled.

To specify the rigidity limited to in-plane directions, select the **XY**, **YZ**, or **ZX** check box. For example, if you have selected **XY** check box, then the structure will be rigid in global X and Z axes with rotation about Y axis. You can also link some specific degrees of freedom by selecting the **FX, FY, FZ, MX, MY,** or **MZ** check box. After specifying the required conditions, choose the **Add** button; the specification will be added to the **Specifications - Whole Structure** window. Now, you can assign specification to the required node(s) by using any of the assignment methods. choose the **STAAD Editor** button from the toolbar; the **STAAD Editor** window will be displayed. In the **STAAD Editor** window, you can view the commands for the Master/Slave specification which will be in the format given next.

```
SLAVE {XY, YX, ZX, RIGID, FX, FY, FZ, MX, MY, OR MZ} MASTER i
JOINT n1, n2, n3,.......
```

In the above command, the **SLAVE** initiates Master/Slave specification. You can specify the slaved directions by specifying any of the directions enclosed in the bracket. The master node is denoted by letter **i** and the slave nodes are denoted by **n1**, **n2**, **n3**, and so on. You can use the **Delete** button to remove any specification from the **Specification** area. After assigning the master slave specification to the desired node, make sure that the **Highlight Assigned Geometry** check box is selected in the **Specifications - Whole Structure** window. On doing so, master nodes and slave nodes will be highlighted. You can also configure the display of the master/slave nodes. To do so, right-click in the main window to display a shortcut menu. Next, choose the **Labels** option from the menu; the **Diagrams** dialog box will be displayed. In this dialog box, select the **Master Slave (L)** check box in the **General** area. Next, choose the **Apply** and **OK** buttons; the dialog box will be closed and you can see the lines emerging from the master node and linking with the slave nodes. The master node is represented by a cube symbol.

You can create rigid floor diaphragm without specifying master joint by using the **Node Specification** window. Choose the **Node** button; the **Node Specification** window will be displayed. Figure 5-2 shows the **Floor Diaphragm** tab in the **Node Specification** window.

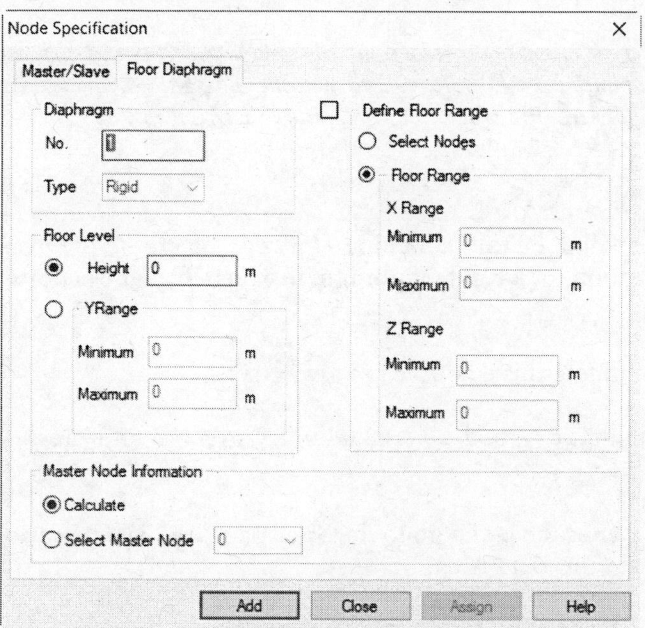

Figure 5-2 *The* ***Floor Diaphragm*** *tab in the* ***Node Specification*** *window*

You can define floor range either by selecting nodes or by providing the range of X and Z coordinates. In both the methods, first ensure that the **Define Floor Range** check box is selected. Now to assign the range using nodes, select the **Select Nodes** radio button from the **Define Floor Range** area. To define floor range by providing range of X and Y coordinates, select the **Floor Range** radio button. As you select the **Floor Range** radio button, the **Minimum** and **Maximum** edit boxes in the **X Range** and **Z Range** areas will become editable. You can enter the required values in the edit boxes in these areas.

After specifying the ranges, select the **Calculate** radio button in the **Master Node Information** area and choose the **Add** button; the specification will be added to the **Specifications -Whole Structure** window and will be assigned to the structure. Choose the **STAAD Editor** button from the toolbar; the **STAAD.Pro Editor** window will be displayed. In the **STAAD.Pro Editor** window, you can view the commands for the Master/Slave specification which will be in the format given next.

DIA i1 TYPE RIG YR f1 f2JOINT XR f3 f4 ZR f5 f6 ni TO nn

In the above command, the **DIA** command is used for initiating the diaphragm specification.**i1** represents diaphragm identification number. **f1** and **f2** represent Global coordinate values for minimum and maximum Y range respectively. **f3** and **f4** represent Global coordinate values for minimum and maximum X range respectively. **f5** and **f6** represent Global coordinate values for minimum and maximum Z range respectively. **ni** represents node one. **nn** represents nth node in the structure.

Note

Floor diaphragm cannot be specified along with the MASTER-SLAVE command.

Note

In this chapter, you need to download the c04_Staad_v8i.zip and c05_Staad_v8i.zip files for the following examples from http://www.cadcim.com. The path of the file is as follows: Textbook > Civil/GIS > STAAD.Pro > Exploring Bentley STAAD.Pro V8i.

Example 1

In this example, you will open the model in *c04_staad_v8i_ex2.std* file. Next, you will define the master-slave specification for a rigid diaphragm in which in-plane actions are rigid but bending actions are flexible.

Steps required to complete this example are given next:

Step 1: Open the model *c04_staad_v8i_ex2.std* in STAAD.Pro and press SHIFT+N to view the node numbers.

Step 2: Choose the **General** tab and go to the **Spec** page; the **Specifications - Whole Structure** window is displayed in the Data Area.

Step 3: Choose the **Node** button; the **Node Specification** dialog box is displayed, refer to Figure 5-3.

Step 4: In this dialog box, select the node number **22** from the **Master Node** drop-down list.

Step 5: Clear the **Rigid** check box in the **Slaved Directions** area and select the **ZX** check box, as shown in Figure 5-3.

Node Specification
Master/Slave Floor Diaphragm
Master Node 22
Slaved Directions
Rigid FX MX
XY FY MY
YZ FZ MZ
ZX
Add Close Assign Help

Figure 5-3 *The* ***Node Specification*** *dialog box*

Step 6: Choose the **Add** button; the **Node Specification** dialog box is closed and the specification is added to the **Specifications - Whole Structure** window.

Step 7: In the **Specifications - Whole Structure** window, ensure that the **SLAVE ZX MASTER 22 JOINT** option is selected. Choose the **View From +Z** button from the toolbar; the front view of the structure is displayed.

Step 8: Ensure that the **Nodes Cursor** is chosen from the side toolbar. Click to begin the selection, hold down the left mouse button, and then drag the pointer over the nodes to select; a selection window is created, refer to Figure 5-4.

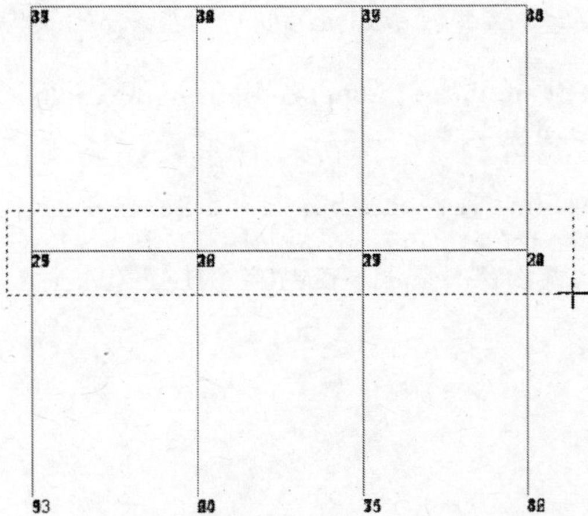

Figure 5-4 *Selecting nodes in the structure*

Step 9: In the **Specifications - Whole Structure** window, ensure that the **Assign To Selected Nodes** radio button is selected and then choose the **Assign** button; the **STAAD.Pro V8i (SELECTseries 6)** window is displayed. Choose the **Yes** button.

Step 10: Choose the **Isometric View** button from the toolbar; the isometric view is displayed. Click in the main window to deselect the nodes.

Step 11: Select the **Highlight Assigned Geometry** check box in the **Specifications - Whole Structure** window; all the slaved nodes as well as the master node is highlighted in the main window. Select the **SLAVE ZX MASTER 22 JOINT** in the specification area; the master node is highlighted with the circles around it.

Step 12: To view the commands for master-slave specification, choose the **STAAD Editor** button; the **Warning** message box is displayed prompting you to save the file. Choose the **Save** button; the **STAAD Editor** window is displayed. In this window, you can view the commands for master-slave specification, refer to Figure 5-5. Next, close the **STAAD Editor** window.

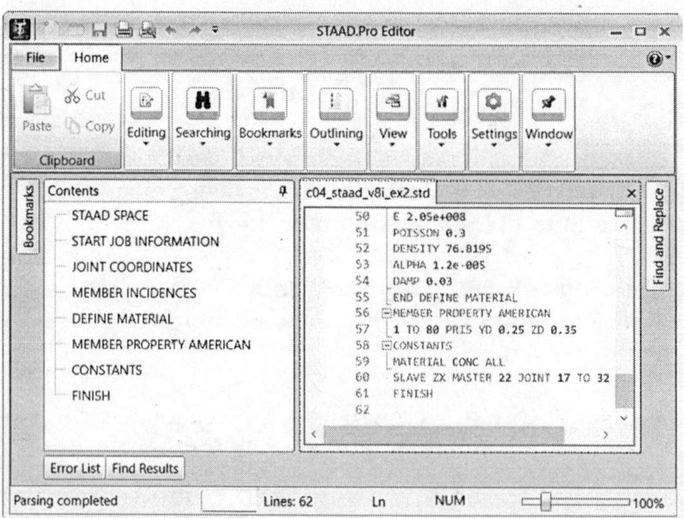

Figure 5-5 The ***STAAD Editor*** *window displaying the specification syntax*

Step 13: Next, choose the **Symbols and Labels** tool from the toolbar; the **Diagrams** dialog box is displayed with the **Labels** tab chosen.

Step 14: Select the **Master Slave (L)** check box in the **General** area of the **Diagrams** dialog box and choose **Apply** and then the **OK** button to close the dialog box; the master/slave nodes are highlighted, refer to Figure 5-6. You can also use the SHIFT+L keys to display master/slave nodes.

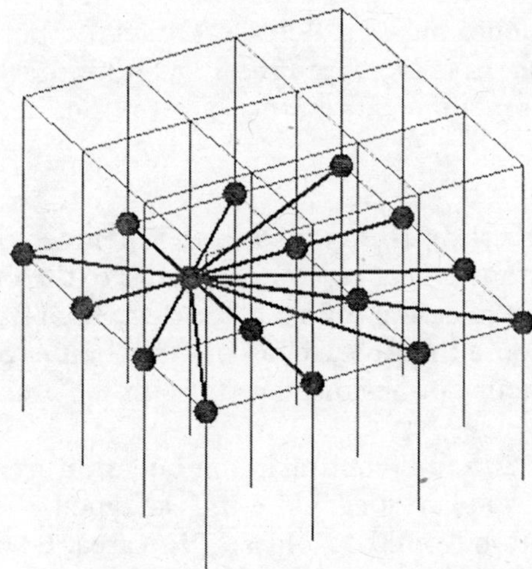

Figure 5-6 *The master/slave nodes*

Step 15: Choose the **Save As** option from the **File** menu; the **Save As** dialog box is displayed. In this dialog box, specify the name *c05_staad_v8i_ex1* in the **File name** edit box and save it at an appropriate location.

MEMBER SPECIFICATION

Member specifications are used to specify the member conditions such as member release, offset, tension, compression, and so on. These conditions can be specified by using the **Beam** button available in the **Specifications - Whole Structure** window. On choosing this button, the **Member Specification** dialog box will be displayed, as shown in Figure 5-7.

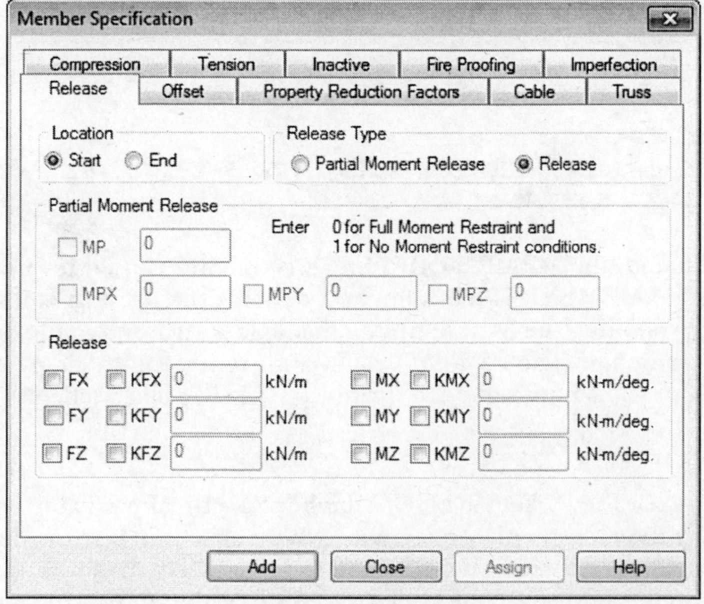

Figure 5-7 *The* ***Member Specification*** *dialog box*

This dialog box comprises of following tabs: **Release, Offset, Property Reduction Factors, Cable, Truss, Compression, Tension, Inactive, Fire Proofing**, and **Imperfection**. Using these tabs, you can define and assign various member conditions. The options in these tabs are discussed next.

Release

In this tab, the release specification is provided in the member end-points to prevent one or more forces/moments to be transferred from one member to the other. You can specify the end conditions for the members by releasing the specified degrees of freedom. To specify the release condition of the member, choose the **Release** tab in the **Member Specification** dialog box, if it is not chosen by default. Various options displayed in this tab are discussed next.

In this tab, select the **Start** or **End** radio button in the **Location** area to define the location of the member end to be released. You can specify the release type by selecting the **Partial Moment Release** or **Release** radio button from the **Release Type** area. If you select the **Partial Moment Release** radio button, then the options in the **Partial Moment Release** area will be enabled. In this area, you can specify the release factor. You can specify a single partial release factor for MX, MY, and MZ moments. To do so, select the **MP** check box; the edit box next to it will be enabled. Specify the required release factor in this edit box. You can specify the independent factors for the moments by selecting the **MPX, MPY**, or **MPZ** check box and then specifying the required factor in the corresponding edit boxes. After specifying the factor, choose the **Add** button; the specification will be added to the **Specifications - Whole Structure** window. Next, assign the specification to the required members by using any of the assignment methods. You can completely release the member end conditions. To do so, select the **Release** radio button. Next, define the release condition by selecting the **FX, FY, FZ, MX, MY**, or **MZ** check box. You can also define the spring constants by selecting the **KFX, KFY, KFZ, KMX, KMY**, or **KMZ** check box and then specifying the value in the corresponding edit box. Next, choose the **Add** button to add the specification and assign it to the required structure members.

The commands for defining and assigning the release specification is given below:

```
MEMBER RELEASE
MEMBER-LIST {START, END, OR BOTH} {FX, FY, FZ, MX, MY, MZ} {KFX,
KFY, KFZ, KMX, KMY, KMZ}
```

In the above command, the **MEMBER RELEASE** command is used for initiating the release command. Next, the **MEMBER-LIST** command denotes the list of members to be released. The commands for defining the location of the member is enclosed in the brackets next to the **MEMBER-LIST** command. The **FX** to **MZ** commands represent the degrees of freedom to be released and **KFX** to **KMZ** represents the spring constants to be attached.

Offset

To define offset, choose the **Offset** tab in the **Member Specification** dialog box. In this tab, first you need to specify the location on the member, where offset will be provided. To do so, select an option from the drop-down list in the **Location** area. Select the **Start** option to provide an offset on the start point of the member. Select the **End** option to provide an offset on the end point of the member. Next, specify the direction for the offset by selecting an option from the drop-down list in the **Direction** area. The **Global** option is selected by default. To assign the offset to a local axis system, select the **Local** option from the drop-down list. Now, specify the offset distance from the start/end node in the three global directions in the **X**, **Y**, and **Z** edit boxes in the **Offsets** area. Next, choose the **Add** button to add the specification in the **Specifications** area of the **Specifications - Whole Structure** window. Now, select the added specification and assign it to the desired member.

Note

*After assigning offset to the structural members, you can notice the difference in the members in the **Rendered View** window. Alternatively, you can view the full section in the main window.*

The commands for defining and assigning the offset is given below:

```
MEMBER OFFSET
MEMBER-LIST {START, END} LOCAL {Xd, Yd, Zd}
```

In the above command, the **MEMBER OFFSET** command is used for initiating the offset specification. In the **MEMBER-LIST** command, the member numbers are to be specified to which the offset will be applied. Next, the location where the offsets will be applied on the member are specified in the same command. The **LOCAL** command is for specifying the local coordinates for the offset location. If you do not specify the **LOCAL** command then the coordinates will be read in global system.

Example 2

In this example, you will open the model in the *c04_staad_v8i_ex3.std* file. Next, you will define and assign offset for the members in a space frame structure.

Steps required to complete this example are given next:

Step 1: Start STAAD.Pro and open the *c04_staad_v8i_ex3.std* file; the model is displayed in the main window refer to Figure 5-8.

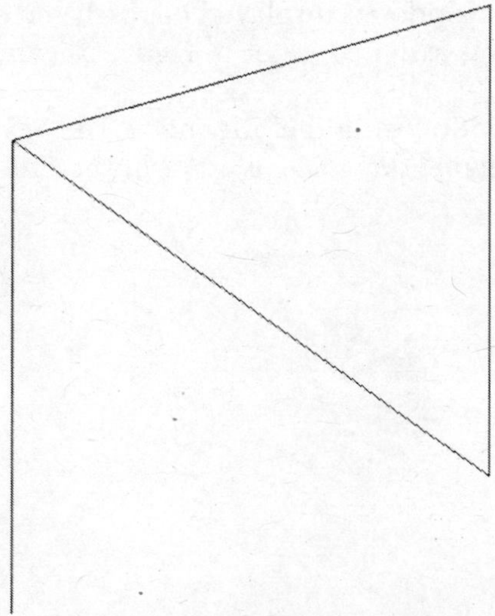

Figure 5-8 *Model displayed in the main window*

Step 2: Select the **Spec** page from the **General** tab; the **Specifications - Whole Structure** window is displayed in the data area of the interface.

Step 3: In the **Specifications - Whole Structure** window, choose the **Beam** button; the **Member Specification** dialog box is displayed.

Step 4: In this dialog box, choose the **Offset** tab and ensure that the **Start** and **Global** options are selected in the drop-down list in the **Location** and **Direction** areas, respectively.

Step 5: Specify the value **0.073** in the **X** edit box in the **Offsets** area and choose the **Add** button; the dialog box closes and the **START 0.073 0 0** offset is added to the **Specification** area in the **Specifications - Whole Structure** window.

Step 6: Repeat the procedure followed in steps 3 and 4 and select the **End** option from the drop-down list in the **Location** area and the **Global** option from the **Direction** area.

Step 7: Specify the value **-0.073** in the **X** edit box in the **Offsets** area. Next, choose the **Add** button; the dialog box closes and the **END -0.073 0 0** offset is added to the **Specification** area in the **Specifications - Whole Structure** window.

Step 8: Invoke the **Beams Cursor** from the side toolbar and click on main window, press **SHIFT+B** and select the member **2** from the structure in the main window.

Step 9: Select the **START 0.073 0 0 Specifications - Whole Structure** window. Next, ensure that the **Assign To Selected Beams** radio button is selected in the **Assignment Method** area and then choose the **Assign** button; the STAADPro.V8i (SELECTseries 6) window message is displayed. Choose the **Yes** button; the offset is assigned at the start of the member.

Step 10: Select the **END -0.073 0 0 Specifications - Whole Structure** and choose the **Assign** button; the **STAADPro.V8i (SELECTseries 6)** window is displayed. Choose the **Yes** button; the offset is assigned at the end of the member. Choose the **3D Rendered View** button from the toolbar; the **Rendered View** window is displayed in which you can notice the difference in the members after the offset is assigned, refer to Figure 5-9 and Figure 5-10.

Step 11: Choose the **Save As** option from the **File** menu; the **Save As** dialog box is displayed. In this dialog box, specify the name *c05_staad_v8i_ex2* in the **File name** edit box and save it at an appropriate location.

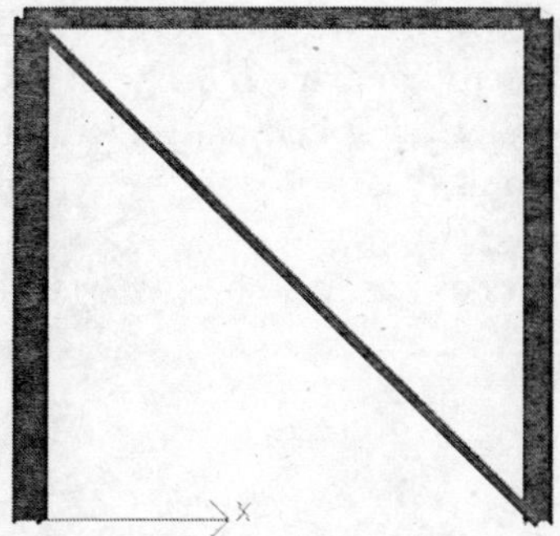

Figure 5-9 The Rendered View before assigning offset

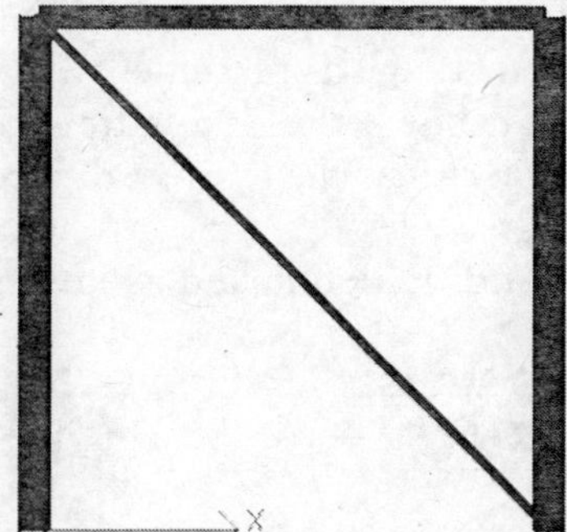

Figure 5-10 The Rendered View after assigning offset

Property Reduction Factors

In the **Property Reduction Factors** tab, you can specify the factors for reducing the cross-section properties. After reducing the cross-section properties, the structure can be reanalyzed and redesigned. In this tab, you can specify the value for the reduction factors for the cross-sectional area, torsional constant, and moment of inertia in the corresponding edit boxes. After specifying the required factors, choose the **Add** button; the reduction factor specification will be added. Next, assign the reduction factor specification to the required structural member.

Cable

In the **Cable** tab, you can define the cable members. In this tab, you need to specify either the initial tension or the unstressed length of the cable. Specify the initial tension value in the **Initial TENSION** edit box. The specified initial tension is applied as an external load on the structure and it also modifies the stiffness of the member. This tension is used to determine the unstressed length. You can also specify the unstressed length value in the **Unstressed Length** value edit box. This length will be used for the non-linear cable analysis. After specifying the required value, choose the **Add** button to add the specification. Select and assign the specification to the required member.

The commands for defining and assigning cable is discussed next.

```
MEMBER CABLE
MEMBER-LIST TENSION f1
```

In the command lines, the **MEMBER CABLE** command is used to start the cable command. In the next line, **MEMBER-LIST** command is used to specify the list of members to be assigned as cables. The **TENSION** f_1 command is used to specify the initial tension in cable members.

Truss

In this tab, truss members are subjected to axial loads only. The only degree of freedom for a truss element is axial displacement at each node. To specify the truss members, choose the **Truss** tab and then choose the **Add** button; the **MEMBER TRUSS** specification will be added to the **Specifications** area. Next, select the truss specification and assign it to the required members.

The commands to define and assign the truss members are as follows:

```
MEMBER TRUSS
MEMBER-LIST
```

In the above lines, the **MEMBER TRUSS** command is used to start with the truss command. In the next line, the **MEMBER-LIST** command represents the list of members that will be assigned as truss members.

Compression

The compression members carry compressive forces only and can be specified using this tab. To specify the compression members, choose the **Compression** tab and then choose the **Add** button; the **MEMBER COMPRESSION** specification will be added to the **Specifications** area. Next, select it and assign it to the required members.

Tension

The tension members carry tensile forces only and can be specified using this tab. To specify the tension members, choose the **Tension** tab and then choose the **Add** button; the **MEMBER TENSION** specification will be added to the **Specifications** area. Next, select the added specification and assign it to the required members.

Note

The commands for specifying tension and compression members is ***MEMBER TENSION*** *and* ***MEMBER COMPRESSION*** *respectively. Similarly, the command* ***MEMBER TRUSS*** *is for specifying truss members.*

Inactive

Using this tab, you can make some members inactive while analyzing a structure. The stiffness contribution of these inactive members will not be considered during the analysis. To make the members inactive, choose the **Inactive** tab and then choose the **Add** button; the **Inactive Member** specification will be added to the **Specifications** area. Next, select the added specification and assign it to the required members.

The command for defining and assigning inactive specification is as follows:

```
INACTIVE MEMBER-LIST
```

You can make the members active again by using the **CHANGE** command. To do so, choose **Analysis > Change** from the **Command** menu. You can specify the **CHANGE** command only after the **PERFORM ANALYSIS** command.

Fire Proofing

In STAAD.Pro, you can calculate the weight of fire proofing material applied to a structure. To do so, choose the **Fire Proofing** tab. In this tab, you can specify two types of fire configurations: Block Fire Proofing and Contour Fire Proofing. In block fire proofing, a rectangular block of fire proofing material will be formed around the steel section. To define block fire proofing, select the **BFP (Block Fire Proofing)** radio button and specify the thickness and density of material in their respective edit boxes.

In contour fire proofing, a coating of fire proofing material will be formed around the steel section. To define contour fire proofing, select the **CFP (Contour Fire Proofing)** radio button and then specify the thickness and density of material in their respective edit boxes.

After specifying the required fire proofing type, choose the **Add** button; the specification will be added to the **Specifications** area of the **Specifications - Whole Structure** window. Next, select the added specification and assign it to the required structure member.

Imperfection

The specifications of the drift and cambers can be defined in the **Imperfection** tab. In this tab, select the **Camber** radio button. On doing so, the related parameters will be displayed in this tab. Next, specify the parameters for the camber and choose the **Add** button to add the camber specification. Next, select the added specification and assign it to the required members.

Similarly to define drift, select the **Drift** radio button and then specify the required parameters and choose the **Add** button to add the drift specification. Next, select the added specification and assign it to the required members.

PLATE SPECIFICATION

The plate specification includes Element Releases, Ignore Inplane Rotation, Rigid Inplane Rotation, Plane Stress, and Ignore Stiffness. These specifications can be defined by choosing the **Plate** button available in the **Specifications - Whole Structure** window. On choosing the **Plate** button, the **Plate Specs** dialog box will be displayed, as shown in Figure 5-11.

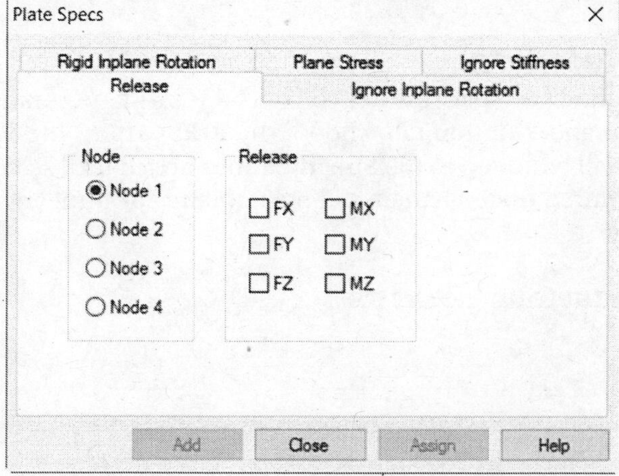

Figure 5-11 *The **Plate Specs** dialog box*

This dialog box comprises of five tabs: **Release**, **Ignore Inplane Rotation**, **Rigid Inplace Rotation**, **Plane Stress**, and **Ignore Stiffness**. Using these tabs, you can define the plate specifications. These tabs are discussed next.

Release

Using the options in the **Release** tab, you can release one or more degrees of freedom at the corner nodes of the plate element. To specify the releases to a node, select the **Node 1**, **Node 2**, **Node3**, or **Node 4** radio button from the **Node** area of the **Plate Specs** dialog box. Next, define the release condition for the translational and rotational degrees of freedom by selecting the corresponding check boxes from the **Release** area. Next, choose the **Add** button to add the release specification and then assign it to the required element.

The commands to define and assign the element release specification is as follows:

```
ELEMENT RELEASE
ELEMENT-LIST {J1, J2, J3, J4} {FX, FY, FZ, MX, MY, MZ}
```

In the above lines, the **ELEMENT RELEASE** command is used for initializing the release specification. In the next line, the **ELEMENT-LIST** command represents the list of element numbers to which release specification will be assigned. The **{J_1, J_2, J_3, J_4}** command represent the nodes to be released and the **{FX, FY, FZ, MX, MY, MZ}** command represent the degrees of freedom to be released.

Ignore Inplane Rotation

In this tab, you can define the specification to ignore the in-plane rotation actions. To do so, in the **Ignore Inplane Rotation** tab, choose the **Add** button; the **Element Ignore Inplane Rotation** specification will be added to the **Specifications** area. Next, select and assign the added specification to the required plate element. The command for applying this specification is as follows:

```
ELEMENT IGNORE INPLANE ROTATION
ELEMENT-LIST
```

Rigid Inplane Rotation

New

In this tab, you can define the specification to rigid the in-plane rotation actions. To do so, in the **Rigid Inplane Rotation** tab, choose the **Add** button; the **Element Rigid Inplane Rotation** specification will be added to the **Specifications** area. Next, select and assign the added specification to the required plate element. The command for applying this specification is as follows:

```
ELEMENT RIGID INPLANE ROTATION
ELEMENT-LIST
```

Plane Stress

The Plane Stress specification is used to model the selected elements for plane stress only. In this case, no bending or transverse shear is applied. To do so, in the **Plane Stress** tab, choose the **Add** button; the **Element Plane Stress** specification will be added in the **Specifications - Whole Structure** window. Assign the added specification to the plate elements. The command for the Plane Stress specification is given next:

```
ELEMENT PLANE STRESS
ELEMENT-LIST
```

Ignore Stiffness

While modeling the plate elements, you might not want to consider the stiffness of some of the plate elements in the analysis. These elements will carry the loads and transfer them to the other parts of the structure but will not provide any additional stiffness to the structure. In this case, you can provide the Ignore Stiffness specification. To do so, in the **Ignore Stiffness** tab, choose the **Add** button; the **IGNORE STIFFNESS ELEMENT** specification will be added to the **Specifications** area of the **Specifications - Whole Structure** window. Assign the added specification to the required plate elements. The command for assigning the Ignore Stiffness specification is as follows:

```
IGNORE STIFFNESS ELEMENT
ELEMENT-LIST
```

SUPPORTS

Generally three types of supports are used to join a structure to its foundation: Fixed, Pinned, and Roller supports. The fourth type is simple support which is not often found in structures. All these supports can be placed anywhere along a structure. For example, these supports can be provided at ends, midpoints, and intermediate points. The support type provided to a structure will determine the type of load a support can resist.

In STAAD.Pro, you can provide different types of supports such as fixed, pinned, roller, inclined, springs, and so on. To define supports, choose the **General** tab and then go to the **Supports** page; the **Supports - Whole Structure** window will be displayed, as shown in Figure 5-12. In this window, choose the **Create** button; the **Create Support** dialog box will be displayed, as shown in Figure 5-13.

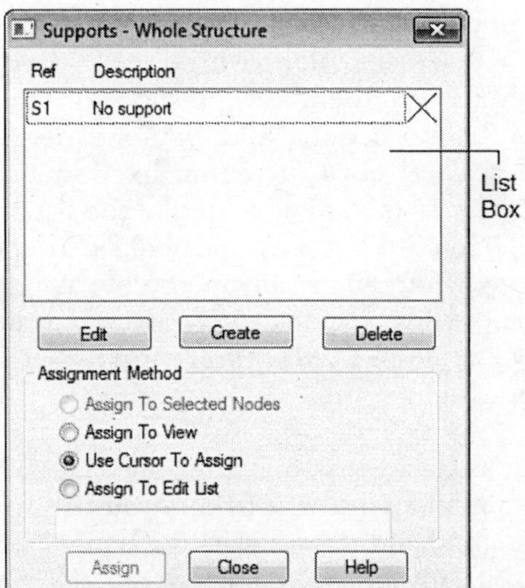

***Figure 5-12** The **Supports - Whole Structure** window*

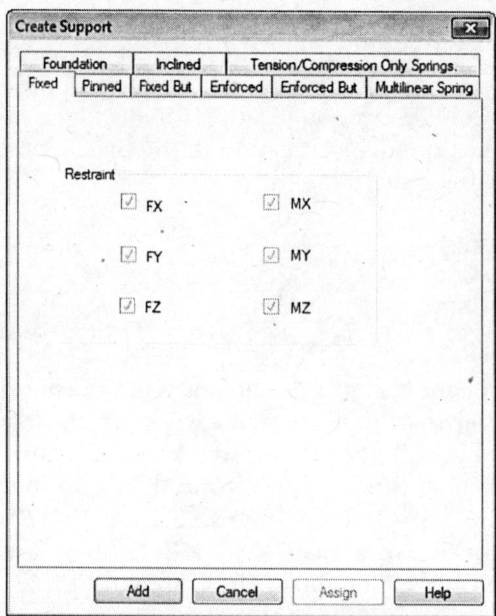

***Figure 5-13** The **Create Support** dialog box*

In this dialog box, all the supports are available in different tabs. These tabs are discussed next.

Fixed

Using this tab, you can define fixed supports. Fixed supports restricts all six degrees of freedom of an element. Along with the moment, they can resist vertical and horizontal forces. So, you can also call them as rigid supports. You will notice that in the **Fixed** tab, all the check boxes for the translational and rotational degrees of freedom are selected by default. You cannot clear these check boxes. To define fixed supports, in the **Fixed** tab, choose the **Add** button; the fixed support will be added to the list box with the name **Support 2**. The fixed support will be represented by a symbol. Next, select the added support and assign it to the appropriate nodes. You can use any method to assign the supports. These methods are already discussed in the previous chapter. After assigning the support, choose the **STAAD Editor** button from the toolbar; the **STAAD Editor** window will be displayed. In this window, you can view the command for assigning the fixed supports.

For assigning supports using the **STAAD Editor** window, first you need to specify the **SUPPORTS** command. In the next line, you will specify the member numbers to which supports will be assigned and then specify the type of support to be assigned. The command for assigning the fixed support is given below:

```
SUPPORTS
MEMBER-LIST FIXED
```

Note

*The commands for the pinned and enforced supports will be same as for the fixed supports. In this case, after specifying the member list, you need to specify the type of support. For example, for the pinned support, the command will be **MEMBER-LIST PINNED**.*

Pinned

Using this tab, you can define pinned supports. Pinned supports restricts the three translational degrees of freedom of an element, but the three rotational degrees of freedom are set free. Pinned supports therefore, allows the structural member to rotate but no translational movement will be possible. To define pinned support, choose the **Pinned** tab. In the **Restraint** area of this tab, you will notice that the check boxes for the translational degrees of freedom are selected and for the rotational degrees of freedom are cleared. Choose the **Add** button in this tab; the pinned support will be added to the list box in the **Supports - Whole Structure** window. Select the added pinned support and assign it to the appropriate nodes.

Fixed But

Using the options in this tab, you can create roller, hinge, and spring supports with specified degrees of freedom for an element. Roller supports are free to rotate and move along the surface on which the support rests. Hinge supports allows rotation only. To define any of the supports mentioned above, choose the **Fixed But** tab; the release check boxes and the define spring options will be displayed. To release any of the six degrees of freedom, select the corresponding check box from the **Release** area of this tab. To define spring support, specify the required value in the appropriate edit box in the **Define Spring** area. Next, choose the **Add** button to add the defined support to the list box in the **Supports - Whole Structure** window. Next, select the added support and assign it to the appropriate nodes. The general format for the command to assign the **Fixed But** support is given next.

```
SUPPORTS
MEMBER-LIST FIXED BUT {RELEASE-SPECIFICATION}{SPRING CONSTANTS}
```

In the above lines, after specifying the **MEMBER-LIST** and **FIXED BUT** commands, you need to specify the degrees of freedom to be released such as FX, FY, FZ, and so on. You can define springs by specifying the spring specification such as KFX, KFY, KFZ, and so on and the constants value next to it. For example, the command for spring constant can be written as KFY 50.

Enforced

Using this tab, you can define enforced supports. Enforced supports also restricts all degrees of freedom of an element alike the fixed supports. They are used while considering support displacement loads in case of plates and solids. Support displacement loads are not allowed if fixed supports are assigned to the plates and solids. To define enforced supports, choose the **Enforced** tab in the **Create Support** window and choose the **Add** button; the support will be added to the list box in the **Supports - Whole Structure** window. Next, select and assign it to the appropriate nodes.

Enforced But

Using the options in this tab, you can define enforced supports with of the required degrees of freedom set free. To define this support, choose the **Enforced But** tab in the **Create Support** window. To release any of the six degrees of freedom, select the corresponding check box from the **Release** area of this tab. Next, choose the **Add** button; the support will be added in the list box in the **Supports - Whole Structure** window. Next, select and assign it to the appropriate nodes. The command to assign the **Enforced But** support is given next.

```
SUPPORTS
MEMBER-LIST ENFORCED BUT {FX,FY,FZ,MX,MY,MZ}
```

Multilinear Spring

Multilinear spring supports are used while applying static load to a structure. They can be used for defining soil spring supports where the behavior in tension zone differs from the behavior in compression zone. To define this support, choose the **Multilinear Spring** tab. Next, in this tab, specify the values for the displacement of support node and the spring stiffness in the **Displacement** and **Spring Stiffness** columns. Next, choose the **Add** button to add the support. Now, select it and assign at the appropriate nodes.

Foundation

You can define spring supports for footings and mat foundation by using the parameters in the **Foundation** tab. To define a spring support for isolated footing, select the **Footing** radio button in the **Foundation** tab. Specify the dimension of the footing in the **L** and **W** edit boxes. Next, specify the direction of spring by selecting the required radio button in the **Direction** area. In this area, if you select the **X**, **Y**, or **Z** radio button, then the spring will be generated in that direction only and the other degrees of freedom will receive fixed support. If you select **X Only**, **Y Only**, or **Z Only** radio button, then the spring support will be generated in the respective direction only and the rest of the degrees of freedom will be free to deform. You can specify the soil subgrade value in the **Subgrade** edit box in the **Subgrade** area.

You can define spring supports for mat foundations by using two methods: Elastic Mat and Plate Mat methods. In both of these methods, STAAD.Pro will calculate the influence area of the nodes that define the surface. Then this influence area will be multiplied with the soil subgrade modulus to calculate spring stiffness value. In the elastic mat method, the influence area will be calculated for the joints, and in the plate mat method, the influence area will be calculated for the plates. To use elastic mat method, select the **Elastic Mat** radio button in the **Foundation** area. Next, specify the direction and soil subgrade values. To use the plate mat method, select the **Plate Mat** radio button in the **Foundation** area and specify the required parameters.

After specifying the desired spring support parameters, choose the **Add** button to add it to the list box of the **Supports - Whole Structure** window. Next, select and assign it to the appropriate nodes.

Inclined

Using the options in this tab, you can define supports that are inclined with respect to the global axis system. To define an inclined support, choose the **Inclined** tab. In this tab, you can define inclined supports in three ways: By specifying the coordinates of the datum, by specifying the coordinates of the reference point which describes the inclined axis system, and by specifying the reference joint of the support.

In the **Inclined** tab, select the **Coordinate** radio button in the **Incline Reference Point** area to specify the coordinates of the datum of the inclined axis system. Next, specify the coordinates in the **X**, **Y**, and **Z** edit boxes. To define the inclined support by specifying the reference point, select the **Ref** radio button and then specify the coordinates in the **X**, **Y**, and **Z** edit boxes. To define the inclined support by specifying the reference joint, select the **RefJt** radio button and then select the joint number from the drop-down list displayed next to the radio button. Next, you can specify the type of support, release conditions, and spring constant in their respective areas. Next, choose the **Add** button; the support will be added to the list box in the **Supports - Whole Structure** window. Next, select and assign it at the appropriate nodes.

The command for assigning the inclined support by specifying the x, y, and z coordinates of the datum is as follows:

```
SUPPORTS
MEMBER-LIST INCLINE x y z{SUPPORT TYPE}{RELEASE SPEC}{SPRING
CONSTANT}
```

Next, you can specify the support type, release specifications, and spring constants, if required.

The command for assigning the inclined support by specifying the coordinates of the point is as follows:

```
SUPPORT
MEMBER-LIST INCLINE REF x y z{SUPPORT TYPE}{RELEASE SPEC}{SPRING
CONSTANT}
```

The command for assigning the inclined support by specifying the reference joint is as follows:

```
SUPPORTS
MEMBER-LIST INCLINE REFJT n{SUPPORT TYPE}{RELEASE SPEC}{SPRING
CONSTANT}
```

Tension/Compression Only Springs

Using this support type, you can define spring supports as tension only or compression only. To define this support, choose the **Tension/Compression Only Springs** tab. Next, specify the degree of freedom by selecting the **Tension Only** or **Compression Only** radio button. Now, specify the degree of freedom which will be set unidirectional by selecting the check boxes in the **Spring Direction** area. Choose the **Add** button; the support will be added to the list box in the **Supports - Whole Structure** window. Next, select and assign it to the appropriate nodes.

The command for assigning the **Tension/Compression Only Springs** support is given as follows:

```
SUPPORTS
SPRING TENSION/COMPRESSION
JOINT-LIST SPRING SPECIFICATION
```

Example 3

In this example, you will create an inclined portal frame structure and define inclined supports for an inclined axis system.

Steps required to complete this example are given below:

Step 1: Start STAAD.Pro and select the **New Project** option from the **Project tasks** area in the STAAD.Pro interface; the **New Model** dialog box is displayed. In this dialog box, select the **Space** check box and specify the name *c03_staad_v8i_ex3* in the **File Name** edit box and browse to the location *C:\ STAAD Examples\c05_staad_v8i* in the **Location** area.

Step 2: Select the **Meter** and **KiloNewton** radio buttons in the **Length Units** and **Force Units** area, respectively and choose the **Next** button; the **Where do you want to go?** window is displayed. In this window, select the **Open STAAD Editor** check box and choose the **Finish** button; the **STAAD.Pro Editor** window is displayed.

Step 3: In this window, specify the commands, as shown in Figure 5-14

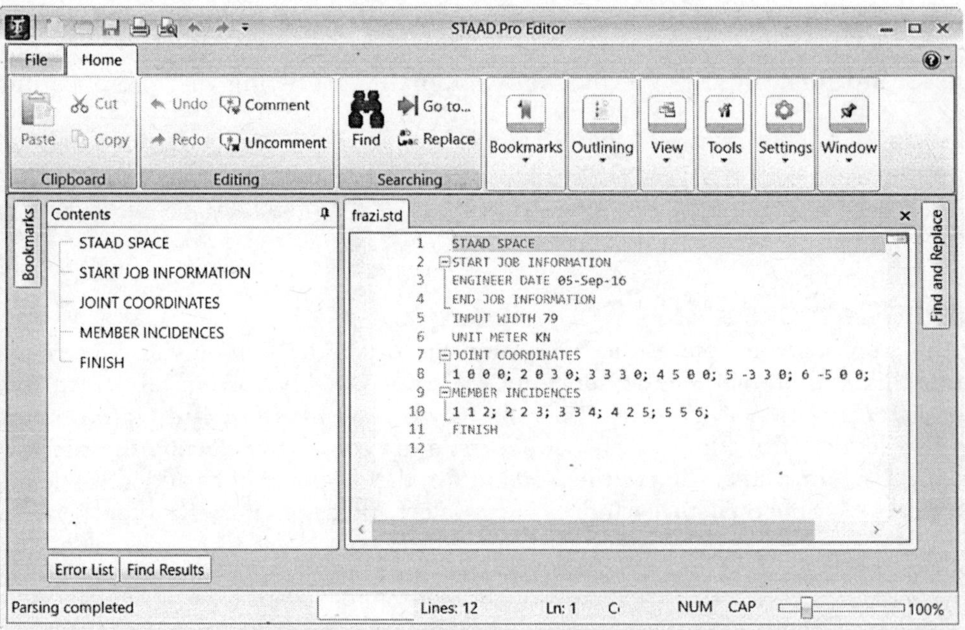

Figure 5-14 Commands specified in the STAAD Editor window

Step 4: Choose the **Save** button from the toolbar in the **STAAD.Pro Editor** window and close it. Press SHIFT+N and SHIFT+B to view the node and beam number. Figure 5-15 shows the model displayed in the main window.

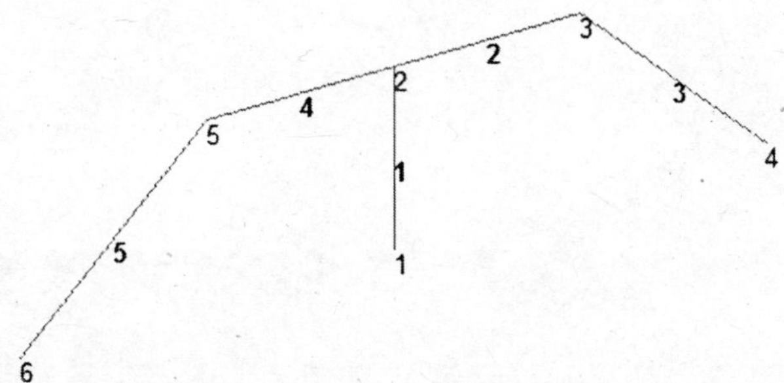

Figure 5-15 Model displayed in the Main Window

Step 5: Choose the **General** tab from the side toolbar and invoke the **Supports** page; the **Supports - Whole Structure** window is displayed in the right area of the interface.

Step 6: In this window, choose the **Create** button from the **Supports - Whole Structure** window; the **Create Support** dialog box is displayed with the **Fixed** tab chosen.

Step 7: Choose the **Add** button; the **Support 2** is added to the list box in the **Supports - Whole Structure** window. Select the added support and assign it to the node **1** using the **Use Cursor To Assign** method.

Step 8: Invoke the **Create Support** dialog box by choosing the **Create** button and then choose the **Inclined** tab. In this tab, select the **Ref** radio button in the **Incline Reference Point** area.

Step 9: Next, specify the values **3**, **3**, and **0** in the **X**, **Y**, and **Z** edit boxes, respectively and then select the **Fixed** radio button in the **Support Type** area. Next, choose the **Add** button; the **Support 3** is added to the list box in the **Supports - Whole Structure** window.

Step 10: Now, select the added support and assign it to the node number **4**.

Step 11: Again, invoke the **Create Support** dialog box by choosing the **Create** button and then choose the **Inclined** tab. In this tab, select the **RefJt** radio button in the **Incline Reference Point** area.

Step 12: Select the node number **5** in the **Node Number** drop-down list and select the **Fixed** radio button in the **Support Type** area. Next, choose the **Add** button; the **Support 4** is added to the list box in the **Supports - Whole Structure** window.

Step 13: Now, select the added support and assign it to the node number **6**. Figure 5-16 shows the model after assigning the supports.

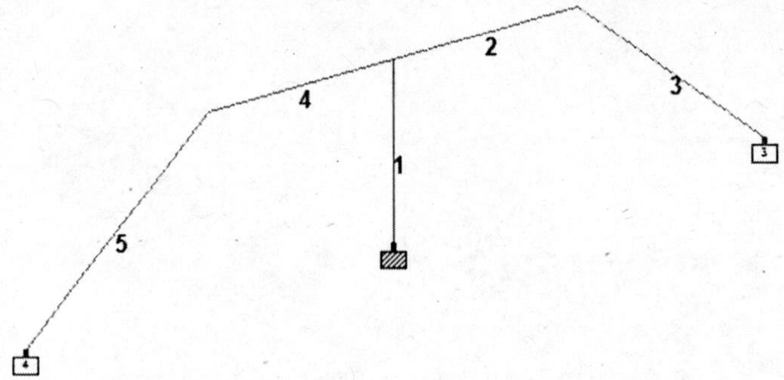

Figure 5-16 Supports assigned to the structure

Step 14: Choose the **STAAD.Pro Editor** button from the toolbar; the **STAAD Editor** window is displayed. In this window, you can view the commands for the added supports as given below:

```
SUPPORTS
1 FIXED
4 INCLINE REF 3 3 0 FIXED
6 INCLINE REFJT 5 FIXED
```

Step 15: Close the **STAAD.Pro Editor** window.

Step 16: Choose the **Save As** option from the **File** menu; the **Save As** dialog box is displayed. In this dialog box, specify the name *c05_staad_v8i_ex3* in the **File name** edit box and save it at an appropriate location.

Self-Evaluation Test

Answer the following questions and compare them to those given at the end of this chapter:

1. Rigid diaphragms are modeled using the __________ specification.

2. The __________ specification is used to release the degrees of freedom at the member ends.

3. The truss members carry __________ loads only.

4. In the __________ tab, you can specify the drift and camber specifications.

5. In cable members, the specified initial tension acts as an external load applied on the structure. (T/F)

6. The **Inactive** specification is used to make the members inactive. (T/F)

7. The compression members carry tensile forces only. (T/F)

Review Questions

Answer the following questions:

1. Which of the following options is used as fire proofing specification?

   (a) **Block Fire Proofing** (b) **Contour Fire Proofing**
   (c) **Cable** (d) Both a & b

2. Which of the following options is used after the **Inactive** command to make the members active again?

   (a) **Offset** (b) **Change**
   (c) **Inactive** (d) **Release**

3. Which of the following options is used to specify supports for static load cases?

   (a) **Fixed** (b) **Multilinear Spring**
   (c) **Enforced** (d) **Pinned**

4. The **Fixed But** tab is used to create roller, spring, and hinge supports. (T/F)

5. Enforced supports are used for support displacement loads. (T/F)

6. The **Ignore Stiffness** specification is used to ignore the stiffness of the plate elements during analysis. (T/F)

7. Fixed supports are restrained in three translational degrees of freedom only. (T/F)

Answers to Self-Evaluation Test

1. **Node**, **2.** **Release**, **3.** axial, **4.** **Imperfection**, **5.** F, **6.** T, **7.** F

Chapter 6

Loads

Learning Objectives

After completing this chapter, you will be able to:

- *Define and assign Primary Loads*
- *Define and generate Seismic Load*
- *Define and generate Wind Load*
- *Define and generate Snow Load*
- *Define and generate Vehicle Load*
- *Define Load Combinations*

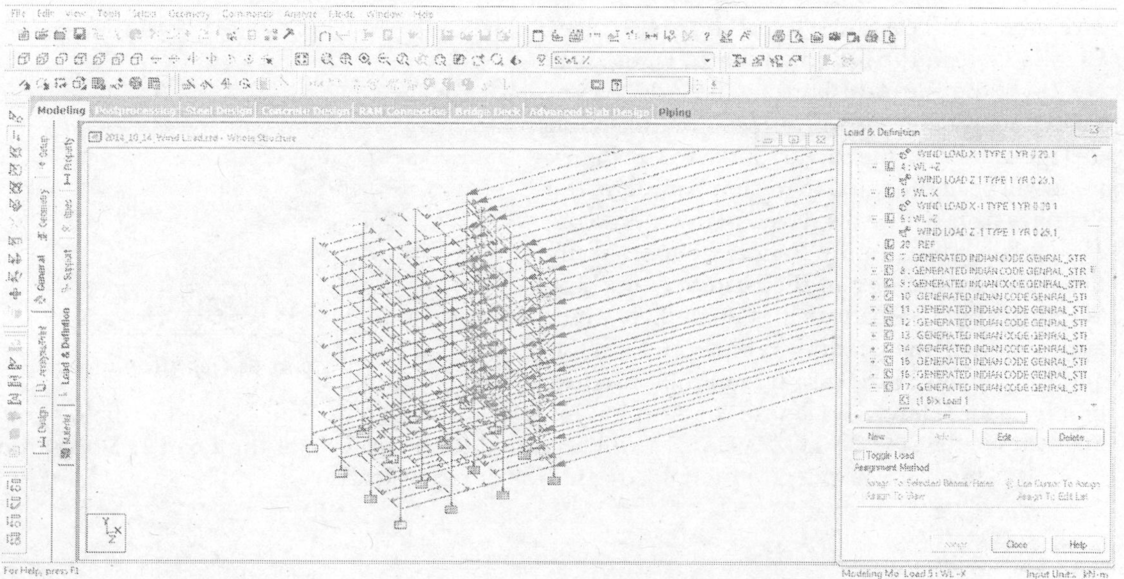

INTRODUCTION

In structural engineering, loads can be classified into different categories: dead loads, live loads, environmental loads, combination loads, and other loads. Dead loads are the loads which remain constant over certain extent of time. It includes weight of the structure such as weight of walls, beams, columns, and so on. Live loads are the moving loads which act for a short duration, for example, a moving vehicle. Environmental loads are the loads which act due to weather and other natural phenomena such as wind, snow, earthquake, and so on. Combination loads are experienced when different types of loads act together. Other loads include support displacement loads, hydrostatic loads, and so on.

Once you model a structure in STAAD.Pro including its cross-sections, supports, and specifications, you can define and assign loads to the structural members. In STAAD.Pro, the above discussed categories are further classified into different groups. These groups are: Primary loads, Load Generation, Combination Loads, and Auto Load Combination, which are discussed next.

PRIMARY LOADS

In STAAD.Pro, primary loads include nodal loads and moment, uniformly distributed loads and moments, area loads, plate loads, wind loads, snow loads, and so on. To define any of the loads, you first need to create the load cases and the loads will be added in these load cases. To define a load case, choose the **General** tab and then go to the **Load & Definition** page; the **Load & Definition** window will be displayed in the Data Area, refer to Figure 6-1. Using the options in this dialog box, you can define different types of primary loads and assign them to the structure.

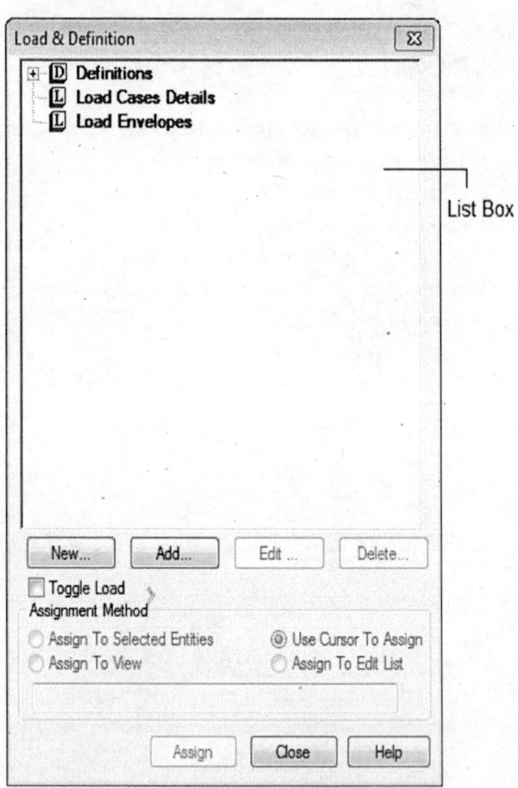

Figure 6-1 The ***Load & Definition*** *window*

To create a load case, first select the **Load Cases Details** node in the list box, refer to Figure 6-1. Next, choose the **Add** button; the **Add New : Load Cases** dialog box will be displayed, as shown in Figure 6-2. In this dialog box, the **Primary** node will be highlighted in the left pane, and the **Primary** page will be displayed in the right pane of the dialog box. In the **Primary** page, specify the load case number in the **Number** edit box. Select the type of load such as dead, live, wind, and so on from the **Loading Type** drop-down list. You can also add load case title in the **Title** text box for your reference. Choose the **Add** button to add the load case and close the dialog box. You can see that the **1 : LOAD CASE 1** will be added to the list box of the **Load & Definition** window. Similarly, you can add more load cases for different loads.

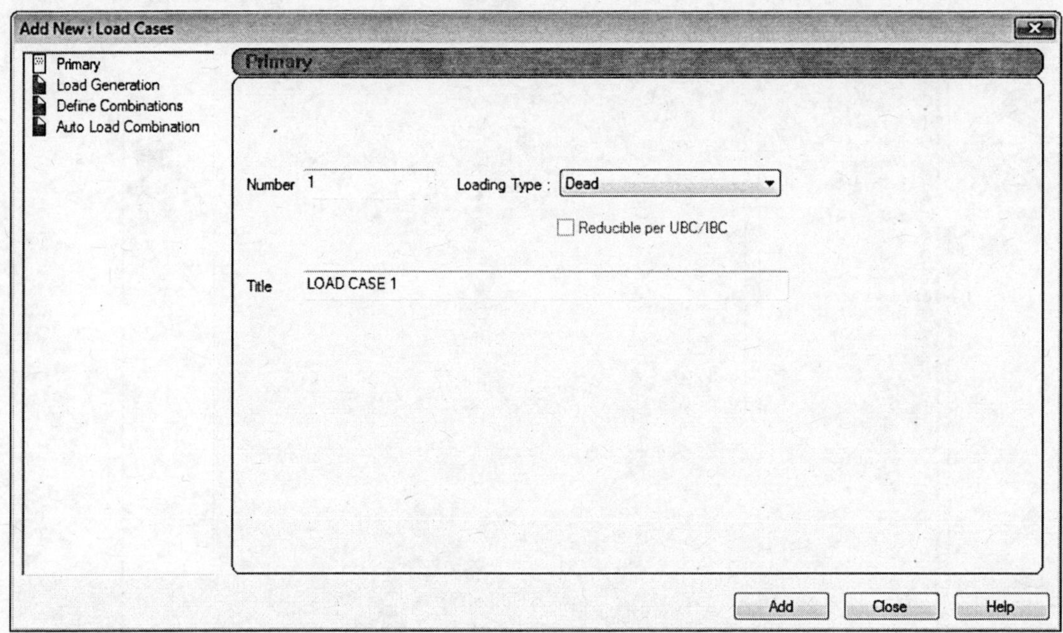

***Figure 6-2** The **Add New : Load Cases** dialog box*

Next, in the added load case, you will define different load types and assign them to the structure. To define these load types, select the required load case from the **Load & Definition** window and choose the **Add** button; the **Add New : Load Items** dialog box will be displayed, as shown in Figure 6-3. In this dialog box, different types of loads are available such as self-weight, nodal load, member load, area load, wind load, and so on. All these loads are discussed next in detail.

Selfweight

The selfweight of a structure consists of a major portion of the dead load in it. To add the self weight of a structure for analysis, expand the **Selfweight** node of the **Add New : Load Items** dialog box; the **Selfweight Load** option will be highlighted and the **Selfweight Load** page will be displayed in the right pane of the dialog box. In this page, you need to specify the direction in which the selfweight will be applied by selecting the required radio buttons from the **Direction** area. Next, specify the factor value in the **Factor** edit box. This value will be multiplied with the selfweight. A -ve sign against the value represents that the load will be applied along the negative direction of the selected axis. Next, choose the **Add** button; **SELFWEIGHT Y -1** will be added to the list box in the **Load & Definition** window. A question mark next to the load added in the **Load & Definition** window indicates the unassigned load. Next, you can assign the added selfweight to a structure using the **Assign To View** method which is discussed in the previous chapters. In STAAD.Pro, selfweight of every structural member will be calculated and applied as uniformly distributed load on the members. The command for assigning the selfweight is given next:

```
SELFWEIGHT {X,Y,OR Z} f MEMBER-LIST
```

In the above command, **X**, **Y**, and **Z** represent the global direction in which the selfweight will act, and **f** represents the factor whose value is multiplied with the selfweight.

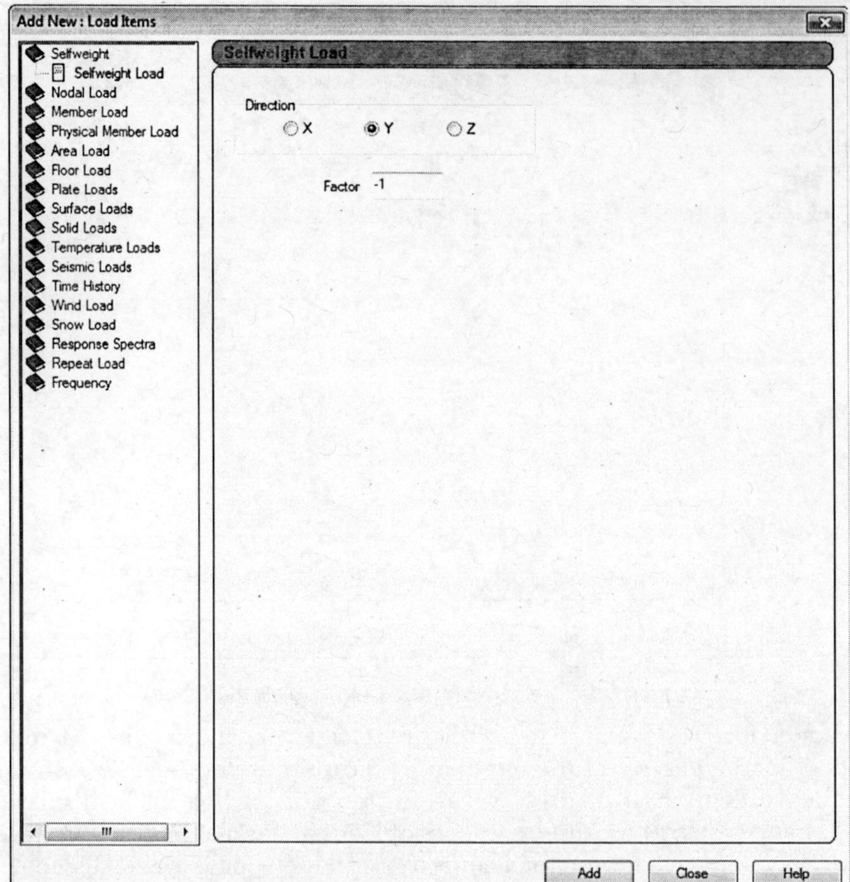

Figure 6-3 *The **Add New : Load Items** dialog box*

Nodal Loads

Nodal loads are used to define and assign the concentrated loads and moments at the joints of a structure. These loads act in the global coordinate system. To define nodal loads, expand the **Nodal Load** node in the left pane of the **Add New : Load Items** dialog box; the **Node** and **Support Displacement** load options will be displayed in the left pane and the **Node** page will be displayed in the right pane of the dialog box. In the **Node** page, specify the values for the forces in the **Fx**, **Fy**, and **Fz** edit boxes. You can specify the values for the concentrated moment in the **Mx**, **My**, and **Mz** edit boxes. After specifying the values, choose the **Add** button; the specified load will be added to the list box in the **Load & Definition** window. A question mark symbol can be seen next to the added load in the **Load & Definition** window. It indicates that the load has not been assigned. Now, select the added load and assign it to the appropriate nodes in the structure using the **Use Cursor To Assign** method, as discussed earlier.

Similarly, you can define and assign support displacement loads. To do so, select the **Support Displacement** load option in the left pane; the **Support Displacement** page will be displayed in the right pane of the dialog box. In the **Support Displacement** page, specify the displacement value in the **Displacement** edit box. Specify the direction of displacement such as translational or rotational by selecting the required radio button in the **Direction** area. Next, choose the **Add** button in the **Add New : Load Items** dialog box to add the load and then assign it at the appropriate nodes.

Note

*After assigning the load, you will notice that the question mark displayed next to the added load in the **Load & Definition** window gets replaced by a green cube which indicates that the defined load has been assigned to the structure.*

Member Loads

Member loads are directly applied to the structural member. They include uniformly distributed loads, concentrated loads, linear varying loads, and so on. Uniform loads act over the full or partial length of the member. Concentrated loads act at a point on the member. Linear varying loads act over the full or partial length of the member. Various types of member loads are discussed next.

Uniform Force and Uniform Moment

To define uniform load, expand the **Member Load** node in the left pane of the **Add New : Load Items** dialog box; the **Uniform Force** load option will be displayed and will be selected by default in the left pane and the **Uniform Force** page will be displayed in the right pane of the dialog box. In this page, specify the load value in the **W1** edit box in the **Force** area. Next, specify the distance between the start point of the member and the start point of the load in the **d1** edit box. Similarly, specify the distance between the start point of the member and the end point of the load in the **d2** edit box. In the **d3** edit box, specify the value which will be considered as the perpendicular distance between member's shear centre to the plane of loading. You can specify the direction of loads by selecting the corresponding radio buttons in the **Direction** area. You can specify direction in the local coordinates by selecting the **X (Local)**, **Y (Local)**, or **Z (Local)** radio button. You can also specify the direction in global coordinates by selecting the **GX**, **GY**, or **GZ** radio button. The **PX**, **PY**, or **PZ** radio button can be selected to define loads along the projected length of the member along the global direction. Next, choose the **Add** button to add the load in the **Load & Definition** list box. Select the added load and assign it to the structural members.

To define uniform moment, select the **Uniform Moment** option under the **Member Load** node in the left pane of the dialog box; the **Uniform Moment** page will be displayed in the right pane. In this page, specify the value of moment in the **W1** edit box in the **Moment** area. Specify the values in the **d1**, **d2**, and **d3** edit boxes. Specify the direction of moment by selecting the corresponding radio buttons in the **Direction** area. Choose the **Add** button to add the moment in the **Load Definition** window. Next, assign the moment to the structural members. Figure 6-4 shows the structure on which uniform load and moment is applied. The command used for assigning uniform force and moment is given next:

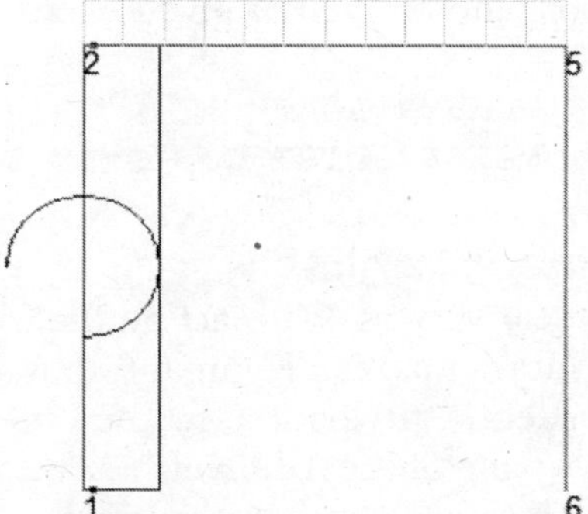

Figure 6-4 *Uniform load and moment applied on the member*

```
MEMBER LOAD
MEMBER-LIST UNI/UMOM DIRECTION-SPEC {W1} {d1,d2,d3}
```

In the command, **UNI** is used for the uniform force and **UMOM** for the uniform moment. The **DIRECTION-SPEC** command is used for specifying the direction. Here, you need to specify the direction such as **GX**, **GY**, and so on. **W1** represents the command for specifying the force or moment value. **d1** and **d2** represent the distance from the start node of the member to the start and end point of the load. And **d3** represents the placement of load in reference to the center line of the member along the cross-section.

Concentrated Force and Concentrated Moment

Concentrated load may act at any point on the structural member. Figure 6-5 shows the concentrated force and moment applied on a structural member. To define concentrated force, select the **Concentrated Force** option from the **Member Load** node in the left pane of the dialog box; the **Concentrated Force** page will be displayed in the right pane of the dialog box. In this page, specify the value of load in the **P** edit box in the **Force** area. Next, specify the distance of load from the start point of the member in the **d1** edit box. Specify the distance from the member's shear centre to the plane of loading in the **d2** edit box. In the **Direction** area, specify the direction in which load will be applied on the member by selecting the desired radio button. Next, choose the **Add** button to add the load and then assign it at an appropriate place in the structure.

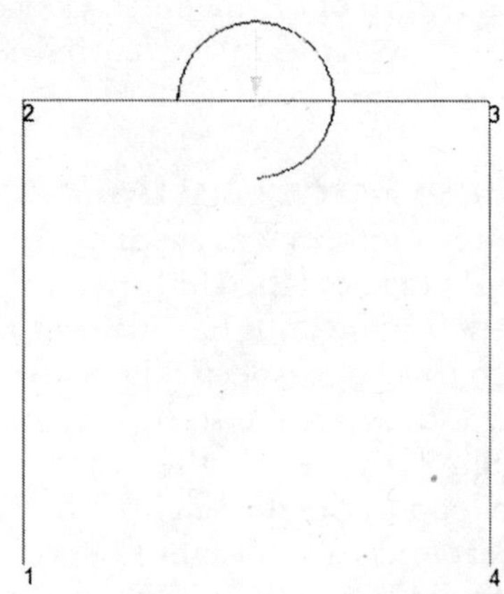

Figure 6-5 *Concentrated force and moment applied on the member*

In the same way, you can define and assign the concentrated moment to a structure. To do so, select the **Concentrated Moment** option under the **Member Load** node; the **Concentrated Moment** page will be displayed. In this page, specify the required values in the same way as discussed earlier for the concentrated force load. The command used for assigning concentrated force and moment is given next:

```
MEMBER LOAD
MEMBER-LIST CON/CMOM DIRECTION-SPEC {W1} {d1,d2,d3}
```

Linear Varying

Linear varying loads act on the whole structural member or on some portion. It acts in a non uniform manner. Figure 6-6 shows the linear varying loads applied on the structural members. To define this load, select the **Linear Varying** load option under the **Member Load** node in the left pane of the **Add New : Load Items** dialog box; the **Linear Varying** page will be displayed in the right pane. In this page, define load in increasing or decreasing manner by specifying the load values in the **W1** and **W2** edit boxes in the **Force** area. In this page, you can also define triangular load. To do so, select the **W3** radio button and specify the load value in the corresponding edit box. Next, specify the direction of loading by selecting the **X (Local)**, **Y (Local)**, or **Z (Local)** radio button. Next, choose the **Add** button to add the load to the **Load & Definition** window and then assign it on the appropriate members. The command used for assigning linear varying load is given next.

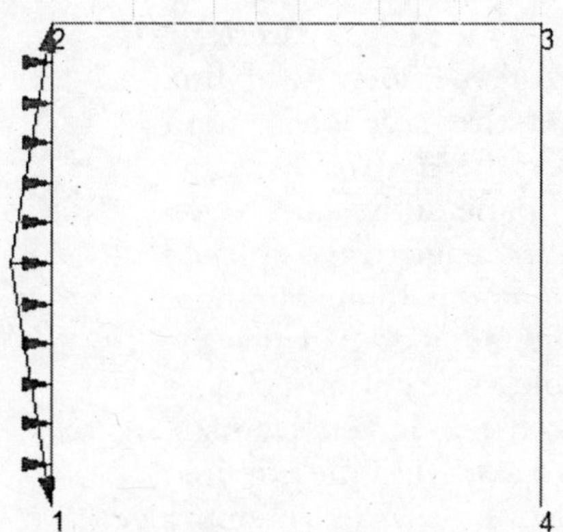

Figure 6-6 Linear varying loads applied on the structure

```
MEMBER LOAD
MEMBER-LIST LIN DIRECTION-SPEC {W1, W2, W3}
```

In the command, **W1** and **W2** represent load values for trapezoidal load and **W3** represents load value for triangular load.

Trapezoidal

Trapezoidal loads are applied in a trapezoidal manner on the structure member. To define trapezoidal load, select the **Trapezoidal** load option available under the **Member Load** node; the **Trapezoidal** page will be displayed in the right pane of the **Add New : Load Items** dialog box. In the **Force** area of this dialog box, specify the value of load intensity in the **W1** and **W2** edit boxes. Next, specify the distance of loading from the start point of the member to the start point of loading in the **d1** edit box, and from the start point of the member to the end point of loading in the **d2** edit box. Next, in the **Direction** area, specify the direction of loading by selecting the required radio buttons. Next, choose the **Add** button to add the load and then assign it to the desired structural members. Figure 6-7 shows the trapezoidal load applied on the structural member. The command used for assigning trapezoidal load is given next.

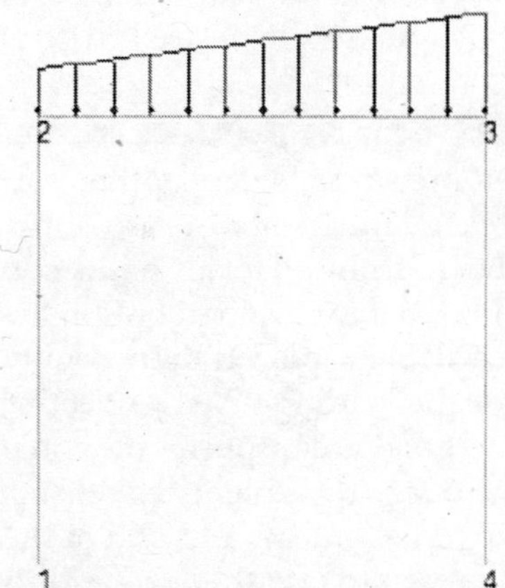

Figure 6-7 Trapezoidal load applied on the structural member

```
MEMBER LOAD
MEMBER-LIST TRAP DIRECTION-SPEC {W1, W2} {W3}
```

Hydrostatic

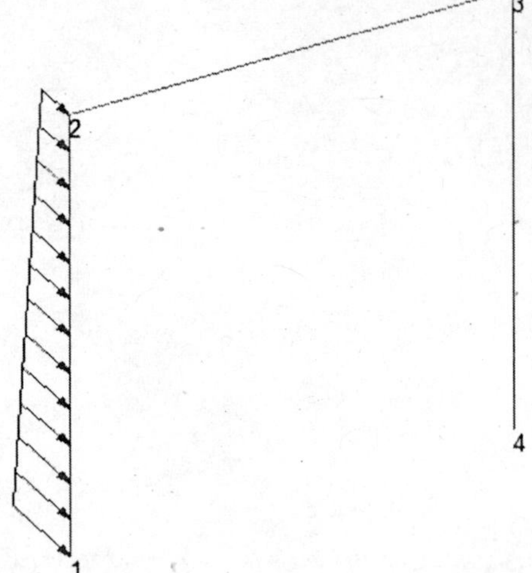

Figure 6-8 Hydrostatic load applied on the structural member

Hydrostatic loads are the loads produced due to hydrostatic pressure. Figure 6-8 shows the hydrostatic load applied on the structural member. To define hydrostatic loads, select the **Hydrostatic** load option under the **Member Load** node; the **Hydrostatic** page will be displayed in the right pane of the **Add New : Load Items** dialog box. In this page, the displayed options will be in an inactive mode. To enable these options, you need to select the member on which the load is to be applied. To enable these options, choose the **Select Member** button; the **Selected Items(s)** dialog box will be displayed. Next, select the required member in the main window; the selected member number will be displayed in the **Selected Items(s)** dialog box. Next, choose the **Done** button; the **Add New : Load Items** dialog box will be displayed again. You will notice that the selected member number will be displayed in the **Member** box. You can deselect any member by clearing the check box displayed corresponding to the member number.

Now, in the **Force** area, specify the load values along the minimum and maximum global axis in the **W1** and **W2** edit boxes, respectively. Specify the direction of loading by selecting the corresponding radio button in the **Direction** area. Next, choose the **Add** button to add the load and assign it to the desired structural members.

Prestress and Poststress

When pre stress load is applied on a structural member, its effect gets transmitted to all other connected members. In case of post stress load, the effect remains on the member itself and is not be transmitted to any of the connecting members. To define pre stress/post stress load, select the **Pre/Post Stress** load option available under the **Member Load** option; the **Pre/Post Stress** page will be displayed in the right pane of the **Add New : Load Items** dialog box. In this page, define the loading type by selecting the **Pre Stress** or **Post Stress** radio button in the **Type** area. In the **Load** area, specify the force value in the **Force** edit box. In the **Eccentricity Distances** area, specify the eccentricity distances with respect to the centre of gravity of the cross-section at the start, middle, and end of the member in the corresponding edit boxes. Next, choose the **Add** button to add the load and then assign it to the desired structural member.

Note

You need to define the pre stress and post stress loads in two different load cases in the ***Load & Definition*** *window.*

The command for assigning the prestress and poststress load is given next.

```
MEMBER PRESTRESS/POSTSTRESS LOAD
MEMBER-LIST FORCE {f1} ES {d1} EM {d2} EE {d3}
```

In the above command, the first line represents the load to be selected: prestress or post stress. In the next line, the **MEMBER -LIST** command represents the list of associated members. The **FORCE** command represents the load to be applied and **{f_1}** represents the force value. **ES, EM,** and **EE** represent the eccentricity distances at the start, middle, and end of the member, respectively. Similarly, **{d_1}**, **{d_2}**, and **{d_3}** represent the values of the eccentricity distances. Note that you do not need to include the parentheses while using the commands in the STAAD Editor window.

Fixed End Loads

Fixed end loads are applied at the member ends and are an alternative for the member loads. To define fixed end loads, select the **Fixed End** load option under the **Member Load** node in the left pane of the **Add New : Load Items** dialog box; the **Fixed End** load page will be displayed in the right pane. In this page, specify the force in x, y, and z directions and moments in x, y, and z direction in their corresponding edit boxes in the **Start Node** and **End Node** areas, respectively. Choose the **Add** button to add the load to the **Load & Definition** window and then assign it at the appropriate member ends.

Note

In this chapter, you need to download the c06_Staad_v8i.zip file for the examples from http://www.cadcim.com. The path of the file is as follows: Textbook > Civil/GIS > STAAD.Pro > Exploring Bentley STAAD.Pro V8i.

Example 1

In this example, you will open the *c06_staad_v8i_ex1_start.std* file. Next, you will define some of the member loads and then assign them to the structural members.

Steps to complete this example are given below:

Step 1: Open the file *c06_staad_v8i_ex1_start.std* in STAAD.Pro; the model is displayed in the main window.

Step 2: Invoke the **Load & Definition** page from the **General** tab; the **Load & Definition** window is displayed in the right area of the interface.

Step 3: In this window, select the **Load Cases Details** as the title node and then choose the **Add** button; the **Add New : Load Cases** dialog box is displayed.

Step 4: In this dialog box, enter **Dead Load** in the **Title** edit box and retain the default settings. Next, choose the **Add** button and choose the close button. The load case is added in the **Load & Definition** window. Similarly, add another load case as **Live Load** and then close the **Add New : Load Cases** dialog box.

Step 5: Next, select the **Dead Load** case in the window and choose the **Add** button; the **Add New : Load Items** dialog box is displayed.

Step 6: In this dialog box, expand the **Member Load** node; the **Uniform Force** page is displayed. In this page, specify the value **-15** in the **W1** edit box and specify **1** and **2** in the **d1** and **d2** edit boxes, respectively and choose the **Add** button to add the load.

Step 7: Select the **Concentrated Force** in the left pane of the **Add New : Load Items** dialog box; the **Concentrated Force** page is displayed in the right pane.

Step 8: In this page, specify the value **-10** in the **P** edit box in the **Force** area and choose the **Add** button to add the load.

Step 9: Select the **Concentrated Moment** in the left pane of the dialog box; the **Concentrated Moment** page is displayed in the right pane. In this page, specify the value **22** in the **P** edit box and select the **GZ** radio button in the **Direction** area. Choose the **Add** button to add the moment and then close the dialog box.

Step 10: Now, select the load which was added first and then select the **Use Cursor To Assign** radio button. Next, choose the **Assign** button. Next, click on the members 2 and 3, refer to Figure 6-9; the load is assigned on these members.

Step 11: Repeat the procedure followed in step 10 to assign the second and third load on the 11 and 12 members, respectively.

Step 12: Choose the **Scale** button from the toolbar to scale the visibility arrows representing **Point Force** and **Point.Moment**. Figure 6-9 shows the dead load applied on the structure.

Step 13: Repeat the previous steps to add the **Uniform Force** of **20kN/m** in the **Live Load** case and assign it to the members 2, 3, 6, 8, 11, and 12. Figure 6-10 shows the live load applied on the structure.

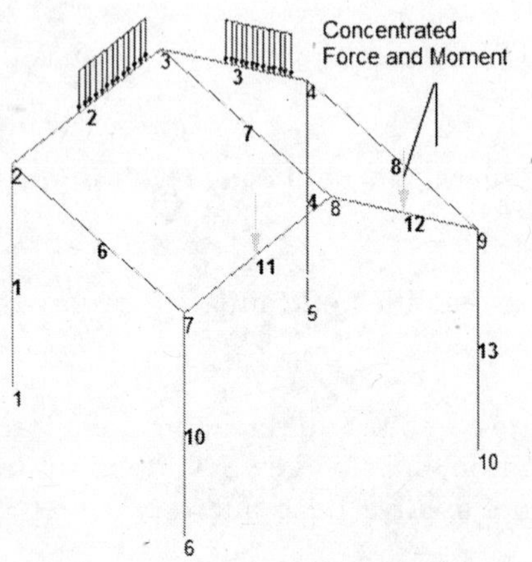

Figure 6-9 Dead load applied on the structure

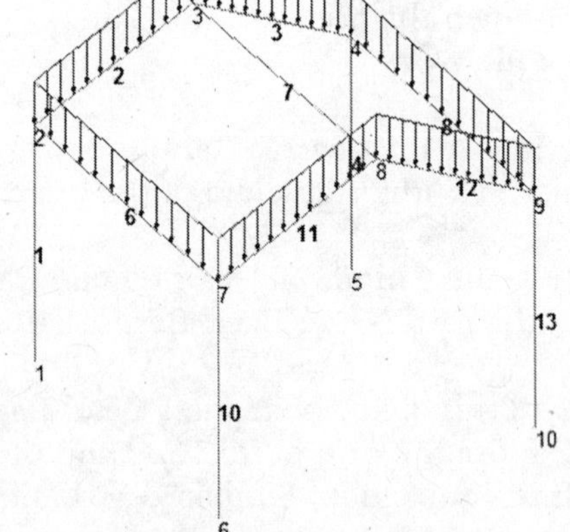

Figure 6-10 Live load applied on the structure

Step 14: Choose the **Save As** option from the **File** menu; the **Save As** dialog box is displayed. In this dialog box, specify the name *c06_staad_v8i_ex1* in the **File name** edit box and save it at an appropriate location.

Area Load

Area load is applied on closed panel structures and is used for one way distribution. In STAAD.Pro, to define area load, you need to define pressure intensity and the direction in which load will be applied. The program will then automatically calculate the tributary area and the loads will be applied on the individual members of the closed panel as uniformly distributed loads. To define area load, select the **Area Load** option from the left pane of the **Add New : Load Items** dialog box; the **Area** page will be displayed. In this page, specify the pressure intensity in the **Pressure** edit box. Specify the direction by selecting the required radio button in the **Direction** area. By default, the direction will be in the local z direction. Next, choose the **Add** button to add the load and then assign it to the structure. After assigning the load to the closed panel structure, you will not be able to view the applied loads in the main window. You can view the applied area load on the structure only after the analysis has been performed. After the analysis, the loads will be applied on the members as member loads. You can also use the commands given next to define and assign area load.

```
AREA LOAD
MEMBER-LIST ALOAD {f} DIRECTION-SPECIFICATION
```

Floor Load

Floor load is used for two way distribution and is applied on closed panel structures. Figure 6-11 shows the floor load acting on a structure. To define floor load, define a load case as discussed earlier. Then, select the defined load case and choose the **Add** button; the **Add New : Load Items** dialog box will be displayed. In this dialog box, select the **Floor Load** option in the left pane; the **Floor** page will be displayed in the right pane. The parameters in this page are discussed next.

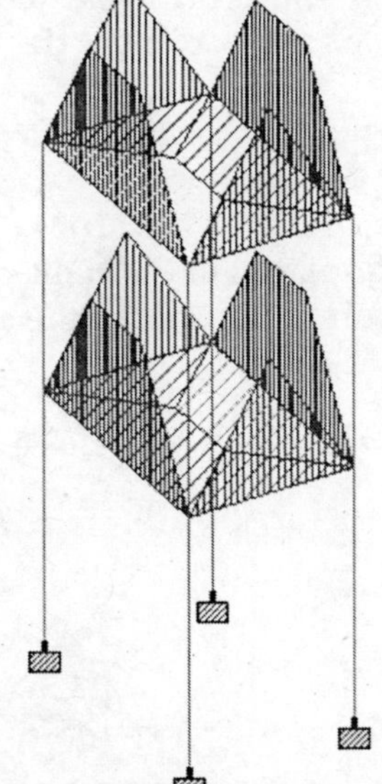

Figure 6-11 Floor load acting on the structure

In the **Floor** page, the **YRANGE** radio button will be selected by default and the related options will be displayed in the **Range** area. In the **Range** area, define **Y Range**, **X Range**, and **Z Range** by specifying the appropriate values in their corresponding **Minimum** and **Maximum** edit boxes. Specify the pressure intensity in the **Pressure** edit box in the **Load** area. Next, specify the direction of loading by selecting the corresponding radio button in the **Direction** area. Select the **One Way Distribution** check box for one way distribution of loading. In this case, loads will be distributed on the longer side of the panel. You can also select the **Group** radio button in the **Floor** page. In this case, first you have to define the members forming the closed panel as **Floor** group. To create a group, first select the members forming the closed panel in the main window. Next, choose the **Create New Group** option from the **Tools** menu; the **Define Group Name** dialog box will be displayed. Specify the desired name in the **Group Name** text box and select the **Floor** option from the **Select Type** drop-down list. Choose the **OK** button; the **Create Group** dialog box will be displayed. In this dialog box, choose the **Associate** button and then choose the **Close** button to close the dialog box. Now, select the **Group** radio button in the **Add New : Load Items** dialog box; the floor groups will be displayed in the **Member Group** list. Next, select the required group from this list box. Choose the **Add** button to add the loading in the **Load & Definition** window. The floor load will be automatically assigned to the structure.

Note

After assigning the loads to a structure, when you click on the defined loads in the ***Load & Definition*** *window, the assigned load will be highlighted in blue color in the main window.*

Example 2

In this example, you will open the *c06_staad_v8i_ex2_start.std* file. Next, you will define floor load and assign it to the structure.

Steps to complete this example are given below:

Step 1: Open file *c06_staad_v8i_ex2_start.std* in STAAD.Pro; the model is displayed in the main window.

Step 2: Invoke the **Load & Definition** page from the **General** tab; the **Load & Definition** window is displayed.

Step 3: Select the **Load:CASE 1** under the **Load Cases Details** head and choose the **Edit** button. The **Edit : Primary Load** dialog box is displayed, edit the name in the **Title** edit box to **Floor Load** and choose **Close** button.

Step 4: Select the created load case and choose the **Add** button; the **Add New : Load Items** dialog box is displayed.

Step 5: In this dialog box, the **Selfweight Load** page is displayed in the right pane.

Step 6: In the **Add New : Load Items** dialog box, expand the **Floor Load** node; the **Floor** page is displayed in the right pane. In this page, specify the values for the parameters, as shown in Figure 6-12. Choose the **Add** button to add the load.

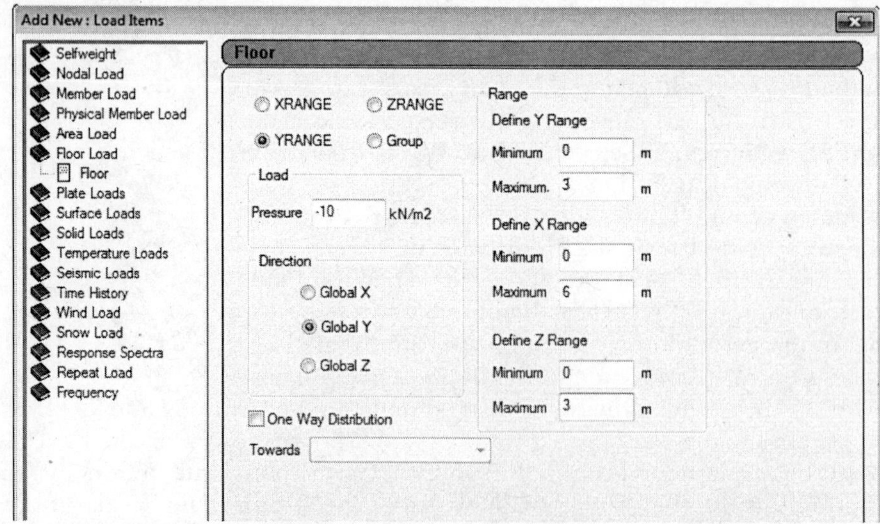

Figure 6-12 *Values specified in the* ***Add New : Load Items*** *dialog box for the 1st floor*

Step 7: In the **Floor** page of the **Add New : Load Items** dialog box, specify the values for the second floor load, as shown in Figure 6-13. Choose the **Add** button to add the load and close the dialog box by choose the **Close** button.

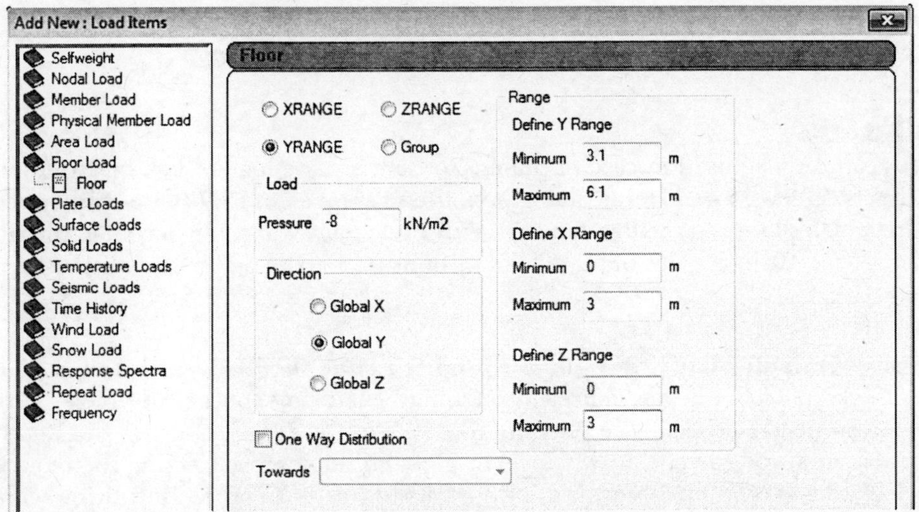

*Figure 6-13 Values specified in the **Add New : Load Items** dialog box for the 2nd floor*

Step 8: Now, click on both the loads one by one in the **Load & Definition** window to view the applied loads on the structure. Figure 6-14 shows the applied floor loads on the structure.

Step 9: Choose the **Save As** option from the **File** menu; the **Save As** dialog box is displayed. In this dialog box, specify the name *c06_staad_v8i_ex2* in the **File name** edit box and save it at an appropriate location.

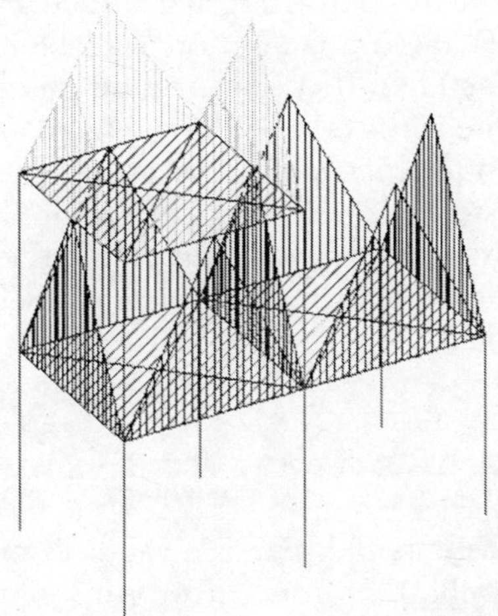

Figure 6-14 Floor loads applied on the structure

The command for the assigned floor load is given next:

```
LOAD 1 LOADTYPE None TITLE Floor Load
SELFWEIGHT Y -1 LIST 1 TO 5 7 8 10 12 TO 24
FLOOR LOAD
YRANGE 0 3 FLOAD -10 XRANGE 0 6 ZRANGE 0 3 GY
YRANGE 3.1 6.1 FLOAD -8 XRANGE 0 3 ZRANGE 0 3 GY
```

Plate Loads

Plate loads can only be used in case of plates. To define plate loads, click on the **Plate Loads** node in the **Add New : Load Items** dialog box; the **Pressure On Full Plate** load option will be selected in the left pane and the **Pressure On Full Plate** page will be displayed in the right pane of the dialog box. Various types of plate load options in this dialog box are discussed next.

Pressure On Full Plate

The **Pressure On Full Plate** load option is used to define the load which will act on the full surface of the plate element. In the **Pressure On Full Plate** page of the **Add New : Load Items** dialog box, you need to specify the pressure intensity in the **W1** edit box in the **Load** area. In the **Direction** area, you can specify the local or global direction by selecting the required radio button. Next, choose the **Add** button to add the load in the **Load & Definition** window and then close the dialog box. You can assign the added load to the desired plate using any of the assigning options. By default, pressure will be applied in the local z direction. Figure 6-15 shows the pressure acting on a plate in the local z direction. The command to define and assign this load is given next.

```
ELEMENT LOAD
   ELEMENT-LIST PRESSURE DIRECTION-SPEC P1
```

Concentrated Load

Concentrated load is used to define the load acting at a particular point in a plate. You can define this load by selecting the **Concentrated Load** option available under the **Plate Loads** node in the **Add New : Load Items** dialog box; the **Concentrated Load** page will be displayed. In this page, specify the force value in the **Force** edit box in the **Load** area. Specify the location of load on the plate by specifying the distance of coordinates from the origin in the **X** and **Y** edit boxes. Next, specify the direction of loading by selecting the required radio button in the **Direction** area. Add the defined load by choosing the **Add** button and then assign it to the desired plate. Figure 6-16 shows the concentrated load acting on a plate in the local z direction. The command for assigning this load is given next.

```
ELEMENT LOAD
ELEMENT-LIST PRESSURE DIRECTION-SPEC P1 X Y
```

In the above command, $\mathbf{P_1}$ represents the pressure value. **X** and **Y** represent the distance of coordinates of a point of load application from the origin.

Note

To apply load on a node in a plate, you can use the **Node** *option under the* **Nodal Load** *node as explained earlier in this chapter.*

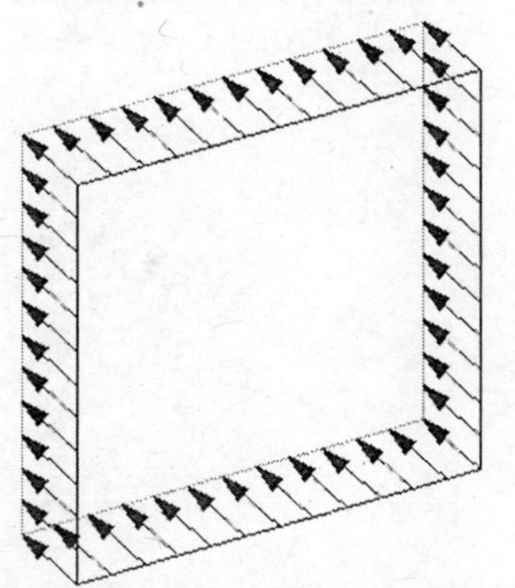

Figure 6-15 *Pressure acting on full plate in the local z direction*

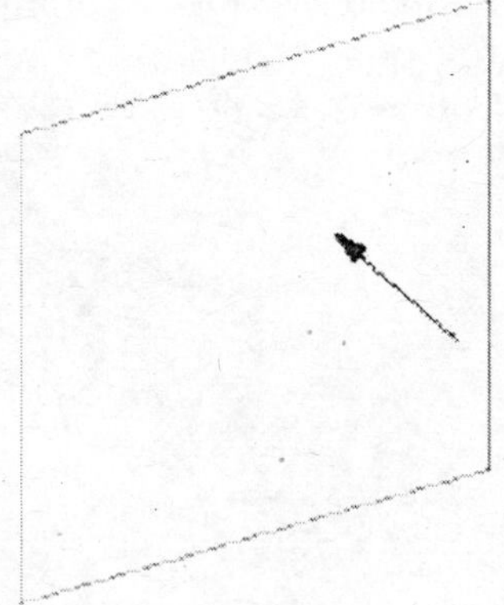

Figure 6-16 *Concentrated load acting on a plate*

Partial Plate Pressure Load

You can use this option to define the load acting partially on the plate element in the area defined by the user. To define this load, select the **Partial Plate Pressure Load** option from the left pane in the **Add New : Load Items** dialog box; the **Partial Plate Pressure Load** page will be displayed in the right pane. In this page, specify the pressure intensity in the **W1** edit box in the **Load** area. Specify the coordinates for the area in the **X1**, **Y1**, **X2**, and **Y2** edit boxes. Next, specify the direction of loading in the **Direction** area. Add and assign the load to the plate in the same way as discussed earlier. The command to define and assign this load is given next.

```
ELEMENT LOAD
ELEMENT-LIST PRESSURE DIRECTION-SPEC P1 X1 Y1 X2 Y2
```

In the above commands, $\mathbf{X_1}$, $\mathbf{Y_1}$, $\mathbf{X_2}$, and $\mathbf{Y_2}$ represent the coordinate value for the enclosed area in the plate.

Trapezoidal Load

The trapezoidal load type is used to apply the trapezoidally varying pressure on a plate. To define this load, select the **Trapezoidal** option from the left pane of the **Add New : Load Items** dialog box; the **Trapezoidal** page will be displayed in the right pane of the dialog box. In this page, first you will specify the direction in which the pressure will act. To do so, select the required radio button in the **Direction of pressure** area. By default, the **Local Z** radio button is selected which shows that the pressure will be applied normally to the plate element in the local z direction. Next, you will specify the direction in which pressure will vary by selecting the **X** or **Y** radio button in the **Variation along element** area. If you select the **Joint** radio button from this area then you need to specify the pressure value for each node in the corresponding edit box. Specify the pressure intensity at the start and end in the **Start (f1)** and **End (f2)** edit boxes. Now, choose the **Add** button to add the load and then assign it to the desired plates. You can use the command given next to assign the trapezoidal load. Figures 6-17 and 6-18 show partial plate pressure and trapezoidal load acting on a plate.

```
ELEMENT LOAD
ELEMENT-LIST TRAP {GX, GY, OR GZ} {X, Y, OR JT} f1 f2
```

In the above command, the **TRAP** command is used in case of trapezoidal load. **GX, GY**, or **GZ** represent the direction in which pressure will be applied. **X, Y**, or **JT** represent the direction in which pressure will vary. $\mathbf{f_1}$ and $\mathbf{f_2}$ represent the pressure values.

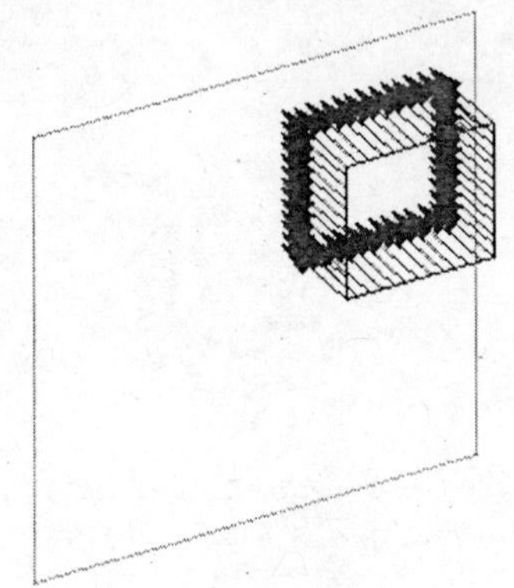

Figure 6-17 Partial plate pressure load acting on a plate

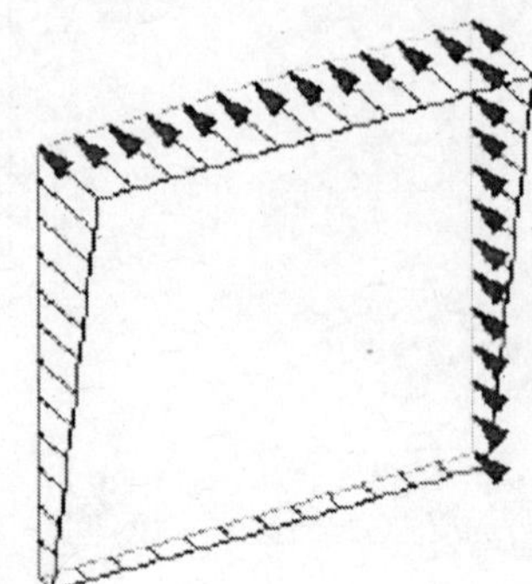

Figure 6-18 Trapezoidal load acting on a plate

Hydrostatic Load

Using hydrostatic load, you can define hydrostatic pressure on plate elements. To define hydrostatic load, select the **Hydrostatic** load option from the left pane of the **Add New : Load Items** dialog box; the **Hydrostatic** page will be displayed in the right pane. In this page, you need to specify the values for the parameters in the same way as discussed earlier for the member loads. This load is converted to trapezoidal load on the plate elements. Figure 6-19 shows the hydrostatic load acting trapezoidally on a plate. The command for the hydrostatic load will be the same as for the trapezoidal load mentioned before.

Element Joint Load

You can define varying pressure on each joint in a plate element using the Element Joint Load. To do so, select the **Element Joint Load** option from the left pane of the **Add New : Load Items** dialog box; the **Element Joint Load** page will be displayed. In this page, first you have to specify the plate type whether it is three or four noded. To do so, select the **Three Noded Facet** or **Four Noded Facet** radio button in the **Joint Load Data** area. Next, specify the node numbers and the corresponding pressure intensity in their respective columns in the table. Specify the direction of pressure acting on the element in the **Direction** area. Now, choose the **Add** button; the load will be added to the **Load & Definition** window. The **Element Joint Load** will be assigned automatically to the specified plate. Figure 6-20 shows the element joint load acting on a plate element. The command for assigning this load is given next.

```
ELEMENT LOAD JOINT
n1 n2 n3 n4 FACETS f PRESSURE p1 p2 p3 p4
```

In the above command, $\mathbf{n_1}$, $\mathbf{n_2}$, $\mathbf{n_3}$, and $\mathbf{n_4}$ represent the four nodes of the plate on which load will be applied and $\mathbf{p_1}$, $\mathbf{p_2}$, $\mathbf{p_3}$, and $\mathbf{p_4}$ represent the pressure values at the four nodes.

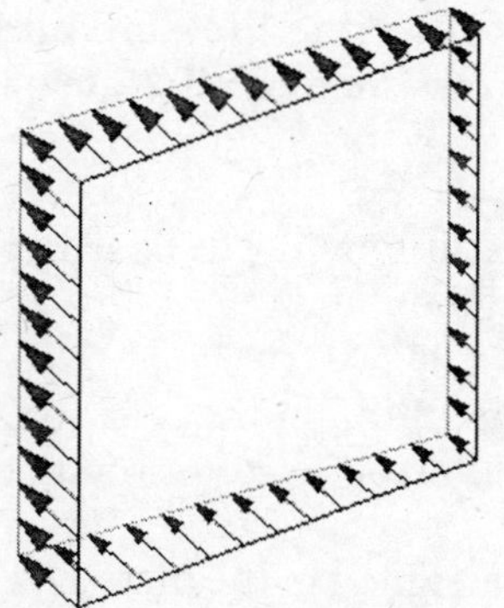

Figure 6-19 Hydrostatic load acting on a plate

Figure 6-20 Element joint load acting on a plate

Example 3

In this example, you will open the *c06_staad_v8i_ex3_start.std* file. Next, you will define pressure acting on a full plate and then assign it to the plate.

Steps required to complete this example are given below:

Step 1: Open the file *c06_staad_v8i_ex3_start.std* in STAAD.Pro; the model is displayed in the main window, as shown in Figure 6-21.

Step 2: Next, click in the main window and press SHIFT+P to view the plate numbers.

Figure 6-21 Model displayed in the Main Window

Step 3: Invoke the **General** tab and then choose the **Load & Definition** page; the **Load & Definition** window will be displayed.

Step 4: In this window, create a load case with the name **Plate Load**. Next, select the created load case and choose the **Add** button; the **Add New : Load Items** dialog box is displayed.

Step 5: In this dialog box, expand the **Plate Loads** node; the **Pressure on Full Plate** load is highlighted in the left pane of the window and the **Pressure on Full Plate** page is displayed in the right pane.

Step 6: In this page, specify the value **1** in the **W1** edit box in the **Load** area and choose the **Add** button to add the load and then close the dialog box.

Step 7: Select the added load and choose the **Assign** button in the **Assignment Method** area. Click in the main window and using the left and right arrow buttons, rotate the model.

Step 8: Next, click on the plate 1; the pressure load is assigned to the plate 1, refer to Figure 6-22.

Step 9: Similarly, assign the pressure load to all the plates in the first row, refer to Figure 6-23.

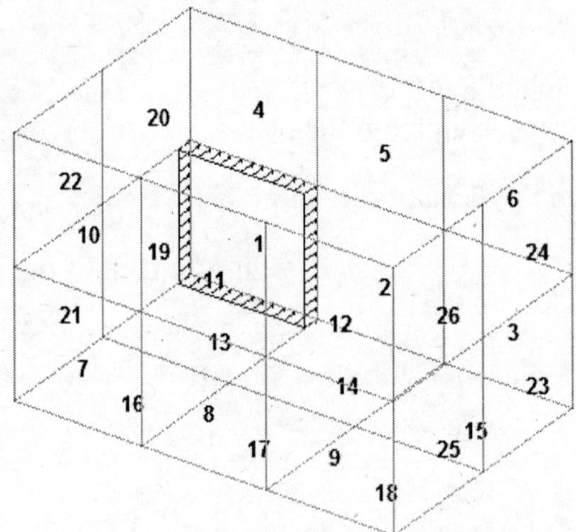

Figure 6-22 *Pressure load assigned to the plate 1*

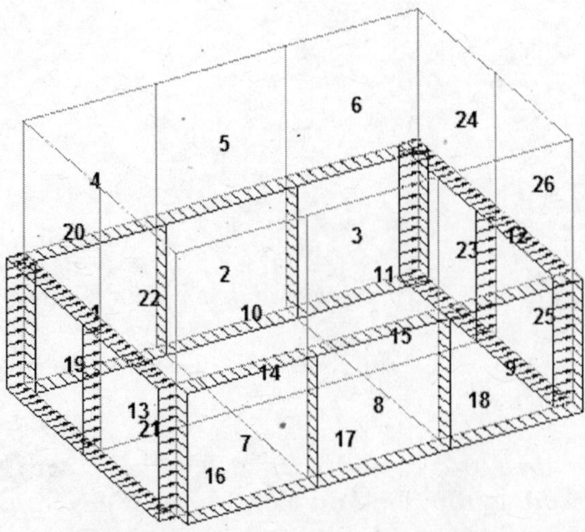

Figure 6-23 *Pressure load applied on all the first row plates*

Step 10: Choose the **Save As** option from the **File** menu; the **Save As** dialog box is displayed. In this dialog box, specify the name *c06_staad_v8i_ex3* in the **File name** edit box and save it at an appropriate location.

Surface Loads

Surface loads allows you to define uniform pressure on surface elements in various ways. This will be discussed later in this chapter. To define a surface load, expand the **Surface Loads** node in the left pane of the **Add New : Load Items** dialog box; the **Concentrated Load** option will be selected in the left pane and the **Concentrated Load** page will be displayed in the right pane of the dialog box. The options in this page are discussed next.

Concentrated Load

Concentrated load will be applied at a particular point on the surface element. You need to specify the x and y coordinates of the point where the load will be applied. Note that the coordinates of this point will be taken with respect to local coordinate system and the first node of the surface element will be taken as the origin. In the **Load** area of the **Concentrated Load** page, specify the force value in the **Force** edit box. Next, specify the distance of the point from the first node in the **X** and **Y** edit box. Next, specify the direction of load by selecting the required radio button in the **Direction** area. After specifying the parameters, choose the **Add** button; the load will be added to the **Load & Definition** window. Now, you can assign the added load to the desired surface element. Figure 6-24 shows the concentrated load applied on a surface element.

Pressure on Full Surface Load

The pressure on full surface can be defined using the **Pressure on Full Surface** load option. To define this load, click on the **Pressure on Full Surface** load option available under the **Surface Loads** node in the left pane of the **Add New : Load Items** dialog box; the **Pressure on Full Surface** page will be displayed in the right pane of the dialog box. In the **Load** area of this page, you will specify the pressure intensity in the **W1** edit box. Next, specify the direction in which load will act by selecting the required radio buttons such as **Local Z**, **GX**, **GY**, or **GZ** in the **Direction** area. Next, choose the **Add** button to add the load to the **Load & Definition** window. Now, you can assign the added load to the desired surface element. Figure 6-25 shows the pressure applied on the full surface element.

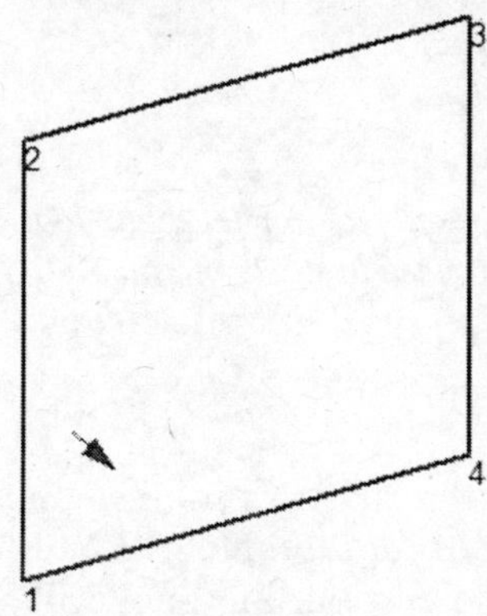

Figure 6-24 *Concentrated force applied on surface*

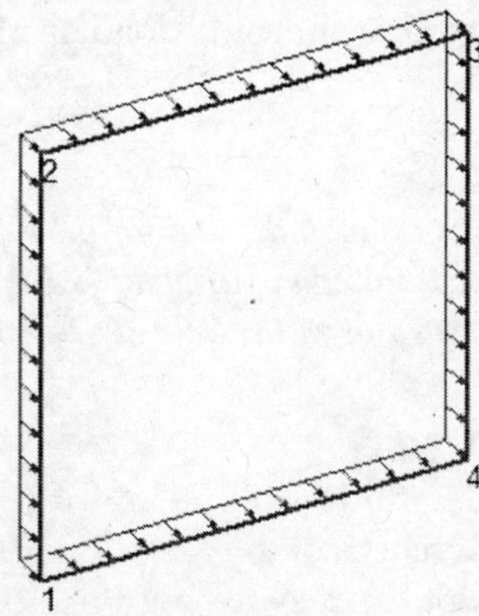

Figure 6-25 *Uniform pressure applied on surface*

Partial Surface Pressure Load

Pressure can also be applied on a surface element partially but in a uniform manner. To do so, click on the **Partial Surface Pressure Load** option in the left pane of the **Add New : Load Items** dialog box; the **Partial Surface Pressure Load** page will be displayed in the right pane of the dialog box. In the **Load** area of this page, specify the pressure intensity in the **W1** edit box. Next, specify the coordinates for the enclosed surface on which load will be applied in the **X1**, **X2**, **Y1**, and **Y2** edit boxes. Specify the direction of loading in the **Direction** area and then choose the **Add** button to add the load to the **Load & Definition** window. Assign the added load to the surface element. Figure 6-26 shows the partial surface pressure load applied on the surface.

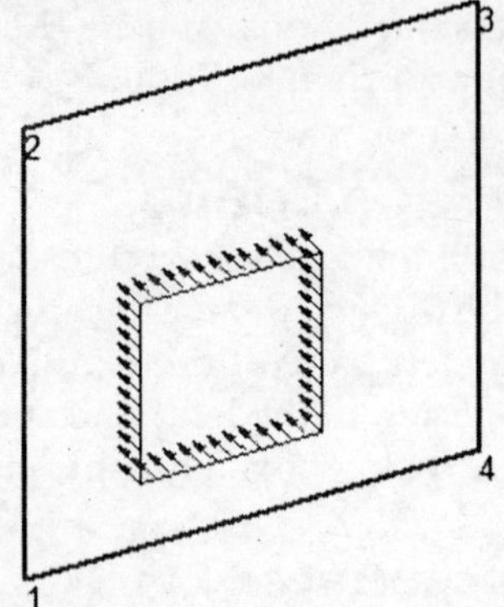

Figure 6-26 *Partial surface pressure applied on a surface*

Partial Surface Trapezoidal Load

When you need to apply the pressure loading on a surface partially in a non-uniform manner, you can use the **Partial Surface Trapezoidal Load** option. To do so, click on the **Partial Surface Trapezoidal Load** option in the left pane of the **Add New : Load Items** dialog box; the **Partial Surface Trapezoidal Load** page will be displayed in the right pane of the dialog box. In the **Direction of Pressure** area, specify the direction of loading by selecting the required radio buttons. In the **Load Position** area, specify the coordinates to define the load area. Next, specify the pressure values at the four corners of the loaded area in the edit boxes in the **Variation along Element** area. Next, choose the **Add** button to add the load and then assign it to the surface. Figure 6-27 shows the partial surface trapezoidal load applied on a surface.

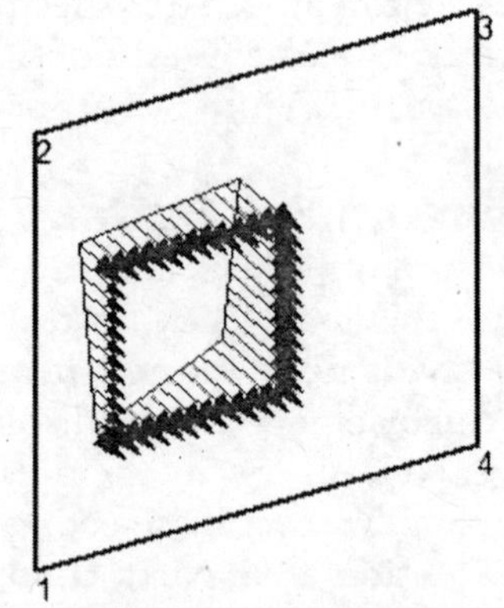

Figure 6-27 *Partial surface trapezoidal load applied on the surface element*

Note

The commands used for all the surface loads will be the same as for the plate loads. For surface loads instead of using the ***PLATE LOAD*** *command, you need to start with the* ***SURFACE LOAD*** *command in the* ***STAAD Editor*** *window.*

Solid Load

Solid load is used to define uniform or varying pressure on the faces of a solid element. To define solid loads, click on the **Solid Loads** node in the left pane of the **Add New : Load Items** dialog box; the **Solid pressure load** option is selected and the corresponding page will be displayed in the right pane of the dialog box. In this page, select the required face number on which the load will be applied from the **Face number** drop-down list. Next, specify the pressure acting at each node in the **Node 1**, **Node 2**, **Node 3**, and **Node 4** edit boxes. Select the required radio button in the **Direction** area to specify the direction of pressure. Next, choose the **Add** button to add the load and then assign it to the required solid element. Figure 6-28 shows the load applied on a solid element.

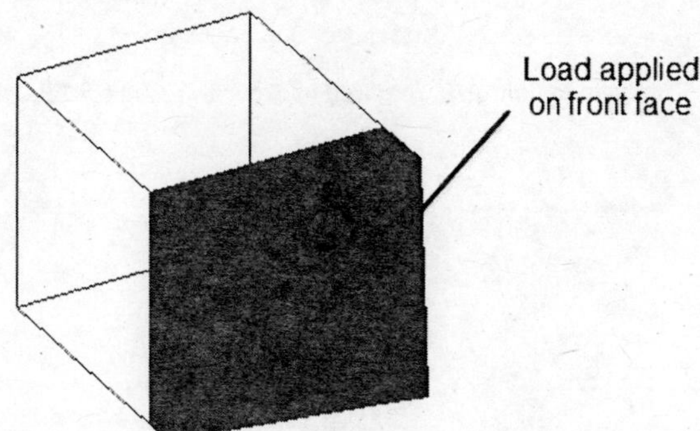

Figure 6-28 *Pressure applied on front face of a solid element*

Temperature Load

In a structural member, temperature differs throughout the member length which causes thermal stress/strain in a building. In STAAD.Pro, to define temperature load, click on the **Temperature Loads** node in the left pane of the **Add New : Load Items** dialog box; the **Temperature** load option will be selected in the left pane and the **Temperature** page will be displayed in the right pane of the dialog box. In this page, specify the value for the axial elongation in the **Temperature Change for Axial Elongation** edit box. Similarly, specify the required values in the **Temperature Differential from Top to Bottom** and **Temperature Differential From Side to Side (Local Z)** edit boxes. Next, choose the **Add** button to add the load and then assign it to the required member or element.

In the left pane of the **Add New : Load Items** dialog box, the **Strain** load option is also available under the **Temperature** load node. To specify a strain load, select the **Strain** option available under the **Temperature Loads** node in the left pane of the dialog box; the **Strain** page will be displayed in the right pane. In this page, specify the value for initial elongation or shrinkage caused in the member in the **Initial Axial Elongation (+) or Shrinkage (-)** edit box. Choose the **Add** button to add the load and then assign it to the structure.

Seismic Load

When an earthquake occurs, a building is subjected to inertia forces acting in opposite direction of earthquake acceleration, which further subjects the building to dynamic motion. This inertia force is known as seismic load.

In STAAD.Pro, to define seismic load, click on the **Seismic Loads** node in the left pane of the **Add New : Load Items** dialog box; the **Factor & Direction** option will be selected in the left pane and the **Factor _Direction** page will be displayed in an inactive state in the right pane of the dialog box and it will look similar to the one shown in Figure 6-29. The options in this page are disabled because no seismic load has been defined yet. The method of defining seismic load is discussed next.

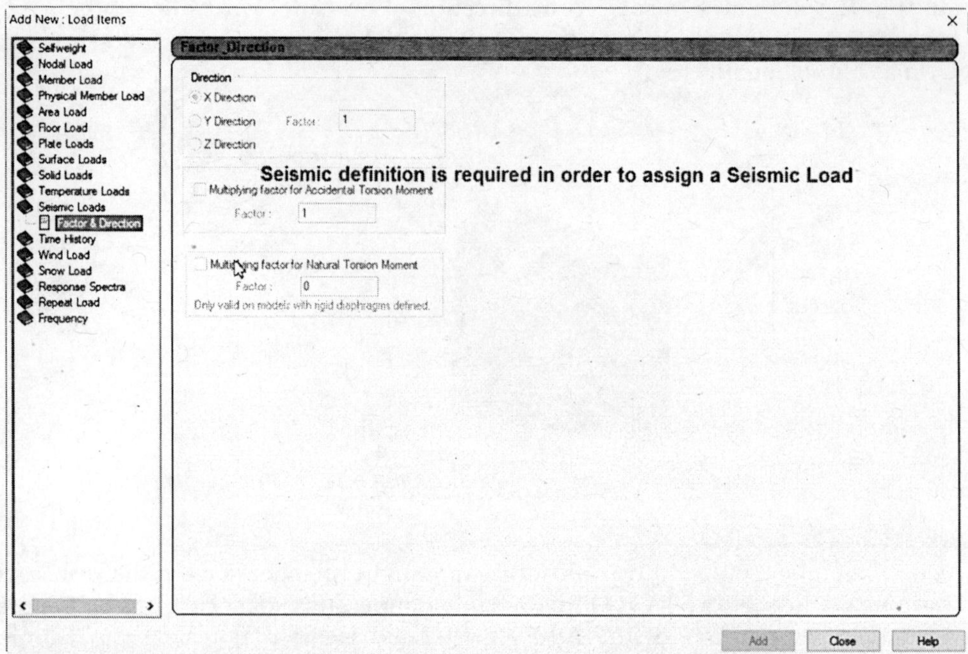

*Figure 6-29 The **Factor _Direction** page in the **Add New : Load Items** dialog box*

Defining Seismic Load

In STAAD.Pro, seismic load is defined to perform the dynamic analysis using various codes. To define seismic load, in the **Load & Definition** window, expand the **Definitions** node. Next, select the **Seismic Definitions** option and choose the **Add** button; the **Add New : Seismic Definitions** dialog box will be displayed, as shown in Figure 6-30.

In this dialog box, select the required code from the **Type** drop-down list. Select the **Include Accidental Load** check box to calculate the accidental torsion component as per the selected code. The various parameters associated with the selected code will be displayed in the table of the **Seismic Parameters** page. For example, if you have selected the **UBC 1997** code, then the related parameters will be displayed in a table, as shown in Figure 6-30. In this table, you need to specify the values for the given parameters.

After specifying the values for the parameters, choose the **Add** button; the seismic parameters will be added and the **Self Weight** page will be displayed in the **Add New : Seismic Definitions** dialog box, refer to Figure 6-31. Now, you will specify the structural weight for calculating the Base Shear. The options used for defining the structural weight are discussed next.

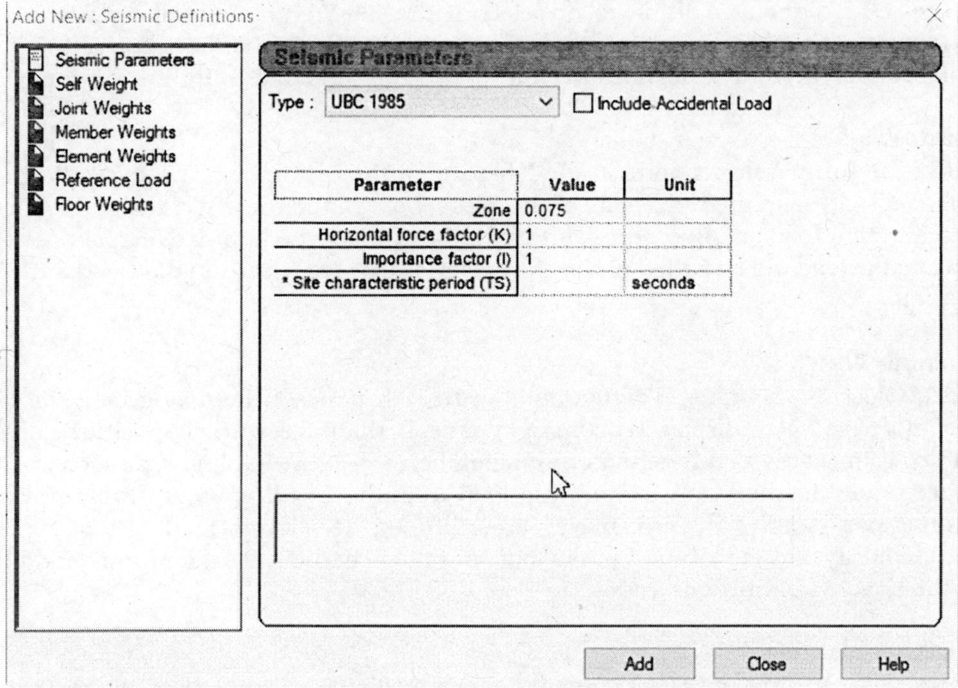

*Figure 6-30 The **Add New : Seismic Definitions** dialog box*

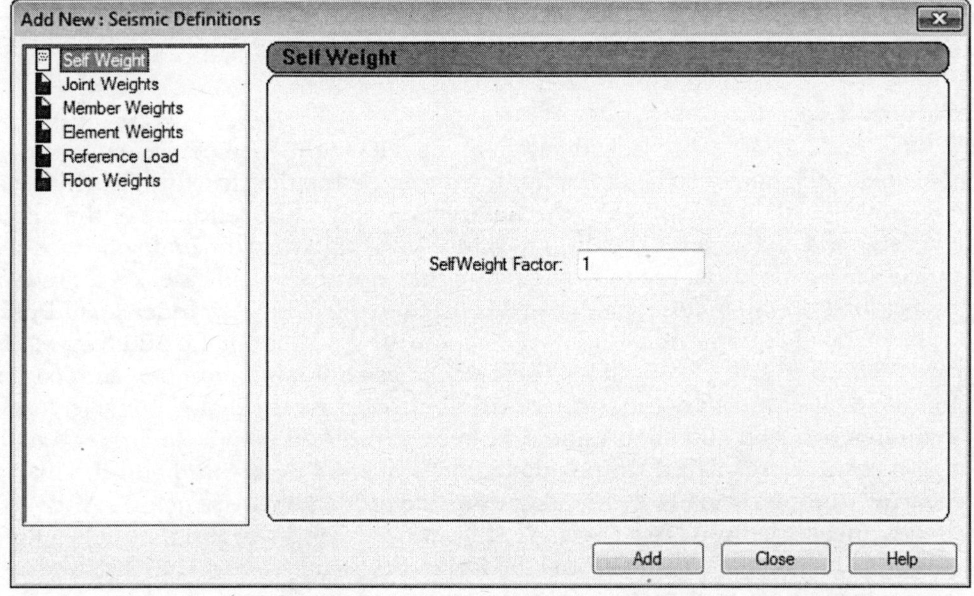

*Figure 6-31 The **Self Weight** page in the **Add New : Seismic Definition** dialog box*

Self Weight

In the **Self Weight** page displayed on selecting the **Self Weight** node, specify the self weight factor in the **SelfWeight Factor** edit box and choose the **Add** button; the self weight load will be added under the **Seismic Definition** node in the **Load & Definition** window.

Joint Weights

Select the **Joint Weights** node in the left pane of the dialog box; the **Joint Weights** page will be displayed in the right pane of the dialog box. In the **Joint Weights** page, specify the concentrated load acting on the joint in the **Joint Weight** edit box. Next, choose the **Add** button; the load will be added under the **Seismic Definition** node in the **Load & Definition** window.

Member Weights

Next, select the **Member Weights** node in the left pane of the dialog box; the **Member Weights** page will be displayed in the right pane. In this page, you will specify the distributed and concentrated weights acting on the member. Select the loading type such as **CON** for concentrated load or **UNI** for uniform load from the **Loading Type** drop-down list. The loading parameters will be displayed according to the selected loading type. Specify the load intensity and the location of the load and then choose the **Add** button to add the load in the **Load & Definition** window.

Element Weights

In case of floor slabs and other structural models which consists of plate elements, you need to define the element weight. To do so, select the **Element Weights** node in the left pane of the dialog box; the **Element Weights** page will be displayed in the right pane of the dialog box. Specify the pressure intensity in the **Pressure** edit box and choose the **Add** button; the load will be added under the **Seismic Definition** node in the **Load & Definition** window.

Reference Load

In seismic loading, instead of individually defining self weight, member weights, joint weights, and element weights for structural weight, you can define the structural weight by adding the reference load. To do so, select the **Reference Load** in the left pane of the dialog box; the **Reference Load** page will be displayed in the right pane of the dialog box, as shown in Figure 6-32. Now, you can see from the figure that a primary load case is required to add a reference load. To do so, close this dialog box first and select the **Reference Load Definitions** node in the **Load & Definition** window and choose the **Add** button; the **Add New : Reference Load Definitions** dialog box will be displayed. Specify the title, number, and loading type in this dialog box and after choosing the **Add** button, close the dialog box. Next, select the added reference load and choose the **Add** button; the **Add New : Reference Load Items** dialog box will be displayed. In this dialog box, you will define and add the loads which are similar to primary loads. Next, assign the added load to the structure. After assigning the loads, invoke the **Add New : Seismic Definitions** dialog box and then select **Reference Load** in the left pane of the dialog box; the **Reference Load** page will be displayed, as shown in Figure 6-33. Now, in this dialog box, select the reference load case from the **Available Load Cases** list box and choose the forward button to move it to the **Referenced Load** list box. Next, specify the required factor to be multiplied with the reference load in the **Factor** column. Select the direction from the **Along** drop-down list and choose the **Add** button to add the reference load. Next, close the dialog box.

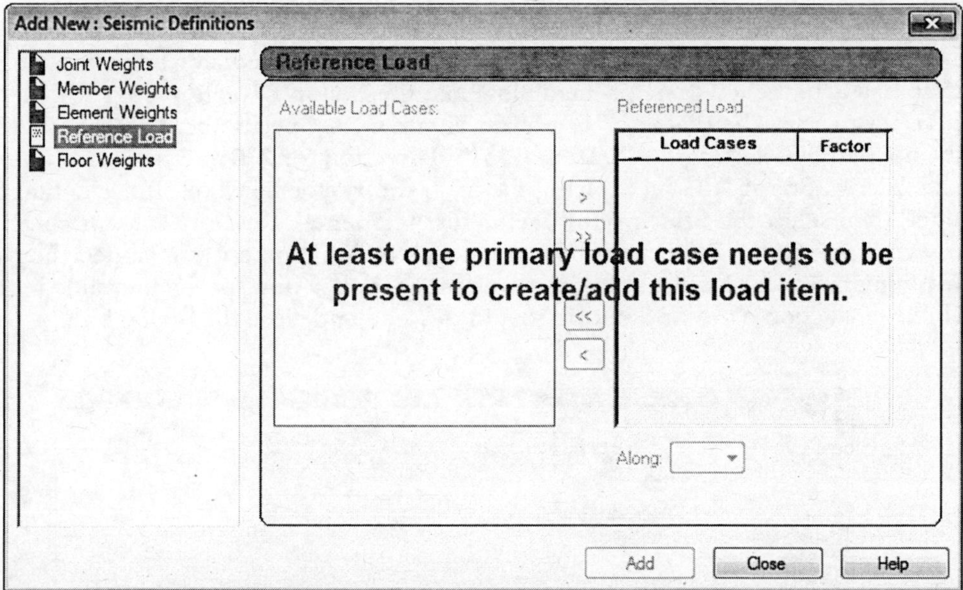

*Figure 6-32 The **Reference Load** page in the **Add New : Seismic Definitions** dialog box*

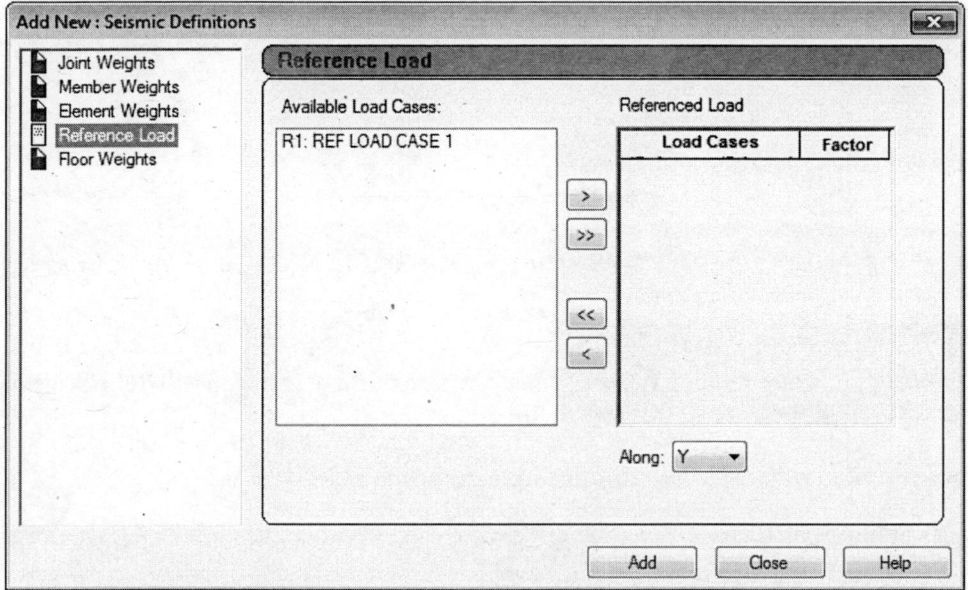

*Figure 6-33 The **Reference Load** page in the **Add New : Seismic Definitions** dialog box*

Floor Weights

You can define floor weights in case of a structure consisting of beams and columns instead of floor slab. To define floor weight, select the **Floor Weight** load option in the left pane of the dialog box; the **Floor Weights** page will be displayed in the right pane of the dialog box. Specify the value for load and the load location, as discussed in the **Floor Load** section. Choose the **Add** button to add the load in the **Load & Definition** window.

After defining seismic loads, you need to define the factor and global direction in which the load will be applied. To do so, invoke the **Add New : Load Items** dialog box and then select the **Seismic Loads** in the left pane of the dialog box; the **Factor_Direction** page will be displayed in the right pane of the dialog box, refer to Figure 6-34. Specify the direction in which load will be applied by selecting the **X Direction**, **Y Direction**, or **Z Direction** radio button in the **Direction** area. Specify the multiplying factor in the **Factor** edit box. If accidental torsion is included then select the **Multiplying factor for Accidental Torsion Moment** check box and specify the value in the **Factor** edit box. If natural torsion moment is included then select the **Multiplying factor for Natural Torsion Moment** check box and specify the value in the **Factor** edit box. Next, choose the **Add** button to add the load and close the dialog box.

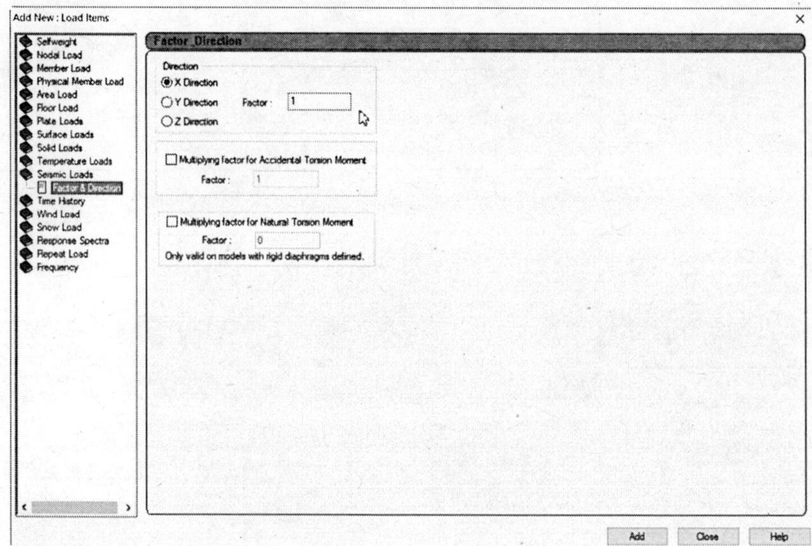

***Figure 6-34** The **Factor_Direction** page in the **Add New : Load Items** dialog box*

Example 4

In this example, you will open the *c06_staad_v8i_ex2.std* file. Next, you will define seismic loading as per IBC 2006 for a space frame structure.

Steps are required to complete this example are given below.

Step 1: Open the file *c06_staad_v8i_ex2.std* in STAAD.Pro; the model is displayed in the main window, as shown in Figure 6-35.

Step 2: In the **General** tab, choose the **Load & Definition** page; the **Load & Definition** window is displayed.

Step 3: Expand the **Definitions** node in the **Load & Definition** window and select the **Seismic Definitions** option. Next, choose the **Add** button; the **Add New : Seismic Definitions** dialog box is displayed.

Step 4: In the right pane of the dialog box, select the **IBC 2006** code from the **Type** drop-down list.

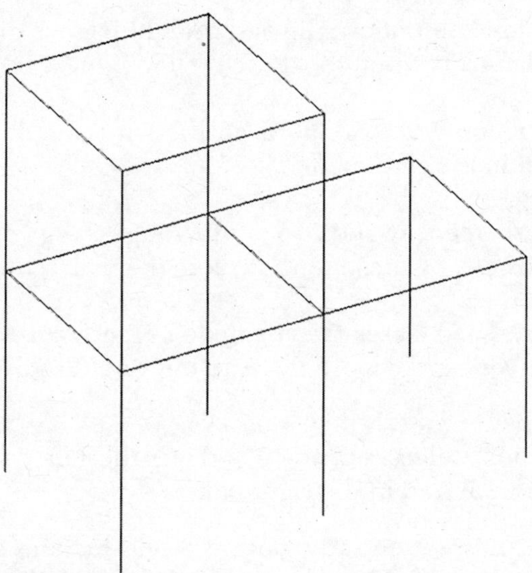

Figure 6-35 Model displayed in the main window

Step 5: Select the **Include Accidental Load** check box to calculate the accidental torsion component as per the IBC 2006 code.

Step 6: Specify **46201** in the **Value** column of the **Zip Code, 10** in the **Value** column of **TL, 1.2** in the **Value** column of $\mathbf{F_a}$, and **1.7** in the **Value** column of $\mathbf{F_v}$, refer to Figure 6-36. After specifying the parameters, choose the **Add** button to add the load definition.

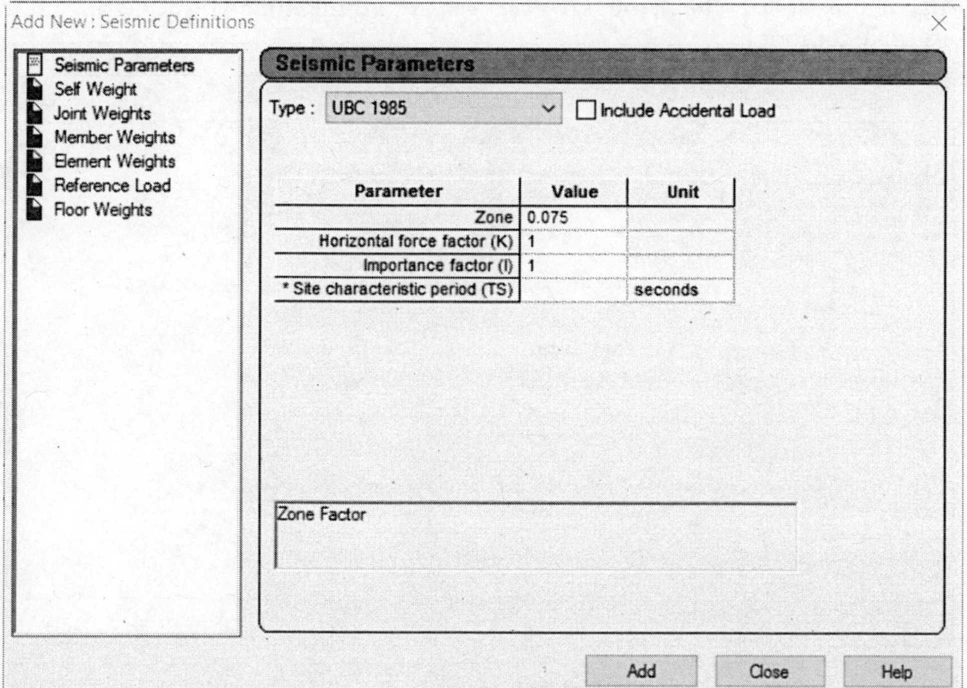

*Figure 6-36 The **Seismic Parameters** page in the **Add New : Seismic Definitions** dialog box*

Step 7: After adding the load definition, the **Self Weight** page is displayed in the left pane of the dialog box. Choose the **Add** button to add the self weight.

Step 8: Next, select the **Floor Weights** option in the left pane of the dialog box; the **Floor Weights** page is displayed in the right pane.

Step 9: Specify the pressure intensity and X, Y, and Z ranges, as given in Figures 6-37 and 6-38. Add both the floor weights one by one and then close the dialog box.

Step 10: Next, expand the **Load Cases Details** node in the **Load & Definition** window, select the **FLOOR LOAD** sub node, and choose the **Add** button; the **Add New : Load Items** dialog box is displayed.

Step 11: In this dialog box, select **Seismic Loads** in the left pane of the dialog box; the **Factor_Direction** page is displayed in the right pane.

Step 12: Ensure that the **X Direction** radio button is selected and specify **1** in the **Factor** edit box in **Direction** area. Choose the **Add** button to add the loading and close the dialog box. The **IBC LOAD X 1** is added under the **FLOOR LOAD** sub node in the **Load & Definition** window.

Step 13: Now, choose the **STAAD Editor** button from the toolbar; the **STAAD Editor** window is displayed. In this window, select the **UBC LOAD X 1** command. Cut and paste this command below the **LOAD 1 LOADTYPE None TITLE FLOOR LOAD** command. The commands should be in the sequence given next. Choose the **Save** button and close the **STAAD Editor** window.

Step 14: Choose the **Save As** option from the **File** menu; the **Save As** dialog box is displayed. In this dialog box, specify the name *c06_staad_v8i_ex4* in the **File name** edit box and save it at an appropriate location.

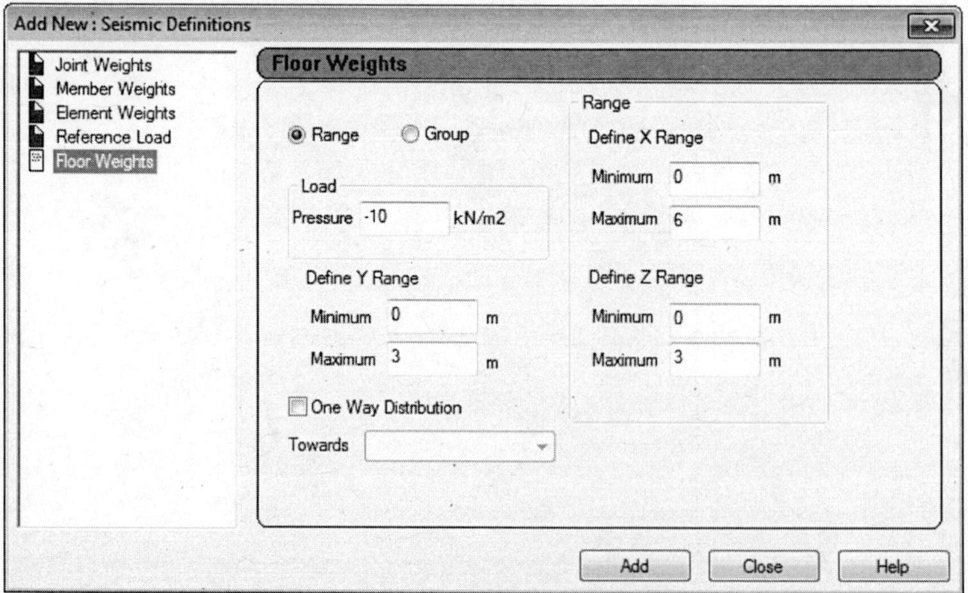

Figure 6-37 *Values for the floor weight 1*

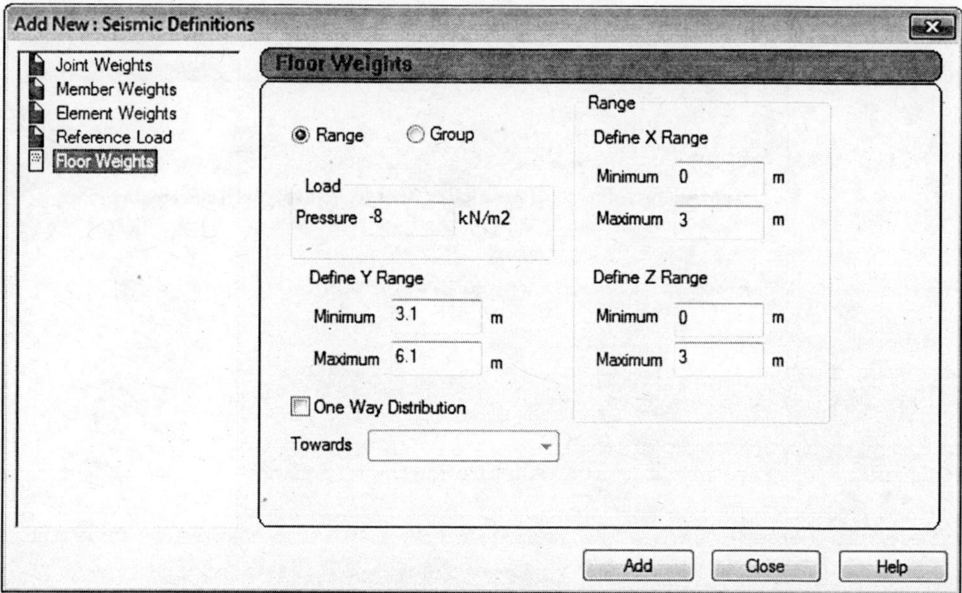

Figure 6-38 *Values for floor weight 2*

Time History Load

Time history load provides for linear or non-linear analysis of dynamic structural response under loading which may vary according to the time. To use this type of load, select the **General** page, then select the **Loads & Definition** page; the **Load & Definition** window will be displayed. Select the **Load Cases Details** node in the list box, next choose the **Add** button; the **Add New: Load Cases** dialog box will be displayed. In the **Primary** page, specify the load case number in the **Number** edit box. Select load type from the **Load Type** drop down list. Add title for the load case in the **Title** text box for reference. Select the **Title** text box for reference. Choose add button to add the load case and close the dialog box. Select the load case you add to the list box of the Load & Definition window, and choose Add button; the Add New : Load Items dialog box will be displayed, select the **Time History** node from the left pane of the **Add New : Load Items** dialog box; the **Time History** page will be displayed in the right pane, as shown in Figure 6-39. The options in this page are inactive. To activate the options, you need to define the time history loading, which is discussed next.

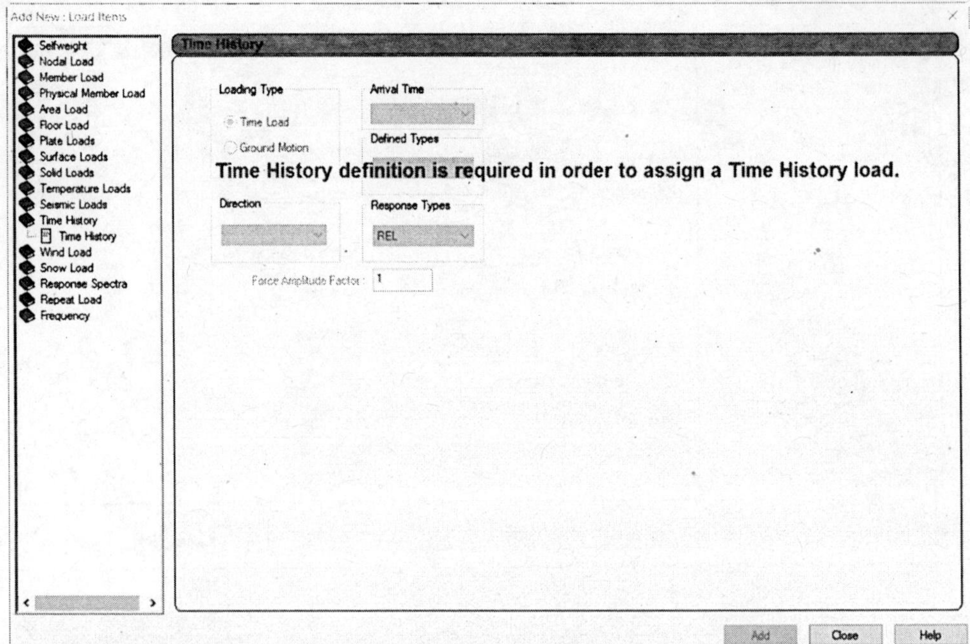

*Figure 6-39 The **Time History** page in the **Add New : Load Items** dialog box*

Defining Time History Load

To define time history load in the **Load & Definition** window, expand the **Definitions** node. Next, select the **Time History Definitions** sub-node and choose the **Add** button; the **Add New : Time History Definitions** dialog box will be displayed, as shown in Figure 6-40. The options in this dialog box are discussed next.

Type

In the **Type** edit box, you will specify the number of the defined load type.

Loading Type

In the **Loading Type** area, you will define the type of function being used for defining time history loading by selecting the **Acceleration**, **Force**, or **Moment** radio button. On selecting any of the radio buttons, the selected options will be displayed in the table below. For example, if you have selected the **Force** radio button then the **Define Time vs Force** table will be displayed. Select the **Save** check box to create an external input file with the *.tmh* extension. This file will contain the history of displacements of each node of the structure.

Function Options

In the **Function Options** area, there are three types of functions. The options displayed in the **Loading Type** area depend on the type of function selected in this area. These functions are discussed next.

Define Time vs Acceleration: This radio button is selected by default in the **Function Options** area. In this function type, you need to specify the values for the time and corresponding acceleration, force, or moment. The time history forcing function will be plotted as per specified values.

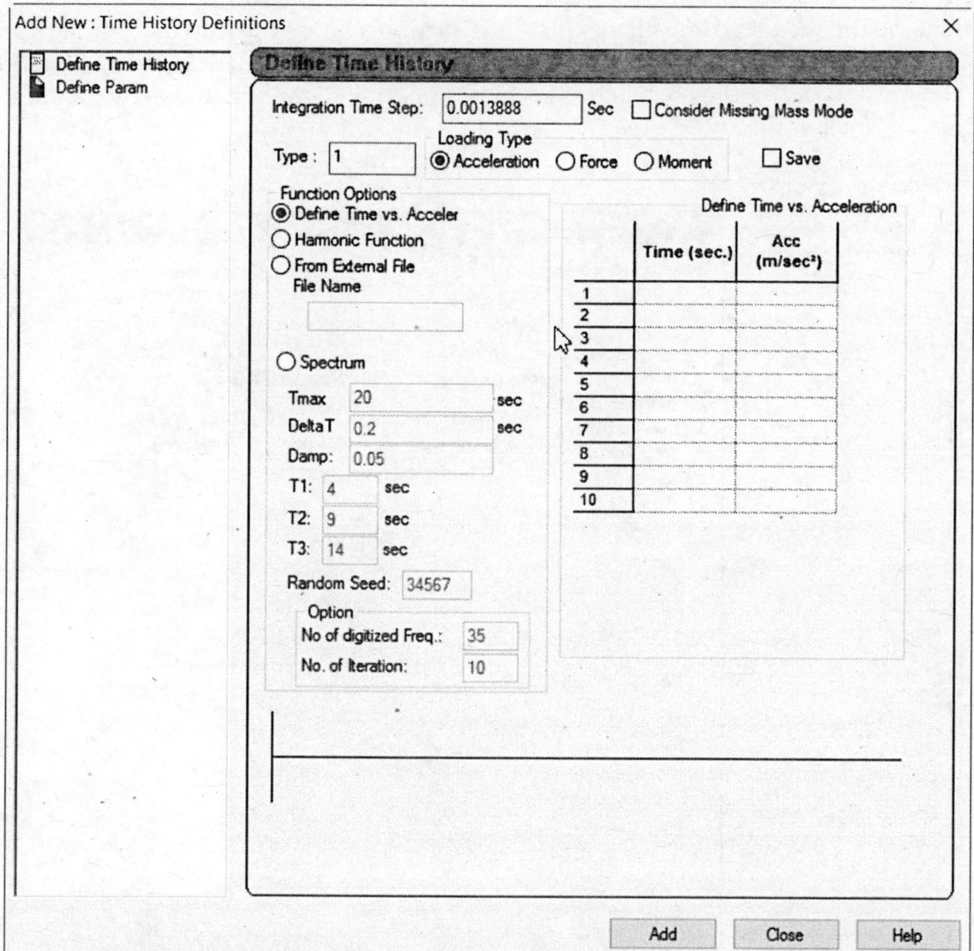

Figure 6-40 The ***Define Time History*** *page in the* ***Add New : Time History Definitions*** *dialog box*

Harmonic Function: Harmonic function is used to define time history harmonic function. When you select this radio button, the related options will be displayed in the **Loading Type** area, as shown in Figure 6-41. In the **Others** area, you will define the sine or cosine function by selecting the **SINE** or **COSINE** radio button. Specify the frequency in cycles per second in the edit box below the **Frequency** radio button. You can also specify the revolutions per minute in the edit box below the **RPM** radio button. Similarly, specify the values for the **Amplitude**, **Phase**, **Cycles**, **Step**, and **SubDiv** in their corresponding edit boxes.

From External File: Select the **From External File** radio button to load an external file containing the time history data. On selecting this radio button, the **File Name** edit box will be activated. In this edit box, specify the file name which should not be more than 8 characters. The file should be placed in the same directory.

After defining the required time history loading function, choose the **Add** button; the definition will be added under the **Time History Definitions** node in the **Load & Definitions** window. Next, you need to define the parameters such as time step, damping, and arrival time for time history load, which is discussed next.

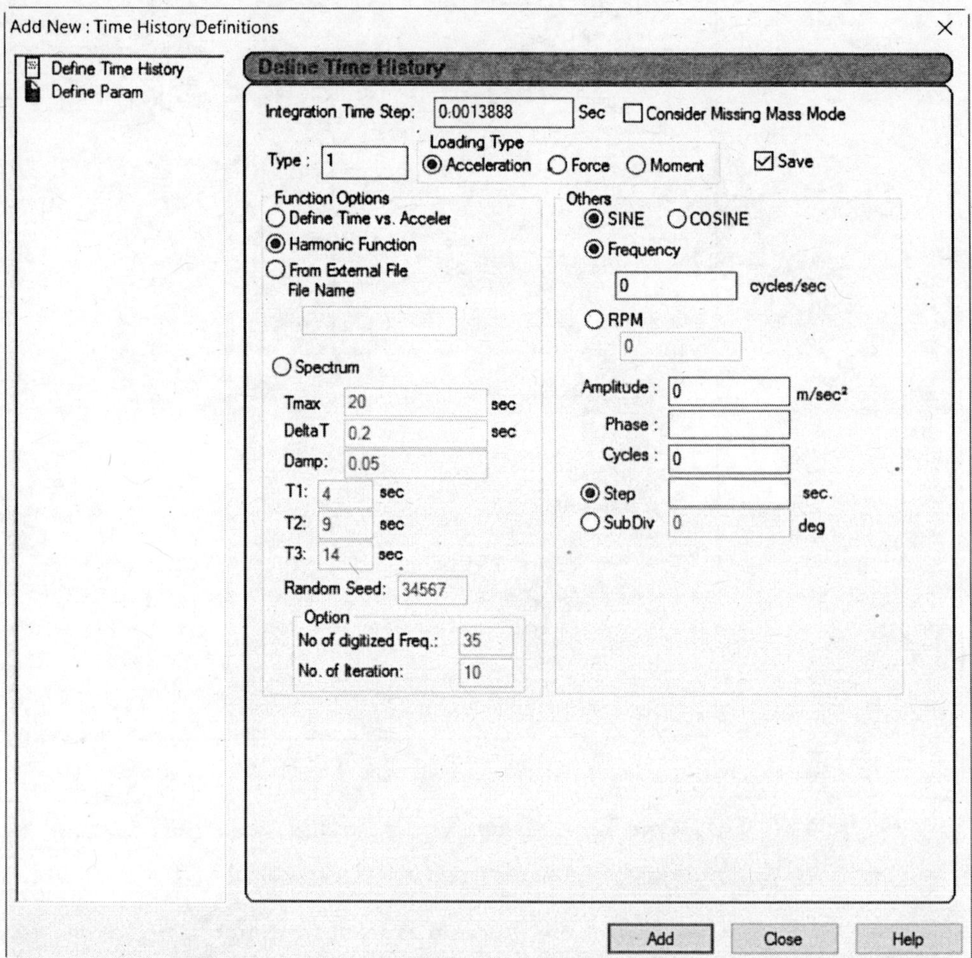

Figure 6-41 *Options displayed on selecting the* ***Harmonic Function*** *radio button*

Defining Parameters

In the left pane of the **Add New : Time History Definitions** dialog box, select the **Define Param** option; the **Define Param** page will be displayed in the right pane of the dialog box, as shown in Figure 6-42. In this page, you will define the time step, damping, and arrival time for time history load, which is discussed next.

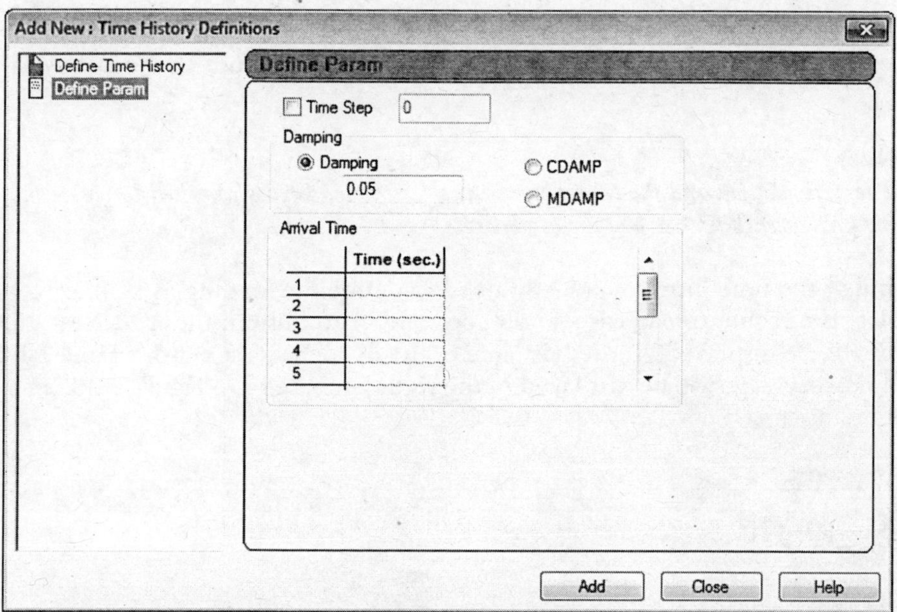

*Figure 6-42 The **Define Param** page in the **Add New : Time History Definitions** dialog box*

Time Step

To specify the value for solution time step to be used in step by step integration of uncoupled equations, first select the **Time Step** check box and then specify a value in the edit box next to it.

Damping

In the **Damping** area, you will specify the damping ratio which will be applied to all the modes. To specify a single modal damping ratio, select the **Damping** radio button, if it is not selected by default. Next, specify a value in the edit box below the **Damping** radio button. The default value in this edit box is **0.05**.

If the damping ratio is already defined in the type of material used in the structure, then, you can use that value for the time history analysis. In such a case, you need to select the **CDAMP** radio button.

You can also use the individual damping ratios for individual modes. To do so, first you need to define the individual damping ratios. Individual damping ratios can be defined in the **Modal Damping** dialog box. This dialog box can be invoked by choosing the **Define Damping for Dynamics** option from the **Commands** menu. After defining the values, you need to select the **MDAMP** radio button in the **Define Param** page of the **Add New : Time History Definitions** dialog box.

Arrival Time

In this area, you will specify the possible arrival time of various dynamic load types in the **Time (sec.)** column. The arrival time is the time at which the load type will begin to act at the joint or at the base of the structure.

After defining the required time history loading function, choose the **Add** button; the defined parameters will be added under the **Time History Definitions** node in the **Load & Definitions** window.

Note

The arrival time and the time-force values for the load types are used to create the load vector required at each time step of the analysis.

After defining the time history load, you need to define the loading as primary load type. To do so, select the required load case, and choose the **Add** button; the **Add New : Load Items** dialog box will be displayed. In the left pane of the dialog box, select the **Time History** node; the **Time History** page will be displayed in the right pane, refer to Figure 6-43. The options in this page are discussed next.

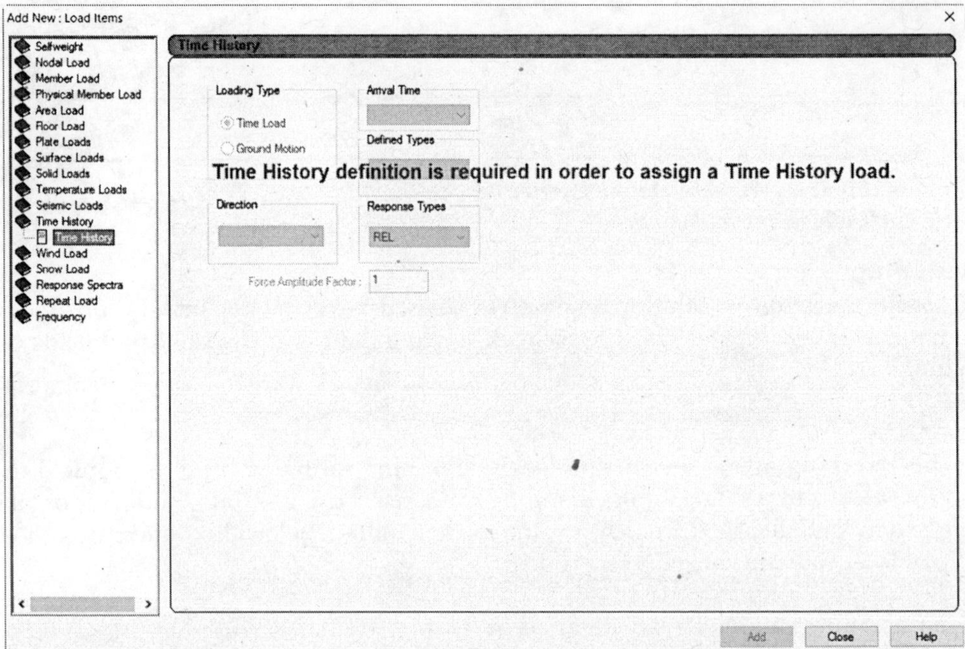

***Figure 6-43** The **Time History** page in the **Add New : Load Items** dialog box*

In the **Loading Type** area, select the **Time Load** radio button to apply the time history load to the joints in the structure. Select the **Ground Motion** radio button to apply the load at the base of the structure. From the drop-down list in the **Arrival Time** area, you need to select the arrival time at which the load begins to act. Select the required time from the drop-down list. In the **Direction** area, specify the global direction in which the load will be applied by selecting an appropriate option from the drop-down list. In the **Defined Types** area, select the previously defined type number from the drop-down list. Specify a value in the **Force Amplitude Factor** edit box. This value will be multiplied with the previously defined force or acceleration values.

Wind Load

Wind load allows you to define the parameters for automatic generation of wind load as joint load on the structure. To define this load, select the **Wind Load** node from the left pane of the **Add New : Load Items** dialog box; the **Wind Load** page will be displayed in the right pane, as shown in Figure 6-44. The options in this page are inactive. To activate the options, you need to define the wind load. The process to do so is discussed next.

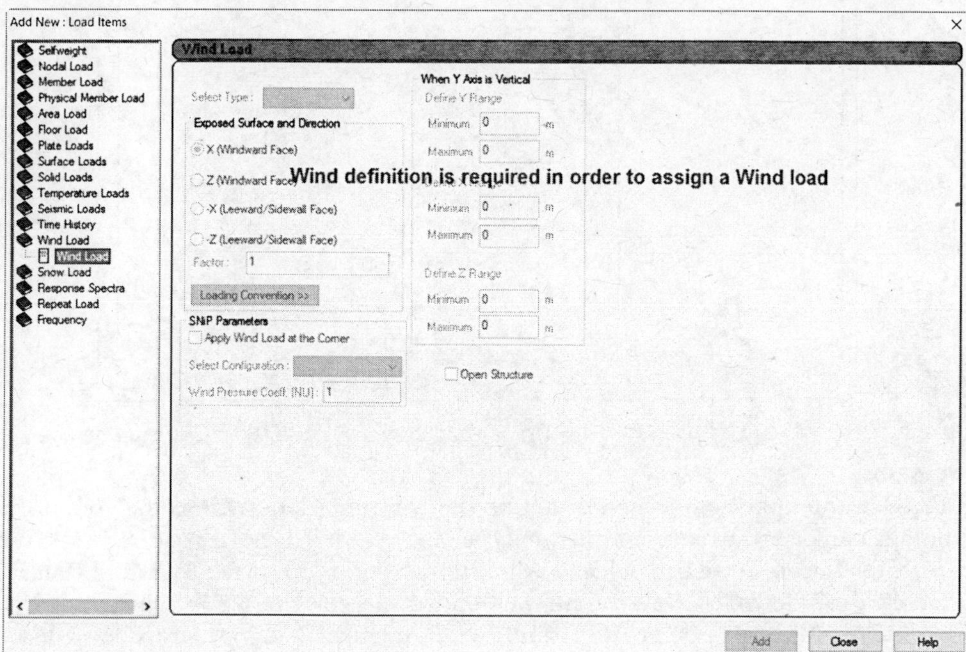

*Figure 6-44 The **Wind Load** page in the **Add New : Load Items** dialog box*

Defining Wind Load

To define wind load, expand the **Definition** node in the **Load & Definition** window and then select the **Wind Definitions** option. Next, choose the **Add** button; the **Add New : Wind Definitions** dialog box will be displayed. In this dialog box, the wind load type number and the comments will be specified by default in the **Type No** and **Comments** edit boxes, respectively. Choose the **Add** button to add the type and close the dialog box; **TYPE 1 : WIND 1** will be added under the **Wind Definitions** option in the **Load & Definition** window. Next, select the **TYPE 1 WIND 1** definition and choose the **Add** button; the **Intensity** page in the **Add New : Wind Definitions** dialog box will be displayed, as shown in Figure 6-45. In this page, the **Intensity vs. Height** table is displayed where you need to enter the values for the wind intensity and the height above the ground. You can also calculate these values as per ASCE - 7. To do so, choose the **Calculate as per ASCE - 7** button; the **Common** page in the **ASCE - 7 : Wind Load** dialog box will be displayed, as shown in Figure 6-46. There are three pages displayed on choosing the options available in the left pane of the dialog box. The options in these pages are used to define the wind intensity. These pages are discussed next.

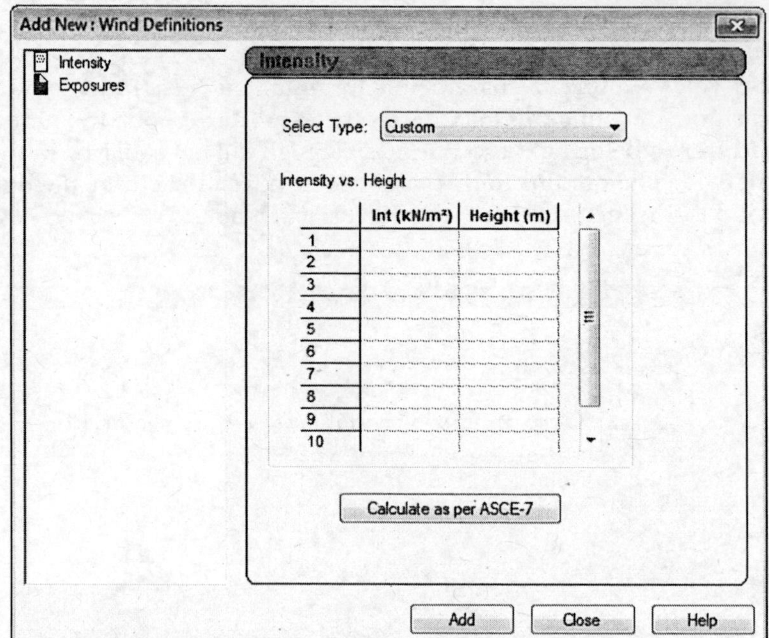

Figure 6-45 The ***Intensity*** *page in the* ***Add New : Wind Definitions*** *dialog box*

Common

In the **Common** page, you need to define the common data such as the code to be used, building category, wind speed, structure type, and so on. Select the required code type from the **ASCE - 7** drop-down list. Select the building category from the **Building Classification Category** drop-down list. Specify the wind speed value in the **Basic Wind Speed** edit box. Select the wind exposure category from the **Exposure Category** drop-down list. Specify the type of structure such as chimney, tanks, tower, and so on by selecting the appropriate option from the **Structure Type** drop-down list. If there are changes in the topography such as hills or escarpments, then select the **Yes** radio button for considering the wind speed over hills or escarpments. The options under the radio button become active. Next, select the type of the hill or the escarpment from the **Type of Hill or Escarpment** drop-down list. Specify the height of hill or escarpment in the **Height of Hill or Escarpment (H)** edit box. Specify the distance upwind of crest in the **Distance upwind of crest (Lh)** edit box. Similarly, specify the distance from the crest to the building site in the **Distance from the crest to the building (x)** edit box. After specifying all the parameters, choose the **OK** button; the intensity and height values will be displayed in the **Intensity** page of the **Add New : Wind Definitions** dialog box.

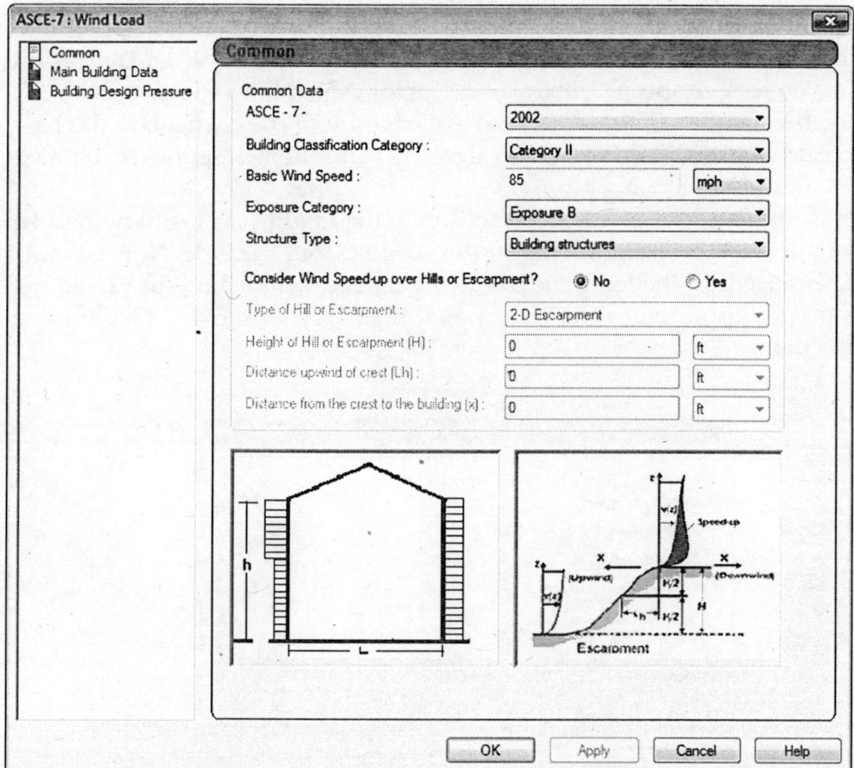

*Figure 6-46 The **ASCE - 7 : Wind Load** dialog box*

Main Building Data

The intensity vs height values can also be defined using the options available in the **Main Building Data** page. To do so, choose the **Main Building Data** node in the left pane of the **ASCE - 7 : Wind Load** dialog box; the **Main Building Data** page will be displayed. In this page, you will specify the building height, building length along the direction of the wind, building length normal to the direction of wind, building natural frequency, damping ratio, and type of enclosure. These parameters will calculate the wind intensity according to the height. After specifying all the parameters, choose the **OK** button; the intensity and height values will be displayed in the **Intensity** page of the **Add New : Wind Definitions** dialog box.

Building Design Pressure

The options in this page are used to calculate the intensity vs height values. To do so, choose the **Building Design Pressure** node in the left pane of the **ASCE - 7 : Wind Load** dialog box; the **Building Design Pressure** page will be displayed in the right pane. To calculate the design wind pressure for the windward, leeward, or sidewall, select the corresponding radio button from the **Generate Wind Load On Wall** area. To include the gust effect factor, external pressure coefficient, and internal pressure coefficient, select the ***G***, C_p, and GC_{pi} check boxes and then specify the value in the corresponding edit boxes. Next, choose the **OK** button; the wind intensity at various heights will be displayed in the **Intensity** page of the **Add New : Wind Definitions** dialog box.

Next, choose the **Add** button to add the load definition in the **Load & Definition** window. On doing so, the **Exposures** page will be displayed in the **Add New : Wind Definitions** dialog box. In this page, you have to specify the exposure factor value in the **Factor** edit box. This exposure value is the influence area of the wind load associated with the particular joints in the structure. Choose the **Add** button to add the exposure factor and then close the dialog box.

After defining the wind load, you need to define the loading as primary load type. To do so, select the required load case and choose the **Add** button; the **Add New : Load Items** dialog box will be displayed. In the left pane of the dialog box, select the **Wind Load** node; the **Wind Load** page will be displayed in the right pane, refer to Figure 6-47. The options in this page are discussed next.

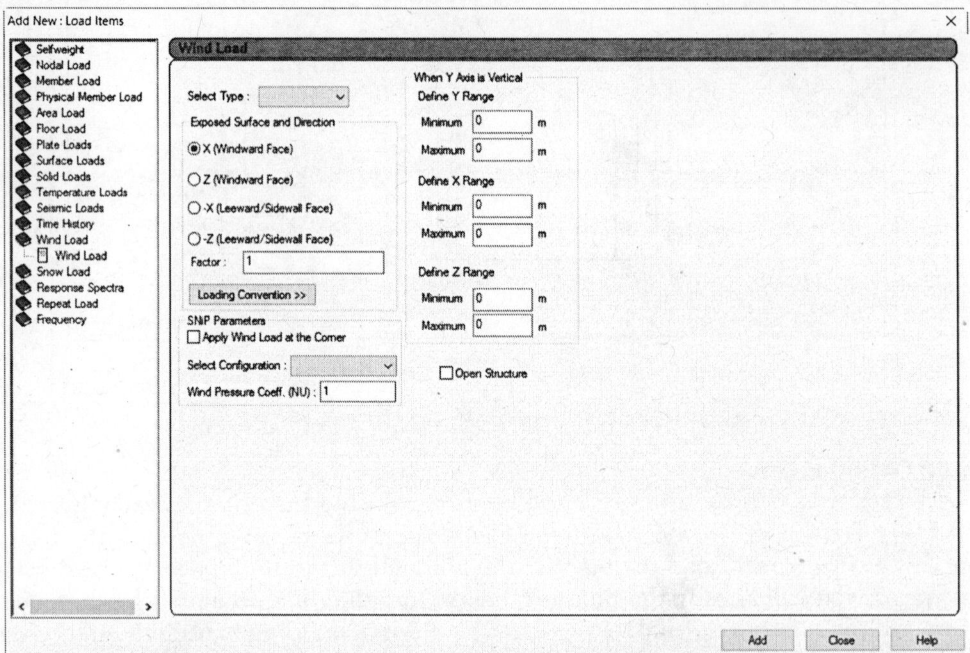

***Figure 6-47** The **Wind Load** page in the **Add New : Load Items** dialog box*

Select the previously defined wind load type in the **Select Type** drop-down list. In the **Direction** area, to specify the global direction in which the wind load is to be applied, select the **X**, **Z**, **-X**, or **-Z** radio button. To specify the multiplying factor to calculate the wind loads in the **Factor** edit box. In the **When Y Axis is Vertical** area, you will define the X, Y, and Z range of the structure. To generate wind load on open structures such as transmission towers, bridges, or any other open structure, select the **Open Structure** check box. By default, the structures are considered as closed structure. Next, choose the **Add** button; the load will be added under the selected load case and then close the **Add New : Load Items** dialog box. Now, click on the added load; the wind load will be displayed at the joints in the structure, refer to Figure 6-48.

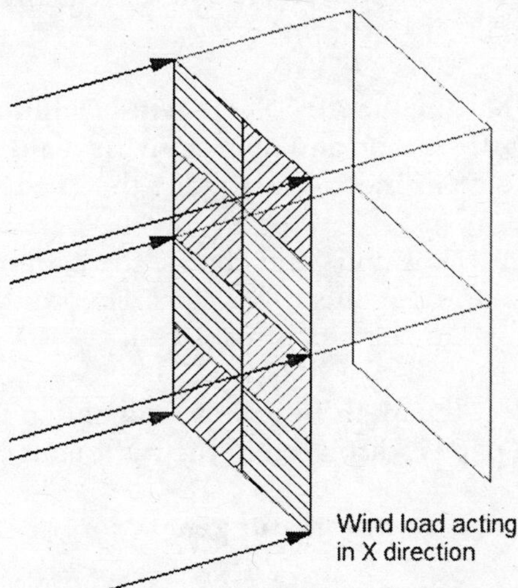

Figure 6-48 *Wind load acting in the X direction*

Example 5

In this example, you will open the *c06_staad_v8i_ex5_start.std* file. Next, you will define wind loads for a space frame structure as per ASCE 7-2002.

The following steps are required to complete this example:

Step 1: Open the file *c06_staad_v8i_ex5_start.std* in STAAD.Pro, press Shift+N; the model is displayed in the main window, as shown in Figure 6-49.

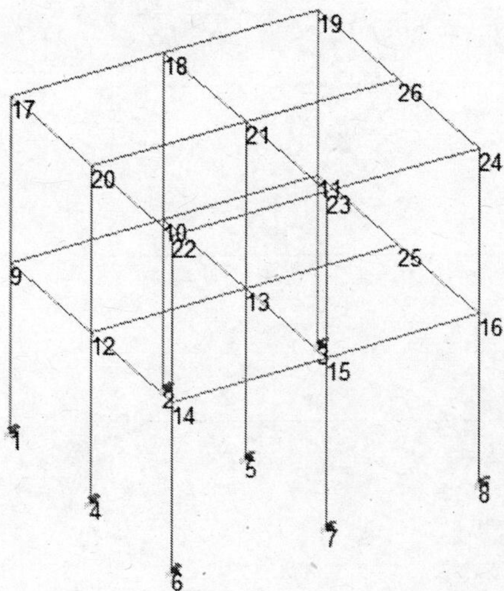

Figure 6-49 *Model displayed in the Main Window*

Step 2: Choose the **General** tab and open the **Load & Definition** page; the **Load & Definition** window is displayed. In the **Load & Definition** window, expand the **Definitions** node and select the **Wind Definitions** sub node.

Step 3: Next, choose the **Add** button; the **Add New : Wind Definitions** dialog box is displayed. In this dialog box, choose the **Add** button and then close the dialog box; the **TYPE 1 : WIND 1** node is added under the **Wind Definitions** sub node in the **Load & Definition** window.

Step 4: Select the **TYPE 1 : WIND 1** node and choose the **Add** button; the **Add New : Wind Definitions** dialog box is displayed. In this dialog box, choose the **Calculate as per ASCE-7** button; the **ASCE 7 : Wind Load** dialog box is displayed.

Step 5: In this dialog box, select the **Main Building Data** option in the left pane of the dialog box; the **Main Building Data** page is displayed in the right pane of the dialog box.

Step 6: Specify the parameters for automatic generation of the wind load, as shown in Figure 6-50.

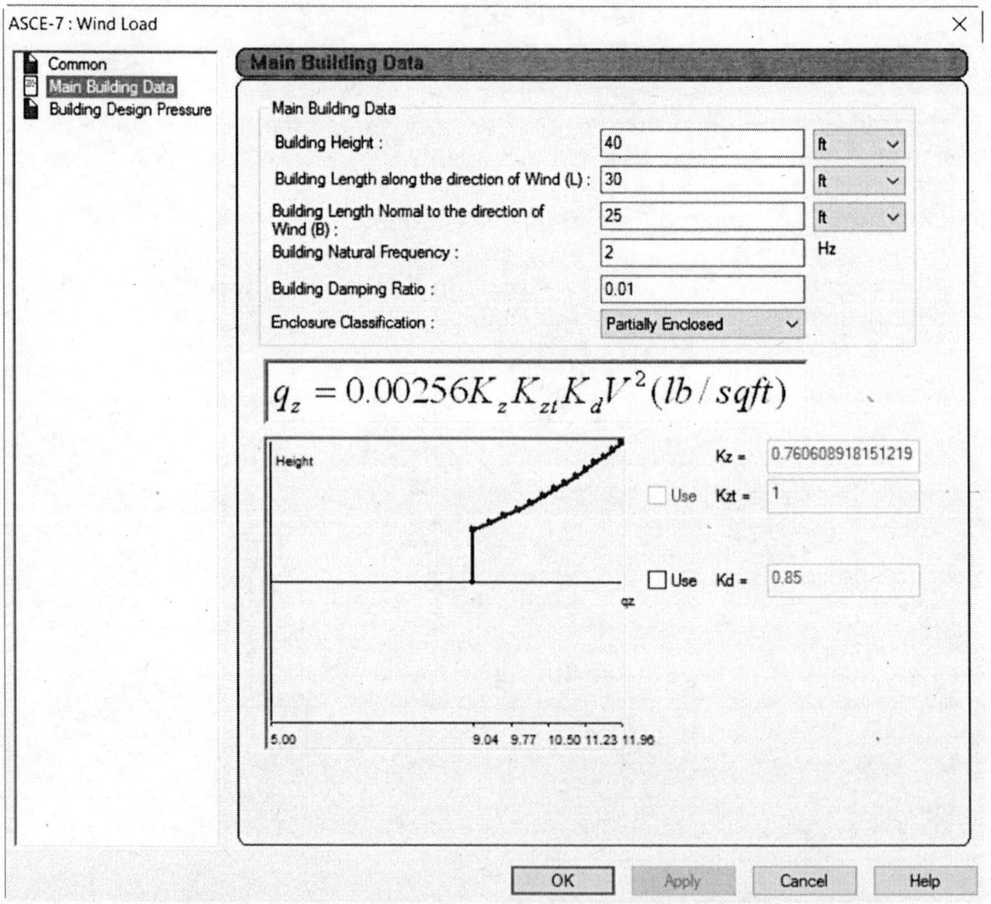

Figure 6-50 Values specified in the ***Main Building Data*** *page*

Step 7: Choose the **Apply** and then **OK** button; the intensity vs height data is added to the **Intensity** previous page of the **Add New : Wind Definitions** dialog box, as shown in Figure 6-51.

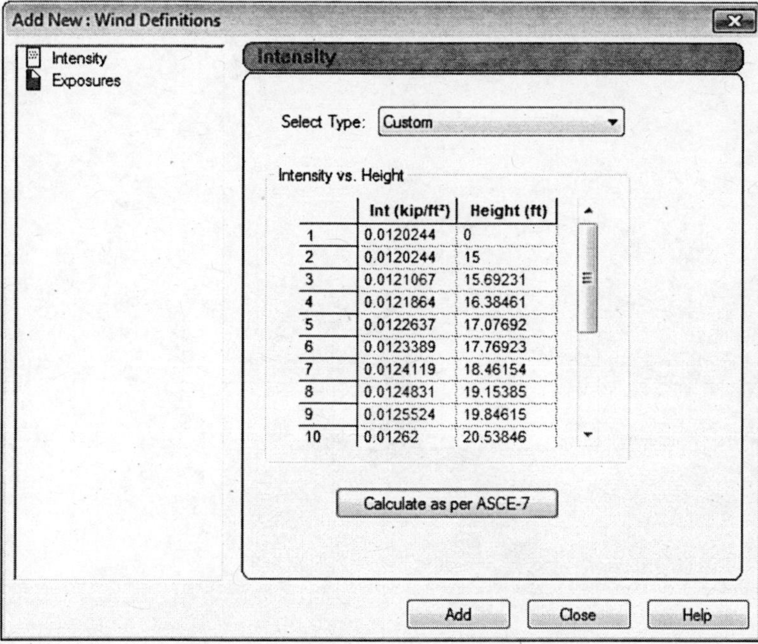

	Int (kip/ft²)	Height (ft)
1	0.0120244	0
2	0.0120244	15
3	0.0121067	15.69231
4	0.0121864	16.38461
5	0.0122637	17.07692
6	0.0123389	17.76923
7	0.0124119	18.46154
8	0.0124831	19.15385
9	0.0125524	19.84615
10	0.01262	20.53846

Figure 6-51 *Values specified in the **Intensity vs. Height** table in the **Intensity** page*

Step 8: Choose the **Add** button; the **Exposures** page is displayed. Specify the value **0.75** in the **Factor** edit box and then choose the **Add** button.

Step 9: Again, specify the value **0.8** in the **Factor** edit box and choose the **Add** button to add the exposure factor. Next, close the **Add New : Wind Definitions** dialog box.

Step 10: Assign the exposure factor 0.75 to the nodes 1, 4, 6, 9, 12, and 14 and assign exposure factor 0.8 to the nodes 17, 20, and 22 using the **Use Cursor to Assign** method in the main window.

Step 11: Select the **Load Cases Details** node in the **Load & Definition** window and choose the **Add** button; the **Add New : Load Cases** dialog box is displayed.

Step 12: Enter the text **WL +X** in the **Title** text box and select **Wind** from the **Loading Type** drop-down list. Next, choose the **Add** button to add the load case and close the dialog box.

Step 13: Select the **WL +X** load case available under the **Load Cases Details** node and then choose the **Add** button; the **Add New : Load Items** dialog box is displayed.

Step 14: Select the **Wind Load** option in the left pane of the dialog box; the **Wind Load** page is displayed in the right pane of the dialog box.

Step 15: In this page, ensure that **1 : Regular** is selected in the **Select Type** drop-down list and **X (Windward Face)** radio button is selected in the **Direction** area. Specify **1.1** in the **Factor** edit box.

Step 16: Choose the **Add** button; the wind load is added under the **WL +X** load case in the **Load & Definition** window. Next, close the **Add New : Load Items** dialog box.

Step 17: Select the added load under the **WL +X** load case; the wind load is applied as joint load on the left wall of the structure, as shown in Figure 6-52.

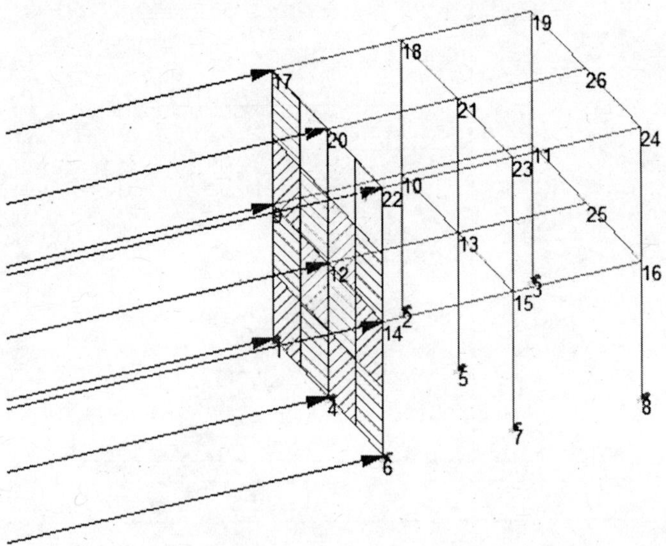

Figure 6-52 *Wind load applied on the left wall of the structure*

Step 18: Choose the **Save As** option from the **File** menu; the **Save As** dialog box is displayed. In this dialog box, specify the name *c06_staad_v8i_ex5* in the **File name** edit box and save it at an appropriate location.

Snow Load

Snow load allows you to generate snow loading on the structure as per the code ASCE-7-2002. To generate snow load, select the **Snow Load** node in the left pane of the **Add New : Load Items** dialog box; the **Snow Load** page will be displayed in the right pane of the dialog box, refer to Figure 6-53. The options in this page are inactive. To activate these options, first you need to define the snow load, which is discussed next.

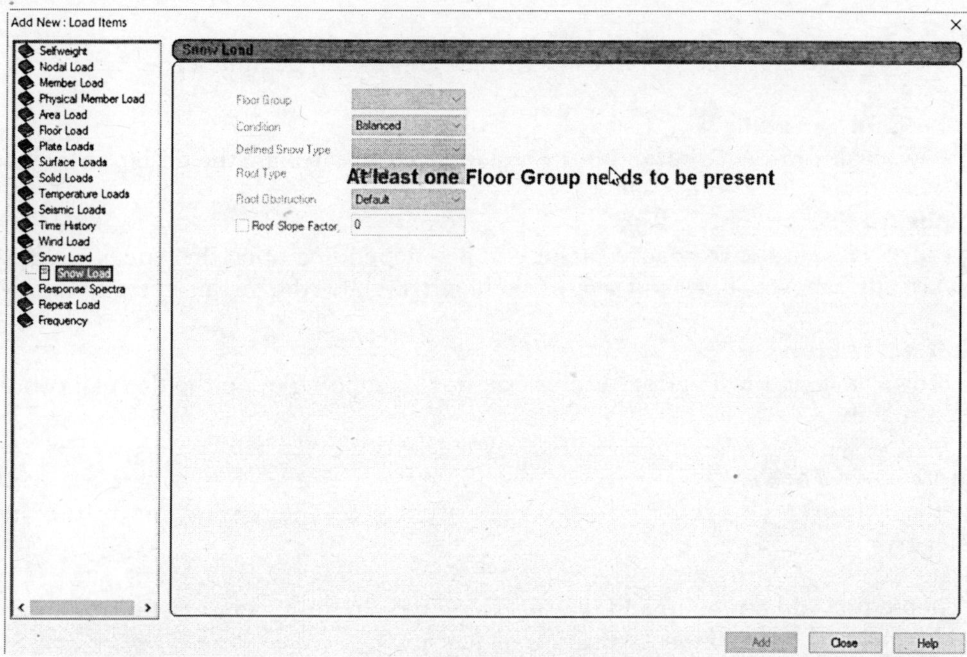

*Figure 6-53 The **Snow Load** page in the **Add New : Load Items** dialog box*

Defining Snow Load

To define snow load, expand the **Definition** node in the **Load & Definition** window and then select the **Snow Definition** option and choose the **Add** button; the **Add New : Snow Definition** dialog box will be displayed, as shown in Figure 6-54. The options in this dialog box are discussed next.

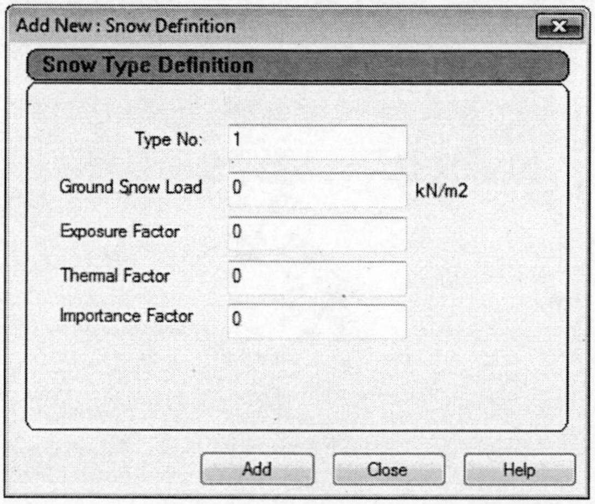

Add New : Snow Definition
Snow Type Definition
Type No: 1
Ground Snow Load 0 kN/m2
Exposure Factor 0
Thermal Factor 0
Importance Factor 0
Add Close Help

*Figure 6-54 The **Add New : Snow Definition** dialog box*

Type No
In the **Type No** edit box, you will specify the snow load type number.

Ground Snow Load
Specify a value in the **Ground Snow Load** edit box to calculate the design snow load.

Exposure Factor
Specify a value in the **Exposure Factor** edit box depending upon the type of exposure such as partially exposed, fully exposed, or sheltered and also the terrain category.

Thermal Factor
Specify a value in the **Thermal Factor** edit box depending upon the thermal condition of the structure.

Importance Factor
In the **Importance Factor** edit box, specify a value depending upon the structure category.

Next, choose the **Add** button to add the snow load type in the **Load & Definition** window and then close the **Add New : Snow Definition** dialog box.

Note

Before defining snow load as primary load, you need to create floor groups. The process to do so has been discussed earlier in this chapter.

After defining the snow load, you need to define it as primary load. To do so, select the required load case under the **Load Cases Details** in the **Load & Definition** window, and choose the **Add** button; the **Add New : Load Items** dialog box will be displayed. In the left pane of the dialog box, select the **Snow Load** option; the **Snow Load** page will be displayed in the right pane, refer to Figure 6-55. The options in this page are discussed next.

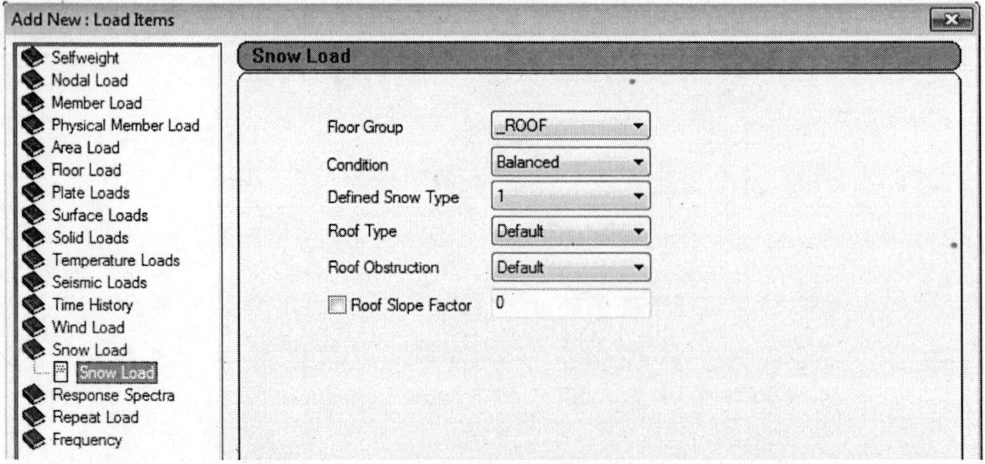

***Figure 6-55** The **Snow Load** page in the **Add New : Load Items** dialog box*

Select the floor group on which the snow load will be applied from the **Floor Group** drop-down list. Here, make sure that the members on which loading will be applied are defined as floor groups. Select the desired option from the **Condition** drop-down list. Select the previously defined load type number from the **Defined Snow Type** drop-down list. Specify the roof type such as mono, hipped, or gable by selecting an appropriate option from the **Roof Type** drop-down list. Select an option for the obstructed or unobstructed roof from the **Roof Obstruction** drop-down list. For sloped roofs, select the **Roof Slope Factor** check box and then specify the slope factor in the edit box next to the check box. Next, choose the **Add** button; the snow loads will be added under the selected load case and it will be automatically assigned to the structure.

Note

You can refer to ASCE 7-2002 code of standard for parameters required for defining the snow load.

Response Spectra

In the response spectrum method, you can analyze a structure dynamically. In this method, the dynamic response of a structure is calculated on the basis of the natural response of individual mode of vibration. The resultant is the summation of responses of each individual mode of vibration. To define response spectra loading, select the required load case in the **Load & Definition** window and then choose the **Add** button; the **Add New : Load Items** dialog box will be displayed. In this dialog box, select the **Response Spectra** node in the left pane; the **Response Spectrum** page will be displayed in the right pane of the dialog box, refer to Figure 6-56. The options displayed in this page are discussed next.

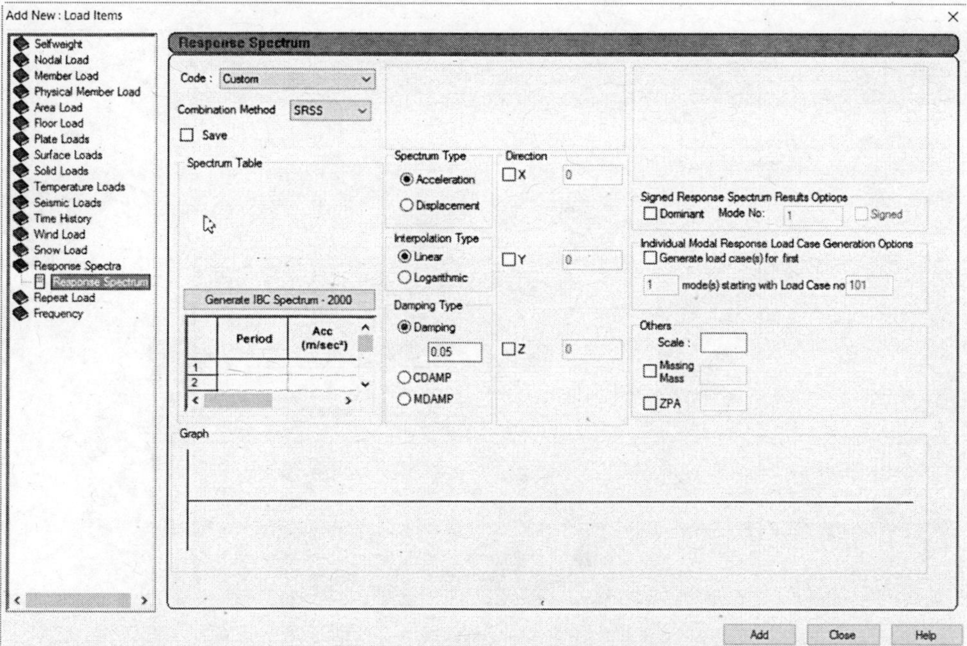

*Figure 6-56 The **Response Spectrum** page in the **Add New : Load Items** dialog box*

Select the required code from the **Code** drop-down list. Select the desired combination method from the **Combination Method** drop-down list. These combination methods are SRSS (Square root of summation of squares), ABS (Absolute sum method), CQC (Complete quadratic combination), TEN (Ten percent method), ASCE (as per ASCE-48 manual), and CSM (Closely spaced modes method). In the **Spectrum Type** area, select the **Acceleration** radio button for the period vs acceleration response spectrum curve or select the **Displacement** radio button for the period vs displacement curve. Specify the global direction in which spectrum will be applied by selecting **X**, **Y**, or **Z** check box and specify the factor applicable to each direction in their respective edit boxes. In the **Interpolation Type** area, specify the interpolation method to be used for the spectral value. The **Linear** radio button is selected by default. In the **Damping Type** area, specify the damping type to be used in the response spectrum analysis. In the **Others** area, specify a value in the **Scale** edit box. This value will get multiplied with the spectral data during the analysis. Select the **Missing Mass** check box to apply the missing mass correction. Select the **ZPA** check box to use the zero period acceleration. Enter the period vs acceleration or period vs displacement value in the table. Note that the spectral data values should be in the increasing order of the period. As you provide the values, the curve will be displayed at the bottom in the dialog box. Next, choose the **Add** button to add the load in the **Load & Definition** window.

STAAD.Pro also allows you to automatically generate the response spectrum data as per IBC/ ASCE code. To generate the data automatically, choose the **Generate IBC Spectrum - 2000** button in the **Response Spectrum** page of the **Add New : Load Items** dialog box; the **Spectrum Parameters::IBC 2000** dialog box will be displayed, as shown in Figure 6-57. The options in this dialog box are discussed next.

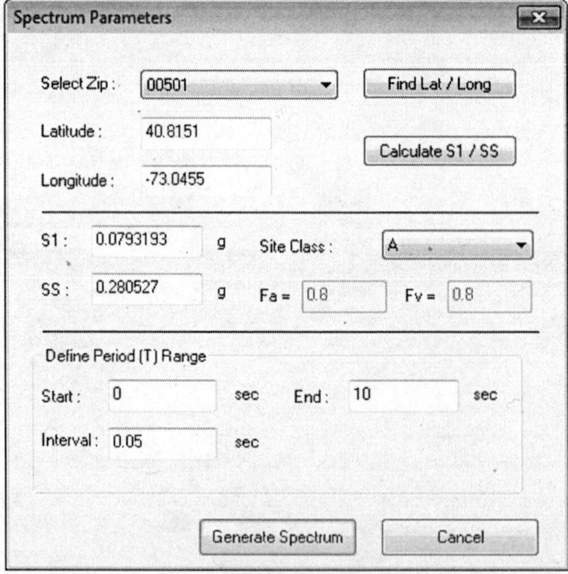

Figure 6-57 *The* ***Spectrum Parameters*** *dialog box*

Select the required zip code from the **Select Zip** drop-down list. On selecting the zip code, the latitudinal and longitudinal values get updated automatically in the **Latitude** and **Longitude** edit boxes. If you do not know the zip code, then enter the latitudinal and longitudinal values in their corresponding edit boxes. After specifying the values manually in the **Latitude** and

Longitude edit boxes, choose the **Calculate S1/SS** button; the site coefficient values of S1 and SS will be filled automatically in the **S1** and **SS** edit boxes. If the zip code is known, then the site coefficient value gets filled automatically. Select the required site class based on the soil type from the **Site Class** drop-down list; the values in the **F**$_a$ and **F**$_v$ edit boxes will be set automatically.

In the **Define Period (T) Range** area, specify the start time of the period for creating the response spectrum in the **Start** edit box. Similarly, specify the end value of the time period in the **End** edit box. Specify the time interval at which the spectral data will be calculated in the **Interval** edit box.

After specifying all the parameters, choose the **Generate Spectrum** button; the spectrum based on the specified data will be displayed in the **Generated Spectrum** dialog box, as shown in Figure 6-58. Next, close the **Generated Spectrum** dialog box and then choose the **Add** button in the **Add New : Load Items** dialog box. The load will be added under the selected load case in the **Load & Definition** window and the added load will be automatically assigned to the structure. Close the **Add New : Load Items** dialog box.

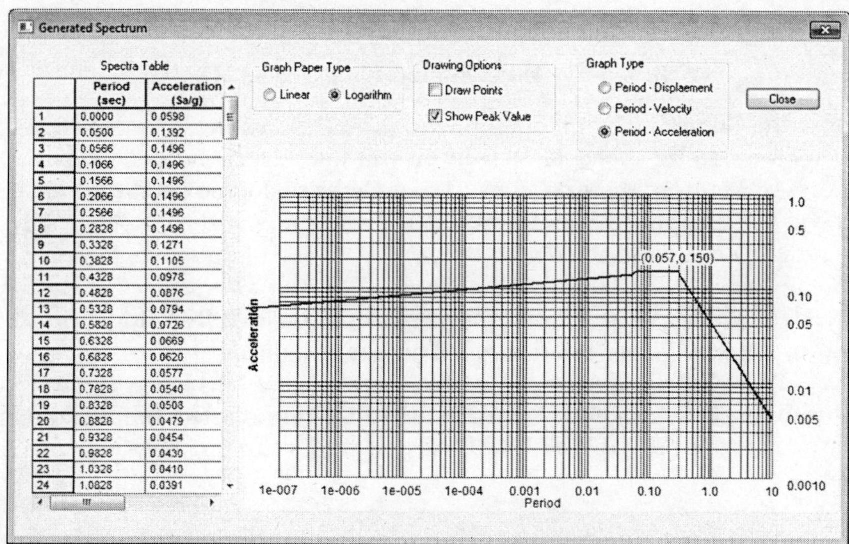

	Period (sec)	Acceleration (Sa/g)
1	0.0000	0.0598
2	0.0500	0.1392
3	0.0566	0.1496
4	0.1066	0.1496
5	0.1566	0.1496
6	0.2066	0.1496
7	0.2566	0.1496
8	0.2828	0.1496
9	0.3328	0.1271
10	0.3828	0.1105
11	0.4328	0.0978
12	0.4828	0.0876
13	0.5328	0.0794
14	0.5828	0.0726
15	0.6328	0.0669
16	0.6828	0.0620
17	0.7328	0.0577
18	0.7828	0.0540
19	0.8328	0.0508
20	0.8828	0.0479
21	0.9328	0.0454
22	0.9828	0.0430
23	1.0328	0.0410
24	1.0828	0.0391

Figure 6-58 *The response spectrum curve generated in the* ***Generated Spectrum*** *dialog box*

Example 6

In this example, you will open the *c06_staad_v8i_ex4.std* file. Next, you will define the response spectrum loading as per IBC 2006.

The following steps are required to complete this example:

Step 1: Open the file *c06_staad_v8i_ex4.std* in STAAD.Pro ; the model is displayed in the main window, as shown in Figure 6-59.

Figure 6-59 Model displayed in the Main Window

Step 2: Choose the **General** tab and open the **Load & Definition** page; the **Load & Definition** window is displayed. In the **Load & Definition** window; select the **Load Cases Details** node and choose the **Add** button; the **Add New : Load Cases** dialog box is displayed. In this dialog box, specify the title **Response Spectra** in the **Title** text box and choose the **Add** button; the load case is added. Next, close the dialog box.

Step 3: Now, select the **Response Spectra** load case in the **Load & Definition** window and choose the **Add** button; the **Add New : Load Items** dialog box is displayed.

Step 4: In this dialog box, specify **1** in the **Factor** edit box and select the **X** radio button. Next, choose the **Add** button; the **SELFWEIGHT X 1** is added under the **Response Spectra** load case.

Step 5: Repeat the procedure followed in step 4 and add the self weight in **Y** and **Z** direction for factor 1 and close the **Add New : Load Items** dialog box.

Step 6: Next, select the **Floor Load** node in the left pane of the dialog box; the **Floor** page is displayed in the right pane of the dialog box. In this page, specify the values as given in Figure 6-60.

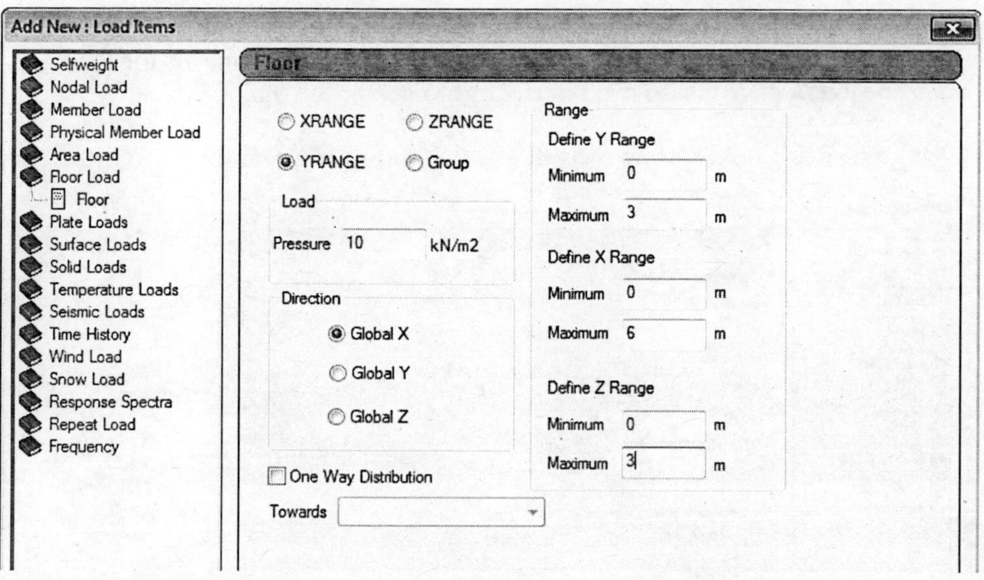

Figure 6-60 *Values specified for a floor load in the* ***Floor*** *page*

Step 7: Choose the **Add** button to add the floor load. Similarly, add the same load intensity in the **Y** and **Z** directions.

You need to select the **Global Y** radio button for the second floor loading and the **Global Z** radio button for the third floor loading.

Step 8: Next, define a different load with the load intensity **8**, as shown in Figure 6-61.

Add New : Load Items
Selfweight
Nodal Load
Member Load
Physical Member Load
Area Load
Floor Load
Floor
Plate Loads
Surface Loads
Solid Loads
Temperature Loads
Seismic Loads
Time History
Wind Load
Snow Load
Response Spectra
Repeat Load
Frequency
Floor
XRANGE
ZRANGE
YRANGE
Group
Load
Pressure 8 kN/m2
Direction
Global X
Global Y
Global Z
One Way Distribution
Towards
Range
Define Y Range
Minimum 3.1 m
Maximum 6.1 m
Define X Range
Minimum 0 m
Maximum 3 m
Define Z Range
Minimum 0 m
Maximum 3 m

Figure 6-61 *Values specified for another floor load in the* ***Floor*** *page*

Step 9: Choose the **Add** button to add the load. Similarly, add two more loads for **Y** and **Z** directions. Next, select the **Response Spectra** node in the left pane of the dialog box; the **Response Spectrum** page is displayed in the right pane of the dialog box.

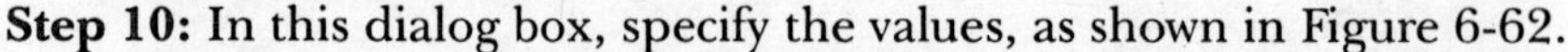

Step 10: In this dialog box, specify the values, as shown in Figure 6-62.

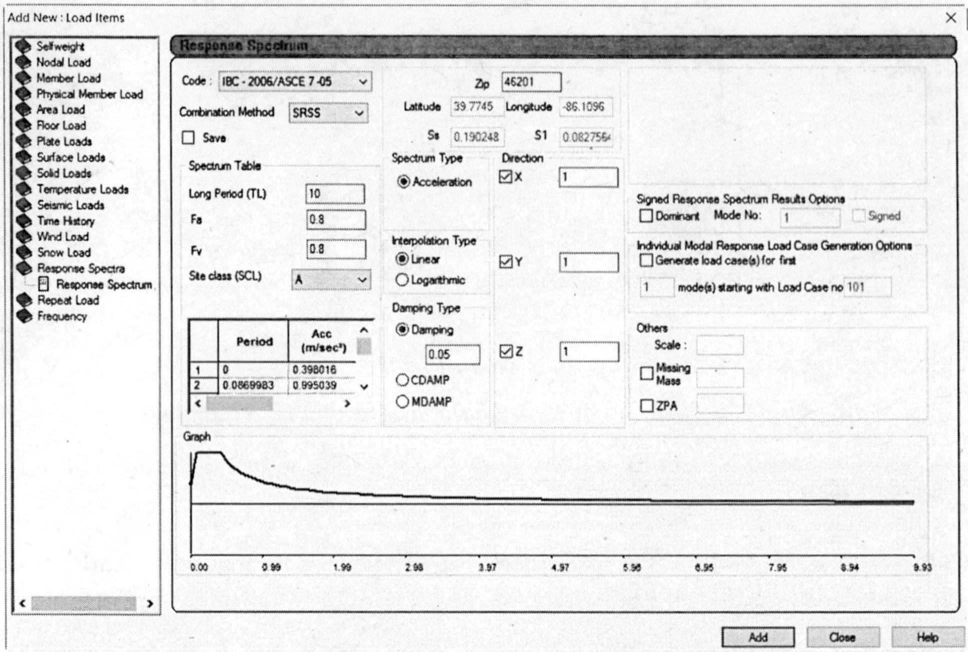

*Figure 6-62 Values specified in the **Response Spectrum** page*

Step 11: Choose the **Add** button to add the load and close the dialog box. Next, using the **Assign To View** method, assign the added self weights to the structure.

Step 12: Choose the **STAAD Editor** button from the toolbar; a **Warning** message box is displayed. Choose the **Save** button; the **STAAD Editor** window is displayed. In this window, the command for the **Response Spectra** load case is displayed as given next:

```
LOAD 2 LOADTYPE None TITLE RESPONSE SPECTRA
SELFWEIGHT X 1 LIST 1 TO 5 7 8 10 12 TO 24
SELFWEIGHT Y 1 LIST 1 TO 5 7 8 10 12 TO 24
SELFWEIGHT Z 1 LIST 1 TO 5 7 8 10 12 TO 24
FLOOR LOAD
YRANGE 0 3 FLOAD 10 XRANGE 0 6 ZRANGE 0 3 GY
YRANGE 0 3 FLOAD 10 XRANGE 0 6 ZRANGE 0 3 GX
YRANGE 0 3 FLOAD 10 XRANGE 0 6 ZRANGE 0 3 GZ
YRANGE 3.1 6.1 FLOAD 8 XRANGE 0 3 ZRANGE 0 3 GX
YRANGE 3.1 6.1 FLOAD 8 XRANGE 0 3 ZRANGE 0 3 GY
YRANGE 3.1 6.1 FLOAD 8 XRANGE 0 3 ZRANGE 0 3 GZ
SPECTRUM SRSS IBC 2006 X 1 Y 1 Z 1 ACC DAMP 0.05 LIN
ZIP 46201 SITE CLASS C TL 10.000
```

Step 13: Choose the **Save As** option from the **File** menu; the **Save As** dialog box is displayed. In this dialog box, specify the name *c06_staad_v8i_ex6* in the **File name** edit box and save it at an appropriate location.

Repeat Load

A repeat load is a primary load case created using a combination of previously defined primary load cases for which STAAD.Pro analyses the structure. To define this load type, select the **Repeat Load** node in the left pane of the **Add New : Load Items** dialog box; the **Repeat Load** page will be displayed in the right pane of the dialog box. In this page, all the primary load cases defined earlier will be displayed in the **Available Load Cases** list box. To include a primary load case, first select it from the list box and then choose the forward button; the load will be shifted to the **Repeat Load Definition** list box, refer to Figure 6-63. Next, specify a multiplying factor in the **Factor** edit box in the **Repeat Load Definition** list box. You can use the CTRL key and select as many load cases as you want. To shift all the load cases at a time, choose the [>>] button. Next, choose the **Add** button to add the load case. Two more options are displayed under the **Repeat Load** node in the left pane of the **Add New : Load Items** dialog box. These options are : **Reference Load** and **Notional Load**. The **Reference Load** has been discussed earlier in this chapter.

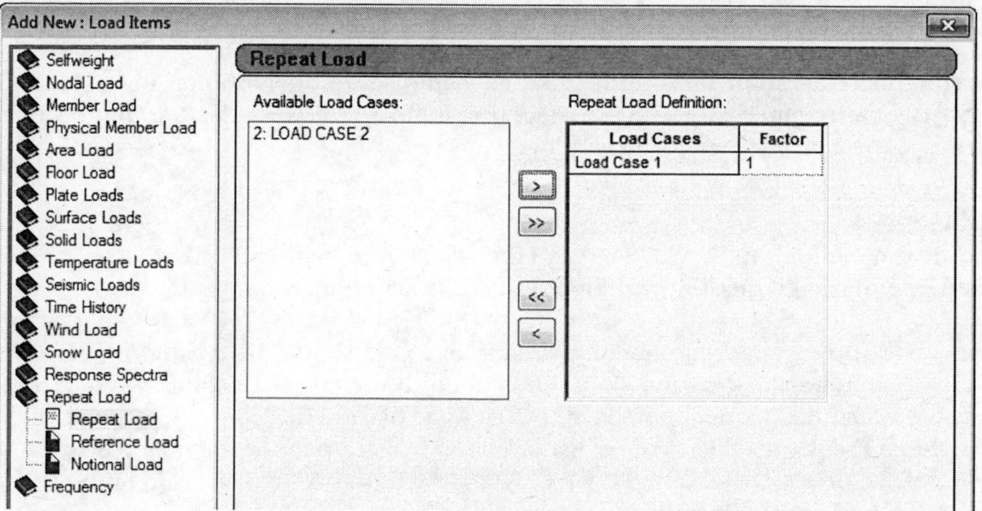

*Figure 6-63 The **Repeat Load** page in the **Add New : Load Items** dialog box*

The **Notional load** is defined as a percentage of gravity loads. In this load type, the primary and reference load cases can be selected from the **Primary Load Cases** and **Reference Load Cases** area and a percentage of them will get applied to the structure. To add this load type, select it; the **Notional Load** page will be displayed, as shown in Figure 6-64.

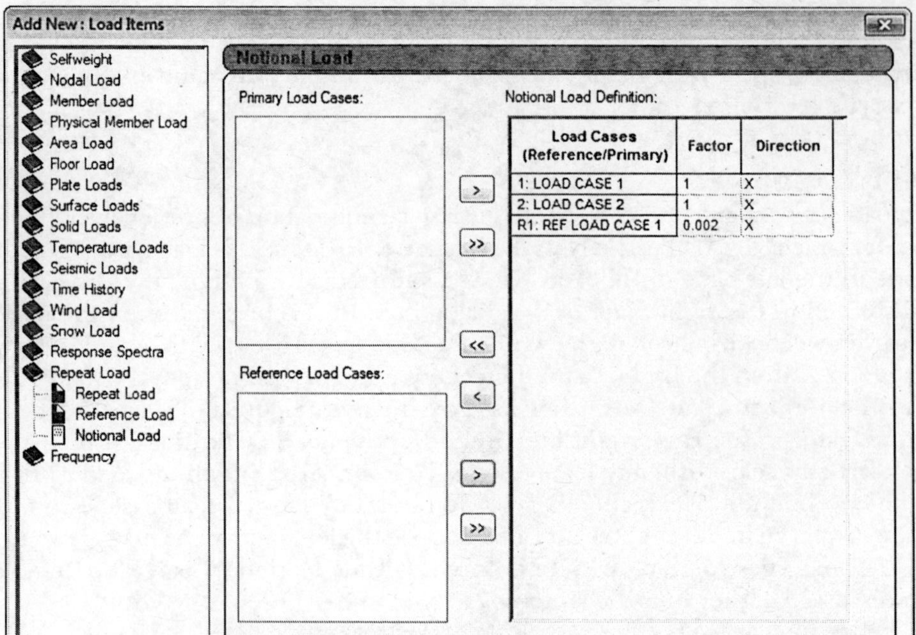

*Figure 6-64 The **Notional Load** page in the **Add New : Load Items** dialog box*

Next, shift the required primary and reference load cases to the **Notional Load Definition** list box. Specify the required factors in the **Factor** column and choose the **Add** button to add the load case in the **Load & Definition** window.

Frequency

There are two methods in STAAD.Pro used for calculating the frequencies of a structure. These methods are: Rayleigh method and EigenValue Extraction method.

To use Rayleigh Frequency method, a primary load case should be created first and then the **Rayleigh Frequency** load option should be added to the created load case. To add Rayleigh Frequency, select the **Frequency** node in the left pane of the **Add New : Load Items** dialog box; the **Rayleigh Frequency** page will be displayed in the right pane of the dialog box. Choose the **Add** button to add the **CALCULATE RAYLEIGH FREQUENCY** command under the selected load case in the **Load & Definition** window.

EigenValue Extraction method is used to calculate relevant frequencies and mode shapes. To use this method, select the **Modal Calculation** option available under the **Frequency** node in the left pane of the **Add New : Load Items** dialog box; the **Modal Calculation** page will be displayed in the right pane of the dialog box. Next, choose the **Add** button; the **MODAL CALCULATION REQUESTED** command will be added under the selected load case in the **Load & Definition** window.

LOAD GENERATION

The **Load Generation** option is used to create primary load case using the data of pre defined vehicle load definitions. To use this option, first select the **Load Cases Details** node in the **Load & Definition** window and then choose the **Add** button; the **Add New : Load Cases** dialog box will be displayed. In this dialog box, select the **Load Generation** node in the left pane of the dialog box; the **Load Generation** page will be displayed in the right pane of the dialog box. In this page, you can define the number of loads to be generated only after defining the vehicle load which is discussed next.

Defining Vehicle Loading

In STAAD.Pro, different types of moving loads can be defined. To define a vehicle load, expand the **Definitions** node in the **Load & Definition** window and select the **Vehicle Definitions** option. Next, choose the **Add** button; the **Add New : Vehicle Definitions** dialog box will be displayed, as shown in Figure 6-65. In this dialog box, you can use any of the three nodes to define the moving load. These nodes are discussed next.

Define Load

The **Define Load** option is selected by default in the left pane of the dialog box and the **Define Load** page will be displayed in the right pane of the dialog box, refer to Figure 6-65. In the **Vehicle Type Ref** edit box of this page, the reference number will be specified by default. Specify the spacing between the wheels in the **Width** edit box. Here, width is the distance between the parallel wheels. Next, you have to specify the value of the concentrated loads acting on the wheels and the distance between them in the **Load (kN)** and **Dist (m)** columns. After specifying the values, choose the **Add** button; the vehicle type will be defined and added under the **Vehicle Definitions** node in the **Load & Definition** window.

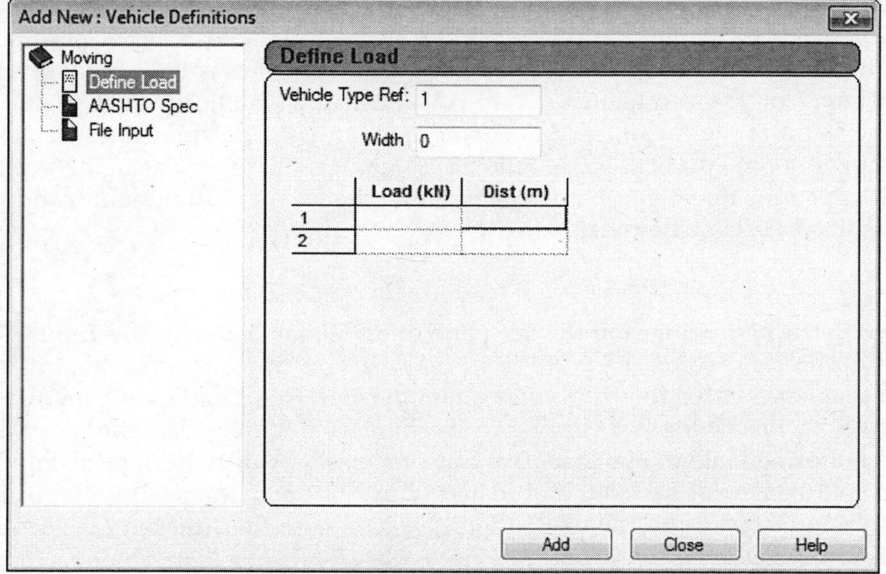

***Figure 6-65** The **Add New : Vehicle Definitions** dialog box*

AASHTO Spec

The vehicle loading can also be defined using the AASHTO specifications, which are available in the **AASHTO Spec** page. To access this page, select the **AASHTO Spec** option in the left pane of the dialog box; the **AASHTO Spec** page will be displayed in the right pane, as shown in Figure 6-66.

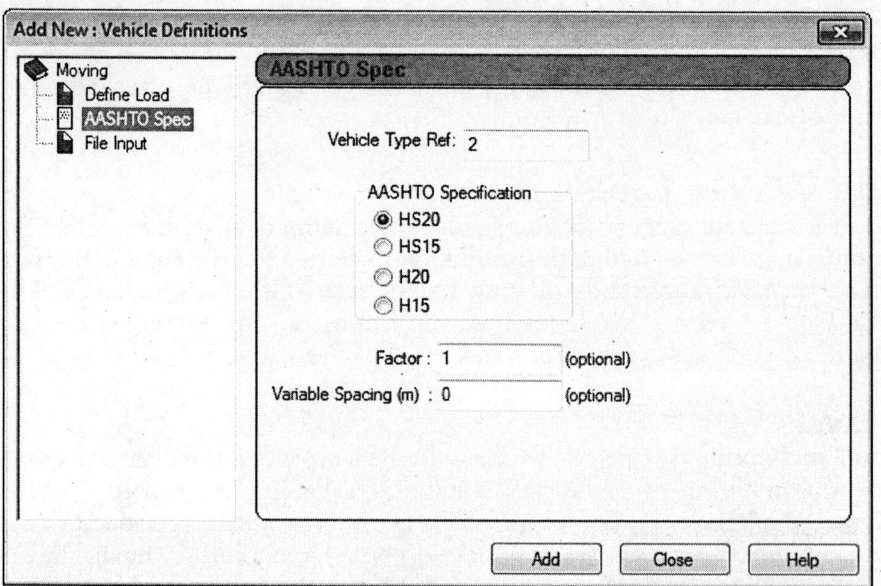

***Figure 6-66** The **AASHTO Spec** page in the **Add New : Vehicle Definitions** dialog box*

The vehicle type reference number will be specified by default in the **Vehicle Type Ref** edit box. In the **AASHTO Specification** area, specify the type of loading by selecting the **HS20**, **HS15**, **H20**, or **H15** radio button. These are the series of truck loadings as per the AASHTO (American Association of State and Highway Transportation Officials) specifications. Here, HS20 means a 20 ton heavy semi-trailer truck and H20 means a 20 ton heavy truck. Next, specify the multiplying factor in the **Factor** edit box. You can also use the default value, which is **1**. In the **Variable Spacing (m)** edit box, specify the wheel spacing. It is the spacing between the loads perpendicular to the direction of movement. Next, choose the **Add** button to add the vehicle type in the **Load & Definitions** window.

File Input

Select the **File Input** option from the left pane of the dialog box; the **File Input** page will be displayed in the right pane, refer to Figure 6-67. In this page, you can import the moving load data from an external file. To do so, choose the **Import** button; the **Open** dialog box will be displayed. In this dialog box, browse to the file location and select the file. Next, choose the **Open** button; the file will be loaded and its name will be displayed in the **File Name** text box. The load name will be filled automatically in the **Load Name** drop-down list. Specify the multiplying factor in the **Factor** edit box. Next, choose the **Add** button; the load will be added under the **Vehicle Definitions** node in the **Load & Definition** window. Next, close the **Add New : Vehicle Definitions** dialog box.

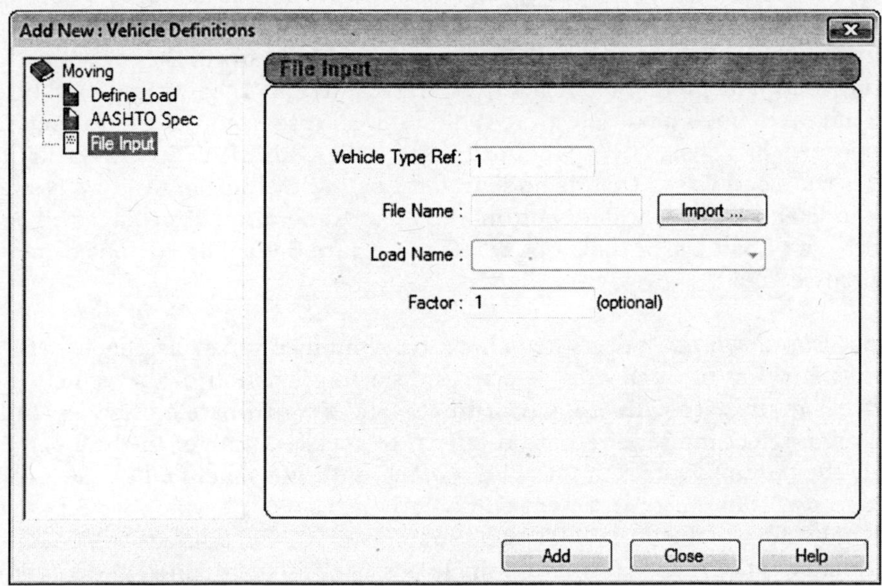

***Figure 6-67** The **File Input** page in the **Add New : Vehicle Definitions** dialog box*

After defining the vehicle type, go to the **Load Generation** page in the **Add New : Load Cases** dialog box, as discussed earlier. Figure 6-68 shows the **Load Generation** page in the **Add New : Load Cases** dialog box.

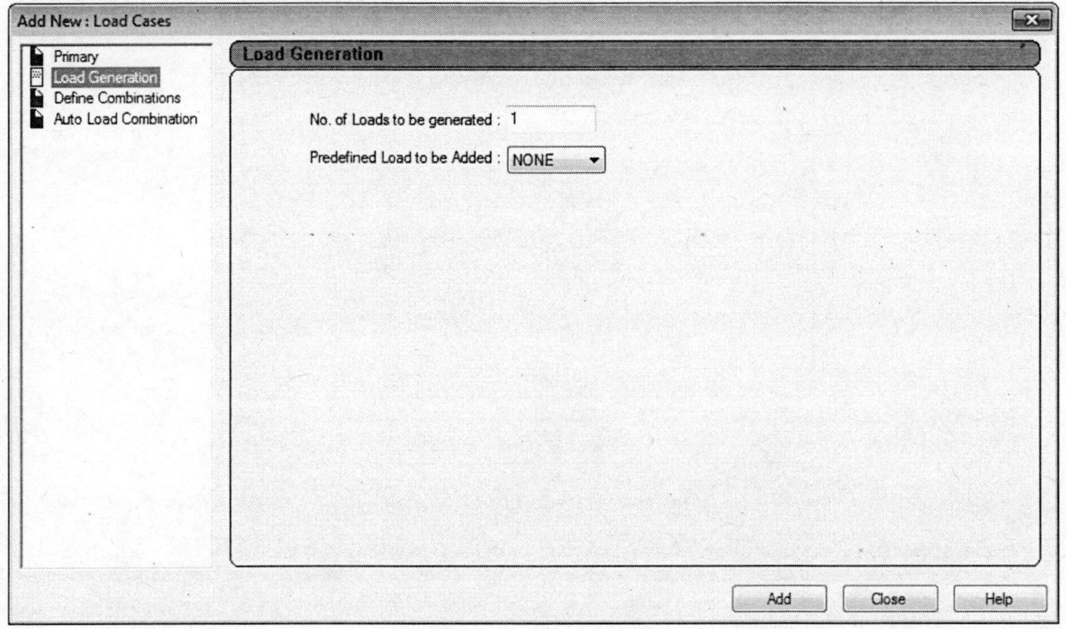

***Figure 6-68** The **Load Generation** page in the **Add New : Load Cases** dialog box*

In the **Load Generation** page, specify the number of load cases to be generated in the **No. of Loads to be generated** edit box. The number of load cases represent the number of positions for the vehicle on the structure. You can also include any of the predefined load cases in the moving load. The predefined load can be the self weight of the structure or the dead load. To include the predefined load, select the required load case from the **Predefined Load to be Added** drop-down list. Next, choose the **Add** button; the **GENERATE LOAD** sub node will be added under the **Load Cases Details** node in the **Load & Definition** window. Now, select this added sub-node and choose the **Add** button; the **Load Generation Type** page will be displayed in the **Add New : Load Cases** dialog box, refer to Figure 6-69. The options displayed in this page are discussed next.

In the **Type** drop-down list, select the vehicle type number which has been defined earlier. In the **Initial Position of Load** area, specify the starting location of the vehicle. Specify the required values in the **x coordinate**, **y coordinate**, and **z coordinate** edit boxes. In the **Range (Optional)** area, select the required radio button to specify a range. In the **Load Increment** area, specify the required values in the **x increment** and **z increment** edit boxes. For example, if you will specify **3ft** in the **z increment** edit box then the vehicle will move 3ft at a time. The vehicle will only move in the horizontal plane so the **y increment** edit box will be in the inactive mode. Next, choose the **Add** button; the vehicle position will get defined and added under the **GENERATE LOAD** sub node in the **Load & Definition** window and then close the **Add New : Load Cases** dialog box.

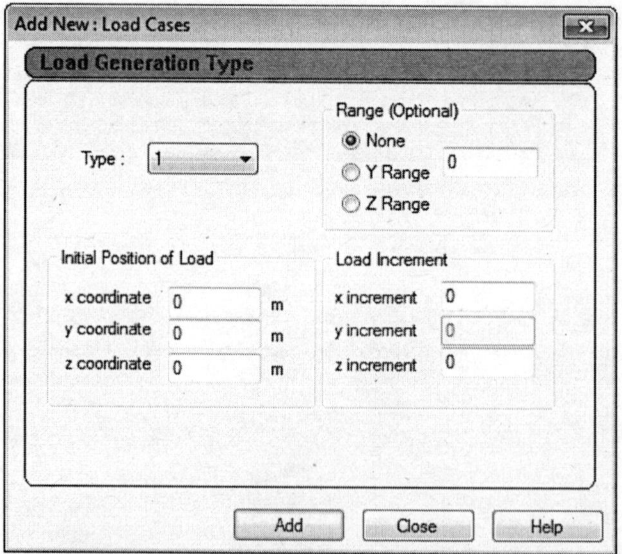

Figure 6-69 The ***Load Generation Type*** *page in the* ***Add New : Load Cases*** *dialog box*

Example 7

In this example, first you will open the *c06_staad_v8i_ex7_start.std* file. Next, you will define vehicle loading as per AASHTO specifications and then define its position on a bridge deck.

Steps required to complete this example are given next:

Step 1: Open the file *c06_staad_v8i_ex7_start.std* in STAAD.Pro; the model is displayed in the main window, as shown in Figure 6-70.

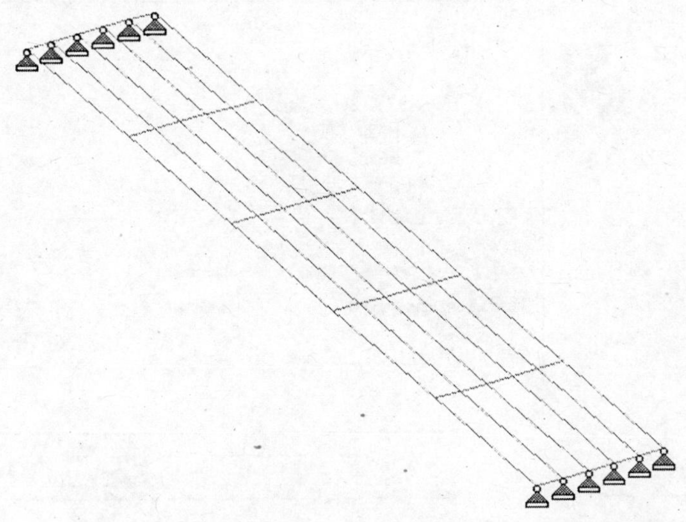

Figure 6-70 *The Bridge Deck model*

Step 2: Go to **General > Load & Definition** in the menu bar; the **Load & Definition** window is displayed. In this window, expand the **Definitions** node and select the **Vehicle Definitions** sub node.

Step 3: Next, choose the **Add** button; the **Add New : Vehicle Definitions** dialog box is displayed. In this dialog box, select the **AASHTO Spec** option; the **AASHTO Spec** page is displayed in the right pane of the dialog box.

Step 4: In this page, specify the values for the vehicle type, as shown in Figure 6-71. Next, choose the **Add** button; the **TYPE 1 HS20 1 4.2** type is defined and added under the **Vehicle Definitions** sub node. Now, close the **Add New : Vehicle Definitions** dialog box.

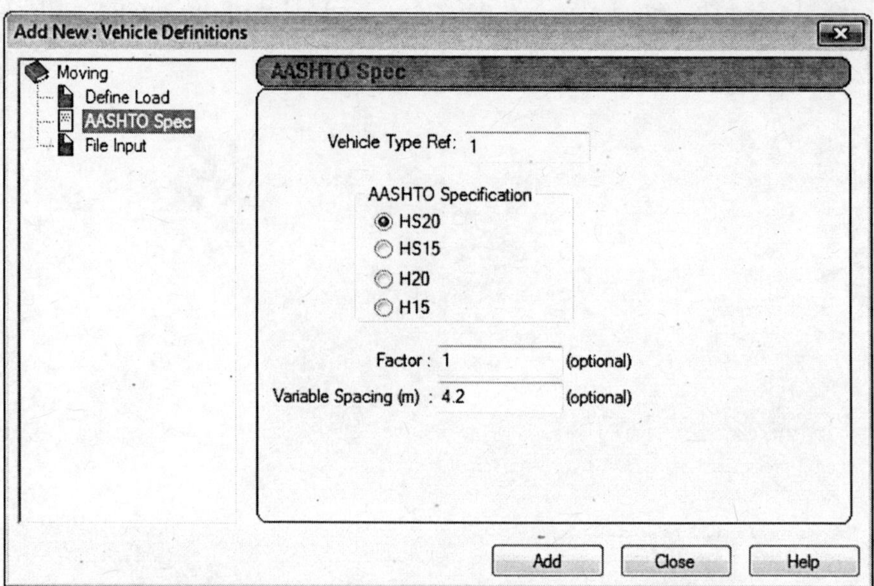

*Figure 6-71 Values specified in the **AASHTO Spec** page*

Step 5: Next, select the **Load Cases Details** node in the **Load & Definition** window and then choose the **Add** button; the **Add New : Load Cases** dialog box is displayed.

Step 6: In this dialog box, select the **Load Generation** node in the left pane; the **Load Generation** page is displayed in the right pane.

Step 7: In this page, specify **10** in the **No. of Loads to be generated** edit box and select **1** in the **Predefined Loads to be Added** drop-down list. Next, choose the **Add** button; the **GENERATE LOAD, ADD LOAD 1** is added under the **Load Cases Details** node. Now, close the **Add New : Load Cases** dialog box.

Step 8: Select the **GENERATE LOAD, ADD LOAD 1** in the **Load & Definition** window and choose the **Add** button; the **Add New : Load Cases** dialog box is displayed.

Step 9: In this dialog box, specify the values for the vehicle position, as shown in Figure 6-72. Next, choose the **Add** button; the position will be defined and added under the **GENERATE LOAD, ADD LOAD 1** in the **Load & Definition** window. Close the **Add New : Load Cases** dialog box.

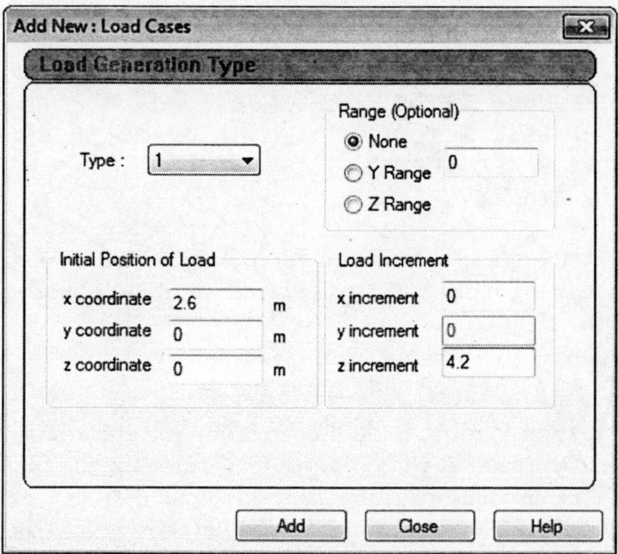

*Figure 6-72 Values specified in the **Add New : Load Cases** dialog box*

Step 10: Now, click on the defined position available under the **GENERATE LOAD, ADD LOAD 1** in the **Load & Definition** window; the vehicle is displayed and placed on the bridge, as shown in Figure 6-73.

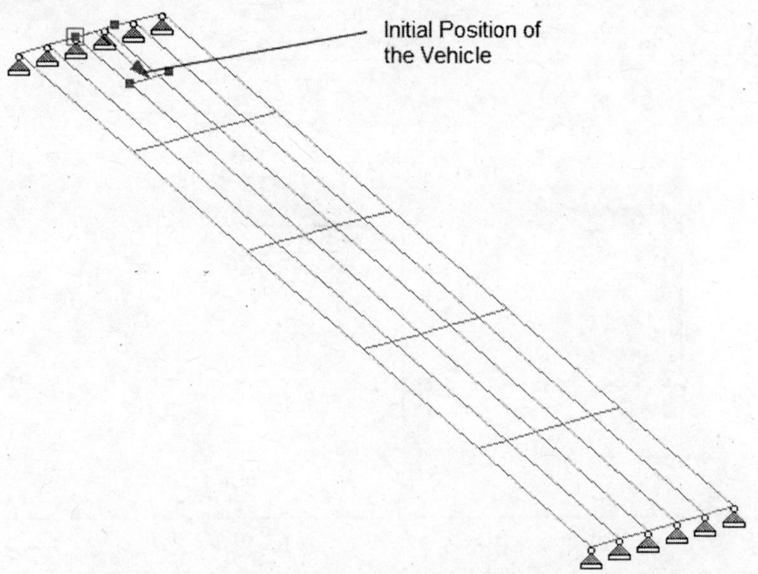

Figure 6-73 Initial position of the vehicle on the bridge

Step 11: Choose the **STAAD Editor** button from the toolbar; the **Warning** message box is displayed. Choose the **Save** button in this message box; the **STAAD Editor** window is displayed. In this window, the command for the vehicle load case is displayed as given next:

```
DEFINE MOVING LOAD
TYPE 1 HS20 1 4.2
LOAD 1 LOADTYPE None TITLE LOAD CASE 1
SELFWEIGHT Y -1 LIST 1 TO 27 33 TO 43 49 TO 59 65 TO 75
LOAD GENERATION 9 ADD LOAD 1
TYPE 1 2.6 0 0 ZINC 4.2
```

Step 12: Choose the **Save As** option from the **File** menu; the **Save As** dialog box is displayed. In this dialog box, specify the name *c06_staad_v8i_ex7* in the **File name** edit box and save it at an appropriate location.

DEFINING LOAD COMBINATIONS

In STAAD.Pro, combination loading is defined to combine the result of analysis performed for different primary load cases. A combination load sums up the analysis results of certain individual load cases. This summation is suitable for linear analysis in which the results of analysis are superimposed. To define combination loading, select the **Load Cases Details** node in the **Load & Definition** window and then choose the **Add** button; the **Add New : Load Cases** dialog box will be displayed. In this dialog box, select the **Define Combinations** node in the left pane of the dialog box; the **Define Combinations** page will be displayed in the right pane, refer to Figure 6-74. The options displayed in this page are discussed next.

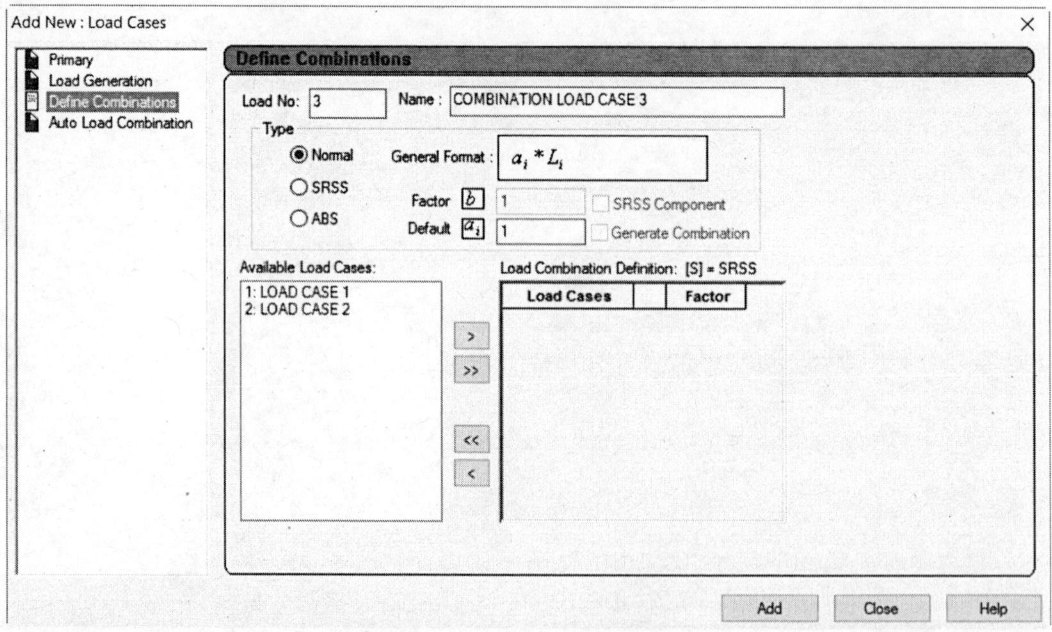

*Figure 6-74 The **Define Combinations** page in the **Add New : Load Cases** dialog box*

The load case number will be automatically filled in the **Load No** edit box. Specify the desired name in the **Name** text box. In the **Type** area, three radio buttons for three combination methods are available. These methods are: Normal, SRSS, and ABS, and are discussed next.

The **Normal** radio button is selected by default. This method uses the combination a_i*L_i. Here, $\mathbf{a}_i$ denotes the multiplying factor and $\mathbf{L}_i$ denotes the load case number. Now, to define this loading, select the load cases individually in the **Available Load Cases** area and move them to the **Load Combination Definition** area using the single arrow button. Next, specify their multiplying factors in the **Factor** column. Choose the **Add** button to add the combination loading in the **Load & Definition** window.

The SRSS (Square root sum of squares) method is required for nuclear codes such as ASCE 4-98. To use this method, select the **SRSS** radio button; the combination expression will be displayed in the **General Format** box. Now, select the required load cases from the **Available Load Cases** area and move them to the **Load Combination Definition** area using the single arrow button. Next, specify their multiplying factors in the **Factor** column.

To use the ABS (Absolute) combination method, select the **ABS** radio button; the combination expression will be displayed in the **General Format** box. The method for defining this combination is same as discussed above. Choose the **Add** button to add the required combination loading in the **Load & Definition** window. Next, close the **Add New : Load Cases** dialog box.

DEFINING LOAD COMBINATIONS AUTOMATICALLY

STAAD.Pro automatically creates load combinations based on the standard load combination factors using the codes like ACI, AISC, UBC, IBC, Indian Code, British, and NBCC 1995. To define auto load combinations, first ensure that the primary loads have been created. Next, select the **Load Cases Details** node in the **Load & Definition** window and choose the **Add** button; the **Add New : Load Cases** dialog box will be displayed. In this dialog box, select the **Auto Load Combination** option from the left pane; the **Auto Load Combination** page will be displayed in the right pane, refer to Figure 6-75. The options displayed in this page are discussed next.

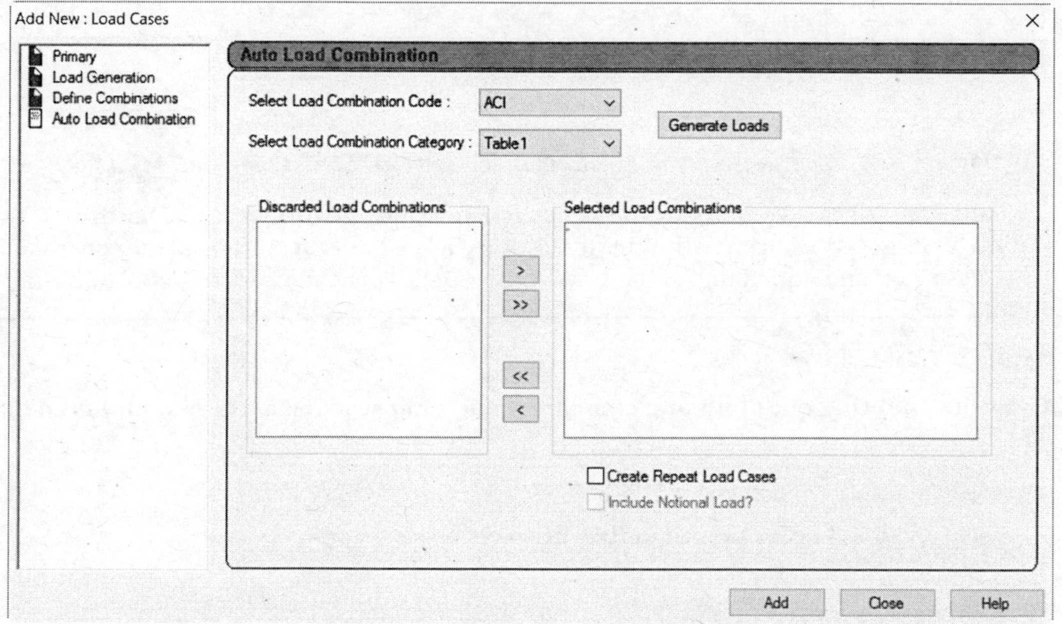

*Figure 6-75 The **Auto Load Combination** page in the **Add New : Load Cases** dialog box*

Note

While creating primary load cases, do not forget to define load category such as wind, seismic, and so on.

Select the required combination code from the **Select Load Combination Code** drop-down list. Next, select the required load combination category from the **Select Load Combination Category** drop-down list. Now, choose the **Generate Loads** button; various combinations will be generated and displayed in the **Selected Load Combinations** list box, as shown in Figure 6-76.

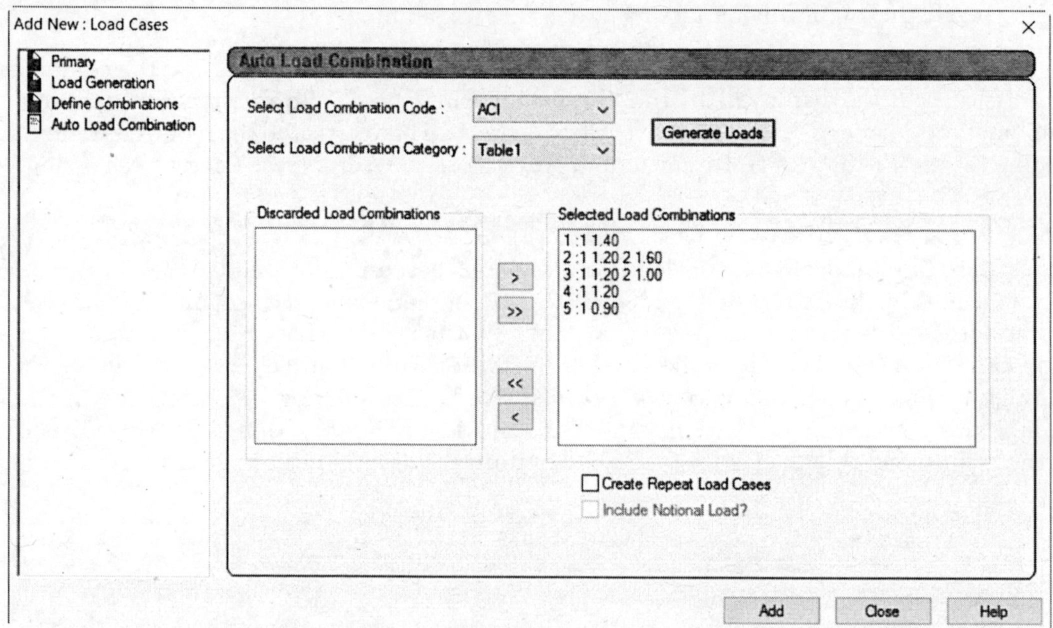

Figure 6-76 *Load combinations generated in the* ***Selected Load Combinations*** *list box*

To exclude any of the combinations, select it and then move it to the **Discarded Load Combinations** list box using the arrow button. Next, choose the **Add** button; all the combinations will be generated and added under the **Load Cases Details** in the **Load & Definition** window.

Self-Evaluation Test

Answer the following questions and compare them to those given at the end of this chapter:

1. Nodal loads are applied at the __________ in a structure.

2. __________ loads act at a point in the structure.

3. The__________ option is used to define uniform pressure on surface elements.

4. The__________ option is used to define varying pressure on each joint in a plate element.

5. The loading effect in poststress load gets transmitted to the connected structural members. (T/F)

6. You cannot define the pressure acting partially on a surface element. (T/F)

7. Before creating the seismic load, you first need to define the seismic parameters. (T/F)

Review Questions

Answer the following questions:

1. Which of the following options is used to define temperature loading?

   (a) **Temperature Load** (b) **Solid Load**
   (c) **Wind Load** (d) None of these

2. Which of the following loadings is defined to perform dynamic analysis?

   (a) Vehicle (b) Temperature
   (c) Snow (d) Seismic

3. Which of the following loading options varies with time?

   (a) **Nodal Load** (b) **Time History**
   (c) **Surface Load** (d) None of these

4. Which of the following options is used to define snow loading?

   (a) **Plate Load** (b) **Member Load**
   (c) **Snow Load** (d) **Wind Load**

5. In STAAD.Pro, wind load is applied as nodal load in a structure. (T/F)

6. The repeat load combines the results of analysis performed for different primary load cases. (T/F)

7. The **Auto Load Combination** option creates load combinations automatically. (T/F)

Answers to Self - Evaluation Test

1. joints, **2.** Concentrated, **3. Pressure on Full Surface**, **4. Element Joint Load**, **5.** F, **6.** F, **7.** T

Chapter 7

Performing Analysis, Viewing Results, and Preparing Report

Learning Objectives

After completing this chapter, you will be able to:

- *Apply various pre analysis print commands*
- *Apply various perform analysis commands*
- *Apply various post analysis print commands*
- *View the results*
- *Create a customized report*

INTRODUCTION

In previous chapter, you learnt to assign different types of loads to a structure. In this chapter, you will learn to perform different types of analysis to view the structural behavior after application of these loads. After the analysis, you will view the results graphically and numerically for support reactions, member forces, bending moments, deflection, and so on. Later on, you will prepare a report which will include the graphical and numerical results, structural model, properties, and loading information.

In this chapter, all the above discussed steps are categorized into five groups: Pre Analysis Print, Performing Analysis, Post Analysis Print, Viewing Results, and Preparing Report. These steps are discussed in detail in this chapter.

PRE ANALYSIS PRINT

In STAAD.Pro, after assigning loads and other properties, you will specify the commands for displaying some specific information about the structure in the STAAD Output file. These commands are known as Pre Print commands. To specify Pre Print commands, choose the **Analysis/Print** tab; the **Analysis/Print Commands** dialog box will be displayed. Close this dialog box and then invoke the **Pre-Print** page; the **Pre Analysis Print - Whole Structure** window will be displayed. In this window, choose the **Define Commands** button; the **Analysis/Print Commands** dialog box will be displayed, as shown in Figure 7-1. This dialog box comprises of several tabs which are used for adding Pre-Print commands. These tabs are discussed next.

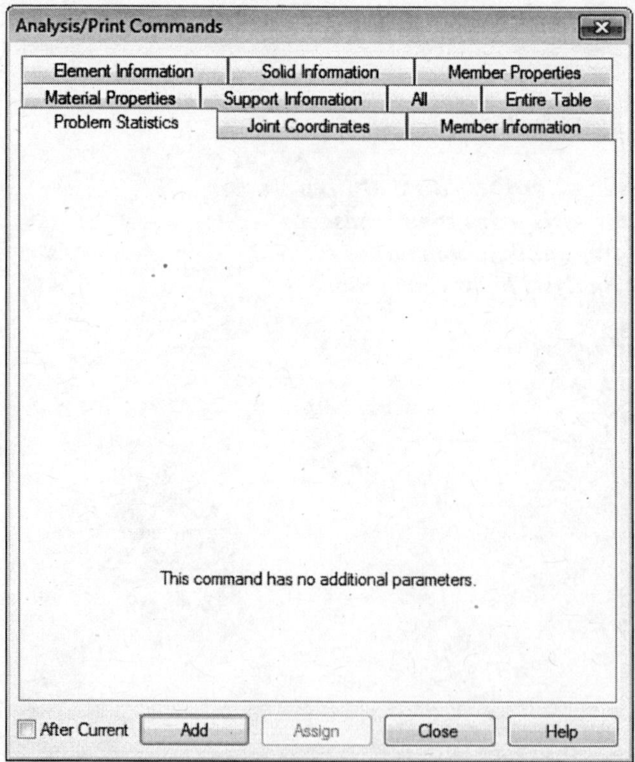

*Figure 7-1 The **Analysis/Print Commands** dialog box*

Problem Statistics

The **Problem Statistics** tab is chosen by default. In this tab, choose the **Add** button; the **PRINT PROBLEM STATISTICS** command will be added to the **Pre Analysis Print - Whole Structure** window. This command is used to print the structural information such as total number of nodes, members, supports, disk space requirement, and other information of the output file.

Joint Coordinates

You can print the joint coordinate values in the output file. To do so, choose the **Joint Coordinates** tab in the **Analysis/Print Commands** dialog box. Next, choose the **Add** button; the **PRINT JOINT COORDINATES** command will be added to the **Pre Analysis Print - Whole Structure** window. You can see a question mark displayed before the **PRINT JOINT COORDINATES** command in the **Pre Analysis Print - Whole Structure** window. This shows that the command has not been assigned to the structure. You can assign the command by using any of the four assignment methods which have been discussed earlier.

Member Information

Member information such as member length, member incidences, beta angles, member specifications, and so on can be printed in the output files. To do so, choose the **Member Information** tab and then choose the **Add** button; the **PRINT MEMBER INFORMATION** command will be added to the **Pre Analysis Print - Whole Structure** window.

Material Properties

You can also print the material properties such as Young's Modulus, Shear Modulus, and so on in the output file. To do so, choose the **Material Properties** tab and then choose the **Add** button; the **PRINT MATERIAL PROPERTIES** command will be added to the **Pre Analysis Print - Whole Structure** window.

Support Information

You can print the information regarding the supports such as restraints, releases, and spring constant values in the output file. To do so, choose the **Support Information** tab and then choose the **Add** button; the **PRINT SUPPORT INFORMATION** command will be added in the **Pre Analysis Print - Whole Structure** window.

Member Properties

Member properties such as cross-sectional area, moment of inertia, and section modulus can also be printed in the output file. To do so, choose the **Member Properties** tab. Next, choose the **Add** button; the **PRINT MEMBER PROPERTIES** command will be added to the **Pre Analysis Print - Whole Structure** window.

Element Information

You can print element related information such as element incidences, thickness of element, and Poisson ratio in the output file. To do so, choose the **Element Information** tab and then choose the **Add** button; the **PRINT ELEMENT INFORMATION** command will be added to the **Pre Analysis Print - Whole Structure** window.

Solid Information

You can also add solid information such as element incidences and Poisson ratios for solid elements in the output file. To do so, choose the **Solid Information** tab and then choose the **Add** button; the **PRINT ELEMENT INFORMATION SOLID** command will be added to the **Pre Analysis Print - Whole Structure** window.

All

You can also print joint coordinates, member information, member properties, material properties, and support information together in the output file. To do so, choose the **All** tab and then choose the **Add** button; the **PRINT ALL** command will be added to the **Pre Analysis Print - Whole Structure** window.

Entire Table

The content of the selected steel section table can also be printed in the output file. For example, if you have selected American Steel Table then it will be printed in the output file. To print the steel section table, choose the **Entire Table** tab and then choose the **Add** button; the **PRINT ENTIRE TABLE** command will be added to the **Pre Analysis Print - Whole Structure** window.

PERFORMING ANALYSIS

In STAAD.Pro, after specifying the pre print commands, you have to specify the commands for the type of analysis to be performed. To perform an analysis, choose the **Analysis/Print** tab; the **Analysis/Print Commands** dialog box will be displayed, as shown in Figure 7-2. In this dialog box, different types of analysis are available as tabs. These tabs are: **Perform Analysis**, **PDelta Analysis**, **Perform Cable Analysis**, **Perform Direct Analysis**, **Perform Imperfection Analysis**, **Perform Buckling Analysis**, and **Perform Pushover Analysis**. These tabs are discussed next.

Perform Analysis

Using the **Perform Analysis** tab, you can add the **PERFORM ANALYSIS** command to the **Analysis - Whole Structure** window which will direct the program to proceed with the analysis. In the **Print Option** area of this tab, different print options are available which allow you to specify the analysis related data to be printed in the output file. These options are discussed next.

Select the **Load Data** radio button to print the entire load data in the output file. Select the **Statics Check** radio button to print the summation of the applied loads and support reactions along with the summation of moments of the loads and reactions taken around the origin in the output file. Select the **Statics Load** radio button to print the statics check results along with the summation of all the internal and external forces at each joint. Select the **Mode Shapes** radio button to print the mode shape values in the output file. Select the **Both** radio button to print both the statics check and load data results in the output file. Select the **All** radio button to print both the statics load and load data results in the output file. Next, choose the **Add** button; the **PERFORM ANALYSIS** command will be added to the **Analysis - Whole Structure** window. You can choose the **Close** button to close the **Analysis/Print Commands** dialog box.

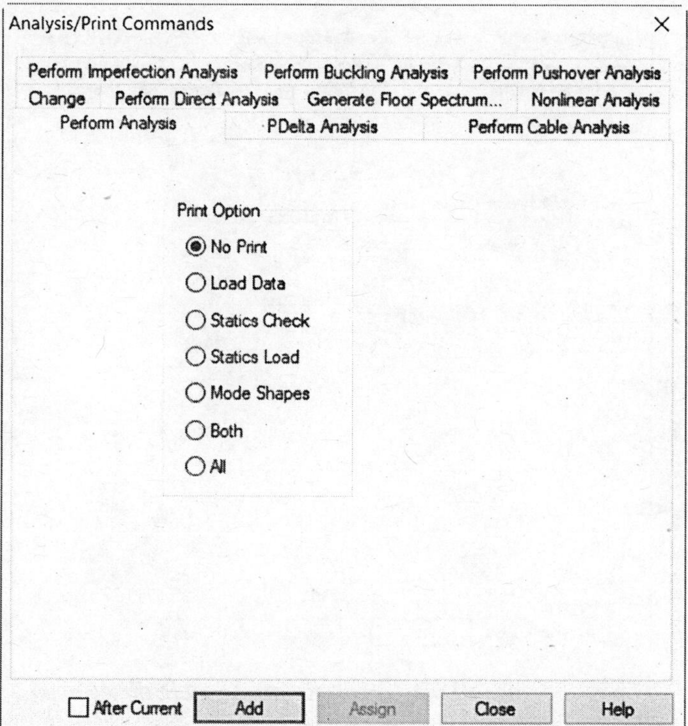

*Figure 7-2 The **Analysis/Print Commands** dialog box with the **Perform Analysis** tab chosen*

PDelta Analysis

Using the **PDelta Analysis** tab, you can add the **PDELTA ANALYSIS** command to the **Analysis - Whole Structure** window. PDelta analysis is used for the structures subjected to lateral loads such as seismic loads. In this type of analysis, multiple iterations are required to produce accurate results. In this tab, specify the required number of iterations in the **Number of Iterations** edit box, refer to Figure 7-3. Alternatively, select the **Converge** check box and specify the number of iterations in the corresponding edit box. To include the geometric stiffness in the analysis, select the **Use Geometric Stiffness (K_g)** check box. To include the small delta effect, select the **Small Delta** check box. Select the required option from the **Print Option** area. Choose the **Add** button; the **PDELTA ANALYSIS** command will be added to the **Analysis - Whole Structure** window.

Perform Cable Analysis

The **PERFORM CABLE ANALYSIS** command is used to perform analysis for the cable members. In the **Perform Cable Analysis** tab, specify the maximum number of iterations per step in the **Eq-Iterations** edit box. Specify the convergence tolerance value in the **Eq-tolerance** edit box, refer to Figure 7-4. Specify the artificial stabilizing stiffness value in the **Stability Stiffness** edit box. Specify the minimum sag value in the **Sag Minimum** edit box. Specify the number of load steps to be applied in the **Load Steps** edit box. Specify the minimum amount of stiffness remaining after a cable sags in the **KSMALL** edit box. In the **Print Option** area, select the required option. Next, choose the **Add** button; the **PERFORM CABLE ANALYSIS** command will be added to the **Analysis - Whole Structure** window.

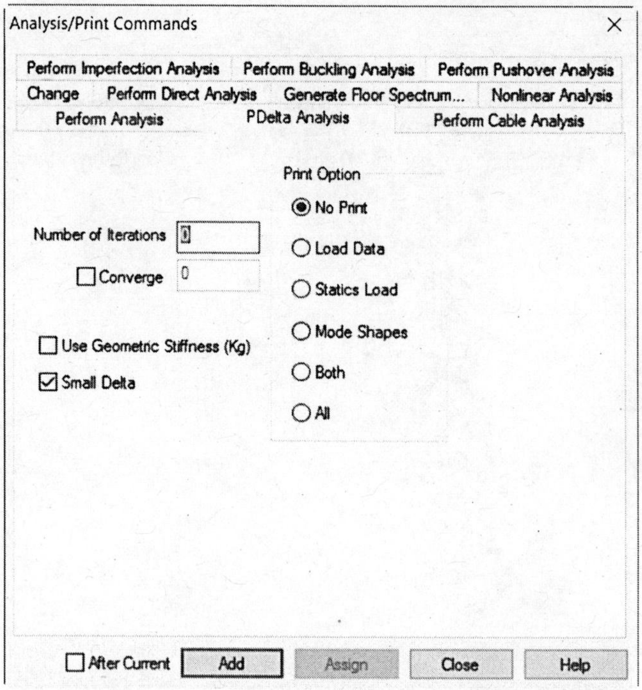

Figure 7-3 *The* ***PDelta Analysis*** *tab chosen in the* ***Analysis/Print Commands*** *dialog box*

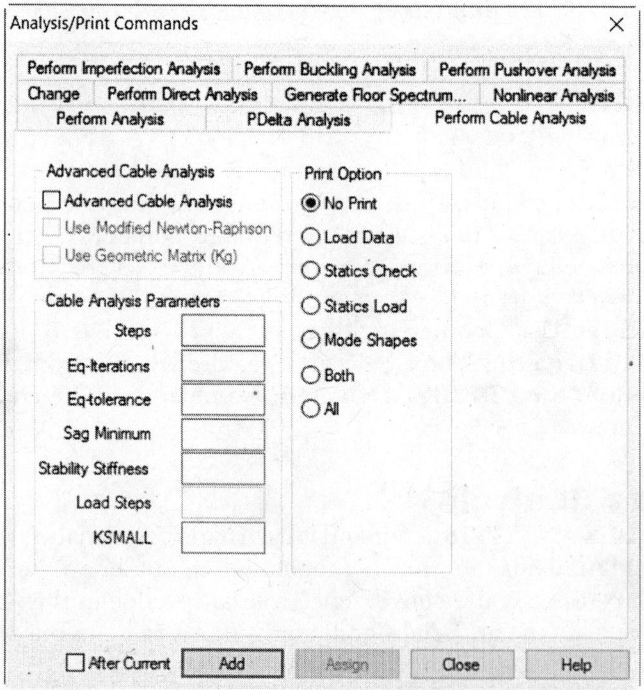

Figure 7-4 *The* ***Perform Cable Analysis*** *tab chosen in the* ***Analysis/Print Commands*** *dialog box*

Perform Direct Analysis

This analysis is a non-linear iterative analysis in which stiffness of the members is dependent upon the forces generated by the load. To perform direct analysis, first you need to define the **Direct Analysis Definition** in the **Load & Definition** window, as discussed in the previous chapters. After defining the **Direct Analysis Definition**, you will add the **PERFORM DIRECT ANALYSIS** command. To do so, choose the **Perform Direct Analysis** tab in the **Analysis/Print Commands** dialog box, refer to Figure 7-5. The options displayed in this tab are discussed next.

In the **Option** area, select the required code by selecting the **LRFD** or **ASD** radio button. In the **Tolerances** area, specify the tau tolerance and displacement tolerance values in their respective edit boxes. Specify the required number of iterations for the analysis in the **Number of Iterations** edit box. Select the required option from the **Print Option** area. Next, choose the **Add** button; the **PERFORM DIRECT ANALYSIS** command will be added to the **Analysis - Whole Structure** window.

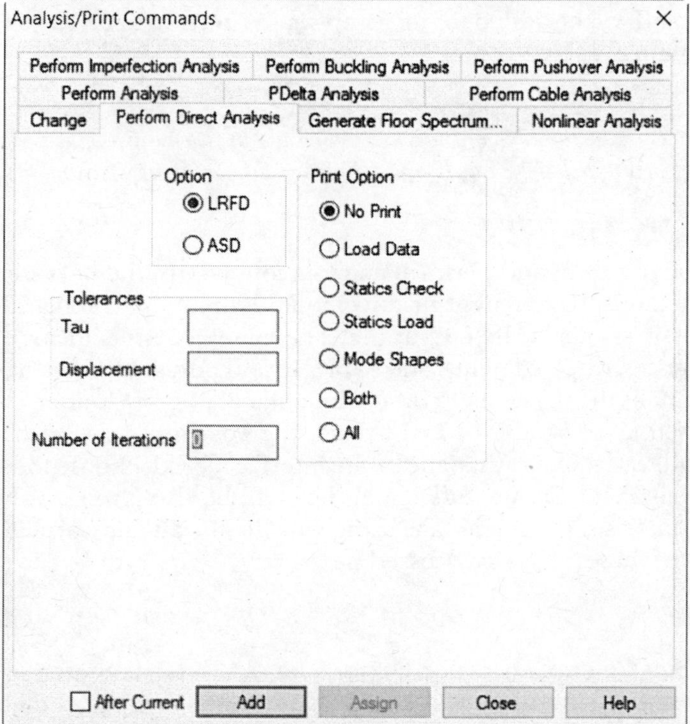

Figure 7-5 *The* ***Perform Direct Analysis*** *tab chosen in the* ***Analysis/Print Commands*** *dialog box*

Perform Imperfection Analysis

Imperfection analysis is performed for the structural members that experience secondary forces due to imperfections in their geometry. The geometry imperfections are due to the curvature imperfection in the columns and beams. To perform the imperfection analysis, choose the **Perform Imperfection Analysis** tab in the **Analysis/Print Commands** dialog box. In this tab, select the required print option from the **Print Option** area and then choose the **Add** button; the **PERFORM IMPERFECTION ANALYSIS** command will be added to the **Analysis - Whole Structure** window.

Perform Buckling Analysis

While performing the buckling analysis, STAAD.Pro performs the PDelta analysis including the geometric stiffness of plates and members due to large and small PDelta effects. To add **PERFORM BUCKLING ANALYSIS** command, choose the **Perform Buckling Analysis** tab in the **Analysis/Print Commands** dialog box. In this tab, specify the number of iterations in the **Number of Iterations** edit box. Next, select the required print option from the **Print Option** area and then choose the **Add** button; the **PERFORM BUCKLING ANALYSIS** command will be added to the **Analysis - Whole Structure** window.

Perform Pushover Analysis

The pushover analysis is performed by subjecting a structure to a consistently increasing pattern of lateral loads. Pushover analysis allows you to determine the non-linear force-displacement relationship. To perform this analysis, choose the **Perform Pushover Analysis** tab in the **Analysis/Print Commands** dialog box. In this tab, choose the **Add** button; the **PERFORM PUSHOVER ANALYSIS** command will be added to the **Analysis - Whole Structure** window. Next, close the **Analysis/Print Commands** dialog box.

Tip

*You can also add the above analysis commands by selecting the required options from the cascading menu displayed on choosing **Commands > Analysis** from the menu bar.*

POST ANALYSIS PRINT

After specifying the pre print and perform analysis commands, the next step is to add the post analysis print commands. Post analysis print commands are those commands which are used to print various analysis results in the output file. The analysis results include support reactions, member forces, stresses, displacements, and so on. To add post analysis print commands, choose the **Analysis/Print** tab; the **Analysis/Print Commands** dialog box will be displayed. Close this dialog box and then invoke the **Post-Print** page; the **Post Analysis Print - Whole Structure** window will be displayed in the right pane of the interface. Next, choose the **Define Commands** button; the **Analysis/Print Commands** dialog box will be displayed, as shown in Figure 7-6. This dialog box comprises of several tabs using which you can add various post analysis print commands. Some of these tabs are discussed next.

Load List

In the **Analysis/Print Commands** dialog box, the **Load List** tab is chosen by default. The **Load List** command is used to activate some of the load cases. By specifying the **Load List** command, the analysis will be performed only for the activated load cases. To add this command, first ensure that the **Load List** tab is chosen. Next, select the required load cases from the **Load Cases** area and then shift them to the **Load List** area. Next, choose the **Add** button; the **LOAD LIST** command will be added to the **Post Analysis Print - Whole Structure** window.

Joint Displacement

The joint displacements for all the specified joints of all the specified load cases can be printed in the STAAD output file. To do so, choose the **Joint Displacement** tab from the **Analysis/Print Commands** dialog box and then choose the **Add** button; the **PRINT JOINT DISPLACEMENTS** command will be added to the **Post Analysis Print - Whole Structure** window.

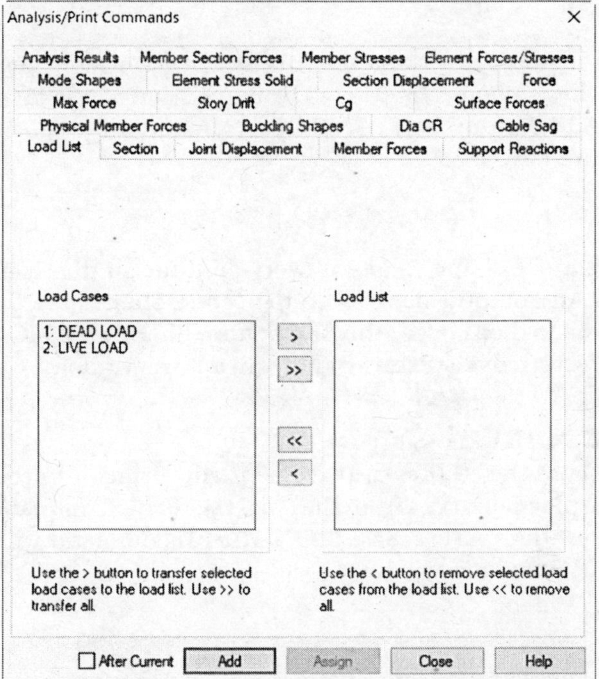

*Figure 7-6 The **Analysis/Print Commands** dialog box*

Member Forces

Member forces such as axial force, shear force in local Y and Z axes, torsional moment, and moments about local Y and Z axes can be calculated and printed in a tabular format in the STAAD output file. To do so, choose the **Member Forces** tab from the **Analysis/Print Commands** dialog box and then choose the **Add** button; the **PRINT MEMBER FORCES** command will be added to the **Post Analysis Print - Whole Structure** window. Next, assign this command to the required members in the structure.

Support Reactions

Support reactions such as F_x, F_y, F_z, M_x, M_y, and M_z can be calculated and printed in a tabular format in the output file. To do so, choose the **Support Reactions** tab from the **Analysis/Print Commands** dialog box and then choose the **Add** button; the **PRINT SUPPORT REACTIONS** command will be added to the **Post Analysis Print - Whole Structure** window. Next, assign this command to the required joints in the structure.

Story Drift

You can also print the average lateral displacement of all the joints at each vertical level of the structure in the output file. To do so, choose the **Story Drift** tab from the **Analysis/Print Commands** dialog box and then choose the **Add** button; the **PRINT STORY DRIFT** command will be added to the **Post Analysis Print - Whole Structure** window.

Cg

You can print the coordinates of the point where centre of gravity is experienced on the structure in the output file. To do so, choose the **Cg** tab from the **Analysis/Print Commands** dialog box and then choose the **Add** button; the **PRINT CG** command will be added to the **Post Analysis Print - Whole Structure** window.

Mode Shapes

You can also print the mode shape values at every joint for all the calculated modes. To print mode shape values in the output file, choose the **Mode Shapes** tab from the **Analysis/Print Commands** dialog box and then choose the **Add** button; the **PRINT MODE SHAPES** command will be added to the **Post Analysis Print - Whole Structure** window.

Section Displacement

STAAD.Pro also calculates the section displacement and prints it in the output file. To do so, choose the **Section Displacement** tab from the **Analysis/Print Commands** dialog box and then choose the **Add** button; the **PRINT SECTION DISPL** command will be added to the **Post Analysis Print - Whole Structure** window.

Force

You can also print the maximum and minimum force/moment envelope values for every section in each specified load case. To do so, choose the **Force** tab from the **Analysis/Print Commands** dialog box. Next, specify the number of sections in the **Number of Sections** edit box. Choose the **Add** button; the **PRINT FORCE ENVELOPE** command will be added to the **Post Analysis Print - Whole Structure** window. Next, assign this command to the required members in the structure.

Analysis Results

If you want to print the joint displacements, support reactions and member forces for all the specified joints/members with the load cases then choose the **Analysis Results** tab from the **Analysis/Print Commands** dialog box. Next, choose the **Add** button; the **PRINT ANALYSIS RESULTS** command will be added to the **Post Analysis Print - Whole Structure** window. Next, assign this command to the required members in the structure.

Member Stresses

You can also print member stresses in the output file. Member stresses include axial (axial force over area), bending-y, bending-z, shear stress in both local Y and Z directions, and combined stresses. To print member stresses, choose the **Member Stresses** tab from the **Analysis/Print Commands** dialog box and then choose the **Add** button; the **PRINT MEMBER STRESSES** command will be added to the **Post Analysis Print - Whole Structure** window. Next, assign this command to the required members in the structure.

Element Forces/Stresses

The element forces/stresses can also be printed in the output file. To do so, choose the **Element Forces/Stresses** tab. Next, select the required radio button and then choose the **Add** button; the **PRINT ELEMENT** command will be added to the **Post Analysis Print - Whole Structure** window. Next, assign this command to the required elements in the structure.

VIEWING RESULTS

After specifying the required commands, you need to perform the analysis to view the results. To do so, choose the **Analyze > Run Analysis** option from the menu bar; the **STAAD Analysis and Design** window will be displayed, as shown in Figure 7-7.

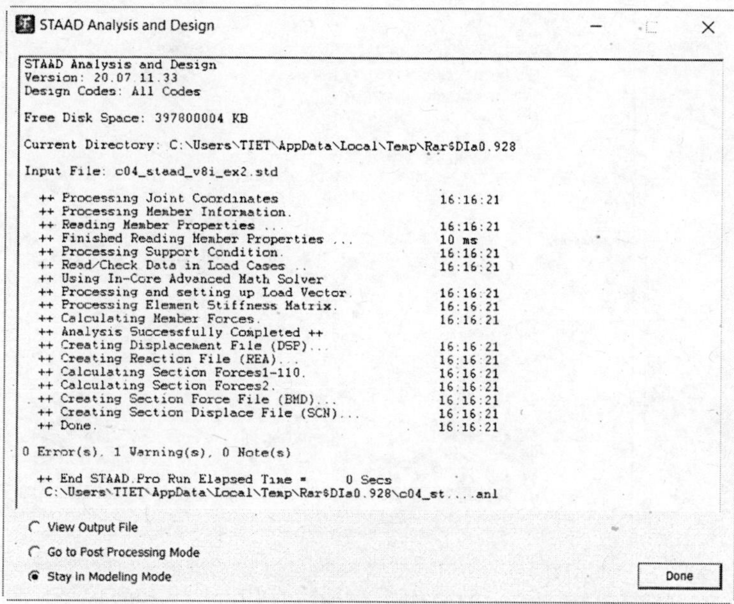

***Figure 7-7** The **STAAD Analysis and Design** window*

In this window, the STAAD.Pro will analyze the structural model and you can view the number of errors and warnings that were generated after the analysis. In this window, three radio buttons are available at the bottom. On selecting these radio buttons, you can view the results numerically, graphically, or you can stay in the modeling mode. The results include displacement, forces, stresses, support reactions, and so on. To remain in the modeling mode, select the **Stay in Modeling Mode** radio button. The other two radio buttons are discussed next.

View Output File

You can view the results numerically in the output file. To display the output file, select the **View Output File** radio button from the **STAAD Analysis and Design** window and then choose the **Done** button; the **STAAD Output Viewer** window will be displayed, as shown in Figure 7-8. This window will display the information related to the structure and their analysis results. When you scroll down in this window, you can view the post analysis results such as support reaction, member forces, element stresses, and so on. Figure 7-9 shows the support reactions displayed in the **STAAD Output Viewer** window.

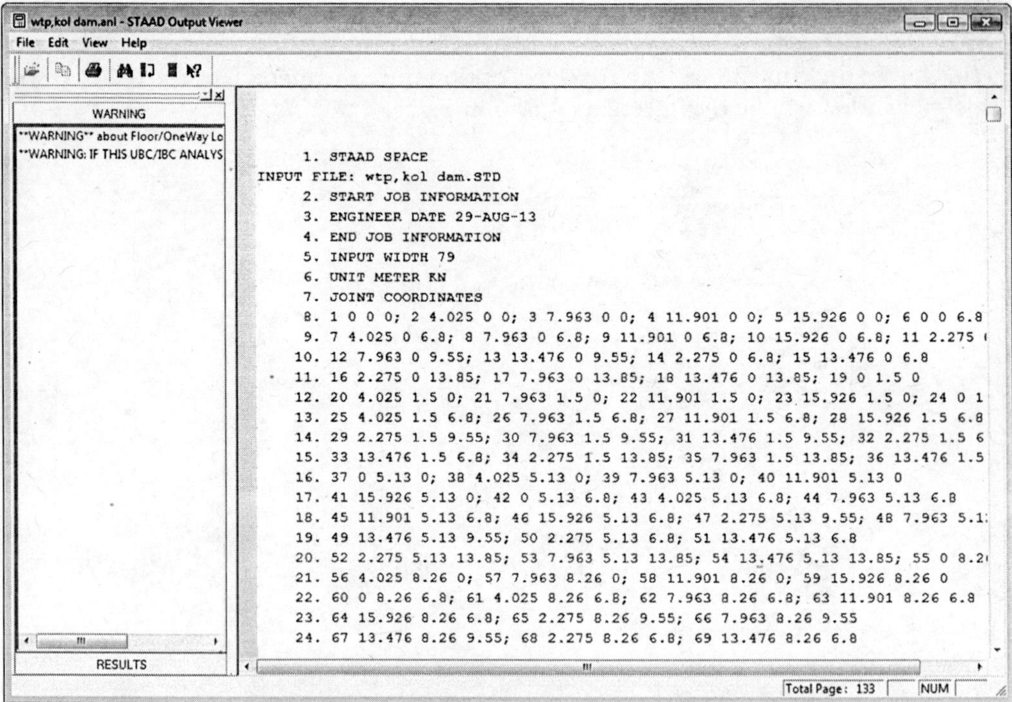

Figure 7-8 *The* ***STAAD Output Viewer*** *window*

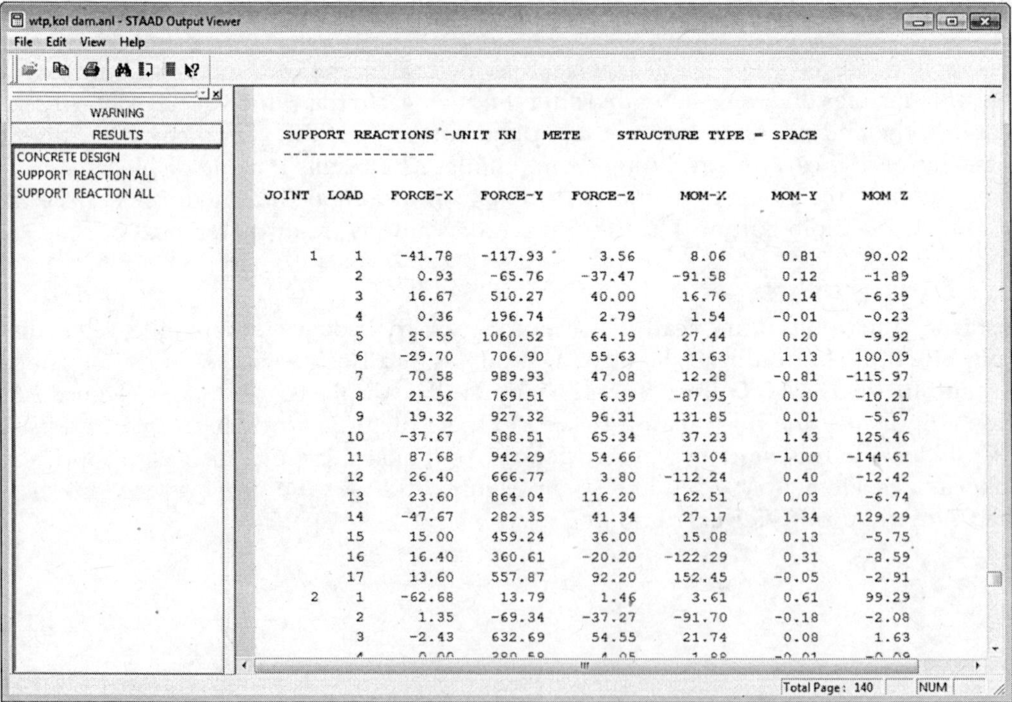

Figure 7-9 *Support reactions displayed in the* ***STAAD Output Viewer*** *window*

Go to Post Processing Mode

In the Post Processing mode, you can view the results graphically. These results include the bending moment diagrams, shear force diagrams, axial forces, deflections, and so on. To view the results graphically, select the **Go to Post Processing Mode** radio button in the **STAAD Analysis and Design** window and then choose the **Done** button; the **STAAD Analysis and Design** window will close and the **Results Setup** dialog box will be displayed, as shown in Figure 7-10.

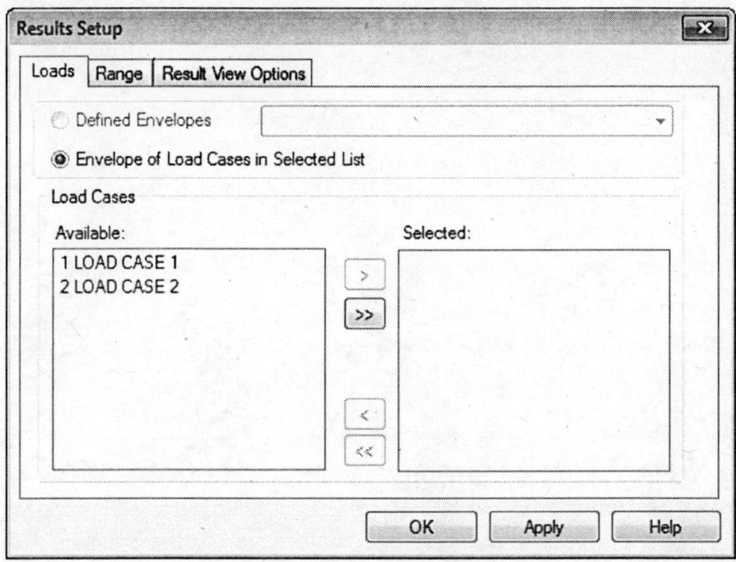

***Figure 7-10** The **Results Setup** dialog box*

In this dialog box, you can select the load cases and structural elements to be included in the post processing operations. In this dialog box, the **Loads** tab is chosen by default. In this tab, you will select the load cases to be included in the post processing operations. Select the required load cases from the **Available** area and then transfer them to the **Selected** area using the arrow buttons.

In the **Range** tab, you can specify the selection conditions based on the attributes for the members, nodes, properties, and so on. These selection conditions will determine whether the results will be displayed for all the members/nodes/properties or only for the selected ones.

In the **Result View Options** tab, you can specify the size for the displacement and moment diagrams to be plotted.

After selecting the required load cases and specifying other options, choose the **Apply** and **OK** buttons; the dialog box will be closed and the **Post Processing** tab will be displayed. In this tab, you can view the results graphically. These results are further categorized into further three tabs: **Node**, **Beam**, and **Animate**. These tabs are discussed next.

Node

On choosing this tab, the **Displacement** page will be displayed. In the **Displacement** page, the node deflection diagram for the selected load cases will be displayed. You need to select the required load case from the **Active Load** drop-down list available in the toolbar; the related node deflection diagram will be displayed in the main window. Figure 7-11 shows the node deflection diagram of a portal frame structure. The node displacement detail and the beam relative displacement detail of the selected load case will be displayed in the **Node Displacements** and **Beam Relative Displacement Detail** windows, respectively. These windows are available on the right side of the interface, refer to Figure 7-12.

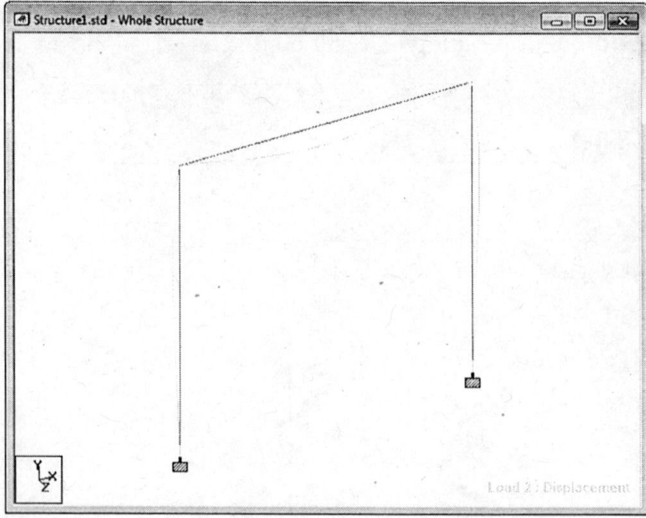

***Figure 7-11** The node deflection diagram in the Main Window*

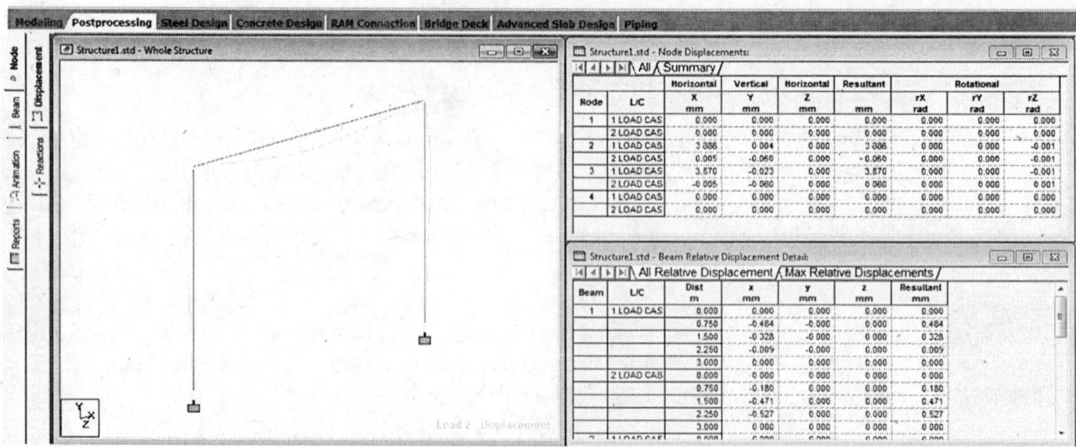

***Figure 7-12** The **Node Displacement** and **Beam Relative Displacement Detail** windows*

You can also view the support reactions in the main window. To do so, invoke the **Reactions** page available under the **Node** tab; the support reactions will be displayed in a box at the nodes where support is provided, refer to Figure 7-13. If you are unable to view the support reactions properly, choose the **Select Text** tool from the side toolbar. Next, press and hold the left mouse button and drag the box displaying the reactions at the desired place in the main window.

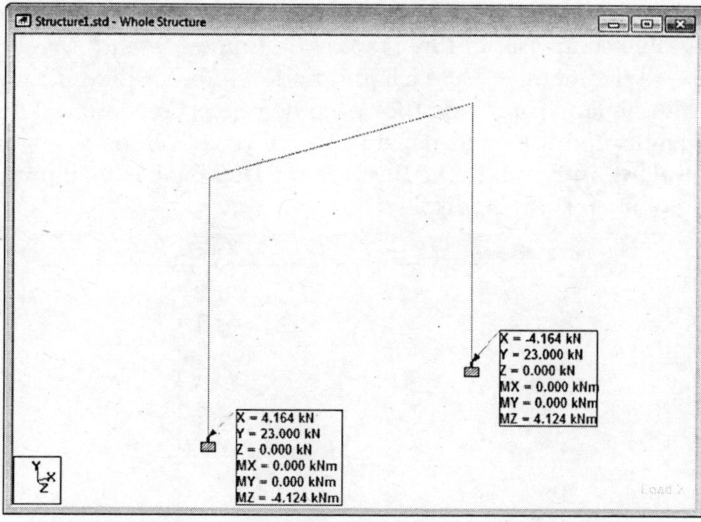

Figure 7-13 *Support reactions displayed at the joints*

Beam

You can view different types of member forces in the **Beam** tab. On choosing this tab, the **Forces** page will be displayed. In this page, you can view the shear force diagram, bending moment diagram, and axial force for different load cases. The bending moment diagram of the structure is displayed by default, refer to Figure 7-14. You can toggle this bending moment diagram on or off by using the **Bending Z Moment** button available in the toolbar, as shown in Figure 7-15. You can view the shear force and axial force diagrams by choosing the **Shear Y Force** and **Axial Force** buttons. Figures 7-16 and 7-17 show the shear force and axial force diagrams of a structure.

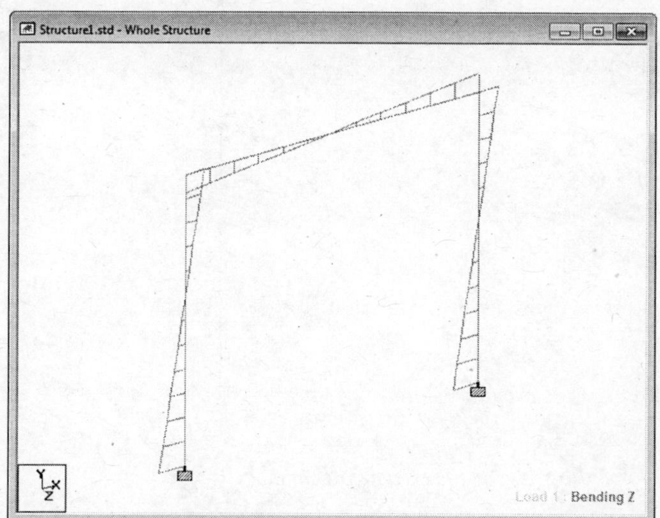

Figure 7-14 *Bending moment diagram of the structural members*

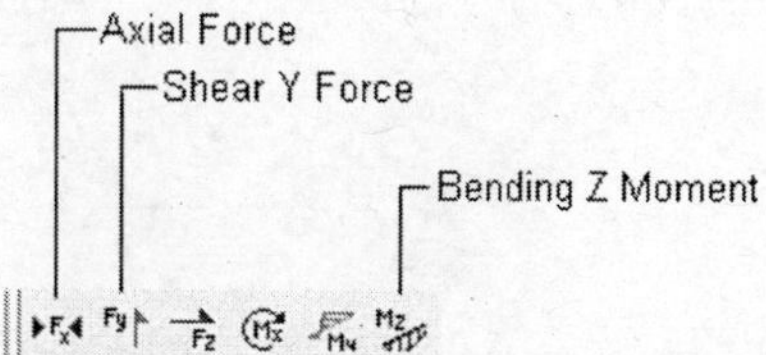

Figure 7-15 *Partial view of the toolbar*

The beam end forces results will be displayed in the **Beam End Forces** table on the right side of the interface. This table comprises of three tabs: **All**, **Summary**, and **Envelope**. In the **All** tab, beam end forces of all the members at each end node will be displayed. In the **Summary** tab, maximum and minimum end force result for each degree of freedom will be displayed. In the **Envelope** tab, maximum positive and negative end force envelope along with the associated load case number will be displayed. In the **Beam Force Detail** table, maximum axial force, shear force, and bending moments will be displayed.

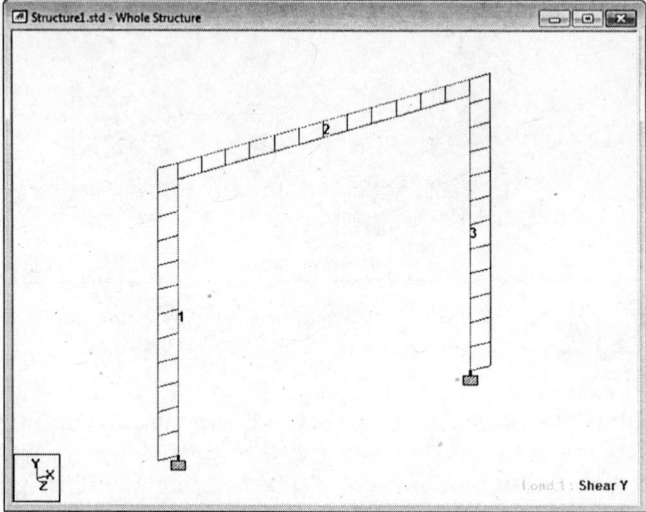

Figure 7-16 *Shear force diagram of the structural members*

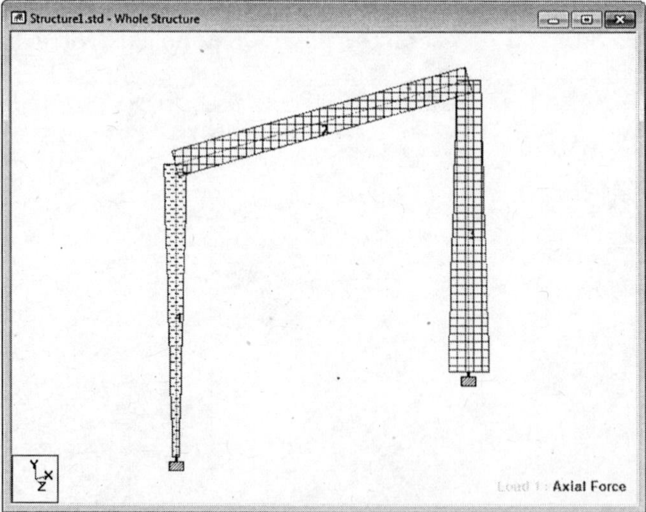

Figure 7-17 *Axial force diagram of the structural members*

In the **Stresses** page of the **Beam** tab, you can view the member stresses both graphically and numerically. The member stresses include combined axial and bending stresses. You can also view the combined stress for the cross-section at any point along the length of the member. When you invoke the **Stresses** page, the main window contains three sub windows: **3D Beam Stress Contour**, **Whole Structure**, and **Beam Combined and Axial Bending Stresses**. The **3D**

Beam Stress Contour window is empty by default. In the **Whole Structure** window, the member stresses diagram will be displayed, as shown in Figure 7-18.

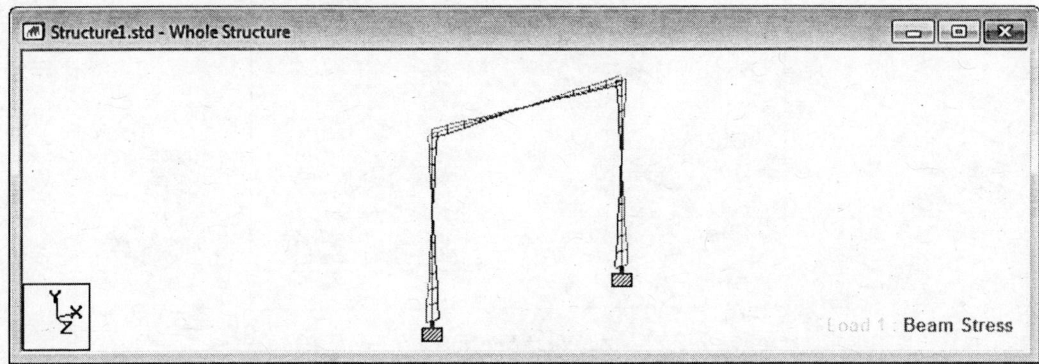

Figure 7-18 *The member stresses diagram displayed in the **Whole Structure** window*

The **Beam Combined Axial and Bending Stresses** window will comprise of three tabs: **All, Max Stresses**, and **Profile Stress Points**. In the **All** tab, the combined axial and bending stresses at the four corners of the member cross section will be displayed. The maximum compressive and tensile stresses are also listed in this window. In the **Max Stresses** tab, maximum compressive and tensile stresses for all members of all load cases will be displayed. The **Profile Stress Points** tab is empty by default. In this tab, you can add forces and stresses (Combined Axial and Bending Stresses) obtained at certain selected points on a cross section. To do so, first select a member in the **Whole Structure** window. On doing so, the stress distribution of the selected member will be displayed in the **3D Beam Stress Contour** window and the **Select Section Plane** dialog box will also be displayed. The **3D Beam Stress Contour** window is divided into two panes. In the left pane, the combined stress distribution along the longitudinal axis of the member will be displayed along with a yellow section plane, refer to Figure 7-19. In the right pane, stress distribution at the yellow section plane will be displayed, refer to Figure 7-19. In the **Select Section Plane** dialog box, you can use the slider to position the yellow rectangle at a certain location, refer to Figure 7-20. On doing so, the cross-sectional stress diagram will be immediately updated in the right pane of the **3D Beam Stress Contour** window.

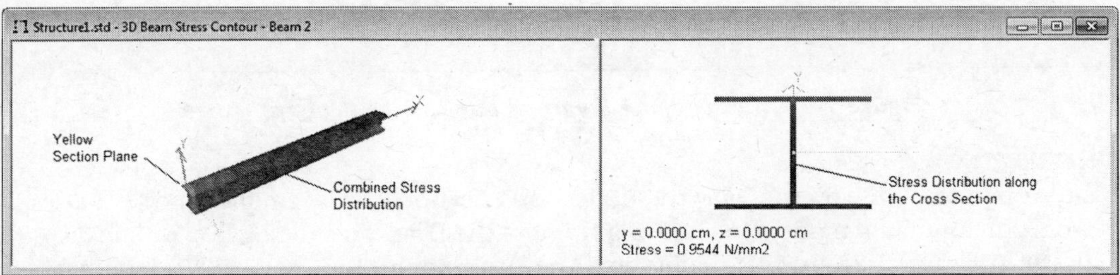

Figure 7-19 *The combined stress distribution in the **3D Beam Stress Contour** window*

Next, in the **Select Section Plane** dialog box, choose the **Add Stress to Table** button; the stresses will be added to the **Profile Stress Points** tab in the **Beam Combined Axial and Bending Stresses** window.

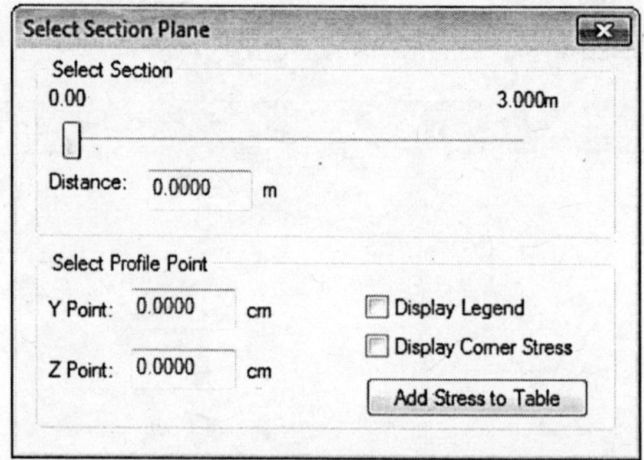

*Figure 7-20 The **Select Section Plane** dialog box*

You can also view the shear force diagram, bending moment diagram, and axial force diagram of each member individually in the **Graphs** page of the **Beam** tab. On invoking the **Graphs** page, you will see the whole structure displayed in the main window and the member force diagrams displayed in the **Graph** area, refer to Figure 7-21. To view the graphs for a particular member, select it in the main window; the corresponding diagrams (Shear Force Diagram, Bending Moment Diagram, and axial force diagram) will be displayed in the **Graph** area.

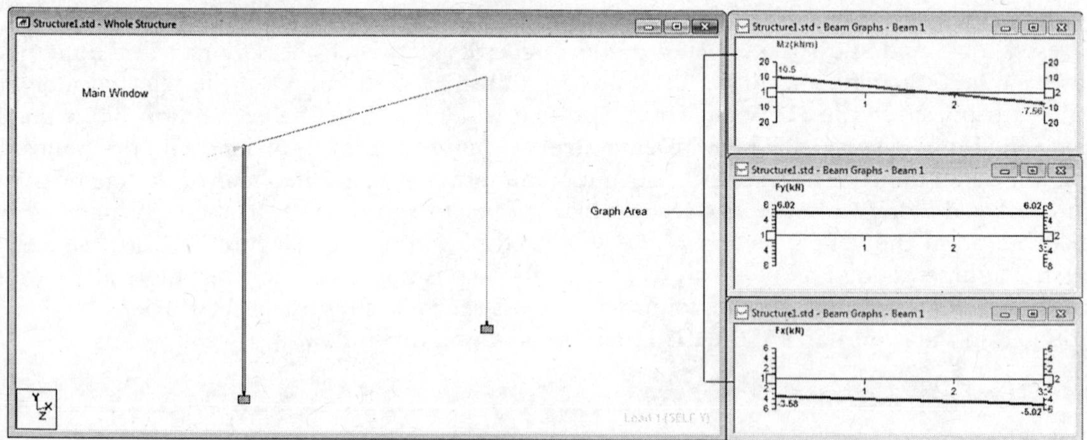

*Figure 7-21 Member force diagrams displayed in the **Graph** area*

Animation

In the **Animation** tab, you can view the deflections, section displacements, mode shapes, and stresses in an animated mode. On choosing this tab, the **Diagrams** dialog box will be displayed, as shown in Figure 7-22. In this dialog box, the **Animation** tab is chosen by default, refer to Figure 7-22. The options displayed in this dialog box are discussed next.

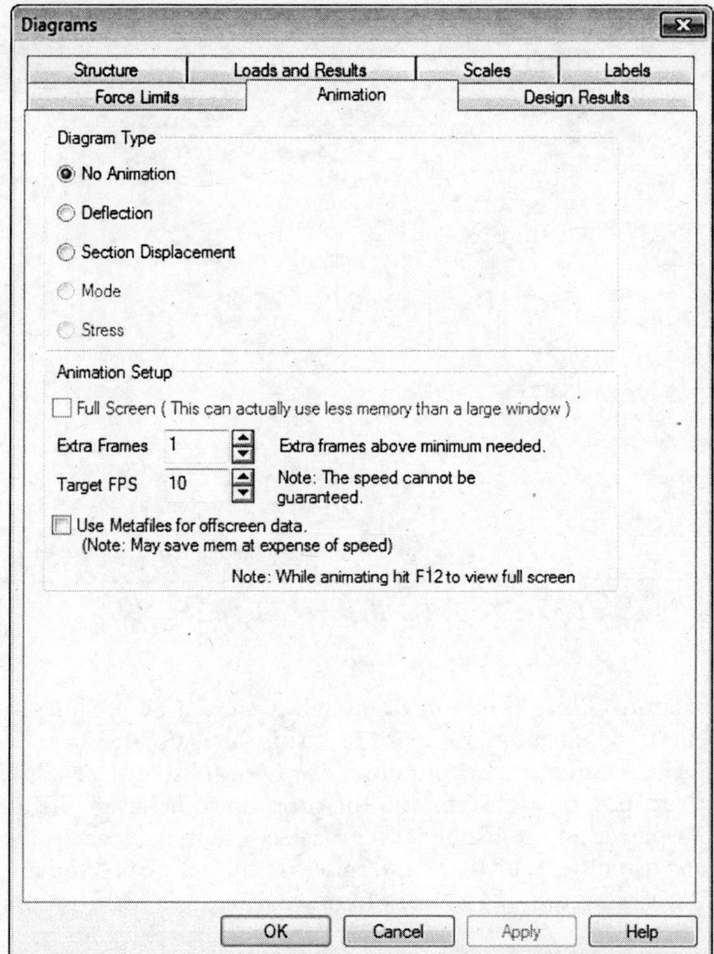

***Figure 7-22** The **Animation** tab in the **Diagrams** dialog box*

Select the type of animation by selecting the required radio button from the **Diagram Type** area. In the **Animation Setup** area, select the **Full Screen** check box to display the animation in full screen rather than inside the window. To enhance the animation, specify the number of extra frames in the **Extra Frames** edit box. To speed up or slow down the animation, specify a value in the **Target FPS** edit box. To save the animated screens as windows metafiles, select the **Use Metafiles for offscreen data** check box.

Note

*Selecting the **Use Metafiles for offscreen data** check box will make the speed of animation slower.*

Reports

In STAAD.Pro, you can generate customized reports. These reports may include load cases, mode shapes, structural elements, numerical and graphical results, and so on. When you choose the **Reports** tab, the **Report Setup** dialog box will be displayed, as shown in Figure 7-23. This dialog box comprises of tabs such as **Items**, **Load Cases**, **Modes**, **Ranges**, **Steel Design**, **Picture Album**, **Options**, **Name and Logo**, and **Load/Save**. These tabs are discussed next.

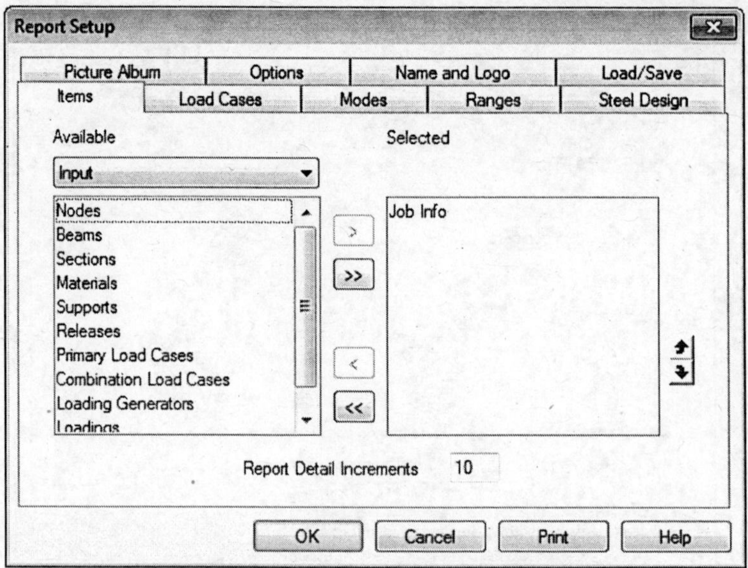

*Figure 7-23 The **Report Setup** dialog box*

Items

In the **Report Setup** dialog box, the **Items** tab is chosen by default. In this tab, you can specify the items to be included in the report. This tab is divided into two areas: **Available** and **Selected**. The **Available** area contains a drop-down list and a list box. Select an option such as **Input**, **Output**, or **Pictures** from the drop-down list available at the top; different items will be displayed in the list box. Next, select the items to be included in the report from the list box using the CTRL key and move them to the **Selected** area using the single forward arrow button. If you want to move the whole list from the **Available** area to the **Selected** area, choose the double forward arrow button.

Load Cases

In the **Load Cases** tab, you can specify which load case results will be included in the report. Then, you can move the required load cases from the **Available** area to the **Selected** area in the same way as discussed in the **Items** tab. You can also group the results table by node/beam numbers or by load cases. Specify the method of grouping using the radio buttons available under the **Grouping for Load Tables** and **Grouping for Result Tables** areas.

Modes

In the **Modes** tab, you can select the mode shape numbers for which the results will be displayed in the report. In this tab, select the required mode shape numbers from the **Available** area using the CTRL key and then move them to the **Selected** area.

Ranges

In the **Ranges** tab, you can specify the nodes, members, and elements to be included in the report. This can be done by selecting the following radio buttons available in this tab: **All**, **View**, **Group**, **Property**, and **Ranges**. These radio buttons are discussed next. You can select the **All** radio button to include all the members in the report. You can also generate a report for the structural element that will appear in a particular view. To do so, select the

View radio button and then select the required view from the drop-down list available next to it. If no view has been saved previously then the **View** radio button will be disabled. You can save a view by selecting the **View Management > Save View** from the **View** menu. The report for a particular group of members/elements can also be generated. To do so, select the **Group** radio button and then select the required group from the drop-down list available next to the **Group** radio button. To include members having certain property in the report, select the **Property** radio button. Next, select the required property from the drop-down list available next to the radio button. Similarly, you can generate a report for a particular set of nodes and members. To do so, select the **Ranges** radio button and then specify the range of nodes and members in the **Nodes** and **Beam/Plates/Solids** edit boxes, respectively.

Picture Album

You can also include the picture of the structure in the report. To do so, choose the **Picture Album** tab and then select the required picture from the **Name** drop-down list, refer to Figure 7-24. To print the picture on an entire page, select the **Full Page** check box or you can print the picture within the dimensions specified in the **Height** and **Width** edit boxes. To change the caption of the picture, specify a name in the **Caption** text box. To delete a picture, choose the **Delete Picture** button.

Note

*You can take a picture by using the **Take Picture** tool from the toolbar.*

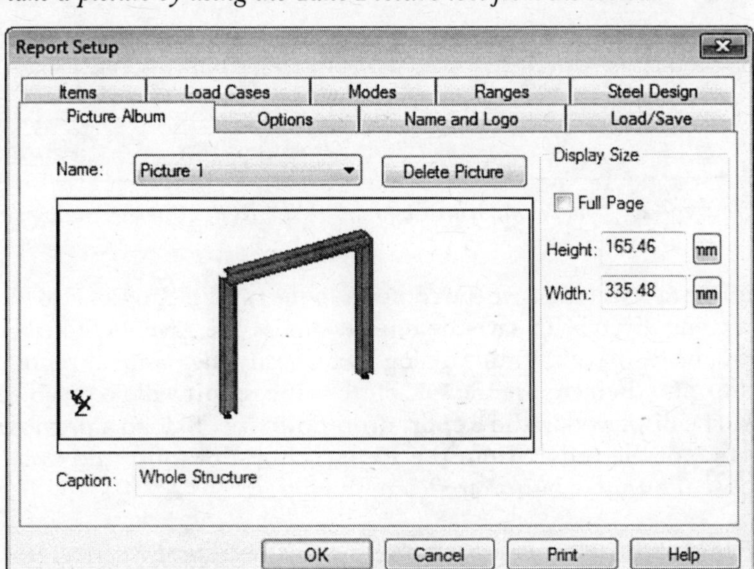

*Figure 7-24 The **Picture Album** tab in the **Report Setup** dialog box*

Options

In the **Options** tab, you can specify various report options. To include page headers, footers, and page outline in the report page, select the **Header**, **Page Outline**, and **Footer** check boxes. To include page numbers in the report, specify the starting page number in the **No. pages from** edit box. You can add prefix and suffix to the page numbers by specifying them in the **Prefix** and **Suffix** edit boxes. To reverse the page numbers, select the **Reverse page order** check box. Similarly, specify other options for the fonts and report table in the **Tables** area.

Name and Logo

In the **Name and Logo** tab, you can add your company's name and logo to the report. You can write the company's name in the viewing area, refer to Figure 7-25. You can change the font of the company name by using the options available in the **Text** area. To include company logo in the report, first save it in bitmap files (.bmp) format. Next, choose the **File** button in the **Graphics** area; the **Open** dialog box will be displayed. Browse to the file location, select the file, and then choose the **Open** button; the logo will be displayed in the **Viewing** area. You can place it at an appropriate place by selecting the **Left**, **Centre**, or **Right** radio button available in the **Graphic** area.

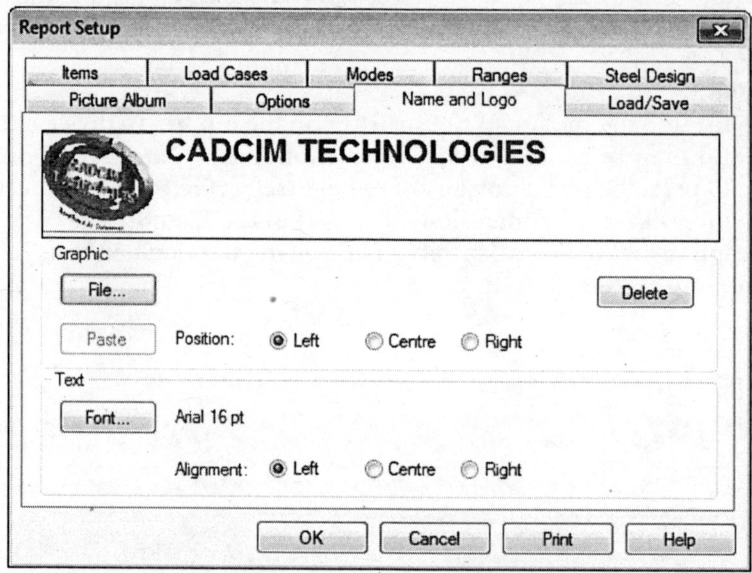

Figure 7-25 *The* ***Name and Logo*** *tab in the* ***Report Setup*** *dialog box*

Load/Save

In the **Load/Save** tab, you can save the contents of the report. You can also load the previously saved report using this tab. To save the report, choose the **Save As** button; the **Save Report** dialog box will be displayed. In this dialog box, specify the name of report in the **Save this report** text box and then choose the **OK** button; the report will be saved with the specified name and will be displayed in the **Report** drop-down list. To load a previously saved report, select the name of the report from the **Report** drop-down list and then choose the **OK** button. Choose the **Delete** button to delete the report.

After specifying all the parameters, choose the **OK** button; the report will be displayed in the main window. You can enlarge the viewing scale of the report. To do so, choose the **Zoom In** button available at the left side in the interface. To print the report, choose the **Print** button; the **Print** dialog box will be displayed. Specify the required settings in this dialog box to print the report or save it in Adobe PDF format. To make any changes in the report, choose the **Setup Report** button.

Note

In this chapter, you need to download the c06_Staad_v8i.zip and c08_Staad_v8i.zip files from http://www.cadcim.com. The path of the file is as follows: Textbook > Civil/GIS > STAAD.Pro > Exploring Bentley STAAD.Pro V8i.

Example 1

In this example, you will open the file *c06_staad_v8i_ex4.std* and then add the pre-print analysis, performing analysis, and the post analysis commands. Next, you will view the results and create a report file.

Steps required to complete this example are given below:

Step 1: Open the file *c06_staad_v8i_ex4.std* in STAAD.Pro; the model is displayed in the main window.

Step 2: Choose the **Analysis/Print** tab; the **Analysis/Print Commands** dialog box is displayed. Select the **All** radio button from the **Perform Analysis** tab in the **Print Option** area and then choose the **Add** button. Choose the **Close** button to close the dialog box.

Step 3: Invoke the **Post-Print** page; the **Post Analysis Print - Whole Structure** window is displayed. Choose the **Define Commands** button available in the **Post Analysis Print - Whole Structure** window; the **Analysis/Print Commands** dialog box will be displayed, as shown in Figure 7-26.

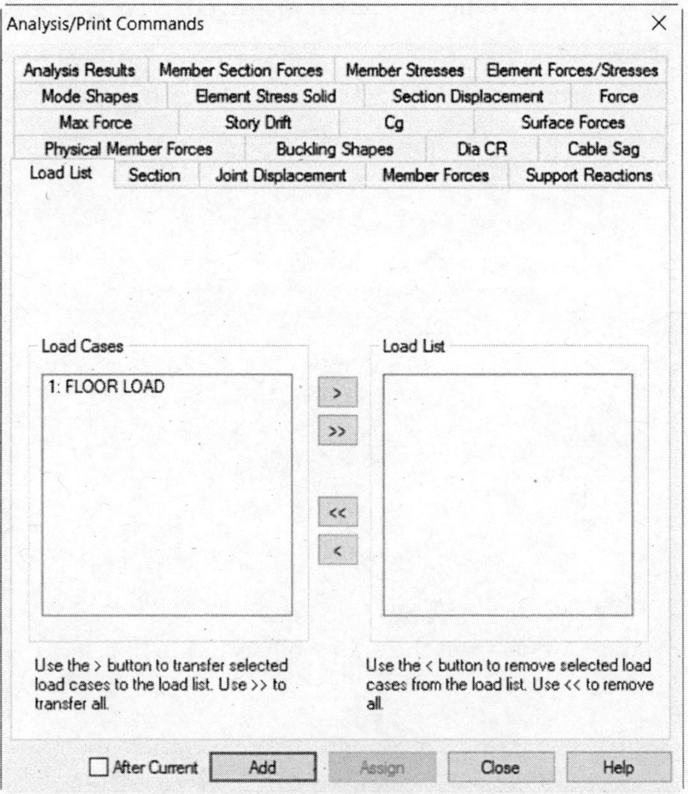

*Figure 7-26 The **Analysis/Print Commands** dialog box*

Step 4: In this dialog box, make sure that the **Load List** tab is chosen and then select the **1: FLOOR LOAD** in the **Load Cases** area. Next, choose the single forward arrow button; the **1: FLOOR LOAD** is moved to the **Load List** area. Choose the **Add** button; the **LOAD LIST** command will be added to the **Post Analysis Print - Whole Structure** window.

Step 5: Choose the **Member Forces** tab in the **Analysis/Print Commands** dialog box and select the **Global** check box. Then, choose the **Add** button to add the command to the **Post Analysis Print - Whole Structure** window.

Step 6: Choose the **Support Reactions** tab. Next, choose the **Add** button and then close the dialog box.

Step 7: Next, select the **PRINT MEMBER FORCES GLOBAL** command in the **Post Analysis Print - Whole Structure** window. Then, select the **Assign To View** radio button and choose the **Assign** button; the **STAAD.Pro V8i (SELECTseries 6)** message box is displayed. Choose the **Yes** button; the command will be assigned to all the members.

Step 8: Next, select the **PRINT SUPPORT REACTION** command from the **Post Analysis Print - Whole Structure** window. Then, choose the **View From +Z** button from the toolbar; the front view of the structure is displayed, refer to Figure 7-27.

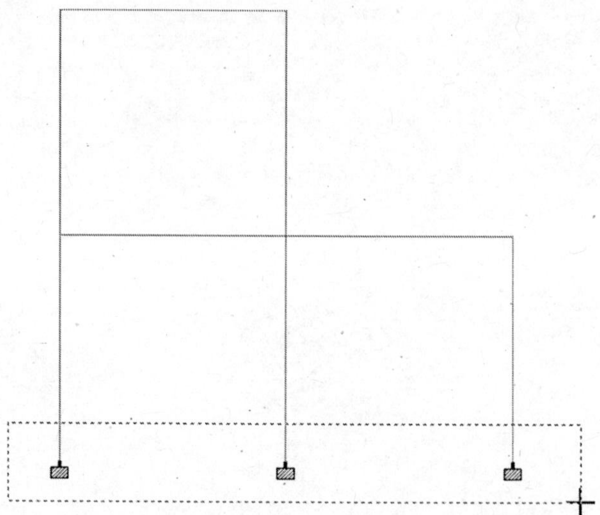

***Figure 7-27** Selecting the lower nodes using the drag box*

Step 9: Select the **Nodes Cursor** from the side toolbar and then select the lower nodes, refer to Figure 7-27.

Step 10: Ensure that the **Assign To Selected Nodes** radio button is selected in the **Assignment Method** area of the **Post Analysis Print - Whole Structure** window. Choose the **Assign** button; the **STAAD.Pro V8i (SELECTseries 6)** message box is displayed. Choose the **Yes** button; the command is assigned to the base nodes.

Step 11: Choose the **Isometric View** button from the toolbar; the isometric view of the structure is displayed in the main window.

Step 12: Choose the **Run Analysis** option from the **Analyze** menu; the **Warning** message box is displayed. In the **Warning** message box, choose the **Save** button; the **STAAD Analysis and Design** message box is displayed. Choose the **OK** button; the **STAAD Analysis and Design** window is displayed.

Step 13: In this window, select the **View Output File** radio button and choose the **Done** button; the **STAAD Output Viewer** window is displayed. In the left pane of this window, click on the **RESULTS** bar and then click on the **MEMBER FORCES GLOBAL LIST**; the member forces of all the members are displayed in the right pane of the window, refer to Figure 7-28.

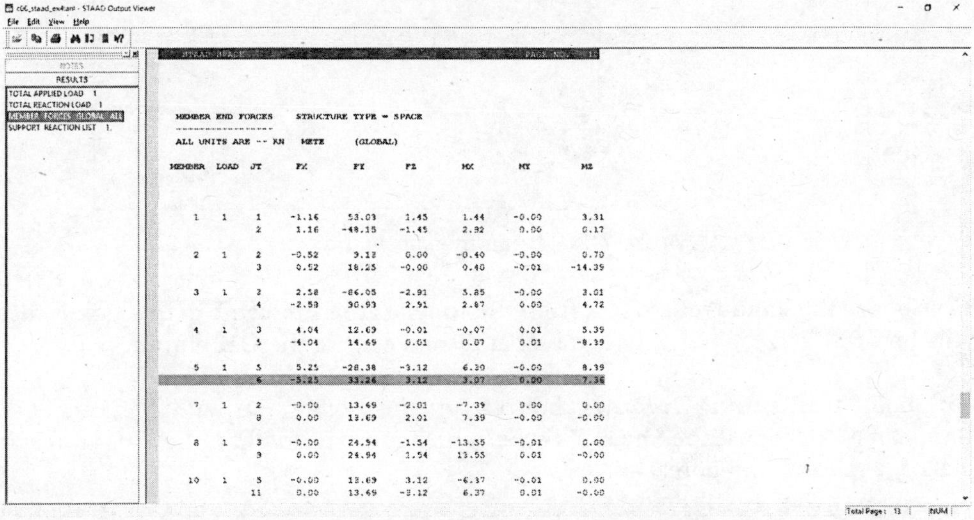
STAAD Output Viewer
File Edit View Help
NOTES
RESULTS
TOTAL APPLIED LOAD 1
TOTAL REACTION LOAD 1
SUPPORT REACTION LIST 1
MEMBER END FORCES STRUCTURE TYPE = SPACE
ALL UNITS ARE -- KN METE (GLOBAL)
MEMBER LOAD JT FX FY FZ MX MY MZ
1 1 1 -1.16 53.03 1.45 1.44 -0.00 3.31
2 1.16 -48.15 -1.45 2.92 0.00 0.17
2 1 2 -0.52 9.12 0.00 -0.40 -0.00 0.70
3 0.52 18.25 -0.00 0.40 -0.01 -14.39
3 1 2 2.58 -86.05 -2.91 5.85 -0.00 3.01
4 -2.58 90.93 2.91 2.87 0.00 4.72
4 1 3 4.04 12.69 -0.01 -0.07 0.01 5.39
5 -4.04 14.69 0.01 0.07 0.01 -8.39
5 1 5 5.25 -28.38 -3.12 6.30 -0.00 8.39
6 -5.25 33.26 3.12 3.07 0.00 7.36
7 1 2 -0.00 13.69 -2.01 -7.39 0.00 0.00
8 0.00 13.69 2.01 7.39 -0.00 -0.00
8 1 3 -0.00 24.94 -1.54 -13.55 -0.01 0.00
9 0.00 24.94 1.54 13.55 0.01 -0.00
10 1 5 -0.00 13.69 3.12 -6.37 -0.01 0.00
11 0.00 13.69 -3.12 6.37 0.01 -0.00
Total Page: 13
NUM

*Figure 7-28 Member forces displayed in the **STAAD Output Viewer** window*

Step 14: Repeat the procedure followed in step 13 and view the support reactions. Next, close the **STAAD Output Viewer** window.
Now, you will view the shear force and bending moment diagrams.

Step 15: Choose the **Post Processing** tab; the **Results Setup** dialog box is displayed. In this dialog box, choose the **Apply** and **OK** buttons; the **Displacement** page is displayed.

Step 16: Choose the **Beam** tab; the **Forces** page is displayed with the bending moment diagram, as shown in Figure 7-29.

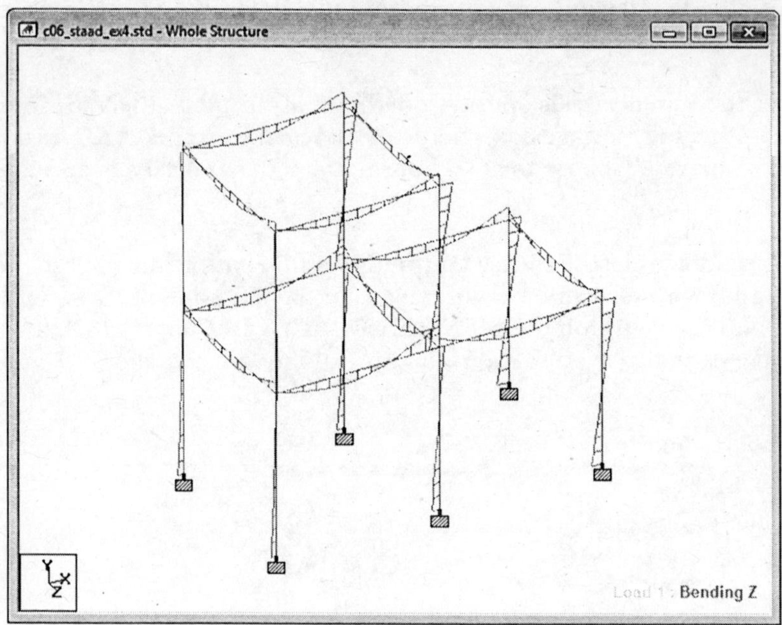

Figure 7-29 Bending moment diagram

Step 17: Choose the **Take Picture** tool from the toolbar; the **Picture 1** dialog box is displayed. Enter the text **BMD** in the **Caption** text box and then choose the **OK** button.

Step 18: Choose the **Bending Z Moment** button from the toolbar; the bending moment diagram will disappear. Next, choose the **Shear Y Force** button from the toolbar; the shear force diagram is displayed, as shown in Figure 7-30.

Step 19: Repeat the procedure followed in step 17 and take a picture with caption **SFD** of the shear force diagram.

Next, you will create a customized report for the structure.

Step 20: Choose the **Reports** tab; the **Report Setup** dialog box is displayed. In the **Items** tab of the dialog box, select the **Input** option from the drop-down list available in the **Available** area. Next, in the **Available** area, select the **Nodes, Beams, Sections, Materials** and **Supports** option from the list box using the CTRL key and then choose the forward button; all the options are moved to the **Selected** area.

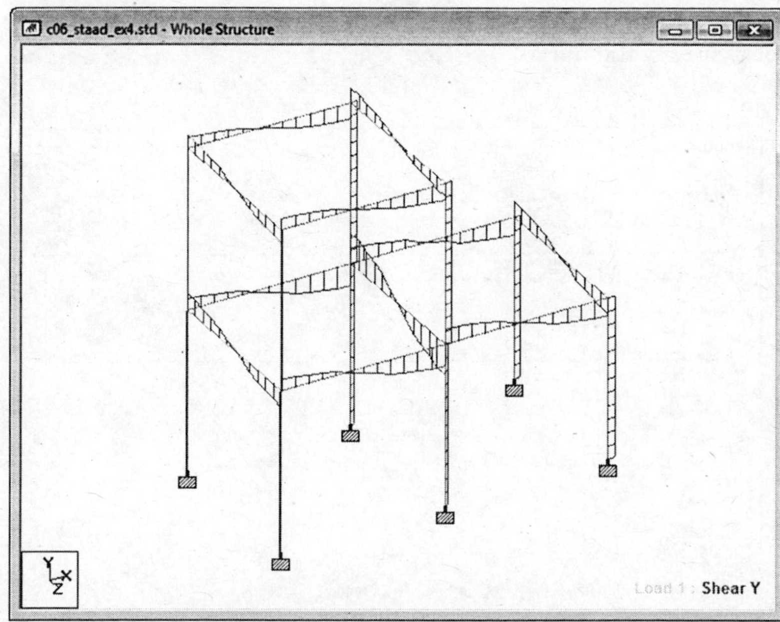

Figure 7-30 Shear force diagram

Step 21: In the **Available** area, select the **Output** option from the drop-down list. Next, select the **Beam End Forces** and **Reactions** options using the CTRL key in the list box and then choose the forward button; the options are moved to the **Selected** area.

Step 22: Similarly, select the **Pictures** option from the drop-down list available in the **Available** area and move **Picture 1** and **Picture 2** to the **Selected** area.

Step 23: Choose the **Load Cases** tab and ensure that the **1 FLOOR LOAD** is available in the **Selected** area.

Step 24: Choose the **Name and Logo** tab and type **CADCIM TECHNOLOGIES** in the Viewing area. Next, choose the **File** button in the **Graphics** area; the **Open** dialog box is displayed.

Step 25: Browse to the folder *c07_Staad_v8i* and then select the *logo.bmp* file. Next, choose the **Open** button; the logo is added to the Viewing area. Ensure that the **Left** radio button is selected in the **Text** area and the **Right** radio button is selected in the **Graphic** area. Figure 7-31 shows the name and logo added in the Viewing area.

Step 26: Choose the **Load/Save** tab and then choose the **Save As** button; the **Save Report** dialog box is displayed. Specify the name *Ex1_report* in the **Save this report as** text box and then choose the **OK** button; the report name is added to the **Report** drop-down list.

Step 27: Choose the **OK** button in the **Report Setup** dialog box. Now, choose the **Print** button from the right side of the interface; the **Print** dialog box is displayed. In this dialog box, select the **Adobe PDF** option from the **Name** drop-down list and then choose the **OK** button; the **Save PDF File As** dialog box is displayed. Browse to an appropriate location and save the file with the name *c07_Staad_v8i_ex1* and then choose the **Save** button; the report is saved as a pdf file, refer to Figure 7-32.

Step 28: Choose the **Save As** option from the **File** menu; the **Save As** dialog box is displayed. In this dialog box, specify the name *c07_staad_v8i_ex1* in the **File name** edit box and save it at an appropriate location.

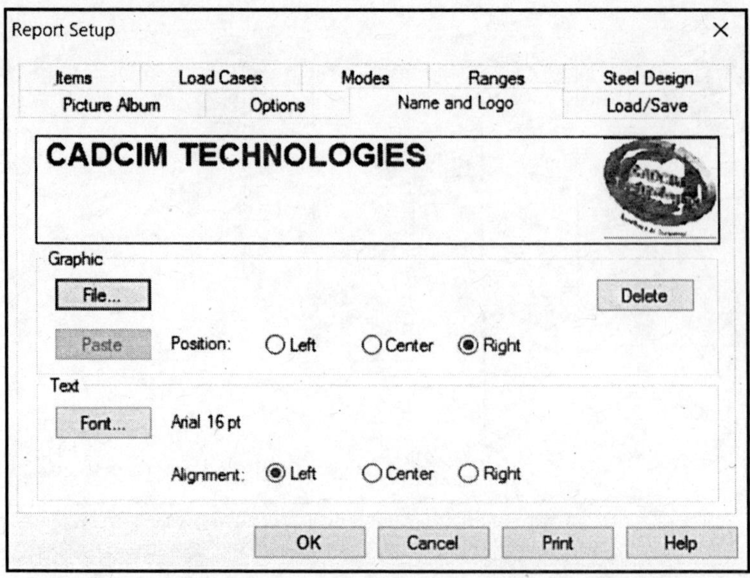

***Figure 7-31** Figure and logo added in the **Viewing** area*

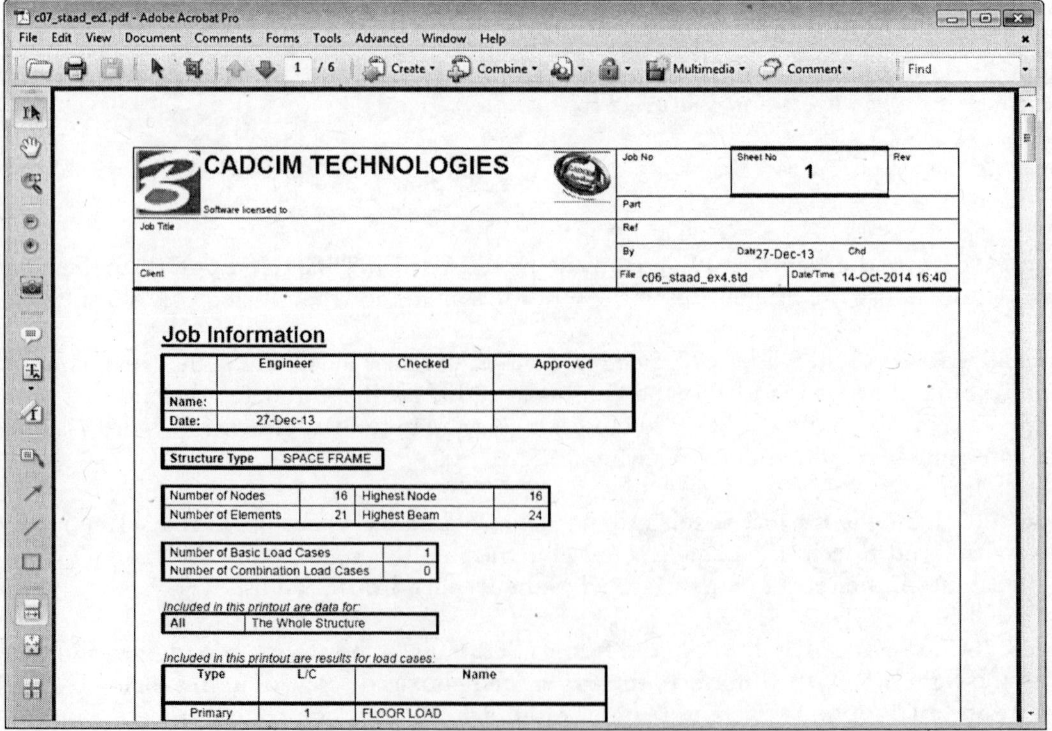

***Figure 7-32** Report file saved as a pdf file*

Self-Evaluation Test

Answer the following questions and compare them to those given at the end of this chapter:

1. The __________ command is used to display basic information about the structure in the output file.

2. The __________ command is used to display entire information about the structure in the output file.

3. You can use the __________ analysis command for the structures subjected to lateral loading.

4. You cannot print mode shape values in the output file. (T/F)

5. In the post processing mode, you cannot view the results graphically. (T/F)

6. You can view the shear force diagram, bending moment diagram, and axial force diagram of each member individually. (T/F)

7. You can toggle on/off the shear force diagram and bending moment diagram of whole structure. (T/F)

8. You can view the stress contours of members and plates graphically. (T/F)

9. You cannot insert pictures of the structural model in the report. (T/F)

10. You can add the company logo with the file extension other than **.bmp*. (T/F)

Review Questions

Answer the following questions:

1. Which of the following options is used to print the coordinates of the centre of gravity of the structure in the output file?

   (a) **Force** (b) **Section Displacement**
   (c) **Cg** (d) None of these

2. Which of the following options is used to calculate the section displacement and print it in the output file?

   (a) **Section Displacement** (b) **Force**
   (c) **Member Stresses** (d) **Mode Shapes**

3. Which of the following options is used to calculate and print the support reactions in the output file?

   (a) **Member Forces** (b) **Support Reactions**
   (c) **Story Drift** (d) None of these

4. You cannot add company's logo to the STAAD report. (T/F)

5. In STAAD.Pro, you cannot create animation of deflection and mode shapes. (T/F)

Answers to Self-Evaluation Test

1. Problem Statistics, **2.** All, **3.** PDelta, **4.** F, **5.** F, **6.** T, **7.** T, **8.** T, **9.** F, **10.** F

Chapter 8

Structural Modeling Using Building Planner

Learning Objectives

After completing this chapter, you will be able to:

- *Create slabs using Building Planner*
- *Create columns using Building Planner*
- *Create beams using Building Planner*
- *Generate a STAAD.Pro model*

INTRODUCTION

Building planner is a new modeling mode introduced in STAAD.pro V8i (SELECTseries 6). In this mode, you can create a structure by using a set of planes. Models generated in the Building Planner mode get quickly defined in STAAD.Pro. Once the model has been defined, the key concrete components are designed and detailed in the RC Designer mode.

Modeling in the Building Planner mode is discussed next.

STRUCTURAL MODELING USING BUILDING PLANNER

To start modeling in the Building Planner mode, you need to choose the **Building Planner** tab in the mode bar from the STAAD interface; the **Start** wizard will be displayed, as shown in Figure 8-1.

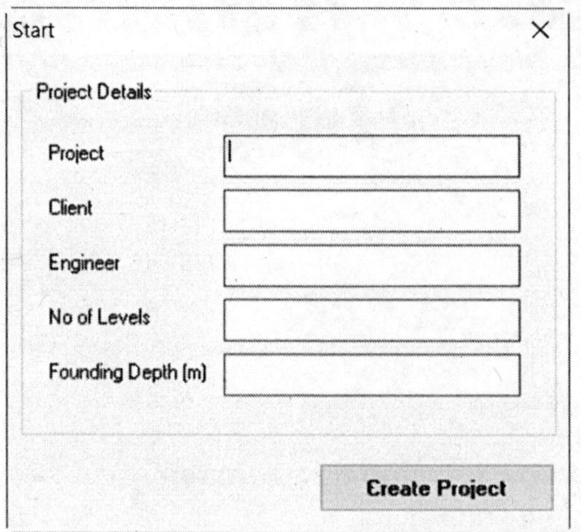

Figure 8-1 *The **Start** wizard*

In this wizard, you can enter general information about the project, such as name of the project, client, engineer and can also define the number of levels in the corresponding edit boxes. After providing the project details, choose the **Create Project** button; the **Start** dialog box will be closed and the **New Plan** dialog box will be displayed, as shown in Figure 8-2.

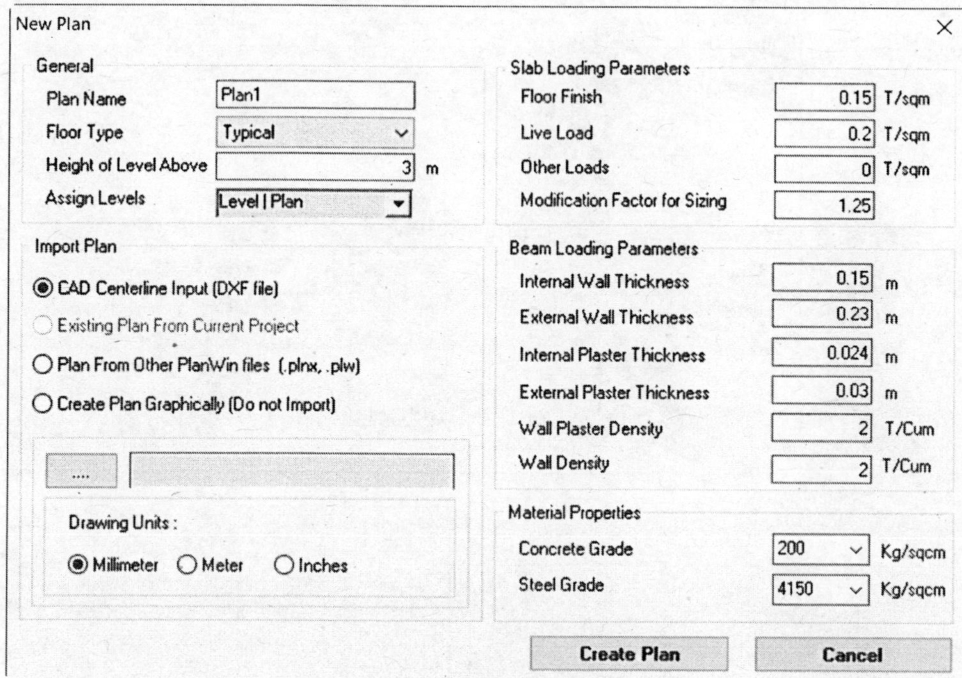

***Figure 8-2** The **New Plan** dialog box*

In this dialog box, specify the name of the plan in the **Plan Name** edit box of the **General** area. Select the floor type as the Ground, Typical, or Roof from the **Floor Type** drop-down list. Specify the height of the level in the **Height of Level Above** edit box. Levels can be assigned by selecting from the **Assign Levels** field. You can import plans from CAD, PlanWin files, and existing plan by selecting the corresponding radio buttons. In the **Slab Loading Parameters** area, you can enter values for various loads in the corresponding edit boxes. Values for loads on beams can be assigned in the **Internal Wall Thickness, External Wall Thickness, Internal Plaster Thickness, External Plaster Thickness, Wall Plaster Density**, and **Wall Density** edit boxes. You can assign grade to both concrete and steel materials by selecting the required values in their corresponding drop-down lists in the **Material Properties** area.

If you want to create plan geometry, select the **Create Plan Graphically (Do not Import)** radio button. After assigning required properties for the plan, choose the **Create Plan** button; the **New Plan** dialog box will be closed and the **Slab Details (Rectangle)** dialog box will be displayed, as shown in Figure 8-3.

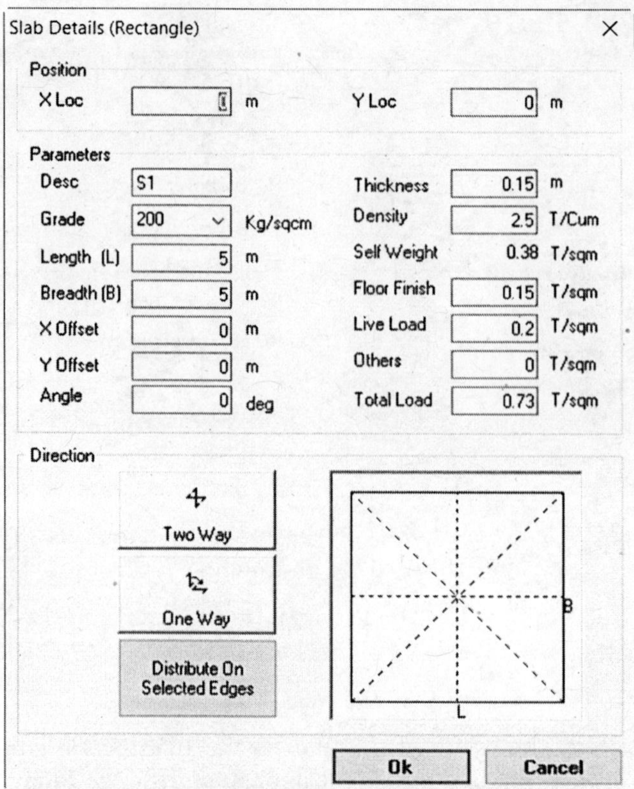

*Figure 8-3 The **Slab Details (Rectangle)** dialog box*

You can assign position of the slab in the **Slab Details (Rectangle)** dialog box. To do so, enter the values in the **XLoc** and **YLoc** edit boxes. Various parameters like grade, length, breadth, and so on for the slab can be assigned in the **Parameters** area. Note that you cannot assign the self weight for the slab. It is calculated by the software on the basis of parameters defined in the **Parameters** area. You can define the nature of slab from the **Direction** area. You can select the **Two Way**, **One Way**, or **Distributed on Selected Edges** button from the **Direction** area. After defining slab specifications, choose the **Ok** button; the **Slab Details (Rectangle)** dialog box will be closed and slab will be added to the working area, refer to Figure 8-4.

Figure 8-4 Slab added to the working area

ADDING SLABS

To add a rectangular slab to the current plan, select the **Create Slab Rectangle** option from the **Slab** menu. Select the start and end corners of the slab from the drawing area. On doing so, the **Slab details (Rectangle)** dialog box will be displayed, refer to Figure 8-3. You can edit parameters in this dialog box as discussed. Next, choose the **Ok** button after assigning the required properties; the **Slab Details (Rectangle)** dialog box will be closed and the slab will be added to the working area.

If the slab is drawn beyond the extents of the window, right-click anywhere in the working area and select the **Zoom Extents** option from the menu; the drawing will now fit in the area. Press **Esc** to quit using this tool.

You can also add irregular slab to the plan view. To add irregular shaped slab, select the **Create Slab Irregular** option from the **Slab** menu. Now, select the top left corner of the slab and then select the bottom right corner of the slab; the **Point Selection** dialog box will be displayed, as shown in Figure 8-5.

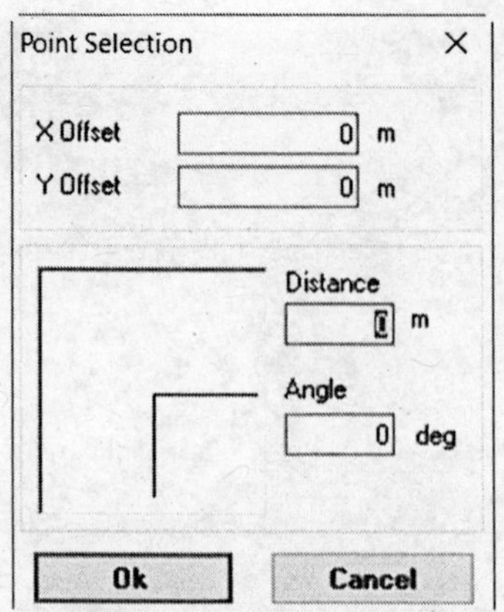

*Figure 8-5 The **Point Selection** dialog box*

You can assign offset values for the slab in x and y direction in the **X Offset** and **Y Offset** edit boxes, respectively. You can enter a value for distance in the **Distance** edit box and angle in the **Angle** edit box. After assigning required values, choose the **Ok** button; the **Point Selection** dialog box will be closed. Now, right-click in the drawing area; the **Slab Details (IRRegular)** dialog box will be displayed, refer to Figure 8-6.

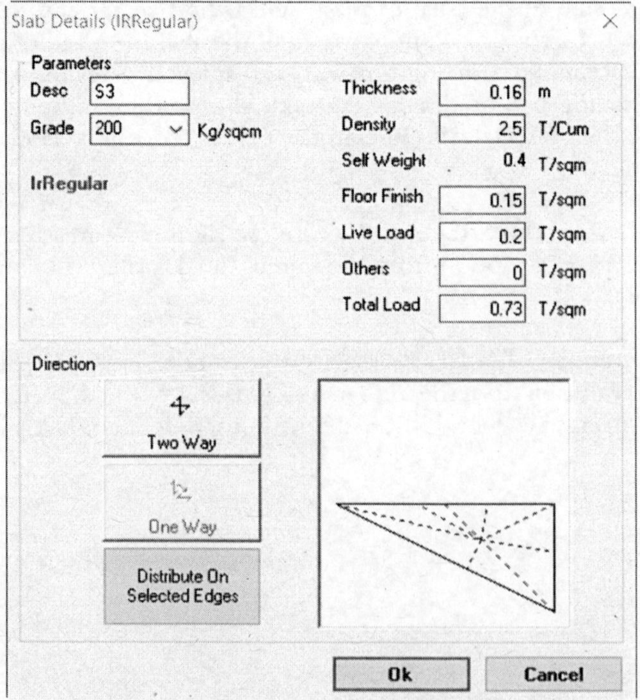

*Figure 8-6 The **Slab Details (IRRegular)** dialog box.*

You can define details in the **Parameters** area for the irregular slab as defined for the rectangular slab. You can also define the direction for the slab in the **Direction** area. After specifying all the required values, choose the **Ok** button; the **Slab Details (IRRegular)** dialog box will be closed. Press **Esc** to exit the current selection.

Editing Slab Properties

You can edit the properties of existing slabs by selecting the **Select/Unselect** option from the **Slab** menu and then select the slab from the **Plan** area; the selected slab is highlighted. Now, select the **Set Property** option from the **Slab** menu; the **Set Slab Property And Loading** dialog box is displayed, as shown in Figure 8-7.

*Figure 8-7 The **Set Slab Property And Loading** dialog box*

Specify the values for each parameter in the **Set Slab Property And Loading** dialog box and then choose the **Ok** button; the **Set Slab Property And Loading** dialog box will be closed and the properties of the selected slab will be modified.

ADDING COLUMNS

To add a column to the current plan, select the **Create Column** option from the **Column** menu and select the nearest point to the slab edge where you want to place the column. On doing so, the nearest slab corner will be highlighted in red circle and the **Column Details** dialog box will be displayed, refer to Figure 8-8.

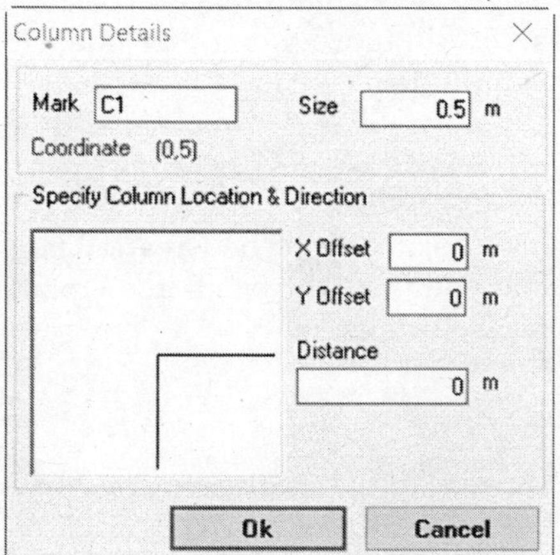

*Figure 8-8 The **Column Details** dialog box*

You can define details for the columns in the **Column Details** dialog box. In this dialog box, edit the mark for the column in the **Mark** edit box. You can define the size of column by entering a value in the **Size** edit box. You can edit the values in the **X Offset** and **Y Offset** edit boxes to place column at an offset from the selected point in the X and Y directions, respectively. You can also place a columns at an assigned distance from the selected point. To do so, edit the value in the **Distance** edit box and select the direction for placement of the column, vertically or horizontally in the preview area of the **Column Details** dialog box. After specifying the values, choose the **Ok** button; the **Column Details** dialog box will be closed and the columns will be placed. These columns will be placed automatically at slab edges by selecting the **Auto Column** option from the column menu. Also, you can specify location for the column by selecting the **Locate Column** option from the **Column** menu. On doing so, the **Locate Column** dialog box will displayed, refer to Figure 8-9.

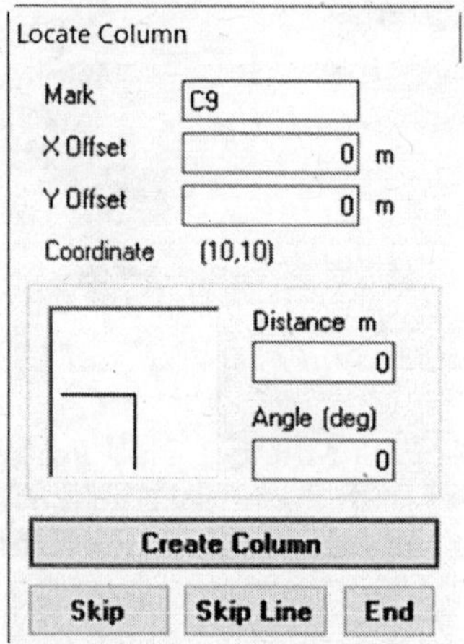

***Figure 8-9** The **Locate Column** dialog box.*

In this dialog box, specify values in the edit boxes to locate the column; a placement marker will be displayed on the edge of the slab. On the located point, create a column by choosing the **Create Column** button. If you want to skip the located point, choose the **Skip** button; the marker will move to another edge where column is not placed. To skip the entire line, choose the **Skip Line** button; the marker will move to another line. Next, choose the **End** button to stop adding columns in the plan window.

ADDING BEAMS

To add single beam to the current plan, select the **Create Beam** option from the **Beam** menu and then select the start and end points for the beam in the plan; the **Beam Details** dialog box will be displayed, refer to Figure 8-10.

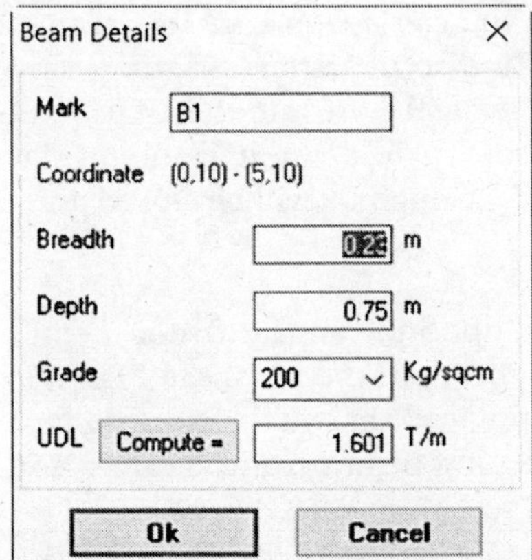

***Figure 8-10** The **Beam Details** dialog box*

In this dialog box, edit the mark property of the beam by entering a value in the **Mark** edit box. To edit the breadth and depth of beam, enter the values in the **Breadth** and **Depth** edit boxes. You can also assign the grade of concrete by selecting required value from the **Grade** drop-down list. You can assign a value for uniformly distributed load in the **UDL** edit box. You can also compute the UDL for a beam. To do so, choose the **Compute** button; the **Beam Load** dialog box will be displayed, as shown in Figure 8-11.

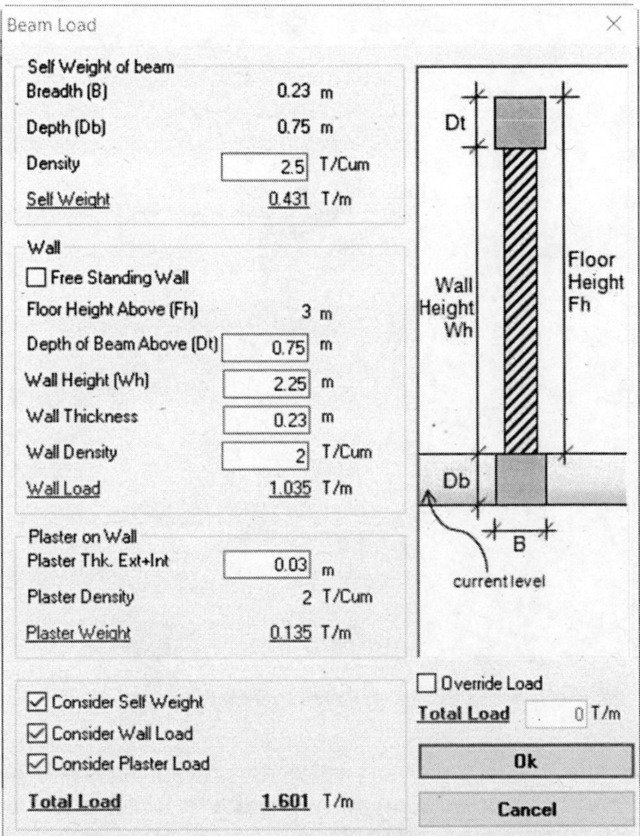

***Figure 8-11** The **Beam Load** dialog box*

In the **Beam Load** dialog box, you can assign various parameters for beam like self weight of beam, breadth, width, density, and so on. After assigning various parameters, choose the **Ok** button; the **Beam Load** dialog box will close and the UDL value corresponding to the assigned value in the **Beam Load** dialog box will be computed and displayed in the **UDL** edit box. Choose the **Ok** button, the **Beam Details** dialog box will be closed and the beam will be drawn in green on the plan window.

You can choose the **Auto Beam** option from the **Beam** menu to place beams automatically in the plan. If there is any existing beam in the plan; the **PlanWin** message box will be displayed, as shown in Figure 8-12, informing you that all the existing beams will be deleted. Next, choose the **Yes** button to delete the existing beams from the plan and the **Auto Beam Details** dialog box will be displayed, as shown in Figure 8-13.

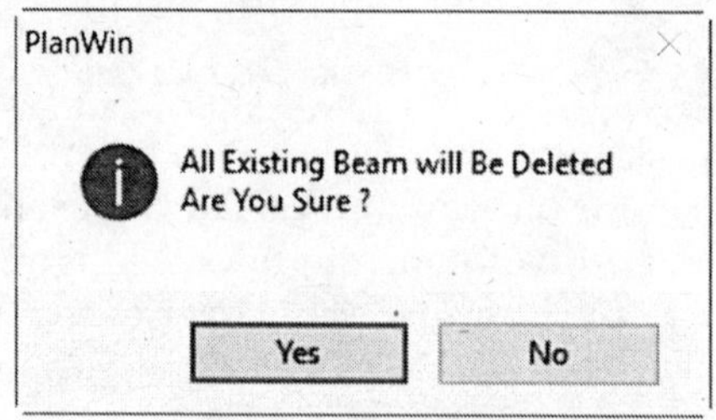

*Figure 8-12 The **PlanWin** message box*

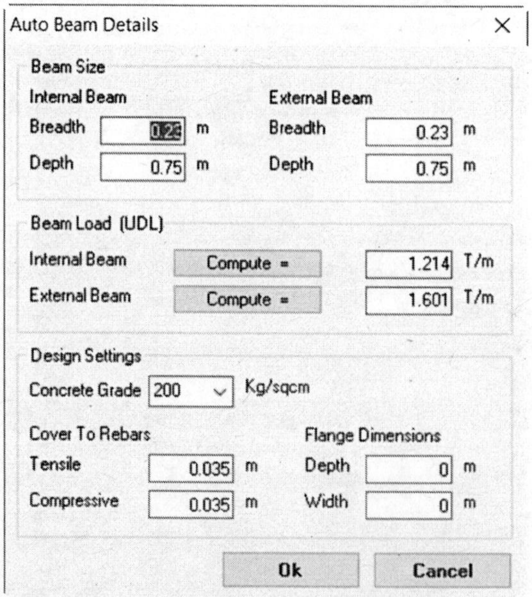

*Figure 8-13 The **Auto Beam Details** dialog box*

In the **Auto Beam Details** dialog box, you will assign the property of beam size, beam load, and design setting. You can assign the breadth and depth for internal and external beams in the **Breadth** and **Depth** edit boxes respectively. You can edit uniformly distributed load on both external and internal beams. To do so, enter the values in the **Internal Beam** and **External Beam** edit boxes in the **Beam Load(UDL)** area. You can also compute the value for beam load automatically by selecting the **Compute** button corresponding to the **Internal Beam** and **External Beam** edit boxes, as discussed earlier. To edit the grade of beam concrete, select a value from the **Concrete Grade** drop-down list in the **Design Settings** area. You can also assign cover for rebars both in tensile and compressive side by entering the **Tensile** and **Compressive** edit boxes. You can also assign the flange dimensions in the **Depth** and **Width** edit boxes under **Flange Dimensions**. Now, choose the **Ok** button; the beams will be automatically added to the plan window.

Note

You can automatically draw individual beams using the Auto Beam feature. If there are any pre existing beams then new beams created using the auto beam feature will replace the existing ones.

Beam Continuity

In the Building Planner mode, you can specify continuous beams over the supports for the entire plan. To do so, choose the **Modify Beam continuity** option from the **Beam** menu; the **Continuous Beam** window will be displayed, refer to Figure 8-14.

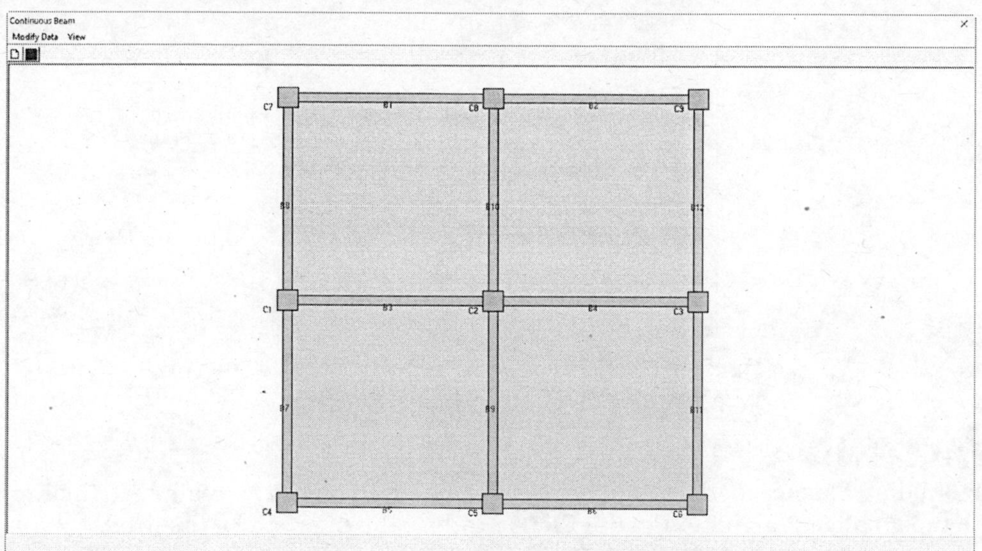

Figure 8-14 *The **Continuous Beam** window*

For better control, you can assign continuity to individual beams or can allow the program to auto assign continuity to all the beams. To assign continuity to individual beams, select the **Mark/Unmark** option from the **Modify Data** menu and select the required beams; the selected beams will be highlighted in red color. Next, choose the **Create** option in the **Modify Data** menu; all the selected beams will be converted into a continuous beam. You can also choose the **Auto Mark Continuous Beam** option from the **Modify Data** menu to automark continuity to the beams. When this option is chosen, the beams get highlighted in purple wherever continuity is possible and becomes continuous. After creating continuous beams, close the **Continuous Beam window**. Next, you must finalize the plan including continuity. To do so, choose **Finalise Plan (With Continuity)** from the **Integrity Check** flyout in the **Plan** menu.

Beam Properties

To edit beam properties, first you need to select the required beams from the entire plan. To do so, choose the **Select/Unselect** option from the **Beam** menu and select the beams. Note that for multiple selection of beams, press the Ctrl key. After selecting the required beams, choose the **Set Property** option from the **Beam** menu; the **Set Beam Property And Loading** dialog box will be displayed, as shown in Figure 8-15. Specify all the required parameters in this dialog box, the properties for the selected beam will be modified. Choose the **Ok** button the dialog box will be closed and the beam will be modified. Now, close the **Continuous Beam** window.

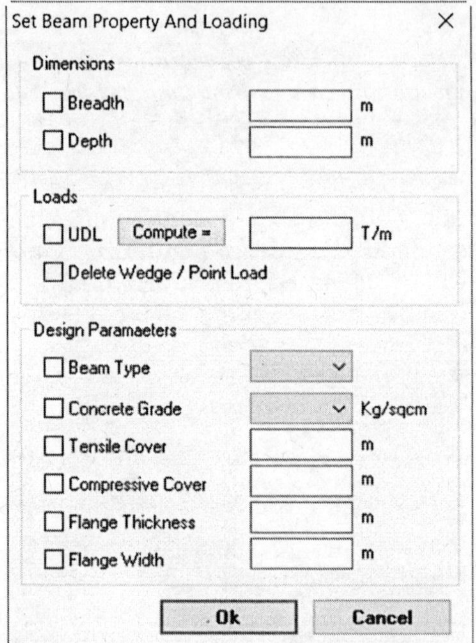

*Figure 8-15 The **Set Beam Property And Loading** dialog box*

FINALIZING A PLAN

In the Building Planner mode, a plan needs to be finalized once it is created. To finalize a plan, choose the **Finalize Plan** button in the **Plans** window; the plan will be finalized.

GENERATING A STAAD.PRO MODEL

You can generate a STAAD.Pro input file in the Building Planner mode. The physical model created using the Building Planner mode can be exported to STAAD.Pro for analysis and design.

To generate a model, choose the **Generate Model** button from the **Level Details** window; the **STAAD.Pro V8i (SELECTseries 6)** message box will be displayed informing you that the existing model will be replaced by the building model. Next, choose the **OK** button; the message box will be closed and the **Space Frame File Generation** dialog box will be displayed, as shown in Figure 8-16

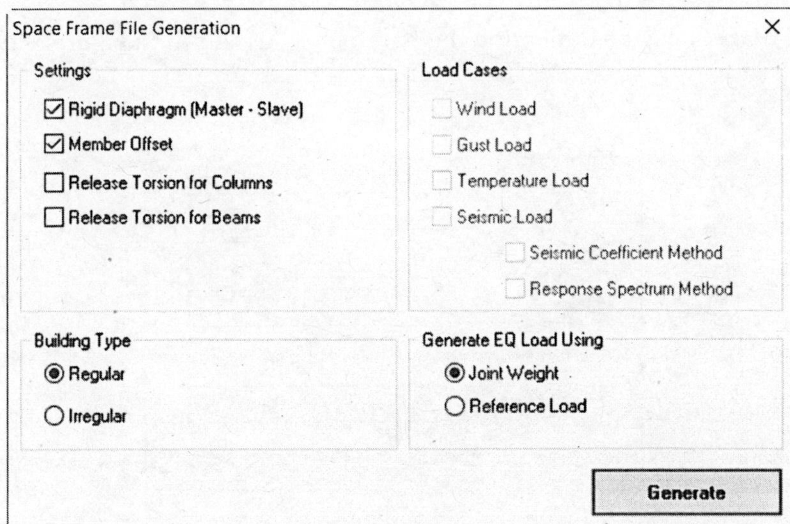

***Figure 8-16** The **Space Frame File Generation** dialog box*

Note

In the STAAD.Pro V8i (SELECTseries 6) message box, never choose the Close button ***X*** *as this will result in an invalid STAAD input file.*

In this dialog box, specify the parameters to be used for the STAAD input file. Select the **Rigid Diaphragm (Master–Slave)**, **Member Offset**, **Release Torsion for Columns**, or **Release torsion for Beams** check box as per the requirement in the **Settings** area. Select the building type by choosing the **Regular** or **Irregular** radio button in the **Building Type** area. Earthquake load can be generated by selecting the **Joint Weight** or the **Reference Load** in the **Generate EQ Load Using** area. Loads can also be imported in a staad model by selecting the corresponding radio button in the **Load Cases** area. After specifying all the values, choose the **Generate** button; the **Space Frame File Generation** dialog box is closed and model is generated in the STAAD.Pro. STAAD.Pro switches from the Building Planner mode to the Modeling mode with the new input file open. You can now make changes to the STAAD.Pro file as necessary. You can perform an analysis by selecting **Run Analysis** from the **Analyze** menu.

Example 1

In this example, you will create a model using Building Planner. The structure will be a space frame structure.

Steps required to complete this example are given below:

Step 1: Start STAAD.Pro, and then, choose the **New Project** option from the **Project Tasks** area in the STAAD.Pro interface; the **New Model** dialog box is displayed. In this dialog box, select the **Space** check box and specify the name as ***c08_staad_v8i_ex1*** in the **File Name** edit box. Choose the **Next** button and select the **Open Building Planner Mode** check box from the **Where do you want to go?** dialog box and then choose the **Finish** button; the **Start** dialog box is displayed.

Step 2: In the **Start** dialog box, mention the parameters, as shown in Figure 8-17.

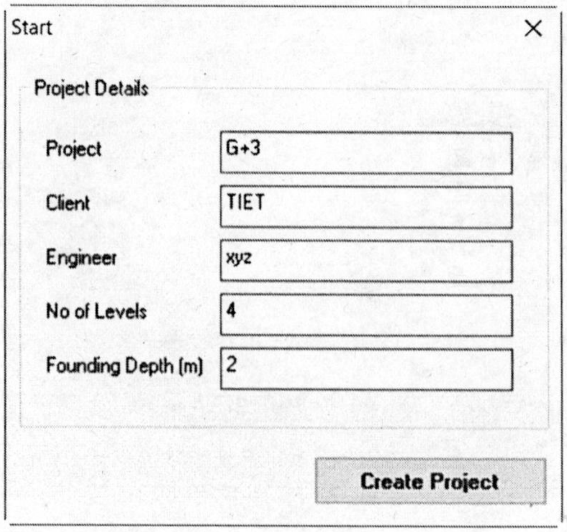

*Figure 8-17 The **Start** dialog box*

Step 3: Choose the **Create Project** button in the **Start** dialog box; the **New Plan** dialog box is displayed. In this dialog box, enter the parameters, as shown in Figure 8-18.

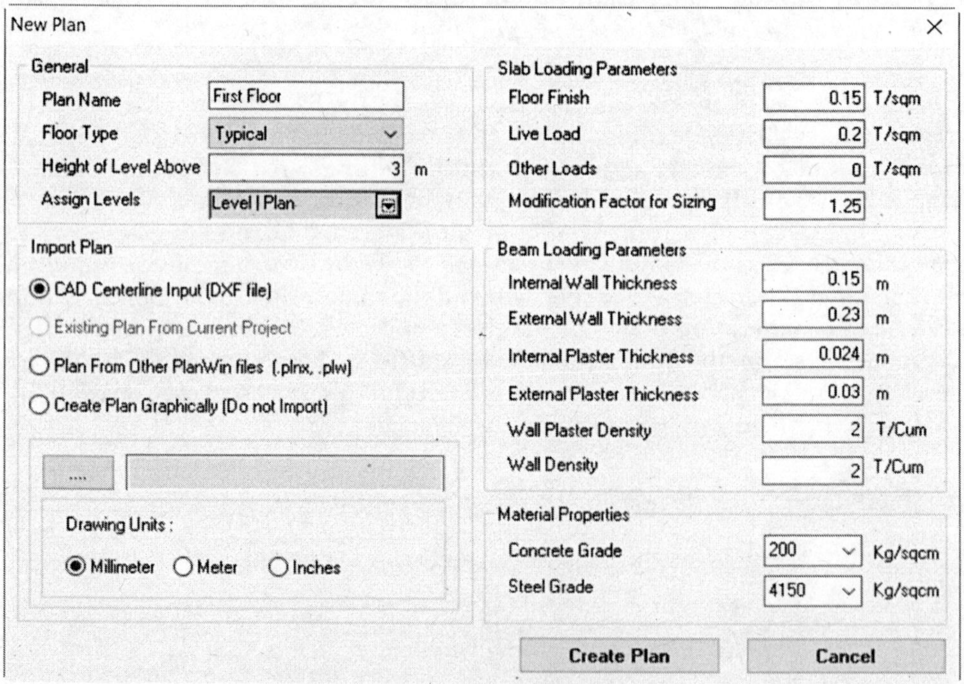

*Figure 8-18 The **New Plan** dialog box*

Step 4: Click in the **Assign Levels** field; a list is displayed. In the displayed list, click on the first field; a Ground Floor name is displayed, as shown in Figure 8-19.

Figure 8-19 The Assign Levels field

Step 5: Choose the **Create Plan** button; the **Slab Details (Rectangle)** dialog box is displayed, as shown in Figure 8-20.

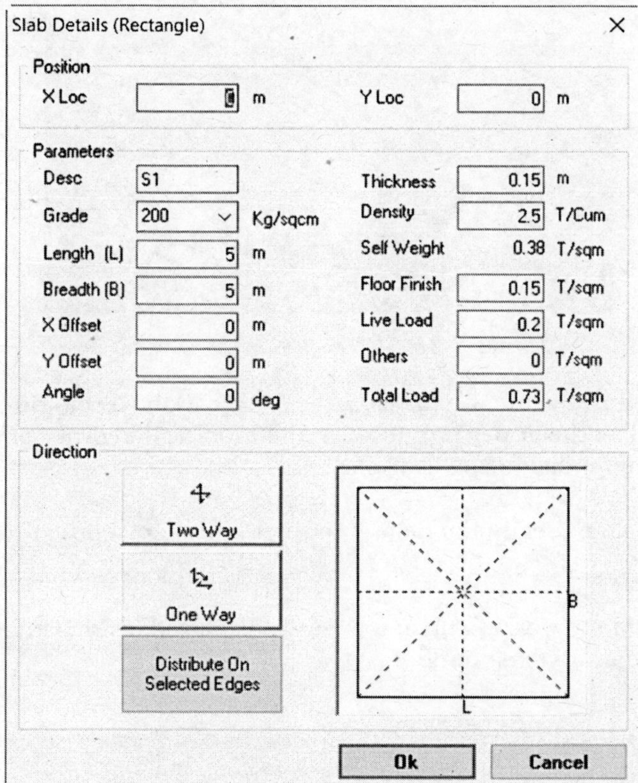

*Figure 8-20 The **Slab Details (Rectangle)** dialog box*

Step 6: In this dialog box, retain all the settings and then choose the **Ok** button; the dialog box is closed and a slab is created on the Ground Floor in the working area, as shown in Figure 8-21.

Figure 8-21 Slab created to the working area

Step 7: Click on the main window and select the **Create Slab Rectangle** option from the **Slab** menu, and then click at the upper right corner and lower right corner of the existing slab; the **Slab Details (Rectangle)** dialog box is displayed.

Step 8: In this dialog box, retain the default settings and then choose the **Ok** button; one slab is added to the right.

Step 9: Right-click on the working area; a flyout is displayed, as shown in Figure 8-22. In this flyuot, choose the **Zoom Extents** option.

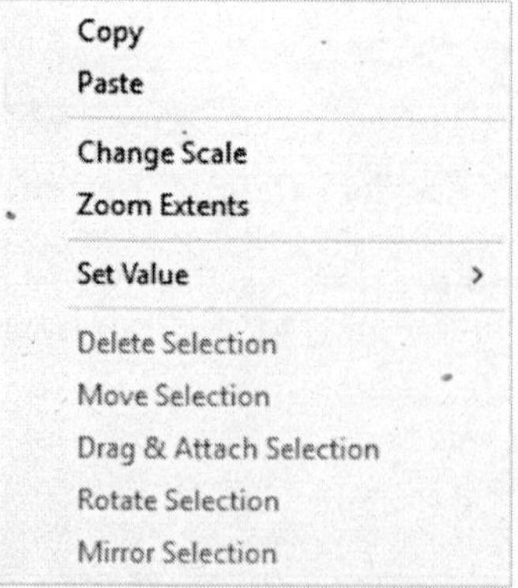

Figure 8-22 Flyout displayed on right-clicking on working area

Step 10: Repeat Step 7 through Step 9 to add other two slabs to the plan, refer to Figure 8-23.

Tip

To fit the slabs within the plan area, right-click on the working area; a flyout will be displayed. Choose the ***Zoom Extents*** *tool; the slabs will be fitted within the working area.*

Figure 8-23 *Slabs created on working area*

Step 11: Select the **Create Slab Irregular** option from the **Slab** menu, and then click on the three corners of the slab, as shown in Figure 8-24; the **Point Selection** dialog box is displayed. Retain the default settings and choose the **Ok** button to close it.

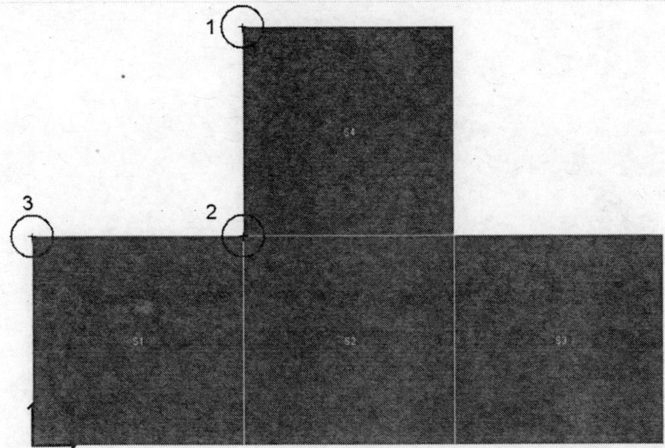

Figure 8-24 *Selected corners of slabs*

Step 12: Right-click on the main window; the **Slab Details (IRRegular)** dialog box is displayed.

Step 13: In this dialog box, enter a value in the **Thickness** edit box, as shown in Figure 8-25, and then choose the **OK** button; an irregular slab is added, as shown in Figure 8-26.

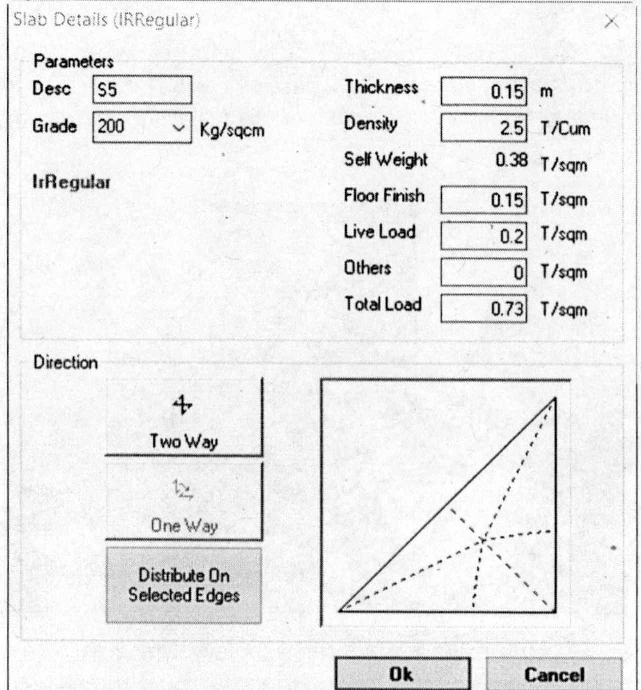

Figure 8-25 *The* ***Slab Details (IRRegular)*** *dialog box*

Figure 8-26 *Slabs created on working area*

Step 14: Similarly, click on the three corners, as shown in Figure 8-27; the **Point Selection** dialog box is displayed. Next, choose the **Ok** button to close the dialog box.

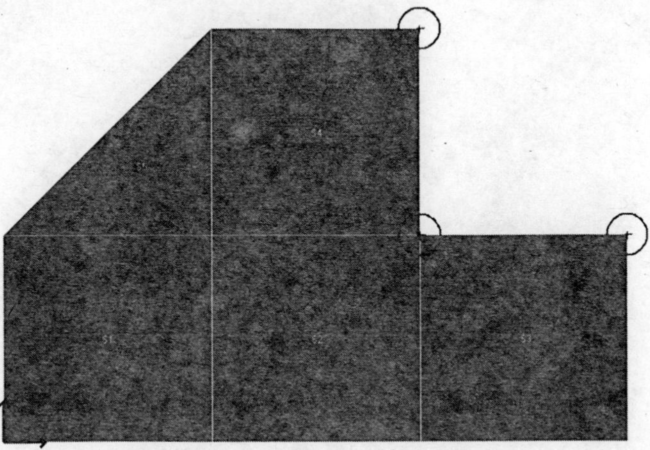

Figure 8-27 *Selected corners of slabs*

Step 15: Repeat the procedure followed in Step 11 through Step 14; an irregular slab is added, as shown in Figure 8-28.

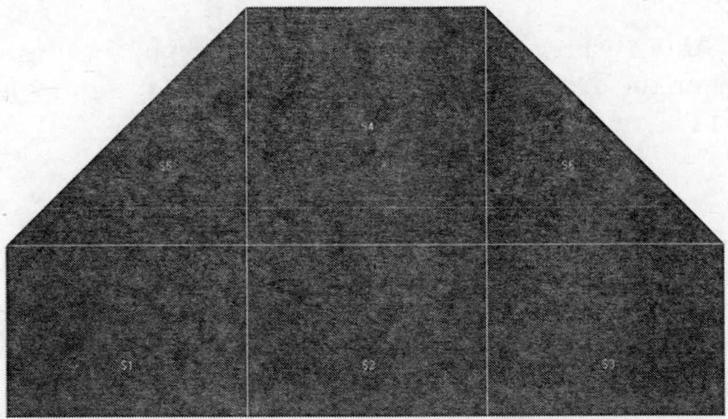

Figure 8-28 *Slabs created on working area*

Step 16: Click on the main window, and then choose the **Auto Column** option from the **Column** menu; columns is created at the joints.

Step 17: Select the **Select/UnSelect** option from the **Column** menu and then select all the columns from the plan area, refer to Figure 8-29.

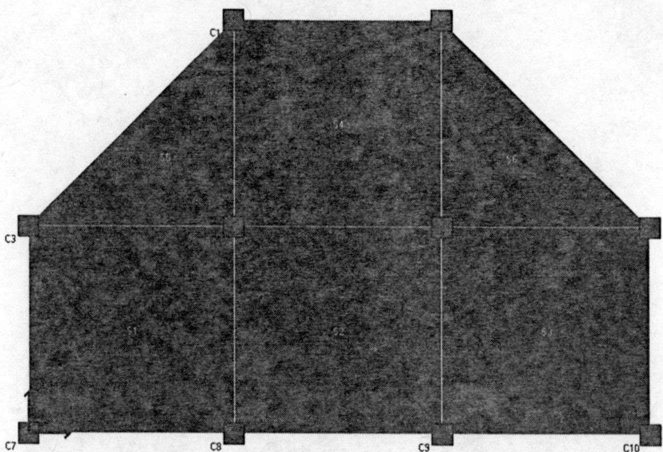

Figure 8-29 *Selected corners of slabs*

Step 18: Right-click on any column; a menu is displayed. Select the **Set Property For Selected Column/s** option from the menu displayed; the **Set Value For Selected Column** dialog box is displayed. Specify **0.6** as the value in the edit box and choose the **Ok** button, the columns get resized.

Step 19: Select the **Auto Beam** option from the **Beam** menu; the **Auto Beam Details** dialog box is displayed. Retain the default settings, and choose the **Ok** button; beams get added to the structure, as shown in Figure 8-30.

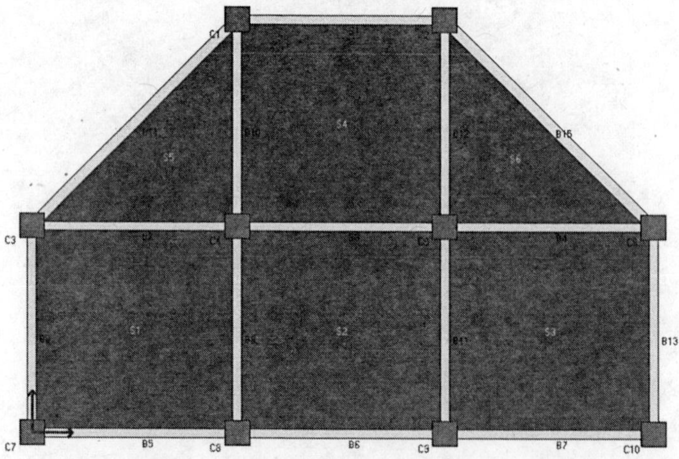

Figure 8-30 *Beams created on structure*

Step 20: Choose the **Finalize Plan** button from the **Plans** area of the **Plans** window; the **PlanWin** message box is displayed with the message that the plan is finished. Choose the **OK** button.

Step 21: Choose the **New Plan** button from the **Plan** area of the **Plan** window; the **New Plan** dialog box is displayed. In this dialog box, rename the plan as **Second Floor** in the **Plan Name** edit box.

Step 22: Click in the **Assign levels** field; a list is displayed. Click on the second row; the Second Floor is assigned in the list.

Step 23: In the **New Plan** dialog box, choose the **Existing Plan From Current Project** radio button from the **Import Plan** area and then choose the **Create Plan** button; the **New Plan** dialog box is closed and the second floor is created and added to the plan.

Step 24: Repeat the procedure followed in Step 21 through Step 23 to create **Thirf Floor** and **Roof**.

Step 25: After creating all the plans, choose the **Finalize Plan** button in the **Plans** area of the **Plans** window; the **PlanWin** message box is displayed. Choose the **OK** button.

Step 26: Choose the **Frame** tab in the Building Planner mode.

Step 27: Choose the **Generate Model** button in the **Level Details** window to generate the model; the **STAAD.Pro V8i (SELECTseries 6)** warning message box is displayed, as shown in Figure 8-31.

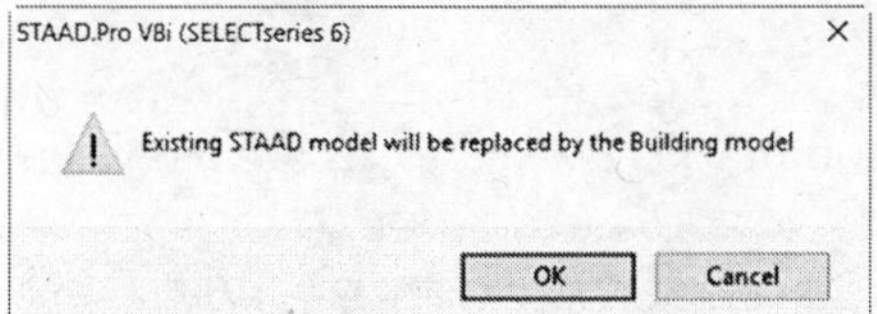

Figure 8-31 *Warning message box*

Step 28: Choose the **OK** button; the **Space Frame File Generation** dialog box is displayed. Clear the **Member Offset** check box in the **Settings** area and choose the **Generate** button; a model is generated in STAAD, as shown in Figure 8-32.

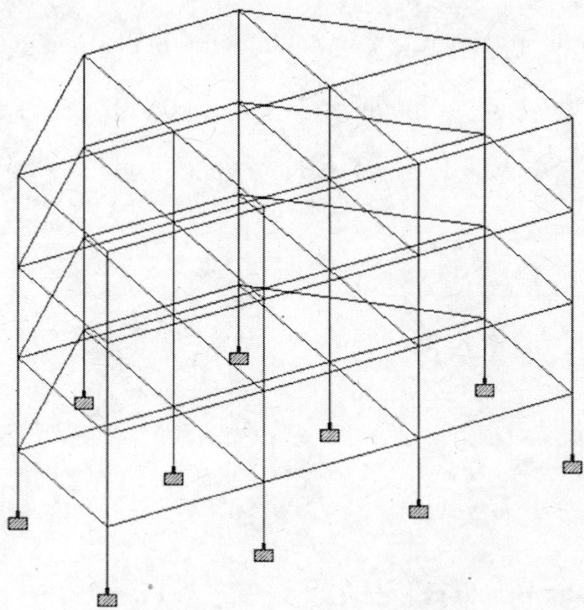

Figure 8-32 *Model generated in STAAD*

Self-Evaluation Test

Answer the following questions and then compare them to those given at the end of this chapter:

1. The _________ option is used to create columns automatically.

2. The _________ option is used to finalize the plan.

3. The _________ option is used for specifying beam continuity.

4. Building Planner mode is used for steel design. (T/F)

5. You can undo the changes in the Building Planner mode. (T/F)

Review Questions

Answer the following questions:

1. Which of the following commands is used to create irregular slab?

   (a) **Create Slab** (b) **Create Slab Irregular**
   (c) **Irregular Slab** (d) None of these

2. Which of the following pages is available in the **Plan** tab in the Building Planner mode?

   (a) **Beam** (b) **Slab**
   (c) **Column** (d) All of these

3. Grids are compulsory to generate a model in building planner. (T/F)

4. Model from Building Planner mode can be exported with offset specifications. (T/F)

5. You cannot directly copy and paste a slab in a plan. (T/F)

Answers to Self-Evaluation Test

1. **Auto Column**, **2.** **Finalize Plan**, **3.** **Modify Beam Continuity**, **4.** F, **5.** F

Index

L

M

N

P

R

S

T

U

V

W

CAD/CAM/CIM/GIS/ANIMATION/CIVIL BOOKS

by **Prof. Sham Tickoo** (Purdue University, USA and Autodesk Authorised Author)

Autodesk
3ds Max 2018
A Comprehensive Guide
ISBN 978-93-8655-168-9
Price: ₹ 999/-

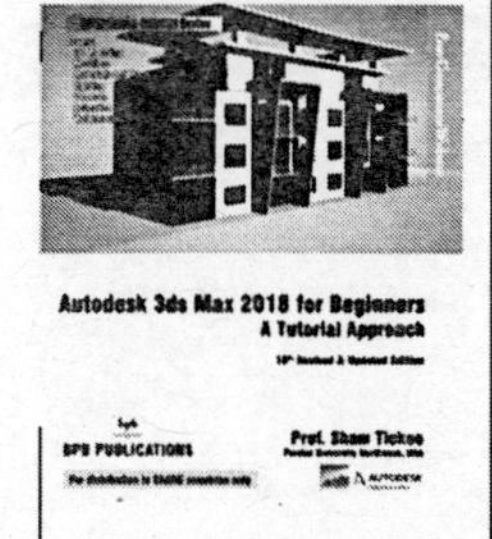

Autodesk
3ds Max 2018 For Beginners
A Tutorial Approach
ISBN 978-93-8655-167-2
Price: ₹ 899/-

Autodesk
3ds Max 2017
A Comprehensive Guide
ISBN 978-93-8655-113-9
Price: ₹ 999/-

Autodesk
3ds Max 2017 For Beginners
A Tutorial Approach
ISBN 978-93-8655-112-2
Price: ₹ 999/-

Autodesk
3ds Max 2019
A Comprehensive Guide
ISBN 978-93-8817-627-9
Price: ₹ 999/-

Blender
For Digital Artists
ISBN 978-93-8817-626-2
Price: ₹ 599/-

Autodesk
Maya 2018
A Comprehensive Guide
ISBN 978-93-8655-170-2
Price: ₹ 899/-

Autodesk
Maya 2017
A Comprehensive Guide
ISBN 978-93-8655-114-6
Price: ₹ 899/-

Pixologic Zbrush 4R8
A Comprehensive Guide
ISBN 978-93-8728-412-8
Price: ₹ 899/-

Pixologic Zbrush 4R7
A Comprehensive Guide
ISBN 978-93-8655-115-3
Price: ₹ 899/-

AutoCAD 2018
Basic and Intermediate
ISBN 978-93-8655-163-4
Price: ₹ 1299/-

Advanced AutoCAD 2018
3D and Advanced
ISBN 978-93-8655-160-3
Price: ₹ 899/-

Available on **www.bpbonline.com** and all leading book stores.

#1 Publisher of Computer Books | 62 Years of Excellence | OVER 90 Million Books Sold Worldwide

CAD/CAM/CIM/GIS/ANIMATION/CIVIL BOOKS

by **Prof. Sham Tickoo** (Purdue University, USA and Autodesk Authorised Author)

Exploring Autodesk
Revit 2017
For Structure
ISBN 978-81-8333-506-5
Price: ₹ 899/-

Exploring Autodesk
Revit 2018
For Architecture
ISBN 978-93-8655-172-6
Price: ₹ 999/-

Exploring Autodesk
Revit 2018
For MEP
ISBN 978-93-8655-173-3
Price: ₹ 799/-

Exploring Autodesk
Revit 2018
For Structure
ISBN 978-93-8655-174-0
Price: ₹ 799/-

Exploring Autodesk
Revit 2019
For Architecture
ISBN 978-93-8817-633-0
Price: ₹ 1199/-

Exploring Autodesk
Revit 2019
For MEP
ISBN 978-93-8817-635-4
Price: ₹ 899/-

Exploring Autodesk
Revit 2019
For Structure
ISBN 978-93-8817-634-7
Price: ₹ 899/-

Exploring
RISA-3D 14.0
ISBN 978-93-8655-108-5
Price: ₹ 499/-

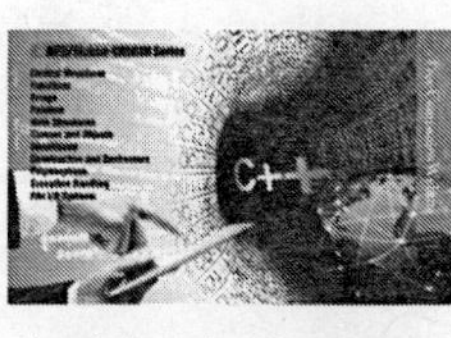

Exploring AutoCAD Raster Design 2017
ISBN 978-93-8655-109-2
Price: ₹ 499/-

Exploring Bentley STAAD.Pro (Select Series 6)
ISBN 978-93-8655-110-8
Price: ₹ 599/-

Exploring Bentley STAAD.Pro (Connect Edition)
ISBN 978-93-8728-414-2
Price: ₹ 499/-

Introduction to C++ Programming
ISBN 978-93-8655-116-0
Price: ₹ 699/-

Available on **www.bpbonline.com** and all leading book stores.

#1 Publisher of Computer Books | 62 Years of Excellence | OVER 90 Million Books Sold Worldwide

CAD/CAM/CIM/GIS/ANIMATION/CIVIL BOOKS

by **Prof. Sham Tickoo** (Purdue University, USA and Autodesk Authorised Author)

Solid Works 2018
For Designers
ISBN 978-93-8728-409-8
Price: ₹ 1299/-

Solid Works Simulation 2018
For Designers
ISBN 978-93-8728-411-1
Price: ₹ 599/-

Solid Works 2018
A Tutorial Approach
ISBN 978-93-8817-631-6
Price: ₹ 799/-

Learning Solid Works 2018
A Project Based Approach
ISBN 978-93-8817-632-3
Price: ₹ 699/-

Exploring AutoCAD Civil 3D 2017
ISBN 978-93-8655-102-3
Price: ₹ 999/-

Exploring AutoCAD Civil 3D 2018
ISBN 978-93-8728-413-5
Price: ₹ 999/-

Exploring AutoCAD Map 3D 2017
ISBN 978-93-8655-103-0
Price: ₹ 875/-

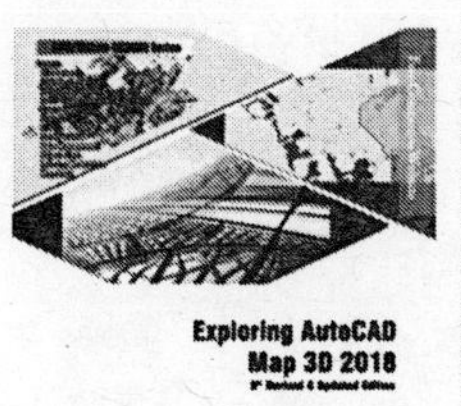

Exploring AutoCAD Map 3D 2018
ISBN 978-93-8655-166-5
Price: ₹ 799/-

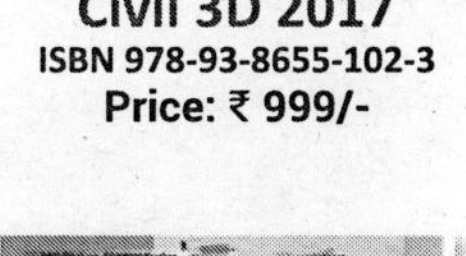

Exploring Autodesk
Navisworks 2017
ISBN 978-93-8655-104-7
Price: ₹ 699/-

Exploring Oracle
Primavera P6 R8.4
ISBN 978-93-8655-105-4
Price: ₹ 599/-

Exploring Autodesk
Revit 2017
For Architecture
ISBN 978-93-8655-106-1
Price: ₹ 999/-

Exploring Autodesk
Revit 2017
For MEP
ISBN 978-93-8655-107-8
Price: ₹ 799/-

Available on **www.bpbonline.com** and all leading book stores.

PUBLICATIONS | #1 Publisher of Computer Books | 62 Years of Excellence | OVER 90 Million Books Sold Worldwide